Merchants and Trade Networks in the Atlantic and the Mediterranean, 1550–1800

T0270722

This collected volume explores the ways merchants managed to connect different spaces all over the globe in the early modern period by organising the movement of goods, capital, information and cultural objects between different commercial maritime systems in the Mediterranean and Atlantic basin.

Merchants and Trade Networks in the Atlantic and the Mediterranean, 1550–1800 consists of four thematic blocs: theoretical considerations, the social composition of networks, connected spaces, and networks between formal and informal exchange, as well as possible failures of ties. This edited volume features eleven contributions which deal with theoretical concepts such as social network analysis, globalisation, social capital and trust. In addition, several chapters analyse the coexistence of monocultural and transnational networks, deal with network failure and shifting network geographies, and assess the impact of kinship for building up international networks between the Mediterranean and the Atlantic. This work evaluates the use of specific network types for building up connections across the Mediterranean and the Atlantic Basin stretching out to Central Europe, the North Sea and the Pacific.

This book will be of interest to those who study the history of economics and maritime economics, as well as historians and scholars from other disciplines working on maritime shipping, port studies, migration, foreign mercantile communities, trade policies and mercantilism.

Manuel Herrero Sánchez is Associate Professor of Early Modern History at Pablo de Olavide University in Seville, Spain.

Klemens Kaps is a post-doc-Researcher at the Institute for Economic and Social History of Vienna University, Austria.

Perspectives in Economic and Social History
Series Editors: Andrew August and Jari Eloranta

For a full list of titles in this series, please visit www.routledge.com/series/PESH.

Merchants and Trade Networks in the Atlantic and the Mediterranean, 1550–1800

Connectors of commercial maritime systems

Edited by Manuel Herrero Sánchez and Klemens Kaps

Routledge
Taylor & Francis Group

LONDON AND NEW YORK

First published 2017 by Routledge

2 Park Square, Milton Park, Abingdon, Oxfordshire OX14 4RN

52 Vanderbilt Avenue, New York, NY 10017

Routledge is an imprint of the Taylor & Francis Group, an informa business

First issued in paperback 2019

British Library Cataloguing in Publication Data
A catalogue record for this book is available from the British Library

Library of Congress Cataloging in Publication Data

Names: Herrero Sánchez, Manuel, editor. | Kaps, Klemens, editor.
Title: Merchants and trade networks in the Atlantic and the Mediterranean, 1550-1800 : connectors of commercial maritime systems / edited by Manuel Herrero Sánchez and Klemens Kaps.
Description: New York : Routledge, 2017.
Identifiers: LCCN 2016009918| ISBN 9781138188730 (hardback) | ISBN 9781315642147 (ebook)
Subjects: LCSH: Mediterranean Sea—Commerce—History. | Atlantic Ocean—Commerce—History. | Merchants—Mediterranean Region—History. | Merchants—Atlantic Ocean Region—History.
Classification: LCC HF381 .M47 2016 | DDC 382.09182/1—dc23
LC record available at http://lccn.loc.gov/2016009918

ISBN: 978-1-138-18873-0 (hbk)
ISBN: 978-0-367-87688-3 (pbk)

Typeset in Times New Roman
by diacriTech, Chennai

Contents

Figures and Maps

Figures

Maps

Tables

Contributors

Bethany Aram
University Pablo de Olavide
Seville, Spain

Eberhard Crailsheim
Institute of History, Spanish National
    Research Council
Madrid, Spain

Ana Crespo Solana
Institute of History, Spanish National
    Research Council
Madrid, Spain

Manuel F. Fernández Chaves
University of Seville
Seville, Spain

Mercedes Gamero Rojas
University of Seville
Seville, Spain

José L. Gasch-Tomás
Institute of History, Spanish National
    Research Council
Madrid, Spain

Sheryllynne Haggerty
University of Nottingham
Nottingham, UK

Pablo Hernández Sau
European University Institute
Florence, Italy

Manuel Herrero Sánchez
University Pablo de Olavide
Seville, Spain

Klemens Kaps
University of Vienna
Vienna, Austria

Xabier Lamikiz
University of the Basque Country
    (UPV/EHU)
Vitoria-Gasteiz, Spain

Margrit Schulte Beerbühl
Heinrich-Heine University of
    Düsseldorf
Düsseldorf, Germany

Montserrat Cachero Vinuesa
University Pablo de Olavide
Seville, Spain

1 Connectors, networks and commercial systems

Approaches to the study of early modern maritime commercial history

Manuel Herrero Sánchez and Klemens Kaps[1]

The study of long-distance maritime trade in the early modern period has gained considerable momentum over the last two decades. Traditionally, research was divided between merchant studies, understood as the analysis of single traders and their companies, and more structural accounts of traded commodities or shipping traffic.[2] By focusing on mercantile agencies and its mechanisms, that is, by combining information from the socio-economic macro-level with a micro-historical approach that puts agents at the centre of research, recent historiography has done much to close this divide. The focus has since been directed to the question of how merchants in the early modern period managed to connect different geographical areas in different parts of the globe and organise the flow of goods, money, information and cultural objects between them.[3] This book aims to contribute to this multilayered debate on trade networks in two important ways: first, it tries to stimulate theoretically driven empirical analyses of merchant networks by linking methodological discussions with case studies; second, it develops these arguments in the study of the Mediterranean Sea and its links with the Atlantic Ocean between the sixteenth and the early nineteenth centuries. We believe that the traditional historiographical view has overemphasised the importance of the North Atlantic in the first globalisation process. Indeed, this book demonstrates the important role played by the Mediterranean and Central Europe in the early steps of globalisation. Consequently, we propose to expand the methodological and theoretical framework devised for the analysis of the transatlantic trade to the Mediterranean and the South Atlantic, and also of trade within the boundaries of the European continent.

This approach is fully concerned with the on-going debates on the origins of globalisation and the importance therein of early modern long-distance trade. While some highly influential authors, such as Fernand Braudel and Immanuel Wallerstein, place the exchange of goods at the core of the origins of the unequal division of labour between north-western and eastern and southern Europe and also between Europe and Latin America in the sixteenth and the seventeenth centuries,[4] other authors have been more sceptical. Thus, Patrick O'Brien stressed the limited weight of foreign, and especially colonial, trade in the overall economic activity of the United Kingdom.[5] Piet Emmer, for his part, took the debate one step further and questioned whether intercontinental trade was a feature of the 'Atlantic System', since transatlantic trade usually did not exceed 2 per cent of the European and American GDPs. Also, trade was exonerated from having caused any lasting negative economic effects in Western Africa, although its devastating consequences, in particular those connected with the slave trade, have been fully recognised. The opposite is true for the Industrial Revolution in Great Britain, which could not have succeeded if the volume of trade had been as small as has been argued.[6] Based on these interpretations, it was only logical to conclude that globalisation did not begin with Columbus' arrival in America in 1492, but only with the emergence of railways, steamships and highly developed financial markets in the late nineteenth century, as Kevin O'Rourke and Jeffrey Williamson argued.[7]

These arguments, in any case, are too reliant on econometrician approaches, especially considering the lack of reliable accounts and the fragmentation of sovereignty that characterise the historical period under analysis. Calculation of such variables as the GDP is problematic, and needs to be supplemented with other evidence capable of offering a qualitative point of view on the quantitative data, for example, letters between private individuals, treaties, and diplomatic negotiations.[8] The opinions of those personally involved in mercantile operations, and of state agents in charge of promoting these operations, and making them more difficult for the enemy, suggests a collective feeling of living in a fully globalised world in which the political and military might of states was the direct result of the state's, or its commercial subjects', ability to operate at an intercontinental level. These endeavours were also behind a large number of technical and naval innovations and fostered the dissemination of cultural and religious traits worldwide. In addition, Serge Gruzinski correctly pointed out that these trends resulted in unprecedented processes of hybridisation and cultural assimilation initiated by the Iberian colonial empires, facilitated by Catholic universalism.[9] Consequently, and despite those like Patrick O'Brien, who tend to underestimate the relevance of colonial trade in the European economy of the period, or those who insist upon focusing on religious and dynastic factors,[10] hegemony seems to have been increasingly related to control over the main raw materials and the key strategic corridors as well as to the strength achieved through the possession of large war navies (the percentage of the budget spent on warships did nothing but increase). The conflict between the powers extended beyond the borders of Europe and became a worldwide struggle. The Dutch East India Company (VOC) became one of the main symbols of the Dutch Republic, but we must not forget that, throughout the seventeenth century, the companies chiefly dealt in high-value trade goods that were transported in no more than 10 to 15 vessels sailing under strong-armed protection; there is no possible comparison with the heavy traffic of the Baltic Sea, on which the original growth of Dutch sea power had been based. This trade played an essential role in the development of a specialised agricultural sector in the Netherlands, but, as noted by Israel, it was infinitely less valuable and less likely to prompt the emergence of the specialised industry on which the economic primacy of the United Provinces was ultimately founded.[11]

In this regard, at the time few doubted that the ability of the United Provinces to challenge their former sovereign was connected with their impressive expansion in the overseas markets. Indeed, colonial expansion allowed the republic to consolidate their recently gained independence and turned the Dutch emporium into a centre for the supply, redistribution and manufacture of both industrial and luxury goods. In this context, it seems questionable to try to minimise the role of overseas exchange for the Dutch economy, especially considering that access to colonial markets and the end of the theoretical Spanish monopoly soon became one of the key issues in the diplomatic exchange between both states and, indeed, a major stumbling block for peace.[12]

Other arguments against the narrow definition of globalisation that was so ostentatiously shaking historical truisms pointed to the effects of the arrival of American silver, not only on the European economy during the so-called 'price revolution' of the sixteenth century but also on seemingly removed phenomena such as demographic trends in China. However, the main argument against those who minimise the importance of international trade in the early modern period is the fact that the world was truly and fully connected only after 1492, so that money, people and commodities could and did flow through worldwide circuits.[13] It is true that most of the money that the Spanish king used to keep his war machine in permanent motion came from the taxes paid by Castilian, Neapolitan and Sicilian peasants. However, it is also true that the Crown's credit, which attracted the arrival of many German and Genoese bankers to the monarchy's financial system, was based on the consolidation of commercial networks throughout the Catholic monarch's widespread possessions and the constant inflow of American silver, which ultimately became the foundation of Castilian imperialism. This explains why the struggle for hegemony not only took place in the Old World but, from the late sixteenth century onwards and especially after the resumption of the Spanish-Dutch war in 1621, in the overseas colonies. In this regard, Flynn followed the opinion of his contemporaries who identified the Indies as the main cause of the decline of Castile, and pointed out that the massive arrival of precious metals became a barrier for economic development and made possible a military effort that was heavily reliant on the Crown's credit and beyond its real capabilities.[14]

In addition, a closer look at the above-mentioned arguments reveals some support for the globalising effects of trade long before the nineteenth century: even Emmer's figures demonstrate that the external trade share of the GDPs of both Portugal and the Netherlands was in excess of 10 per cent, which suggests that commerce had a much larger impact than the aforementioned arguments suggest.[15] The monetary influx that this activity involved played a crucial role in facilitating Dutch merchants in launching other commercial ventures, for example in the Ottoman Levant, the Baltic regions and, especially, in Asia, where American silver was considered among the most valuable goods.[16] The endemic commercial deficit with Asia, therefore, had the effect of stimulating other branches of international Dutch commerce; the long military conflict with Madrid forced the republic to develop direct commercial channels with America via the Dutch–Africa–America triangle, which turned the West India Company (WIC), founded in 1621, into a company that essentially dealt with slaves.[17] The peace in 1648 also made it easier for the VOC to control the silver remittances sent from New Spain to the Philippines.[18] As the work carried out by Bruijn, Gaastra and Schöffer demonstrated, the impact of the VOC on the Dutch economy far exceeded the value of its shares or the profit derived from its transactions, which in absolute terms were, no doubt, lower than those from other economic sectors. The VOC, despite internalising the high protection costs, an essential factor for the consolidation of the independence of the United Provinces, had to overcome, because of Asia, a threefold shortcoming which had an overall negative effect on the republic: in ships, due to the large number of vessels that had to meet the regional trade needs; in personnel, because only one-third of the million Dutch émigrés in Asia returned; and in precious metal, which amounted to two-thirds of the exports shipped to Asia.[19] The growing demand for Asiatic products in Europe was, consequently, a constant drain on cash, which gave the company an important advantage over its competitors, because Amsterdam was the main market for precious metals in the continent.

All of this evidence suggests that some 'hard' globalisation was happening, an idea which is supported by the example of other globally traded commodities that Europe imported from Asia in the eighteenth century, such as tea, coffee, textiles and porcelain. All of these products were directed at the mass consumer markets, and textiles and porcelain openly competed with European industries, one of the features of the modern globalisation processes. Still, in general early modern globalisation adopted 'soft' methods and was mostly regional in scope.[20] The shift in international economic integration caused by the arrival of railways, steamships and telegraphic communication was unquestionably immense, and interregional and international connections grew at an unprecedented speed in their wake. Rather than ushering in an entirely new phase, however, these new developments seem to have prompted new directions within an already interconnected system of information and commodity exchange. This is at least the basis of Christopher Bayly's suggestion differentiating between 'archaic' or early modern globalisation and its modern counterpart: the seventeenth and eighteenth centuries did not see an integrated world-system, but rather witnessed the expansion of pre-existing networks from local and regional levels to interregional and intercontinental exchange.[21] This incipient globalisation process has been masterfully described by Kirti N. Chaudhuri in this illustrative paragraph: 'American treasure helped to finance Spain's balance of indebtedness. The cost advantage enjoyed by the Genoese bankers, and later the Dutch and English in entrepot trade accumulated capital in the hands of Europe's most efficient entrepreneurs. This capital helped to finance the imports of Indian cotton textiles, Asian spices, and Chinese silks and tea. Indian textiles and cowries were in turn exchanged for African slaves who produced new agricultural commodities in the New World for consumption in the Old. The circuit seems to have ended as Barbados sugar sweetened Chinese tea in porcelain cups copied from the products of Ching-te-chen kilns in imperial China'.[22]

In this way, this phase can be seen as a formative stage of later globalisation processes. This perspective seems in line with the most recent historiographical trends in relation to early modern trade, which point out that commerce in the 'first global age'[23] or the 'first global trade'[24] already embraced the whole globe, although its geographical presence was still uneven and its performance was still burdened by uncertainty and trade barriers. It is, at any rate, convenient to avoid the adoption of teleological perspectives derived from the holistic and deterministic arguments that are characteristic of the theoretical premises of the world-system perspective. In their eagerness to explain the origins of the current capitalistic system and of the economic dependence of the Third World, they push the notion of a worldwide division and specialisation of labour – the consequence of the transference of capital gains from the periphery to the centre – as far back as the seventeenth century. As Shannon has rightly pointed out, these theorists 'emphasize that the institutions of society are organized to meet the needs of this global system'.[25] We must not forget that, as Van Leur pointed out in his analysis of the impact of the European presence on Asian society and commerce, the role played by Portuguese, Dutch and British merchants was that of mere middlemen, which also challenges the strongly Eurocentric flavour which is often associated with this early globalisation process.[26] Although the notion that the endemic commercial deficit with Asia forced European commerce to reinforce its position worldwide, especially through the triangular trade with Africa and America in order to accumulate precious metal, seems beyond a doubt, we must not overlook the fact that this process highlighted the European incapacity to flood Asian markets with manufactured goods. This certainly challenges the dominating role associated with the centre and goes a long way to emphasise the limits of its political authority.[27]

Leaving linear conceptions of commercial interactions aside, we find that the spatial and social complexities of commercial interactions in the early modern world can be grasped through the application of social network analysis. Trade networks acted as connectors between consumption and production centres located in different places, although this role was often indirect and involved the participation of a large number of middlemen; these links evolved into complex chains of intermediaries, where a wide range of different services – such as overland and sea transport, wholesaling and retailing, and credit and finances – was needed. Wholesale and retail trade were thus neatly integrated with one another in order to guarantee the fluid transfer of commodities.[28] The aim of these commercial networks was to overcome, or at least to reduce, the risks faced by early modern commercial exchange, including the difficult enforcement of contracts, shipping accidents, delays caused by weather and wars, slowness of information flow and, in relation to this, asymmetric information.[29] It has to be stressed that these barriers were not static and that they did not disappear during the course of the early modern age. Chaudhuri uses the example of the negative effect for security that the expansion of the Ottoman Empire and the Portuguese attacks on Muslim traders had in the late sixteenth century. As a consequence, foreign traders had to bear additional protection costs by contributing to military expenditure, which was at the same time a way for states to redistribute the profits earned by very wealthy merchants.[30] Transaction costs[31] due to slow communication and the subsequent direness of information were among those that could be reduced through social trust, mutual obligations, loyalty and close-knit foreign communities that bound commercial networks together.[32]

As rightly pointed out by Van Zanden, the nature of mercantile capitalism that these businessmen represented depended on a well-oiled relationship with pre-capitalist modes of production, a relationship that was established on very unequal terms, owing to the merchants' ability to place agricultural surplus in the most advantageous markets and to efficiently meet the demand for luxury goods which the privileged groups required in order to maintain their status[33] In addition, the naval and financial services provided by the merchants were in high demand in Europe, which was permanently at war and eminently aristocratic in character. Until well into the eighteenth century, merchants found their most profitable bases of action in the zealously free and autonomous small urban republics.[34] These urban republics set up original institutional solutions to offset the negative effects of war on their respective markets.[35] The rivalry between cities and international conflicts had a considerable impact on the strategies of commercial agents, who were forced to face the rising cost of insurance and the instability of sea routes by organising convoys or by putting together other solutions, which also increased protection costs. The systematic application of economic warfare strategies and the declaration of commercial embargoes deeply affected the normal course of mercantile transactions and acted as a stimulus for the search for alternative markets and the use of straw men and contraband.

In order to promote trust and overcome the multiple risks and uncertainties that were inherent to their business, especially the principal-agent problem, merchants followed multiple strategies. Most merchant organisations were built around kinship, which was followed in importance by cultural and, finally, cross-cultural relationships. Family relations were often regarded as the best guarantee of trustworthy relationships; in these instances, the different roles involved in commercial mediation, such as agents, correspondents and consignees, were assumed by family members who migrated to different harbours and thereby connected different regions. By keeping brokerage within the family, transaction costs could be partially internalised.

The role of kinship and family relations in the formation of networks is even more pronounced if we take into consideration that commercial networks are often not formed within the lifespan of a single trader, but over much longer periods.[36] The intergenerational survival of contacts contributed to creating very strong networks; a long common history and shared habits and knowledge were the raw materials with which very solid networks capable of connecting traders from different backgrounds and families could be made. Despite their efficiency, however, family networks had their limitations, and trust and mutual obligations could break down or bring about quite different results from those envisaged by the network's prime movers.[37] This point was stressed by Sheryllynne Haggerty in her analysis of a trading company in eighteenth-century Liverpool. In this particular case, family networks turned out to be not only of no use for the company but actually harmful because of the moral hazards associated with socially bound mutual obligations.[38] Thus, network failure and collapse could well occur, which stresses the temporal dimension of relationships that were far from having the static character so often invoked for analytical purposes.

Cultural ties were the basis for the formation of so-called 'national' or 'ethnic' merchant networks. These terms should, however, be used with caution, not only because they project an idea of identity that belongs to the modern homogenised nation state onto early modern societies but also because the traders' identity was a very fluid reality. Cultural ties were essentially dependent on a shared geographical origin; merchants tended to develop commercial relationships with their co-naturals and to choose them as consignees and correspondents. A shared language and religion were among the factors that contributed to the formation of early modern trading communities. This form of cooperation was usually backed by an institutional setting, generally embraced under the term 'nation': chapels, confraternities, hospitals and maritime consulates.[39] Maritime consulates, one of the key trade institutions, were established by different governments in order to guarantee the rights and privileges of their merchants and sailors abroad, according to the stipulations of commercial treaties. However, consuls were multipolar figures; they were not always citizens of the nation they represented, and they formed their own mercantile networks, thus acting as commercial agents rather than as mere government officials or institutional representatives.[40]

A number of studies have delved into the support mechanisms set in motion by trading communities in the international arena: in the seventeenth and eighteenth centuries, the Huguenot community in Hamburg traded in French colonial products, especially sugar, but also exported textiles from Central Europe to the overseas colonies. They exploited old networks in their country of origin but also created new ties in Hamburg, thus combining ethnic and transnational ties. They successfully replaced the Sephardic merchants, most of whom were of Portuguese origin and had, up until that time, connected the Hanseatic port with the sugar plantations in Brazil, as well as with other colonial destinations.[41]

This example underlines the importance of religion in the formation of cultural ties and underlines its impact on the changing spatial configuration of networks: the routes and products traded by merchant communities of different origins changed over time in a fluid motion, resulting in a much more dynamic system than classic definitions of trade diasporas suggest.[42] There are a large number of case studies of successful trading communities in the early modern period, including the Armenians,[43] the Sephardic Jews in seventeenth- and eighteenth-century Livorno,[44] the Maltese in eighteenth-century Spain and the Germans, Flemings and Genoese in eighteenth-century Cádiz.[45]

Each of these communities followed their own organisational model and network strategies. Thus, close ties with the province or country of origin, for example, among the Germans and the Flemish in Cádiz and the centre of the Bourbon's mercantilist system in Spain in the eighteenth century, resulted in a general rejection of the idea of naturalisation; indeed, Germans were not particularly willing to become subjects of the Spanish king – mainly due to their Protestant or Lutheran beliefs – while the Genoese were much more eager to obtain official status as Spanish subjects, as their links with their homeland were few and they formed only a loose-knit national group in Cádiz.[46] Another case in point is that posed by the Milanese merchants in eighteenth-century Cádiz, who, in spite of their weak intra-group integration, did not show much interest in Spanish citizenship, preferring instead to build up their transnational networks.[47]

Naturalisations were the ultimate expression of changing identities and are a good reminder of the degree of complexity, fluidity and ambivalence of merchants' identities, which were often reshaped and reconceptualised over time and space.[48] This is in part related to the practice of network building, as is demonstrated by the example posed by Jewish-convert merchants in sixteenth-century Burgos (northern Castile), whose network disintegrated quickly as short-term individual profit maximisation proved to have more weight than group solidarity.[49] Unsurprisingly, cultural networks were also in a permanent flux of contraction, expansion and spatial shifts. Thus, for instance, throughout the eighteenth century the Germans extended their networks from Hamburg, Lübeck and Bremen to London, Bordeaux and Cádiz,[50] while Basque traders managed to establish direct trade links between Cádiz and Peru after 1739.[51]

These last two examples also underline the fact that different network types were not mutually exclusive but could work perfectly well in combination. Thus, the Germans and the Basques used both family- and culture-based networks to build up and expand their enterprises by connecting their home regions with British and Spanish Atlantic markets respectively. These relationships with their respective homelands have aroused much interest among scholars who are interested in researching the identity of merchant communities. While many studies tend to focus on the ways foreign merchants tried to integrate into their host societies, it is important not to forget the rejection suffered and the obstacles faced by these merchants. This is, for example, the case posed by the French in Spain, and especially in Cádiz, whence they were expelled after the onset of the Spanish-French war in 1793. Despite all of the reprisals that were unleashed upon them, the French stayed loyal to their country,[52] a reminder that legal status and social practice among merchants were in a constant state of renegotiation due to the ever-shifting political, economic, social and cultural landscape.

More recently, the analytical focus has shifted towards transnational networks and cross-cultural trade relationships. Networks that included only co-naturals and family members were limited in their ability to set up wide-ranging business relations: relationships with members of different cultures were needed to make truly international trade possible. María Fusaro, who has also worked on the interdependence between Greek and English merchants in the Eastern Mediterranean,[53] has recently taken an original approach to the commercial interaction between

Venice and England and revealed the cosmopolitism that prevailed within these two communities, which certainly did not feel constrained by any nationality-inspired limitations.[54]

The new cross-cultural stance, however, represented with special clarity by Francesca Trivellato's work on Sephardic traders in seventeenth- and eighteenth-century Livorno, implies a profound theoretical and methodological critique of the community approach. Instead of taking 'internally homogeneous and externally bounded'[55] groups as the basic organisational feature of early modern trade, 'communitarian cosmopolitism' is claimed as the most appropriate description of cultural and economic exchange 'within the framework of a corporatist society of unequal and separate groups'.[56] Instead of communities living and coexisting side by side, polycentric-networked structures evolved among traders from different cultural backgrounds; these networks channelled the transmission of knowledge, money and goods but had to overcome social and legal barriers that were not fully neutralised by the operation of the network.

In sum, several types of networks may be recognised in early modern long-distance trade: ethnic or cultural, family based and transnational or cross-cultural. This raises the question of whether they coexisted and overlapped in time and space or whether there was generally a dominant type, as so many studies appear to assume. It should also be taken into account that the relationships within the network's core (that is, actors which are closely related) and those between the core and the periphery (actors with looser links with the core) may have been very different in nature.[57] For instance, family-based relationships or ethnic connections could bind together the network's core (e.g. the partners of a company), while transnational networks could be the basis for weaker relationships (e.g. partners in one business transaction, occasional correspondents, etc.). Another issue is that of the temporal and spatial dynamics of networks: this topic was addressed by Ana Crespo Solana with the aid of geographic information system (GIS) technology, with which she mapped shipping routes and commercial operations with specific consideration given to their temporal dimensions and shifts. In this way, merchant networks can be perceived and analysed on the macro-level and in their full structural dimensions.[58]

At the same time, it is important to analyse what kind of shifts occurred (e.g. strengthening or weakening of networks) and their causes (e.g. changing trust, failing business operations or political factors, such as peace or war). This kind of analysis requires a precise definition of networks. Critics have stressed the sometimes inflationary use of the term 'network' in studies that focus on social relationships from a historical perspective. The application of social network analysis to historical studies, as proposed by Mark Casson, Andrea Caracausi and Christof Jeggle, is based on a definition of networks that contemplates a minimum of three actors connected with one another by frequent rather than occasional contact. Variables, such as network density, closeness or centrality, are crucial tools for understanding the inner logic that rules the operation of networks, and they can also be useful in the analysis of their spatial and temporal dynamics.[59]

While these concepts basically build on quantitative methods, large datasets and software-aided calculations (e.g. Ucinet or Pajek), the potential of qualitative enquiry should not be forgotten. The use and advantages of quantitative network calculations cannot be questioned, but they must be considered as complementary to qualitative analysis, which remains the best approach for case studies that involve single merchants, companies and mercantile communities. In this way, migration patterns, questions of identity, the type and kind of social relations, the institutional background and the links with political networks and lobbying can be explored. Also, the evidence is often scattered and fragmentary, which poses difficulties for quantification.

While it is clear that this analysis is useful for analysing the inner structures and dynamics of trading houses and agents, the methodological implications also influence the study of the market. Indeed, some scholars have noted a rift between the network approach, which represents social relations based on informal bonds, trust and reciprocity, and impersonal mercantile transactions conducted in the market.[60] We do not want to challenge the notion that social networks and market exchange are different categories, and the relationships between the political economy, trade and mercantile agency; however, it has to be stressed that early modern markets are hardly independent from political interventions, but rather are constituted in tight interrelations with the authorities.[61]

This seems to question the Weberian idea that there is a solid, clear-cut line that divides markets, as abstract and impersonal points of exchange ruled by the laws of supply and demand, from merchant networks, as constituted by personal relationships.[62] These arguments claim that capitalistic economic development demanded the creation of impersonal institutions free from any corporate, ethnic or religious bond, in order to ensure the formation of national markets ruled by increasingly anonymous relationships. We believe, however, that the progressive integration of commercial spaces worldwide was made possible by different mercantile diasporas, which, despite being grouped on the basis of their national character, had a markedly transnational nature and operated with ease within notably heterogeneous political and social contexts.[63] Similarly, merchants are not isolated rational utilitarian agents, but are embedded into all sorts of social surroundings.[64] Thus, commercial networks contribute to the formation of markets by providing the framework for the exchange of information, discourses and trust in a context where reliable information, credit and centralised state authority are lacking.[65]

Seemingly, some find it difficult to distinguish between networks that emerged as a consequence of mercantilist regulations – for example the Spanish *Consulado*, based in Seville between 1543 and 1717, and thereafter in Cádiz – and those created by merchants in order to set up multilayered and polycentric webs that made long-distance commercial exchange and trust possible. Mercantilist monopolies are identified as one of the factors that kept prices – and thus merchants' profits – high and, therefore, impeded market integration, which can be measured by shrinking price differentials.[66] To what extent merchant networks counterbalanced this trend with their multiple strategies to lower transaction costs, and how they acted when they were also part of these mercantilist monopolies, is open to discussion. We must not forget, as Marcello Carmagnani masterfully reminds us, that despite the considerable differences between the Dutch, English and French model – based on the creation of privileged companies – and the Spanish one – based on the theoretical direct control of exchange in the *Carrera de Indias* – both systems were equally monopolistic. Mercantile capital was fragile, and social structure imposed further limits on external commerce, which made the use of armed force and the restriction of the lucrative colonial markets an inescapable necessity for everyone.[67] While Steensgaard's classic arguments underlined the modernity of the VOC and its autonomy with regard to the Dutch state, and compared it with the archaic and feudal structure of the Portuguese *Estado da India*,[68] Subrahmayan, following Meilink-Roelofs, opts for stressing the continuities between both models, and the crucial importance of the Asian regional trade for two models that, at first sight, have very little in common, but which were, in reality, dependent on similar factors.[69]

Thus, we need to know how merchants used different types of networks (kinship, national, cross-cultural) in order to carry out each task involved in commercial transactions (credit, payment, transportation, sale and purchase, etc.), tasks that were a precondition for integrated markets. Another aspect that needs clarification is whether, and to what degree, networks barred competition from outsiders, or whether they simply set up a different competitive environment.

These different conceptualisations of commercial exchange notwithstanding, all approaches have gradually abandoned traditional perspectives based on linear or bilateral exchange relations between regions or states, and focus instead on a multipolar perspective: actors, communities and their networks are conceived as connectors between different commercial systems.[70]

The 'commercial system' concept encompasses the full complexity of international long-distance trade in the context of colonial-mercantilist maritime empires: legal norms, maritime consulates or other corporate institutions such as merchant guilds or fraternities, mercantilist regulations, the acquisition of citizenship, organisation of transport, production and consumption patterns, payment facilities and credit. Commercial systems can be defined as exchange relation structures between and within maritime empires (e.g. Spain, Portugal, France or Great Britain) in the age of mercantilism. Compared with other systemic approaches, such as Wallerstein's World-System[71] or the Atlantic System, the 'commercial system approach' is a rather wide and open way to address and systematise commercial exchange and combine the analysis of trade networks and that of political economies. Some have shown their scepticism: Piet Emmer states that there was no Atlantic System, at least as far as the economy is concerned, because the relationships between the regions that were supposedly part of it were insufficiently 'entangled'. More recently, Horst Pietschmann claimed that a truly mercantilist Spanish empire, and thus a 'Spanish Atlantic' with all the necessary norms and rules, did not emerge until the Bourbonic reforms of the eighteenth century.[72] This idea has been challenged recently by Regina Grafe, who believes that, despite the Bourbonic reforms, the Spanish monarchy retained its essentially polycentric nature in which power was still eminently based on local authority; this is supported by the fact that the Spanish tax systems resembled that in the United Provinces more than those in fully sovereign states such as France and Britain.[73] Also, in her opinion, despite the wishes of the imperial authorities, the Spanish Atlantic system remained very flexible and capable of adapting to the demands of the mercantile networks on which it depended, and was far from being as rigidly mercantilist and authoritarian as is often claimed.[74]

In the United Provinces, there was also no room for the application of protectionist policies due to the pre-eminence of commercial over productive interests, which made it unviable to implement measures that aimed at protecting the domestic market. Local authorities had to make do with ensuring that the strict guild controls were enforced and that guilds monopolised the supply of luxury products to the member of the aristocracy, who were their main customers. This dynamic was reinforced after the signing of the alliance with the Spanish monarchy in 1648, which consolidated the dominant position of merchants in the international markets and brought radical changes to the productive structure, which promoted the industrialisation of the luxury manufacturing sector and imposed very tight quality control systems.[75] The manufacturing sector had been facing increasing difficulties with its competitors because of the high wages demanded by the guilds and the lack of protection in the shape of custom duties, owing to the refusal of the all-powerful commercial sector. The opposite process was, in the meantime, taking place in England, where the parliament imposed stern measures to prevent the arrival of Asian calicoes. In the United Provinces, the internal barriers to the development of free manufacture were combined with the pernicious effect of the mercantilist policies that were followed by the country's main rivals, France and England (Colbert's increase in custom duties and Navigation Acts, respectively),[76] and the aggressive economic warfare measures that culminated with the invasion of the United Provinces in 1672. The war costs and the protection of trade routes forced a considerable increase in taxation. In this regard, against those who, like Brawley, claim that the United Provinces were an island of liberalism based on Grotius' doctrine of *mare liberum*,[77] we follow Fernand Braudel and his authoritative opinion that 'les hollandais ne pouvaient pas échapper à l'esprit de son temps'.[78] The republic, therefore, did not hesitate to protect its markets by force of arms and to apply exclusivist policies in its Asian markets, closing the mouth of the Scheldt in order to slow the recovery of the southern Low Countries and using their powerful fleet to guarantee access to the Baltic Sea or to block Lisbon's harbour. These policies responded to internal vested interests that created important conflicts between the different corporations that held a position of authority within the state. As acutely pointed out by Julia Adams in her analysis of the struggle between the VOC and the WIC, these conflicts were in the end more damaging to the position of the United Provinces in the Atlantic markets in the late seventeenth century than the external attacks.[79] Again, a very different process was unfolding in England, where, as pointed out by Chaudhuri, the strength of the primary sector and the common interests of merchants and major agricultural producers guaranteed the production of agricultural surplus, which stimulated trade and reduced the country's economic dependence on foreign merchants.[80]

Therefore, as with the debate on globalisation, systems can be approached from very different perspectives: early modern trade in the Atlantic world in the seventeenth and eighteenth centuries has been often linked with the role of centralising mercantilist empires such as France and England. These empires aspired to build a territorialised and centralised state, where political institutions could closely control economic resources and impose a homogeneous understanding of political sovereignty. However, besides this model, in which long-distance trade played a decisive role, there existed what we have recently started to refer to as polycentric systems; these complex political structures were far from meeting Bodin's principles of full sovereignty, and enable us to understand that the national, centralised and homogenous French model was not the only – in fact, it was not even the predominant – way to organise a modern state. This is further proven by the close interaction and strong interdependence between some dynastic systems (the Hispanic monarchy, the Holy Roman Empire, the Hanseatic League) and some of the key republican systems (Genoa, the United Provinces, Venice and the Helvetic Confederation) with which they shared a mainly urban and polynuclear constitutional structure, marked by constitutional, legal and cultural diversity.[81]

Challenging the traditional distinction between British parliamentarianism and French absolutism, we believe that, despite having notable differences, both states opted for a process of administrative centralisation and exclusive control of economic resources through the application of rigorous mercantilist measures. While in England and France, the community of the kingdom was increasingly identified with the monarch and the centralised state, in polycentric models, the mechanisms for naturalisation and citizenship continued to be based on the consensus of local communities rather than the orders of the sovereign alone, which guaranteed the autonomy of the different corporations, cities, families and bodies that formed the state.[82] This heterogeneous and flexible space facilitated the participation and inclusion of different transnational mercantile diasporas, which were not only allowed to operate without barriers within this framework of diverse legal and monetary systems but which also acted as connectors between widespread territories and became an essential resource for them. This situation, far from standing as a barrier to economic development, may explain the mercantile and financial vitality experienced in territories which were otherwise characterised by fragmented sovereignty, but which were nevertheless at the roots of the European overseas expansion. Once more, all of this indicates that the centralist and homogenising model of the nation state was far from being the only viable option.[83] As pointed out by Oscar Gelderblom in his analysis of the transformation that the heterogeneous city network of the Netherlands underwent between 1250 and 1650, the fierce defence of urban privileges and political fragmentation was not a burden for economic development, but rather a stimulus to institutional innovation towards efficiency and increasing connectivity with other markets.

Despite the geographical complexity of the country, war-related problems and constant intercity rivalry, municipal governments implemented legal, commercial and financial measures that aimed at developing exchange in the global market.[84] In Israel's opinion, decentralisation acted as a catalyst for the colonial expansion of the republic; the collective nature of decision-making mechanisms turned the drafting of economic policies into a process of long and difficult negotiations and compromises. Both the VOC and the WIC attracted investment from different cities and provinces more efficiently than the privileged companies in England and France, the capital for which was mostly supplied by their respective governments.[85]

Similarly, the Spanish monarchy, which we have recently defined as a monarchy of urban republics, and which for a long time included the Low Countries,[86] was characterised by rigorous respect for the liberty of each of the corporations and bodies that were part of it, as well as for its multi-jurisdictional nature. As demonstrated by Ana Belem Fernández de Castro, the system created a variety of institutional set-ups in order to attract mercantile communities, which were essential for the operation of the empire on a global scale.[87] Another example of this polycentric structure is the role played by the Genoese as both merchants and bankers at the service of the Spanish Crown, especially during the 'Genoese century' in the sixteenth and seventeenth centuries.[88]

Such a perspective on commercial systems also creates the possibility of examining events that crossed the systems' boundaries, that is, inter-imperial trade or commercial exchange between regions under different rulers. These include mercantile republics, but also regions in the interior of Central Europe. It is precisely this connection between the Mediterranean and the Atlantic that some of the book's chapters have picked up on in order to start discussing the aforementioned theoretical approaches. The chapters are organised by topic into four main sections, and by chronological order within each section.

Part I is dedicated to theoretical considerations and historiographical reviews. Xabier Lamikiz and Montserrat Cachero reconsider theoretical concepts associated with network analysis for the study of early modern long-distance trade. Both authors argue for theoretical clarity and a precise definition of terms and concepts; without these, they argue, the application of the tools of social-network analysis to historical narratives and sources, which might be difficult to interpret, can generate distortions. Lamikiz closely examines several relevant works on trade, which argue for the application of network analysis or use different approaches to empirical analysis. He draws particular attention to key concepts for the history of early modern trade, such as trust and social capital, and reaches the conclusion that theoretical concepts are not always applicable to historical data (and sometimes to social data in general) – for example, when it comes to defining the boundaries of a network. While rejecting the use of network merely as a metaphor, Lamikiz agrees with Cachero and calls for an adaption of network analysis to historical trade analysis and, therefore, for a theoretical dialogue between historians and other social scientists.

Lamikiz, in summary, argues for a qualitative approach, insisting on the paucity of sources for the early modern age, while Montserrat Cachero shows that quantitative network analysis can be turned into a workable approach for historians engaged in the analysis of early modern merchant networks. Cachero traces the development of social network analysis and introduces key concepts and quantitative tools, taking the early sixteenth-century Augsburg commercial dynasty of the Welser as an example. This well-known company opened a factory in Seville, run by Hieronymus Sayler, and reached out to Spanish America when granted an *asiento* contract by Charles V, which meant that, in effect, they were ordered to take charge of Venezuela. As a consequence, their ties stretched as far as Santa Marta and later, also Santo Domingo. However, information flows always had to run through Seville, so that (geographical) closeness in the network mattered less than centrality as far as access to information was concerned. Also, Cachero points out that variables such as transitivity can be used in order to indicate which actors had more authority within an enterprise, and which were less connected or even isolated from the rest. When actors were only indirectly connected with one another, structural holes appeared that made it possible for one actor to exercise a considerable degree of power and control. Dense networks, in contrast, strengthened multipolar structures of social interaction. Cachero repeatedly insists, however, that these variables must be complemented with a close scrutiny of the sources: mercantile correspondence, court testimonies and diaries are sources of information on both the quantity and the quality of social relations. While the usefulness of quantitative network theory in the examination of social interactions is demonstrated, the shortcomings and limitations of the approach are also discussed, primarily in relation to limited information, owing to the fragmentary character of historical sources (although this problem still haunts the modern social scientist) and the use of highly abstract and therefore, oversimplified network models, which often lead to spurious results.

The link between transnational trade networks and regional economies is the point of departure for Ana Crespo Solana's analysis of the transmission of social and behavioural change through commercial networks. Drawing on her profound knowledge of the Dutch and Flemish mercantile communities in eighteenth-century Cádiz, Crespo points out the regional embedding of commercial exchange over long distances, which was carried out by 'self-organised networks' that had to bridge the gap between reciprocal exchange within networks and the corporate reality within which merchant communities lived and operated. In fact, both realities were combined and resulted in the construction and extension of networks in which a wide variety of practical arrangements for cooperation converged, including loans and the representation of other merchants. In this way, local interaction produced global coordination, and changes in local merchant families led to changes in transnational trade networks, in a butterfly effect that ended in the emergence of new global cultures and identity-forming spaces.

These behavioural patterns include competition for network resources and cooperation with the political authorities. This underlines the fact that economic networks were not separated from the state and the social environment: in eighteenth-century Spain and western Andalusia, tax farmers and custom officials often belonged to the same network as merchants and moneylenders. Increased cooperation and growth were the driving forces behind the selective expansion of networks, which often led to social stratification and the consolidation of the position of some merchants as members of the social elite.

At the same time, this expansion played a key role in the connection of different ports and the establishment of new transport and shipping routes as well as links between producers and consumers. This is illustrated by the example of a Dutch-Flemish merchant who linked the Mediterranean with Spanish America and the European Atlantic, also reaching the North Sea and the Baltic Sea. Some merchants may have operated within small networks, but in this case the structure and solidity of networks is more relevant than size, as far as commercial efficiency is concerned.

In the opening chapter of Part II, which deals with the social configuration of networks – the polarity between culturally and transnationally oriented networks – Eberhard Crailsheim contributes to the studies that analyse the effect of family and culture on the structure of merchant networks. Through the examination of a sample of notarial documents dated to between 1570 and 1640, and concerning Flemish and French merchants in Seville, the most important trade link between Europe and the Spanish Atlantic, this chapter argues that these two merchant communities had an impact on the Spanish Atlantic system by virtue of immigration flows caused by largely political factors. During the Eighty Years' War with the northern Dutch provinces, many Flemings escaped to the south and settled in Seville, where they established a chapel, and later also a consulate during the Twelve Years' Truce. Between the late sixteenth and the first half of the seventeenth century, their numbers rose considerably, and they became one of the most powerful foreign merchant communities in the city. French traders had started settling earlier, especially in the aftermath of the signing of the Peace Treaty of Cateau-Cambresis. The influx of French immigrants ceased after the Spanish declared war in 1635, after which the sequestration of property, ordered by King Philipp IV, and the systematic policy of commercial embargoes against the enemies of the Crown drove them back to their homeland.[89]

While Flemish merchants, in spite of their organisational structure, sought and achieved quick and close integration with the local Spanish society, as demonstrated by the numerous naturalisation letters and mixed marriages with Castilians, they still built their business networks around their own community. Conversely, the French community was much smaller and had to rely much more on outsiders; the Flemings were, in fact, their most common partners. Only when the French community had grown to a considerable size by the second decade of the seventeenth century did they rely more on mono-ethnic networks. Crailsheim argues that the results of his thorough study underline the principle of homophily as opposed to the stress laid by recent approaches upon cosmopolitan and cross-cultural approaches to trade. He adds, at any rate, that other factors, such as the geopolitical context, are also crucial for a correct understanding of the flexibility and adaptability of merchant communities in their networking strategies.[90]

With his case study on the trajectory of the Seville-born, Mexican-based and Tuscan-in-origin merchant Santi Federighi during the first half of the seventeenth century, José Luis Gasch illustrates the role that merchants played as connectors between different mercantile systems and in the laying down of the foundations of a global market. This example demonstrates not only the fluid character of the identities of merchants and their constant reconceptualisation but also the temporal construction of both cultural and cross-cultural ties of one family over the generations, mainly through marriages of its members. From this solid base, Federighi used his operations in Mexico City, the strategic crossroads for trade between Europe, Africa, Asia and the interior of America, to gain a key position in international trade. He traded in two key products for New Spain and the nascent global economy – cochineal and silver – and he acted as a moneylender and invested in the Manila Galleon, a vehicle of the Philippine trade. In order to manage these vast trade flows, Federighi resorted to different types of networks: while he maintained a direct relationship with the miners of Zacatecas and Aguascalientes, in Oaxaca he relied on representatives. His agents were constantly on the move, providing Federighi with fresh information, while the Veracruz merchants were his brokers for the re-exportation of cochineal to Seville, but not as sources of credit. By relying on family and close political ties, Federighi also intervened directly in the Philippine trade, where he purchased textiles and porcelains, which he distributed between the viceroyalty of New Spain and Seville.

Federighi's example is an eloquent case in point of the polycentric nature of the Spanish monarchy, which was not ruled solely from Madrid, but also from the multiple local and interconnected decision centres, which were united by cosmopolitism. Despite the rigorous rules that prohibited the presence of foreigners in the overseas colonies under the Crown,[91] some merchant networks, for example the Welser's – analysed in this volume by Montserrat Cachero – or Santi Federighi's, were an essential factor in the integration of different territories. The monarchy itself promoted the formation around the different decision centres of a wide variety of overlapping but distinct aristocratic, military, religious and mercantile networks. These networks had to adapt to the laws and privileges of each territory and became, despite their heterogeneous character, the main factor of cohesion within such a complex political structure, along with the obedience to a single monarch and a shared religious faith. The political structure was based on cities, and has been masterfully described by Jack Owens: 'I conceive of Castile and the Hispanic Monarchy of the first global age as a complex array of intricate, overlapping, interlocal, and interactive economic, political, and information networks. The loci connected by these networks were the municipalities whose jurisdictions completely covered many of the larger political regions, and many of the networks involved locations well beyond the territorial boundaries of any part of the Monarchy'.[92] The circulation of elites across these polycentric empires was an essential connecting factor, as well as operating as the main mechanism of social promotion among the merchant groups. Social promotion among the urban oligarchies and the aristocracy has been thoroughly studied,[93] but we are still very much in the dark concerning businessmen and merchants. In this regard, as recently pointed out by Hilario Casado in his study of the role of mercantile colonies in the rest of the Spanish territories between the fifteenth and the sixteenth centuries, it is necessary to focus upon the analysis of preindustrial commerce as a multinuclear phenomenon in which, apart from any bilateral relationships of dependence and domination (centre-periphery, metropolis-colonies, haulers-merchants), we should also consider a multiplicity of multilateral links.[94]

Manuel F. Fernández Chaves and Mercedes Gamero Rojas examine the complexity of the identity of merchants and its constant recontextualisation over time. The Irish community in Seville and Cádiz, which started growing rapidly and steadily from the late seventeenth century onwards, did not organise itself formally as a commercial nation. The Irish adapted to the circumstances and tried to profit from them, either by declaring themselves to be British citizens or by operating independently, or by trying to integrate with the local Spanish society or building transnational ties with Flemish and, to a lesser extent, French merchant families. They occupied the space left by the British merchants who were expelled during the Spanish War of Succession and operated wide Irish networks in France, the Spanish (and also, from 1713, the Austrian) Netherlands and Holland. This allowed them not only to conduct business with Flemish and French traders but also to organise the commodity flows between these regions, for example, the import of wheat and iron to Cádiz and thence towards the Mediterranean and the Spanish Atlantic. These contacts also connected them to the proto-industrial textile regions in the Holy Roman Empire, for example, Elberfeld while contacts with Great Britain never ceased to exist, as shipments of Cornish wheat demonstrate. A share of the wool exports, conducted by mainly Dutch (and to a lesser degree French) merchants went also to Great Britain, alongside with its main destination in these case studies, that is, Holland and a destination in the north of Europe that is not named explicity. However, in insurance businesses, French commercial enterprises and investors largely took the lead for Irish merchants' business, while Dutch investors still played an important role. Finally, there was also some investment in French colonial trade, which underlines the highly permeable character of trade barriers between colonial territories under different empires. This constant circulation of commodities and money was made possible by merchants and their regular migratory flows and marriage strategies; in the case of the Irish, these were chiefly with members of other national groups, mainly the Spanish, French (with and without Irish roots) and Flemish.

In Part III, entitled 'Connecting Spaces: Networks and Systems, Merchants and Political Economies', Margrit Schulte-Beerbühl demonstrates the gradual involvement of German networks between the mid-seventeenth century and the early nineteenth century. Initially, merchants from north-western Germany migrated to the harbours of Bremen and Hamburg and thence to London, thus connecting their home regions with the maritime trade in the North Sea and, therefore, the Atlantic.

While the links with Bremen and Hamburg were being laid down, these merchants were also extending their networks across different interior regions in the Holy Roman Empire.

During a second stage, these networks expanded towards East Germany, as far as Saxony and Silesia, and also, Bohemia, and soon they were in command of the export of the linen produced in several regions of the Holy Roman Empire to both English and Spanish colonial markets, a commercial enterprise that kept growing for a long time. Indeed, despite some setbacks in the second half of the eighteenth century, caused by British industrialisation, this textile trade remained active until the 1830s. During a third stage, these networks reached the Mediterranean and incorporated important harbours such as Livorno, Genoa and Trieste. Their integrating role, therefore, not only united the North Sea and the Mediterranean, but also northern and southern German merchants in the first half of the eighteenth century.

This pattern fits well with the recent reappraisal of the role of traders in the Habsburg monarchy; these were mainly Milanese in origin, and established trade links which included Genoa, Cádiz, Trieste and, crucially, Austria and Bohemia, which they linked with the Spanish Atlantic in the second half of the eighteenth century. They made skilful use of the infrastructure provided by the imperial consulate in Cádiz in terms of legal protection, privileged access to information and political decision-making, and higher social status.[95] In many instances, these mercantile networks were neatly intertwined with financial enterprises, in particular those of which the Habsburg state and the Viennese Court mostly relied.[96]

As Schulte-Beerbühl demonstrates, the networks of German traders were also multilayered webs organised along family and kinship lines, but cross-cultural connections, mainly with British, Dutch and relocated Spanish traders, played an important role as well. The shifting spatial dimensions of their trade led to a constant reshuffling of network structures, and migration was one of their most important tools. Although the Napoleonic Wars and the Continental Blockade seem at first sight to have damaged these connections and caused the initial disintegration of networks, a second glance clearly demonstrates that these networks managed to reorganise quite quickly. They shifted their trade focus (including smuggling) towards the North and Baltic Seas, including smuggling; they were given special treatment by the British government, which applied a stick-and-carrot policy during the war in order to guarantee the supply of food and raw materials necessary for the war effort. After the end of the war, these networks re-established the traditional trade routes between the North and Baltic Seas and the Atlantic and the Mediterranean, and new networks were created between German and US merchants. These networks were to become highly influential in the evolution of bilateral trade in the early nineteenth century.

Over the last few decades, the role of the Mediterranean has been revisited and tested against Braudel's idea of the region's decline, at least after 1650. While historiography has for a long time focused on groups that either operated in the Mediterranean (such as the Greeks and the Jews) or in the Atlantic, recent trends indicate a growing interest in the links that existed between both regions. To date, research has mainly concentrated on the role played by the Genoese in Spain between the sixteenth and the eighteenth centuries. Pablo Hernández Sau explores the potential of a micro-historical approach through an analysis of an Italian-French merchant family, the Bouligny, based in the Spanish city of Alicante. This family operated in several locations that acted as key connectors between the Mediterranean and the Atlantic in the eighteenth century. Hernández Sau frames change in the Mediterranean within a broader context and argues for the relative displacement of traditional Mediterranean merchant communities, such as the Venetians, the Greeks and the Jews, by newcomers, chiefly the French, the English, the Flemish and the Germans, from the seventeenth century onwards. The French community was particularly favoured by political conditions in the Spanish Empire, which is the focus of the chapter, after the Peace of the Pyrenees in 1659 and especially the Peace of Ryswick in 1697, which ended the permanent state of war between Madrid and Versailles. This initiated a period of dynastic rapprochement, which culminated in the recovery of Naples and Sicily by Spain (already under the Bourbons) in 1734. The arrival of the Bouligny family in Alicante in the early eighteenth century is part of a larger phenomenon involving the immigration of French merchants. While the first half of the century witnessed an expansion from the regional to Atlantic-wide networks and a heavy focus on textiles, the second half of the century was characterised by commercial diversification and a parallel shift in the orientation of networks: social networks became wider, assuming a clear transnational character, expanded geographically, especially in the Atlantic, and became more closely integrated into Spanish society.

The last section of the book examines formal and informal exchange mechanisms within networks and the breach of networks. Bethany Aram scrutinises the distribution channels of hides from the Spanish Caribbean – mainly Hispaniola/Santo Domingo, but occasionally also Puerto Rico – to Europe at the turn of the seventeenth century. The attempts of the Spanish Crown to impose a colonial monopoly on bovine hides in the immediate aftermath of the occupation of Santo Domingo had failed, as demonstrated by the lively trade between different Caribbean islands or the direct trade from Hispaniola to European countries, for example France. Emperor Charles V had to accept some exceptions in the commercialisation of this highly profitable product, which was in high demand in many European markets, mainly in France, the Low Countries and England, but also in Italy. Before this traffic was made legal during the reign of Philip II, an enormous amount of contraband hides were smuggled out of the Spanish Caribbean towards the Iberian Peninsula and a range of European harbours, still to the benefit of the Crown. In later years, licences to export hides to European destinations other than the Iberian Peninsula was turned into an instrument for the regulation of relations between the Crown and its most loyal and needy subjects. Thus, trade licences were granted according to social, political and economic criteria, preferably to subjects who were in a precarious financial situation or could support their application with other social and political arguments; at any rate, the licensees were always loyal subjects of the King. With the implementation of this policy, the trade in a colonial product and its distribution from the Spanish Caribbean to Europe was linked with political rule and the (re)production of loyalty, also productively linking trade history and the study of royal courts and their ways. Only in later years, under Philip III's rule, were the negative effects of this policy noticed: trade with hides grew in excess, and many unused licences were resold at rapidly falling prices. This, in addition, also helped to cover renewed smuggling. The Crown seems not to have issued any more licences to export hides after 1621.

Sheryllynne Haggerty stresses the notion that networks did not always work smoothly and that their success should not be considered automatic. Her study of a court process celebrated between 1711 and 1713 and related to a sea voyage in the British Atlantic is a textbook example of the problems that haunted underdeveloped networks in the port of Liverpool during its formative period as an international trading hub. The trip was not successful and encountered several problems, mainly due to the behaviour of the ship's skipper and supercargo. This behaviour was left to run unchecked because of the existence of structural holes in the network, which were being bridged by none other than the captain and the supercargo. One of them was simply incompetent, while the other was acting fiendishly. Although the trip took much longer than originally planned, the Liverpool merchants and the shipowner remained linked to the same business enterprise for many years. By the 1740s, Liverpool had developed into a major Atlantic port. In conclusion, we cannot say the network had failed, but to have shown, at the time of the unsuccessful trip, signs of underdevelopment, which are part of a social learning process.

In summary, this book aims to examine the roles of mercantile connectors and commercial structures that gave shape to the first globalisation process. Beyond a merely quantitative or economistic perspective, we have tried to focus on the complex ways these networks operated, often within the framework of equally complicated political constructs. Despite the growth of centralised government models from the seventeenth century onwards, right up until the end of the eighteenth century, the landscape remained dominated by polycentric and dispersed political structures based on fragmented forms of sovereignty. These heterogeneous structures were the natural environment for the operation of motley and varied mercantile organisations; these cosmopolitan constructs acted as connectors between regions and played an essential role in the circulation of a large variety of goods. The enormous importance of the local scale forced these businessmen to adapt to a great diversity of social circumstances. In order to illustrate the extraordinary versatility that these merchants had to exercise, we have analysed as wide a variety as possible of geographical contexts, which in turn is a good argument against the alleged hegemony of north-western Europe in shaping early modern globalization during this period. Indeed, both the Mediterranean and Central Europe played an important role in the process of global market integration, and we believe more work must go into investigating the connections between these regions and the rest of the world. Only then can we appreciate the complexity and fragmentation that characterised commercial exchange in the age of the first globalisation, as well as underlining the strong links that existed between regions which are often analysed only marginally. Similarly, we have tried to balance methodological considerations and case studies, sometimes approached from theoretically opposed perspectives. Our aim has not been to argue for a homogenous model of analysis or, even less, to reach universal conclusions. We have instead tried to create new spaces for debate and restore spaces and actors that historiography, conditioned by the institutionalist paradigm and by a trend to adopt unilinear narratives in order to explain economic development, had moved away from the focus.

This book results from the combination of several research projects directed by the editors: these projects culminated in an international meeting celebrated in the Escuela de Estudios Hispanoamericanos (CSIC) in June 2014. This conference was preceded by a series of conferences and bilateral meetings celebrated in the Universidad Pablo de Olavide, which were attended and supported by many of our colleagues. We would like to express our warmest thanks to the members of the Early Modern History Area at UPO, and most especially to those, such as Yasmina Ben Yessef Garfia, Natalia Maillard Álvarez, Claudio Marsilio, Orla Power, Alejandro García Montón, Renate Pieper and Fernando Ramos Palencia, who played an active role in the discussions and whose suggestions and contributions have done so much to enrich this volume. Finally, we want to thank David Govantes Edwards for his fine revision and translation of the texts collected in this volume, including this introduction.

Notes

1 This work was carried out within the framework of two projects based in Universidad Pablo de Olavide (Seville) ES-41013, which were conducted by both authors: 'Merchant Networks. Trade Between Spain and Habsburg Monarchy (1725–1815)', funded by the programme PEOPLE, Marie Curie (European Union) (UE PIEF-GA-2011-299469), and 'El modelo policéntrico de soberanía compartida (siglos XVI–XVIII). Una vía alternativa en la construcción del Estado Moderno' (HAR 2013-45357-P), funded by MINECO (Ministerio de Economia y Competitividad del gobierno español) with FEDER funds (European Union).
2 See, for instance: H. Lapeyre, *Simón Ruiz et les "asientos" de Philippe II* (Paris: Armand Colin, 1953); H.-T. Niephaus, *Genuas Seehandel von 1746–1848: Die Entwicklung der Handelsbeziehungen zur Iberischen Halbinsel, zu West und Nordeuropa sowie den Überseegebieten* (Köln, Wien: Böhlau, 1975). In contrast, Ana Sofia Ribeiro's most recent analysis of Simon Ruiz provides a good example of the new mercantile historiography focusing on networks: A.S. Ribeiro, *Early Modern Trading Networks in Europe: Cooperation and the Case of Simon Ruiz* (London: Routledge, 2015).
3 A. Crespo Solana, 'Las comunidades mercantiles y el mantenimiento de los sistemas comerciales de España, Flandes y la República Holandesa, 1648–1750', in A. Crespo Solana and M. Herrero Sánchez (eds.), *España y los diecisiete Países Bajos, siglos XVI–XVIII: una revisión* (Córdoba: Universidad de Córdoba, 2002), pp. 445–446, 453.
4 F. Braudel, *Civilisation matérielle, économie et capitalisme, XVe–XVIIIe siècle*, 3 vols. (Paris: Armand Colin, 1979); I. Wallerstein, *The Modern World-System I. Capitalist Agriculture and the Origins of the European World-Economy in the Sixteenth Century* (New York, San Francisco, London: Academic Press, 1974); idem., *The Modern World-System II: Mercantilism and the Consolidation of the European World-Economy, 1600–1750* (New York: Academic Press, 1980).

5 P.K. O'Brien, 'European Economic Development: The Contribution of the Periphery', *The Economic History Review* 35 (1982).

6 P. Emmer, 'In Search of a System: The Atlantic Economy 1500–1800', in H. Pietschmann (ed.), *Atlantic History. History of the Atlantic System 1580–1830* (Göttingen: Vandenhoeck and Ruprecht, 2002), pp. 169–171.

7 K. O'Rourke and J. Williamson, 'When did Globalization Begin?', *European Review of Economic History* no. 6 (April 2002).

8 Braudel authoritatively challenges the arguments against the economic impact of intercontinental exchange put forth by M. Godinho, J. Heers and O'Brien, 'il y a bien d'arguments pour expliquer que le fait minoritaire puisse l'emporter sur le majoritaire', in F. Braudel (ed.), *Civilisation matérielle*, II, p. 356.

9 S. Gruzinski, *Les quatre parties du monde. Histoire d'une mondialisation* (Paris: La Martinière, 2004).

10 L. Bély, *Les relations internationales en Europe (XVIIe–XVIIIe siècles)* (París: Presses Universitaires de France, 1992).

11 J. Israel, *Dutch Primacy in World Trade, 1585–1740* (Oxford: Clarendon Press, 1989).

12 M. Herrero Sánchez, 'Las Indias y la Tregua de los Doce Años', B. García García (ed.), *Tiempo de Paces. La Pax Hispánica y la Tregua de los Doce Años* (Madrid: Fundación Carlos de Amberes), 2009, pp. 193–229.

13 D.O. Flynn and A. Giráldez, *China and the Birth of Globalization in the 16th Century* (Farnham, Burlington: Ashgate-Variorum, 2010).

14 D.O. Flynn, 'Comparing the Tokuwaga Shogunate with Hapsburg Spain. Two Silver-Based Empires in a Global Setting', in E.H.G. Van Cauwenberghe (ed.), *Money, Coins, and Commerce: Essays in the Monetary History of Asia and Europe (From Antiquity to Modern Times)* (Leuven: Leuven University Press, 1991), pp. 11–46, and especially D.O. Flynn, 'El desarrollo del primer capitalismo a pesar de los metales preciosos del nuevo mundo: una interpretación anti-Wallerstein de la España imperial', *Revista de Historia Económica* 2 (1984), pp. 29–57.

15 P. Emmer, 'Search', p. 172. Klein, for his part, based on Steensgaard's date, estimates that around 1700 the trade of the republic with the rest of Europe was worth 130 million florins, while imports from Asia amounted to 18.4 million and those from the Atlantic, 2.25 million. This means that less than one-quarter of the merchant shipping operated in the non-European markets. However, he concludes that: 'there are reasons to assume that the positive impact of these goods on the Dutch economy was out of proportion' despite the negative effect of Asian trade for the Dutch textile industry'. E. van den Boogaart, P. Emmer, P. Klein and K. Zandvliet, *La expansión holandesa en el atlántico* (Madrid: Mapfre, 1992), p. 53.

16 A. Attman, *Dutch Enterprise in the World Bullion Trade, 1550–1800* (Göteborg: Kugl. Vetenskaps och Vitterhets Samhället, 1983).

17 For the best analysis to date, see J.M. Postma, *The Dutch in the Atlantic Slave Trade 1600–1815* (Cambridge: Cambridge University Press, 1990).

18 F.S. Gaastra, 'Merchants, Middlemen and Money: Aspects of the Trade between the Indonesian Archipelago and Manila in the 17th Century', in G. Schutte and H. Sutherland (eds.), *Papers of the Dutch Indonesian Historical Conference held at Lage Vuursche, The Netherlands 23–27 June 1980* (Leiden/Jakarta: Bureau of Indonesian Studies, 1982), pp. 301–314.

19 J.R. Bruijn, F.S. Gaastra and I. Schöffer, *Dutch Asiatic Shipping in the 17th and 18th Centuries* (La Haya: Martinus Nijhoff, 1987). With 600 million florins sent to Asia, the VOC became the main exporter of gold and silver to the region.

20 J. De Vries, 'The Limits of Globalization in the Early Modern World', *Economic History Review* 63, no. 3 (2009), pp. 719–722.

21 C.A. Bayly, *The Birth of the Modern World, 1780–1914: Global Connections and Comparisons* (Oxford: Blackwell, 2004), pp. 41–43.

22 K.N. Chaudhuri, 'World Silver Flows and Monetary Factors as a Force of International Economic Integration 1658–1758', in W. Fisher, R.M. McInnis and J. Schneider (eds.),

The Emergence of a World Economy, 1500–1914. Papers of the IX International Congress of Economic History (Wiesbaden-Stuttgart: Steiner-Verlag, 1986), p. 76.

23 J.B. 'Jack' Owens, 'Dynamic Complexity of Cooperation-Based Self-Organizing Commercial Networks in the First Global Age (DynCoopNet): What's in a Name?', in A. Crespo Solana and D. Alonso García (eds.), Special Issue: 'Self-Organizing Networks and GIS Tools. Cases of Use for the Study of Trading Cooperation (1400–1800)', *Journal of Knowledge Management, Economics and Information Technology*, (2012).

24 A. Crespo Solana, 'The Iberian Peninsula in the First Global Trade. Geostrategy and Mercantile Network interests (XV to XVIII centuries)', in *Global Trade Before Globalization (VIII–XVIII)* (Madrid: Fundación Cultura de Paz, 2007).

25 T.R. Shannon, *An Introduction to the World-System Perspective* (London, Boulder: Westview Press, 1989), p. 23. It must be stressed, however, that Wallerstein and his followers conceptualised the world-system as progressively expanding space, so that not all regions in the world were part of a worldwide division of labour from the moment the system took off in the sixteenth century, but were instead gradually incorporated. Such a notion of an expanding global space fits much better with realities of Asian hegemony than – paradoxically – Andre Gunder Frank's unique world-system, according to which all of the world has been but a single economic system since very ancient times. See A.G Frank, *ReOrient: The Global Economy in the Asian Age* (Berkeley, Los Angeles, London: University of California Press, 1998).

26 J.C. Van Leur, *Indonesian Trade and Society. Essays in Asian Social and Economic History* (The Hague: W. Van Hoeve Ltd., 1955).

27 See the clarifying debate between Chaudhuri and Blitz: R.C. Blitz, 'Some Reflections on the World Trade of the XVIIth and XVIIIth Century: A Comment on the Findings of Professor Chaudhuri', *The Journal of European Economic History* 7–1 (1978), pp. 214–222; and K.N. Chaudhuri, 'Some Reflection on the World Trade of the XVIIth Century: A Reply', *The Journal of European Economic History* 7–1 (1978), pp. 223–231.

28 J.A. Salas Auséns, 'Pequeños comerciantes extranjeros en la España del siglo XVIII', in A. Crespo Solana (ed.), *Comunidades transnacionales. Colonias de mercaderes extranjeros en el Mundo Atlántico (1500–1830)*, (Madrid: Doce Calles, 2010), pp. 123–125. M. Häberlein and C. Jeggle (eds.), *Praktiken des Handels. Geschäfte und soziale Beziehungen europäischer Kaufleute im Mittelalter und früher Neuzeit*, Irseer Schriften (Konstanz: UVK-Verlagsgesellschaft, 2010), p. 24.

29 X. Lamikiz, *Trade and Trust in the Eighteenth-Century Atlantic World: Spanish Merchants and Their Overseas Networks* (Woodbridge: Royal Historical Society, 2010), p. 13.

30 K.N. Chaudhuri, 'Reflections on the Organizing Principles of Premodern Trade', in J.D. Tracy (ed.), *The Political Economy of Merchant Empires. State Power and World Trade 1350–1750* (Cambridge: Cambridge University Press, 1991), p. 437.

31 D. North, 'Institutions, Transaction Costs, and the Rise of Merchant Empires', in J.D. Tracy (ed.), *The Political Economy of Merchant Empires. State Power and World Trade 1350–1750* (Cambridge: Cambridge University Press, 1991).

32 A. Greif, 'Institutions and International Trade: Lessons from the Commercial Revolution', *The American Economic Review* 82, no. 2 (May 1992), pp. 22–40. A. Crespo Solana, '¿Redes de dependencia inter-imperial? Aproximaciones teóricas en la funcionalidad de los agentes de comercio en la expansión de la sociedades mercantiles', in I. Pérez Tostado and E. García Hernán (eds.), *Irlanda y el Atlántico Ibérico. Movilidad, participación e intercambio cultural* (Valencia: Albatros Ediciones, 2010), pp. 42–43.

33 J.L. Van Zanden, *The Rise and Decline of Holland's Economy. Merchant Capitalism and the Labour Market* (Manchester: Manchester University Press, 1993), pp. 7–8.

34 M. Lindemann, *The Merchant Republics: Amsterdam, Antwerp, and Hamburg, 1648–1790* (Cambridge: Cambridge University Press, 2015). For Genoa, see M. Herrero Sánchez, Y.R. Ben Yessef, C. Bitossi and D. Puncuh (eds.), *Génova y la Monarquía Hispánica (1528–1713)* (Génova: Atti de la Società Ligure di Storia Patria, 2 Vols., 2011). Concerning the relationship between mercantile republics and the Spanish monarchy, see M. Herrero Sánchez, 'Republican Monarchies, Patrimonial Republics. The Catholic Monarchy and the Mercantile Republics of Genoa and the United Provinces', in P. Cardim, T. Herzog, J.J. Ruiz Ibáñez and G. Sabatini (eds.), *Polycentric Monarchies. How did Early Modern Spain and Portugal Achieve and Maintain a Global Hegemony?* (Eastbourne, Sussex: Academic Press, 2012), pp. 181–196. A recent general overview can be found in M. Herrero Sánchez (ed.), *Repúblicas y republicanismo en la Europa Moderna* (Madrid: Fondo de Cultura Económica: 2016).

35 O. Gelderblom, *Cities of Commerce: The Institutional Foundation of International Trade in the Low Countries, 1250–1650* (Princeton and Oxford: Princeton University Press, 2013).

36 K. Weber and M. Schulte-Beerbühl, 'From Westphalia to the Caribbean: Networks of German Textile Merchants in the Eighteenth Century', in A. Gestrich and M. Schulte-Beerbühl (ed.), *Cosmopolitan Networks in Commerce and Society 1660–1914* (London: German Historical Insitute London, 2011), p. 55.

37 C. Álvarez Nogal has demonstrated that the Genoese banking families that dominated Castilian finances between 1600 and 1640 were less kinship-dependent when it came to generating trust and to achieving a competitive position than hitherto believed. C. Álvarez Nogal, 'Las compañías bancarias genovesas en Madrid a comienzos del siglo XVII', *Hispania* LXV/1, 219 (2005), pp. 67–90.

38 S. Haggerty, 'I Could "Do For the Dickmans": When Family Networks Don't Work', in A. Gestrich and M. Schulte-Beerbühl (eds.), *Cosmopolitan Networks in Commerce and Society 1660–1914* (London: German Historical Insitute London, 2011).

39 A. Crespo Solana, 'Redes de dependencia', pp. 43, 45, 49. M. Bustos Rodríguez, *Cádiz en el sistema atlántico. La ciudad, sus comerciantes y la actividad mercantil (1650–1830)* (Madrid, Cádiz: Sílex-Universidad de Cádiz, 2005), pp. 116–118. M. Aglietti, M. Herrero Sánchez and F. Zamora Rodríguez (eds.), *Los consules extranjeros en la edad moderna y a principios de la edad contemporánea (siglos XV–XIX)* (Madrid: Doce Calles, 2013).

40 S. Marzagalli (ed.), *Les Consuls en Méditerranée, agents d'information XVIe–XXe siècle* (Paris: Classiques Garnier, 2015). G. Poumarède, 'Consuls, réseaux consulaires et diplomatie à l'époque moderne', in G. Sabatini and P. Volpini (eds.), *Sulla diplomazia in età moderna. Politica, economia, religione* (Milano: FrancoAngeli, 2011). See also an overview in M. Herrero Sánchez, 'La red consular europea y la diplomacia mercantil en la Edad Moderna', in J.J. Iglesias, R. Pérez García and M. Fernández Chaves (eds.), *Comercio y cultura en la Edad Moderna* (Sevilla: Servicio de Publicaciones de la Universidad de Sevilla, 2015), pp. 135–164.

41 K. Weber, 'La migration huguenote dans le contexte de l'économie atlantique. L'exemple de Hambourg (1680–1800)', in G. Braun and S. Lachenicht (eds.), *Les états allemands et les huguenots* (München: Oldenbourg, 2007), esp. pp. 127–130.

42 R. Cohen, *Global Disaporas: An Introduction* (München: Oldenbourg, 2007); P.J. Curtin, *Cross-Cultural Trade in World History* (London: Routledge, 1997), p. 11.

43 S.D. Aslanian, *From the Indian Ocean to the MediterraneanL The Global Trade Networks of Armenian Merchants from New Julfa* (Berkeley: California World History Library, 2011).

44 F. Trivellato, *The Familiarity of Strangers: The Sephardic Diaspora, Livorno, and Cross-Cultural Trade in the Early Modern Period* (New Haven, London: Yale University Press, 2009).

45 A. Crespo Solana, *Entre Cádiz y los Países Bajos. Una comunidad en la ciudad de la ilustración* (Cádiz: Universidad de Cádiz, 2001); C. Brilli, 'Mercaderes genoveses en el Cádiz del siglo XVIII. Crisis y reajuste de una simbiosis secular', in A. Crespo Solana (ed.), *Comunidades transnacionales. Colonias de mercaderes extranjeros en el Mundo Atlántico (1500–1830)* (Madrid: Doce Calles, 2010); K. Weber, *Deutsche Kaufleute im Atlantikhandel 1680–1830: Unternehmen und Familien in Hamburg, Cádiz und Bordeaux* (München: C.H. Beck, 2004).

46 K. Weber, *Deutsche Kaufleute*, pp. 119–120. C. Brilli, 'La importancia de hacerse español: la élite mercantil genovesa de Cádiz en el siglo XVIII', in I. Lobato Franco and J.M. Oliva Melgar (eds.), *El sistema comercial español en la economía mundial (siglos XVII–XVIII)* (Huelva: Universidad de Huelva, 2012); C. Brilli, 'Administrando la debilidad. Los mercaderes genoveses y sus instituciones en Cádiz durante el siglo XVIII', in F. Ramos Palencia and B. Yun Casalilla (eds.), *Economía política desde Estambul a Potosí. Ciudades estado, imperios y mercados en el Mediterráneo y en el Atlántico ibérico, c.1200–1800* (Valencia: Universität de Valencia, 2012); C. Brilli, 'La nación genovesa de Lisboa y sus cónsules en el último cuarto del siglo XVIII', in M. Aglietti, M. Herrero Sánchez and F. Zamora Rodríguez (eds.), *Los cónsules extranjeros en la edad moderna y a principios de la edad contemporánea (siglos XV–XIX)* (Madrid: Doce Calles, 2013), pp. 213–223.

47 K. Kaps, 'Small But Powerful: Networking Strategies and Trade Business of Habsburg-Italian Merchants in Cadiz in the Second Half of the 18th Century', (Special Issue: *The Business Relations, Identities, and Political Resources of the Italian Merchants in the Early-Modern Spanish Monarchy*), *European Review of History: Revue européenne d'histoire*, 23:3 (2016).

48 See, for the Germans in England: M. Schulte-Beerbühl, *The Forgotten Majority: German Merchants in London, Naturalization and Global Trade 1660–1815* (New York: Berghahn Books, 2014).

49 M. Cachero Vinuesa, 'Redes mercantiles en los inicios del comercio atlántico. Sevilla entre Europa y Amércia, 1520–1525', in N. Böttcher, B. Hausberger and A. Ibarra (eds.), *Redes y negocios globales en el mundo ibérico, siglos XVI–XVIII* (Madrid: Iberoamericana, 2011).

50 K. Weber, *Deutsche Kaufleute*; M. Schulte-Beerbühl, *Forgotten Majority*. In contrast, merchants from the Habsburg Monarchy followed both the Northern path throughout the ports at the Northern Sea and the Mediterranean trade route in order to access Atlantic markets in the eighteenth century. Apart from Trieste, Genoa, Venice and Livorno were important ports that channelled trade links between the Habsburg territories and Spanish Atlantic markets. Kaps, 'Small but powerful'; idem., 'Entre servicio estatal y los negocios transnacionales: El caso de Paolo Greppi, cónsul imperial en Cádiz (1774–1791)', in M. Aglietti, M. Herrero Sánchez and F. Zamora Rodríguez (eds.), *Los cónsules extranjeros en la edad moderna y a principios de la edad contemporánea (siglos XV–XIX)* (Madrid: Doce Calles, 2013), pp. 225–235.

51 X. Lamikiz, *Trade and Trust*; on Basque merchants see: J. P. Priotti, *Bilbao et ses marchands au XVIe siècle. Genèse d'une croissance* (Villeneuve d'Ascq, Presses Universitaires du Septentrion, 2004); H. Casado Alonso, *El triunfo de Mercurio. La presencia castellana en Europa (siglos XV y XVI)* (Burgos: Cajacírculo, 2003).

52 A. Bartolomei, 'Identidad e integración de los comerciantes extranjeros en la Europa Moderna. La colonia francesa de Cádiz a finales del siglo XVIII', in A. Crespo Solana (ed.), *Comunidades transnacionales. Colonias de mercaderes extranjeros en el Mundo Atlántico (1500–1830)* (Madrid: Doce Calles, 2010) pp. 359–376.

53 M. Fusaro, 'Les Anglais et les Grecs. Un réseau de coopération commerciale en Méditerranée vénitienne', *Annales* HSS, 58 (3) 2003, pp. 605–62.

54 M. Fusaro, *Political Economies of Empire in the Early Modern Mediterranean: The Decline of Venice and the Rise of England 1450–1700* (Cambridge: Cambridge University Press, 2015).

55 R. Brubaker, *Ethnicity without groups* (Cambridge: Harvard University Press, 2004), p. 8, quoted in: F. Trivellato, *Familiarity of Strangers: The Sephardic Diaspora, Livorno, and Cross-Cultural Trade in the Early Modern Period* (New Haven, London: Yale University Press, 2009), p. 11.

56 F. Trivellato, *Familiarity of Strangers*, p. 18.

57 For the different definitions of network relations, see: M. Casson, 'Networks in Economic and Business History: A Theoretical Perspective' in A. Gestrich and M. Schulte-Beerbühl (eds.), *Cosmopolitan Networks in Commerce and Society 1660–1914* (London: Deutsches Historisches Institut, 2011).

58 A. Crespo Solana, *Spatial-Temporal Narratives. Historical GIS and the Study of Global Trading Networks (1500–1800)* (Newcastle: Cambridge Scholars Publishing, 2014); A. Crespo Solana and D. Alonso García (eds.), Special Issue: 'Self-organizing Networks and GIS Tools: Cases of Use for the Study of Trading Cooperation (1400–1800)', *Journal of Knowledge Management, Economics and Information Technology*, (2012).

59 M. Casson, 'Theoretical Perspective'; A. Caracausi and C. Jeggle, 'Introduction', in A. Caracausi and C. Jeggle (eds.), *Commercial Networks and European Cities, 1400–1800 Perspectives in Economic and Social History* (London: Routledge, 2014).

60 C. Álvarez Nogal, 'Mercados o redes de mercaderes: el funcionamiento de la feria de Portobelo', in N. Böttcher, B. Hausberger and A. Ibarra (eds.), *Redes y negocios globales en el mundo ibérico, siglos XVI–XVIII* (Madrid: Iberoamericana, 2011), p. 56. E. Van Young, N. Böttcher, B. Hausberger and A. Ibarra (eds.), 'Social Networks: A Final Comment', in *Redes y negocios globales en el mundo ibérico, siglos XVI–XVIII* (Madrid: Iberoamericana, 2011), pp. 294, 298–299.

61 C. Jeggle, 'Interactions, Networks, Discourses and Markets', in A. Caracausi and C. Jeggle (eds.), *Commercial Networks and European Cities, 1400–1800* (London: Routledge, 2014), p. 57; C. Antunes, 'Failing Institutions: The Dutch in Portugal and the Tale of a Sixteenth-Century Firm', in B. Crivelli and G. Sabatini (eds.), *Reti finanziarie e reti commerciali. Operatori economici stranieri in Portogallo (XVI–XVII secolo)*, *Storia Economica XVIII* (Il: Mulino, 2015), Vol. 2, pp. 331–347.

62 F. Trivellato, 'A Republic of Merchants?', in A. Molho and D. Ramada Curto (eds.), *Finding Europe: Discourses on Margins, Communities, Images, 13th to 18th Centuries* (Oxford, New York: Berghahn Books, 2007).

63 Concerning the active role played by networks of Italian businessmen operating within the Spanish monarchy, see the recent monograph edited by C. Brilli and M. Herrero Sánchez, with contributions by Angela Orlandi, Yasmina Ben Yessef, Klemens Kaps and Felipe Gaitán: *The Business Relations, Identities, and Political Resources of the Italian Merchants in the Early-Modern Spanish Monarchy*, in *European Review of History: Revue Européenne d'Histoire*, (2016), 23/3.

64 A. Bartolomei, 'Identidad', in A. Crespo Solana (ed.), *Comunidades transnacionales. Colonias de mercaderes extranjeros en el Mundo Atlántico (1500–1830)* (Madrid: Aranjuez, 2010), p. 360.

65 C. Jeggle, 'Interactions Networks, Discourses and Markets', in A. Caracausi and C. Jeggle (eds.), *Commercial Networks and European Cities, 1400–1800* (London: Pickering & Chatto, 2014), p. 59; E. Van Young, 'Social Networks: A Final Comment', in N. Böttcher, B. Hausberger and A. Ibarra (eds.), *Redes y negocios globales en el mundo ibérico, siglos XVI–XVIII* (Madrid: Iberoamericana, 2011), p. 299.

66 O'Rourke and Williamson, 'When did Globalization begin?' in J. Williamson (ed.), *Globalization and the Poor Periphery before 1950* (Cambridge: The MIT Press 2006), pp. 25–28.

67 M. Carmagnani, 'Capitale mercantile e colonie', in A. Guardicci (ed.), *Atti della "Decima settimana di studio" (7–12 aprile 1978). Sviluppo e sottosviluppo in Europa e fuori d'Europa dal secolo XIII alla Rivoluzione Industriale* (Paris: Le Monnier, 1983), pp. 465–477.

68 N. Steensgaard. 'The Dutch East India Company as an Institutional Innovation', in M. Aymard (ed.), *Dutch Capitalism and World Capitalism* (Cambridge: Cambridge University Press, 1982), pp. 235–257.

69 S. Subrahmanyam, *The Portuguese Empire in Asia, 1500–1700: A Political and Economic History* (London: Longman, 1993); M.A.P. Meilink-Roelofsz, 'The Structures of the Trade in Asia in the Sixteenth and Seventeenth Centuries. A Critical Appraisal', *Mare LusoIndicum*, 4 (1980), pp. 1–43.

70 A. Crespo Solana, 'Sistemas comerciales', in I. Lobato Franco and J. M. Oliva Melgar (eds.), *El sistema comercial español en la economía mundial (siglos XVII–XVIII)* (Huelva: Universidad de Huelva, 2013). For the use of the concept of transnational connectors in the case of the network organised by the Genoese firm Grillo-Lomellino for the management of the slave trade licence (*asiento de negros*) in the Spanish monarchy, see M. Herrero Sánchez and I. Pérez Tostado, 'Conectores del mundo atlántico: los irlandeses en la red comercial internacional de los Grillo y Lomelín', in E. García Hernán and I. Pérez Tostado (eds.), *Ireland and the Iberian Atlantic: Mobility, involvement and cross-cultural exchange (1580–1823)* (Valencia: Albatros ediciones, 2010), pp. 307–322.

71 I. Wallerstein, *The Modern World-System I*.

72 H. Pietschmann, 'Imperio y comercio en la formación del Atlántico español', in I. Lobato Franco and J.M. Oliva Melgar (eds.), *El sistema comercial español en la economía mundial (siglos XVII–XVIII)* (Huelva: Universidad de Huelva, 2013), p. 92; C. Martínez Shaw and J. M. Oliva Melgar (eds.), *El sistema atlántico español (siglos XVII–XIX)* (Madrid: Marcial Pons, 2005).

73 R. Grafe, *Distant Tyranny: Markets, Power, and Backwardness in Spain, 1650–1800* (Princeton, Princeton University Press, 2012); see also R. Grafe, 'Polycentric States. The Spanish Reigns and the "Failures" of Mercantilism', in P.J. Stern and C. Wennerlind (eds.), *Mercantilism Reimagined: Political Economy in Early Modern Britain and Its Empire* (Oxford: Oxford University Press, 2013), pp. 241–262.

74 R. Grafe, 'On the Spatial Nature of Institutions and the Institutional Nature of Personal Networks in the Spanish Atlantic', *Culture & History Digital Journal* 3(1) June 2014, doi: http://dx.doi.org/10.3989/chdj.2014.006.

75 J. Israel, *Dutch Primacy in World Trade* (Oxford: Clarendon Press, 1989); and M. Herrero Sánchez, *El acercamiento hispano-neerlandés (1648–1678)* (Madrid: Consejo Superior de Investigaciones Científicas, 2000).

76 We must not forget that the trade carried out by the United Provinces was, in Colbert's conception, like a physical object, which, like land, could be snatched by force of arms. Indeed, in a letter addressed to Louis XIV, he expressed his conviction about the invasion of the republic in 1672: 'Si le Roy assujettissait toutes les Provinces-Unies de Pays-Bas, leur commerce devenant le commerce des sujets de Sa Majesté, il n'y aurait rien à désirer davantage …' after P. Goubert, *Louis XIV et vingt millions de français* (Paris: Fayard, 1966), p. 95.

77 M.R. Brawley, *Liberal Leadership. Great Powers and Their Challengers in Peace and War* (Ithaca: Cornell University Press, 1993), p. 29

78 F. Braudel, *Civilisation matérielle, II* [11], p. 487. For the persistence of mercantilist and protectionist policies in the United Provinces, see the classic P.W. Klein, 'A New Look at an Old Subject: Dutch Trade Policies in the Age of Mercantilism', in S. Groenveld and M. Wintle, (eds.), *State and Trade. Government and the Economy in Britain and the Netherlands since the Middle Ages. Papers delivered to the Tenth Anglo-Dutch Historical Conference, Nijmegen, 1988* (Zutphen: Walburg Press, 1992), pp. 39–49.

79 J. Adams, 'Trading States, Trading Places: The Role of Patrimonialism in Early Modern Dutch Development', *Comparative Studies in Society and History* 36–2 (1994), pp. 319–355.

80 K.N. Chaudhuri, 'Reflections on the Organizing Principles of Premodern Trade', in J.D. Tracy (ed.), *The Political Economy of Merchant Empires. State Power and World Trade 1350–1750* (Cambridge: Cambridge University Press, 1991), p. 429.

81 For an overview of the concept of polycentric monarchy, see P. Cardim, T. Herzog, J.J. Ruiz Ibáñez and G. Sabatini, (eds.), *Polycentric Monarchies. How did Early Modern Spain and Portugal Achieve and Maintain a Global Hegemony?* (Eastbourne, Sussex: Academic Press, 2012).

82 T. Herzog, *Defining Nations. Immigrants and Citizens in Early Modern Spain and Spanish America* (New Haven: Yale University Press, 2003); M. Herrero Sánchez, 'Foreign Communities in the Cities of the Catholic Monarchy: a Comparative Perspective Between the Overseas Dominions and Crown of Castile', in H. Braun and J. Pérez Magallón (eds.), *The Transatlantic Hispanic Baroque. Complex identities in the Atlantic World* (Farnham: Asghate, 2014), pp. 187–204.

83 K.N. Chaudhuri, 'Reflections on the Organizing Principles of Premodern Trade', pp. 428–429.

84 O. Gelderblom, *Cities of Commerce. The Institutional Foundation of International Trade in the Low Countries 1250–1650* (Princeton and Oxford: Princeton University Press, 2013).

85 See B. van den Hoven and P. Vries's interview to J. Israel in *Het Hollandse wonder. Handel en politiek in de zeventiende eeuw* en *Historisch Tijdschrift*, 1 (1992), pp. 5–21. The clearest illustration of the effects that overbearing control of the state can have on commerce is France, as demonstrated by D. Dessert; J. L. Journet, 'Le lobby Colbert. Un Royaume, ou une affaire de famille?', *Annales. Economies, Sociétés, Civilisations* 30–6 (1975), pp. 1303–1335.

86 M. Herrero Sánchez, 'La Monarquía Hispánica y las repúblicas europeas. el modelo republicano en una monarquía de ciudades', in M. Herrero Sánchez (ed.), *Repúblicas y republicanismo en la Europa moderna* (Madrid: Fondo de Cultura Económica, forthcoming 2016).

87 A.B. Fernández Castro, 'A Transnational Empire Built on Law: the Case of the Commercial Jurisprudence of the House of Trade of Seville (1583–1598)', in T. Duve, (ed.), *Entanglements in Legal History: Conceptual Approaches* (Frankfurt am Main: Max Planck Institute for European Legal History, 2014), pp. 187–212. An eloquent example of this is Alejandro García Montón's recent study on the network of conservative judges created around the aforementioned slave licence in the hands of Grillo and Lomellino: A. García Montón, 'Corona, hombres de negocios y jueces conservadores. Un acercamiento en escala transatlántica (siglo XVII)', *Jerónimo Zurita* 90 (2015), pp. 75–112.

88 M. Herrero Sánchez, 'Génova y el sistema imperial hispánico', in A. Álvarez-Ossorio Alariño and B. García (eds.), *La Monarquía de las naciones. Patria, Nación y Naturaleza en la Monarquía de España* (Madrid: Fundación Carlos de Amberes, 2004), pp. 528–562.

89 This chapter is related to the interesting recent contributions in the volume edited by J.-P. Priotti and G. Saupin. These works analyse the economic circuits that bound French and Spanish ports, through an examination of the role played by social actors in the creation of business networks and of their interpersonal relationships and commercial methods; this perspective does not fail to take into account the crucial importance of political events: J.-P. Priotti and G. Saupin (eds.), *Le commerce atlantique franco-espagnol. Acteurs, négoces et ports (XVe–XVIIIe siècle)* (Rennes: Presses Universitaires de Rennes: 2008).

90 It must not be forgotten that the French community suffered the most from the succession of mercantile embargoes between 1635 and 1697, as illustrated by M. Herrero Sánchez, 'La política de embargos y el contrabando de productos de lujo en Madrid (1635–1673). Sociedad cortesana y dependencia de los mercados internacionales',

Hispania 201 (1999), pp. 171–191. Similarly, it would be interesting to compare Crailsheim's compelling arguments with other communities with strong roots in Seville, for example the Genoese. For this issue, see R. Pike, *Enterprise and Adventure: the Genoese in Seville and the Opening of the New World* (Ithaca: Cornell University Press, 1966); E. Vila Vilar, *Los Corzo y los Mañara. Tipos y arquetipos del mercader con América* (Sevilla: Liquore Editorie, 1991); M.Á. Ladero Quesada, 'I genovesi a Siviglia e nella sua regione: elementi di permanenza e di radicamento (secoli XIII– XVI)', in M. Del Treppo (ed.), *Sistema di rapporti internazionali ed élites economiche in Europa (secoli XII–XVII)* (Naples: Liquore Editorie, 1994), pp. 211–230; C. Álvarez Nogal, *Sevilla y la Monarquía Hispánica en el siglo XVII* (Sevilla: Ayuntamiento de Sevilla, 2000).

91   M. Herrero Sánchez and E. Poggio Ghilarducci, 'El impacto de la Tregua en las comunidades extranjeras. Una visión comparada entre Castilla y Nueva España', in B. García, M. Herrero Sánchez and A. Hugon (eds.), *El arte de la prudencia. La Tregua de los Doce Años en la Europa de los pacificadores (1598–1618)* (Madrid: Doce Calles/ Fundación Carlos de Amberes, 2012), pp. 249–273.

92   J.B. Owens, *"By My Absolute Royal Authority": Justice and the Castilian Commonwealth at the Beginning of the First Global Age* (Rochester: University of Rochester Press, 2005), p. 246.

93   B. Yun Casalilla (ed.), *Las redes del Imperio. Élites sociales en la articulación de la Monarquía Hispánica, 1492–1714* (Madrid: Marcial Pons, 2009); J.F. Pardo Molero and M. Lomas Cortés (eds.), *Oficiales reales. Los ministros de la Monarquía Católica (siglos XVI–XVII)* (Valencia: Universidad de Valencia-Red Columnaria, 2012).

94   H. Casado Alonso, 'El papel de las colonias mercantiles castellanas en el Imperio Hispánico (siglos XV y XVI)', in J.J. Ruiz Ibáñez (Coord.), *Las vecindades de las Monarquías Ibéricas* (Madrid: FCE, 2013), pp. 355–374.

95   K. Kaps, 'Small but powerful'; idem., 'Entre servicio'.

96   K. Kaps, 'Una intermediación entre Europa Central y el Atlántico Hispánico: las repúblicas mediterráneas dentro de la red mercantil de comerciantes milaneses entre Lombardía y Cádiz en la segunda mitad del siglo XVIII', in M. Herrero Sánchez (ed.), *Repúblicas y republicanismo en la Edad Moderna* (Madrid: Fondo de Cultura Económica, forthcoming).

Bibliography

Adams, J., 'Trading States, Trading Places: the Role of Patrimonialism in Early Modern Dutch Development', *Comparative Studies in Society and History* 36–2 (1994), pp. 319–355.

Aglietti, M., Herrero Sánchez, M., and Zamora Rodríguez, F. (eds.), *Los consules extranjeros en la edad moderna y a principios de la edad contemporánea (siglos XV–XIX)*, Madrid: Doce Calles, 2013.

Álvarez Nogal, C., *Sevilla y la Monarquía Hispánica en el siglo XVII*, Sevilla: Ayuntamiento de Sevilla, 2000.

Álvarez Nogal, C., 'Las compañías bancarias genovesas en Madrid a comienzos del siglo XVII', *Hispania* LXV/1, 219 (2005), pp. 67–90.

Álvarez Nogal, C., 'Mercados o redes de mercaderes: el funcionamiento de la feria de Portobelo', in Böttcher, N., Hausberger, B. and Ibarra, A. (eds.), *Redes y negocios globales en el mundo ibérico, siglos XVI–XVIII*, Madrid: Iberoamericana, 2011, pp. 53–86.

Antunes, C., 'Failing institutions: the Dutch in Portugal and the tale of a Sixteenth-Century firm', in Crivelli, B. and Sabatini, G. (eds), *Reti finanziarie e reti commerciali. Operatori economici stranieri in Portogallo (XVI–XVII secolo), Storia Economica* XVIII/2 (2015), pp. 331–347.

Aslanian, S.D., *From the Indian Ocean to the Mediterranean. The Global Trade Networks of Armenian Merchants from New Julfa*, Berkeley: California World History Library, 2011.

Attman, A., *Dutch Enterprise in the World Bullion Trade, 1550–1800*, Göteborg: Kugl. Vetenskaps och Vitterhets Samhället, 1983.

Bartolomei, A., 'Identidad e integración de los comerciantes extranjeros en la Europa Moderna. La colonia francesa de Cádiz a finales del siglo XVIII', in Crespo Solana, A. (ed.), *Comunidades transnacionales. Colonias de mercaderes extranjeros en el Mundo Atlántico (1500–1830)*, Madrid: Doce Calles, 2010, pp. 359–376.

Bayly, C.A., *The Birth of the Modern World, 1780–1914: Global Connections and Comparisons*, Oxford: Blackwell, 2004.

Bély, L., *Les relations internationales en Europe (XVIIe–XVIIIe siècles)*, París: Presses Universitaires de France, 1992.

Blitz, R.C., 'Some Reflections on the World Trade of the XVIIth and XVIIIth Century: A Comment on the Findings of Professor Chaudhuri', *The Journal of European Economic History* 7–1 (1978), pp. 214–222.

Braudel, F., *Civilisation matérielle, économie et capitalisme, XVe–XVIIIe siècle.*, 3 vols., Paris: Armand Colin, 1979.

Brawley, M.R., *Liberal Leadership. Great Powers and Their Challengers in Peace and War*, Ithaca: Cornell University Press, 1993.

Brilli, C., 'Administrando la debilidad. Los mercaderes genoveses y sus instituciones en Cádiz durante el siglo XVIII', in Ramos Palencia, F. and Yun Casalilla, B. (eds.), *Economía política desde Estambul a Potosí. Ciudades estado, imperios y mercados en el Mediterráneo y en el Atlántico ibérico, c.1200–1800*, Valencia: Universität de Valencia, 2012, pp. 109–136.

———. 'La importancia de hacerse español: la élite mercantil genovesa de Cádiz en el siglo XVIII', in Lobato Franco, I. and Oliva Melgar, M. (eds.), *El sistema comercial español en la economía mundial (siglos XVII–XVIII)*, Huelva: Universidad de Huelva, 2012, pp. 225–255.

———. 'Mercaderes genoveses en el Cádiz del siglo XVIII. Crisis y reajuste de una simbiosis secular', in Crespo Solana, A. (ed.), *Comunidades transnacionales. Colonias de mercaderes extranjeros en el Mundo Atlántico (1500–1830)*, Madrid: Doce Calles, 2010, pp. 83–102.

———. 'La nación genovesa de Lisboa y sus cónsules en el último cuarto del siglo XVIII', in Aglietti, M., Herrero Sánchez, M. and Zamora Rodríguez, F. (eds.), *Los cónsules extranjeros en la edad moderna y a principios de la edad contemporánea (siglos XV–XIX)*, Madrid: Doce Calles, 2013, pp. 213–223.

Brilli, C. and Herrero Sánchez, M. (eds.), *The Business Relations, Identities, and Political Resources of the Italian Merchants in the Early-Modern Spanish Monarchy en European Review of History: Revue Européenne d'Histoire*, (2016), 23/3.

Brubaker, R., *Ethnicity Without Groups*, Cambridge: Harvard University Press, 2004.

Bruijn J.R., Gaastra, F.S. and Schöffer, I., *Dutch Asiatic Shipping in the 17th and 18th Centuries*, La Haya: Martinus Nijhoff, 1987.

Bustos Rodríguez, M., *Cádiz en el sistema atlántico. La ciudad, sus comerciantes y la actividad mercantil (1650–1830)*, Madrid, Cádiz: Sílex – Universidad de Cádiz, 2005.

Cachero Vinuesa, M., 'Redes mercantiles en los inicios del comercio atlántico. Sevilla entre Europa y Amércia, 1520–1525', in Böttcher, N., Hausberger, B. and Ibarra, A. (eds.), *Redes y negocios globales en el mundo ibérico, siglos XVI–XVIII*, Madrid: Iberoamericana, 2011, pp. 25–51.

Caracausi, A. and Jeggle. C. 'Introduction', in Caracausi, A. and Jeggle, C. (eds.), *Commercial Networks and European Cities, 1400–1800,* London: Routledge, 2014, pp. 1–12.

Carmagnani. M., "Capitale mercantile e colonie", in Guardicci, A. ed., *Atti della "Decima settimana di studio" (7–12 aprile 1978). Sviluppo e sottosviluppo in Europa e fuori d'Europa dal secolo XIII alla Rivoluzione Industriale*, Paris: Le Monnier, 1983, pp. 465–477.

Casado Alonso, H., *El triunfo de Mercurio. La presencia castellana en Europa (siglos XV y XVI)*, Burgos: Cajacírculo, 2003.

————. 'El papel de las colonias mercantiles castellanas en el Imperio Hispánico (siglos XV y XVI)', in Ruiz Ibáñez, J.J. (coord.), *Las vecindades de las Monarquías Ibéricas*, Madrid: FCE, 2013, pp. 355–374.

Casson, M., 'Networks in Economic and Business History: A Theoretical Perspective', in Gestrich, A. and Schulte-Beerbühl, M. (eds.), *Cosmopolitan Networks in Commerce and Society 1660–1914*, London: Deutsches Historisches Institut, 2011, pp. 17–49.

Chaudhuri, K.N. 'Some Reflection on the World Trade of the XVIIth Century: A Reply', *The Journal of European Economic History* 7–1 (1978), pp. 223–231.

————. 'World Silver Flows and Monetary Factors as a Force of International Economic Integration 1658–1758', in Fisher, W., McInnis, R.M. and Schneider, J. (eds.), *The Emergence of a World Economy, 1500–1914. Papers of the IX International Congress of Economic History*, Wiesbaden, Stuttgart: Steiner-Verlag, 1986, pp. 61–81.

————. 'Reflections on the Organizing Principles of Premodern Trade', in Tracy, J.D. (ed.), *The Political Economy of Merchant Empires. State Power and World Trade 1350–1750*, Cambridge: Cambridge University Press, 1991, pp. 421–442.

Cohen, R., *Global Disaporas: An Introduction*, London: Routledge,1997.

Crespo Solana, A., *Entre Cádiz y los Países Bajos. Una comunidad en la ciudad de la ilustración*, Cádiz: Universidad de Cádiz, 2001.

————. 'The Iberian Peninsula in the First Global Trade. Geostrategy and Mercantile Network Interests (XV to XVIII Centuries)', *Global Trade Before Globalization (VIII–XVIII)*, Madrid: Fundación Cultura de Paz, 2007, pp. 103–127.

————. 'Las comunidades mercantiles y el mantenimiento de los sistemas comerciales de España, Flandes y la República Holandesa, 1648–1750', in Crespo Solana, A. and Herrero Sánchez, M. (eds.), *España y los diecisiete Países Bajos, siglos XVI–XVIII: una revisión historiográfica*, Córdoba: Universidad de Córdoba, 2002, pp. 445–467.

————. '¿Redes de dependencia inter-imperial? Aproximaciones teóricas en la funcionalidad de los agentes de comercio en la expansión de la sociedades mercantiles', in Pérez Tostado, I. and García Hernán, E. (eds.), *Irlanda y el Atlántico Ibérico. Movilidad, participación e intercambio cultural*, Valencia: Albatros Ediciones, 2010, pp. 35–50.

————. *Spatial-Temporal Narratives. Historical GIS and the Study of Global Trading Networks (1500–1800)*, Newcastle: Cambridge Scholars Publishing, 2014.

Crespo Solana, A. and Alonso García, D. (eds.), Special Issue: 'Self-Organizing Networks and GIS Tools. Cases of Use for the Study of Trading Cooperation (1400–1800)', *Journal of Knowledge Management, Economics and Information Technology*, 2012.

Curtin, P.J., *Cross-Cultural Trade in World History*, London: Routledge, 1997.

Dessert D. and Journet J.L. 'Le lobby Colbert. Un Royaume, ou une affaire de famille?", *Annales. Economies, Sociétés, Civilisations* 30–36 (1975), pp. 1303–1335.

De Vries, J., 'The limits of Globalization in the Early Modern World', *Economic History Review* 63, no. 3 (2009), pp. 710–733.

Emmer, P., 'In Search of a System: The Atlantic Economy 1500–1800', in Pietschmann, H. (ed.), *Atlantic History. History of the Atlantic System 1580–1830*, Göttingen: Vandenhoeck and Ruprecht, 2002, pp. 169–178.

Fernández Castro, A.B., 'A Transnational Empire Built on Law: the Case of the Commercial Jurisprudence of the House of Trade of Seville (1583–1598)', in Duve, T., ed., *Entanglements in Legal History: Conceptual Approaches,* Frankfurt am Main: Max Planck Institute for European Legal History, 2014, pp. 187–212.

Flynn, D.O., 'Comparing the Tokuwaga Shogunate with Hapsburg Spain. Two Silver-Based Empires in a Global Setting', in Van Cauwenberghe, E.H.G. (ed.), *Money, Coins, and*

Commerce: Essays in the Monetary History of Asia and Europe (From Antiquity to Modern Times), Leuven: Leuven University Press, 1991, pp. 11–46.

—————. 'El desarrollo del primer capitalismo a pesar de los metales preciosos del nuevo mundo: una interpretación anti-Wallerstein de la España imperial', *Revista de Historia Económica* 2 (1984), pp. 29–57.

Flynn, D.O. and Giráldez, A., *China and the Birth of Globalization in the 16th Century*, Burlington: Ashgate-Variorum, 2010.

Frank, A.G., *ReOrient. The Global Economy in the Asian Age*, Berkeley, Los Angeles, London: University of California Press, 1998.

Fusaro, M., 'Les Anglais et les Grecs. Un réseau de coopération commerciale en Méditerranée vénitienne', *Annales HSS* 58:3 (2003), pp. 605–662.

—————. *Political Economies of Empire in the Early Modern Mediterranean The Decline of Venice and the Rise of England 1450–1700*, Cambridge: Cambridge University Press, 2015.

Gaastra, F.S., 'Merchants, Middlemen and Money: Aspects of the Trade between the Indonesian Archipelago and Manila in the 17th century', in Schutte, G. and Sutherland, H. (eds.), *Papers of the Dutch Indonesian Historical Conference held at Lage Vuursche, The Netherlands 23–27 June 1980*, Leiden, Jakarta: Bureau of Indonesian Studies, 1982, pp. 301–314.

García Montón, A., 'Corona, hombres de negocios y jueces conservadores. Un acercamiento en escala transatlántica (siglo XVII)', *Jerónimo Zurita* 90 (2015), pp. 75–112.

Gelderblom, O., *Cities of Commerce. The Institutional Foundation of International Trade in the Low Countries, 1250–1650*, Princeton and Oxford: Princeton University Press, 2013.

Goubert, P., *Louis XIV et vingt millions de français*, Paris: Fayard, 1966.

Grafe, R., *Distant Tyranny: Markets, Power, and Backwardness in Spain, 1650–1800*, Princeton: Princeton University Press, 2012.

Grafe, R., 'Polycentric States. The Spanish Reigns and the "Failures" of Mercantilism', in Stern, P.J. and Wennerlind, C. (eds.), *Mercantilism Reimagined: Political Economy in Early Modern Britain and Its Empire*, Oxford: Oxford University Press, 2013, pp. 241–262.

—————. 'On the Spatial Nature of Institutions and the Institutional Nature of Personal Networks in the Spanish Atlantic', *Culture & History Digital Journal* 3(1) (June 2014), doi: http://dx.doi.org/10.3989/chdj.2014.006.

Greif, A., 'Institutions and International Trade: Lessons from the Commercial Revolution', *The American Economic Review* 82, no. 2 (May) (1992), pp. 128–133.

Gruzinski, S. *Les quatre parties du monde. Histoire d'une mondialisation*, Paris: La Martinière, 2004.

Häberlein, M. and Jeggle, C. (eds.), *Praktiken des Handels. Geschäfte und soziale Beziehungen europäischer Kaufleute im Mittelalter und früher Neuzeit*, Konstanz: UVK-Verl.-Ges., 2010.

Haggerty, S., 'I could "do for the dickmans": When Family Networks don't Work', in Gestrich, A. and Schulte-Beerbühl, M. (eds.), *Cosmopolitan Networks in Commerce and Society 1660–1914*, London: German Historical Institute London, 2011, pp. 317–342.

Herrero Sánchez, M., 'Génova y el sistema imperial hispánico', in Álvarez-Ossorio, A., García, A. and Garcia, B. (eds.), *La Monarquía de las naciones. Patria, Nación y Naturaleza en la Monarquía de España*, Madrid: Fundación Carlos de Amberes, 2004, pp. 528–562.

—————. 'La política de embargos y el contrabando de productos de lujo en Madrid (1635–1673). Sociedad cortesana y dependencia de los mercados internacionales', *Hispania* 201 (En-Abril 1999), pp. 171–191.

—————. 'Las Indias y la Tregua de los Doce Años', in García García, B. (ed.), *Tiempo de Paces. La Pax Hispánica y la Tregua de los Doce Años*, Madrid: Fundación Carlos de Amberes, 2009, pp. 193–229.

————. 'Republican Monarchies, Patrimonial Republics. The Catholic Monarchy and the Mercantile Republics of Genoa and the United Provinces', in Cardim, P., Herzog, T., Ruiz Ibáñez, J.J. and Sabatini, G. (eds.), *Polycentric Monarchies. How did Early Modern Spain and Portugal Achieve and Maintain a Global Hegemony?*, Eastbourne, Sussex: Academic Press, 2012, pp. 181–196.

————.'Foreign Communities in the Cities of the Catholic Monarchy: A Comparative Perspective Between the Overseas Dominions and Crown of Castile', in Braun, H. and Pérez Magallón, J. (eds.), *The Transatlantic Hispanic Baroque. Complex Identities in the Atlantic World*, Farnham: Asghate, 2014, pp. 187–204.

————. 'La red consular europea y la diplomacia mercantil en la Edad Moderna', in Iglesias, J.J., Pérez García, R. and Fernández Chaves, M. (eds.), *Comercio y cultura en la Edad Moderna*, Sevilla: Servicio de Publicaciones de la Universidad de Sevilla, 2015, pp. 135–164.

————. 'La Monarquía Hispánica y las repúblicas europeas. el modelo republicano en una monarquía de ciudades', in Herrero Sánchez, M. (ed.), *Repúblicas y republicanismo en la Europa moderna*, Madrid: Fondo de Cultura Económica, forthcoming.

————. *Repúblicas y republicanismo en la Europa moderna*, Madrid: Fondo de Cultura Económica, forthcoming.

Herrero Sánchez, M., Ben Yessef, Y.R., Bitossi, C. and Puncuh, D., eds., *Génova y la Monarquía Hispánica (1528–1713)*, 2 Vols., Génova: Atti de la Società Ligure di Storia Patria, 2011.

Herrero Sánchez, M. and Pérez Tostado, I., 'Conectores del mundo atlántico: los irlandeses en la red comercial internacional de los Grillo y Lomelín', in García Hernán, E. and I. Pérez Tostado (eds.), *Ireland and the Iberian Atlantic: Mobility, Involvement and Cross-cultural Exchange (1580–1823)*, Valencia: Albatros ediciones, 2010, pp. 307–322.

Herrero Sánchez, M. and Poggio Ghilarducci, E., 'El impacto de la Tregua en las comunidades extranjeras. Una visión comparada entre Castilla y Nueva España', in García, B., M. Herrero Sánchez, M. and Hugon, A. (eds.), *El arte de la prudencia. La Tregua de los Doce Años en la Europa de los pacificadores (1598–1618)*, Madrid: Doce Calles/ Fundación Carlos de Amberes, 2012, pp. 249–273.

Herzog, T., *Defining Nations. Immigrants and Citizens in Early Modern Spain and Spanish America*, New Haven: Yale University Press, 2003.

Israel, J., *Dutch Primacy in World Trade, 1585–1740*, Oxford: Clarendon Press, 1989.

Jeggle, C., 'Interactions, Networks, Discourses and Markets', in Caracausi, A. and Jeggle, C. (eds.), *Commercial Networks and European Cities, 1400–1800*, London: Routledge 2014, pp. 45–63.

Kaps, K., 'Entre servicio estatal y los negocios transnacionales: El caso de Paolo Greppi, cónsul imperial en Cádiz (1774–1791)', in García, B., M. Herrero Sánchez, M. and Hugon, A. (eds.), *Los cónsules extranjeros en la edad moderna y a principios de la edad contemporánea (siglos XV–XIX)*, Madrid: Doce Calles, 2013, pp. 225–235.

————. 'Small But Powerful: Networking Strategies and Trade Business of Habsburg-Italian Merchants in Cadiz in the Second Half of the 18th Century', (Special Issue: *The Business Relations, Identities, and Political Resources of the Italian Merchants in the Early-Modern Spanish Monarchy), European Review of History: Revue Européenne d'Histoire*, 23:3 (2016).

————. 'Una intermediación entre Europa Central y el Atlántico Hispánico: las repúblicas mediterráneas dentro de la red mercantil de comerciantes milaneses entre Lombardía y Cádiz en la segunda mitad del siglo XVIII', in Herrero Sánchez, M. (ed.), *Repúblicas y republicanismo en la Europa moderna*, Madrid: Fondo de Cultura Económica, forthcoming.

Klein, P.W., 'A New Look at an Old Subject: Dutch Trade Policies in the Age of Mercantilism', in Groenveld, S. and Wintle, M. (eds.), *State and Trade. Government and the Economy in Britain and the Netherlands since the Middle Ages. Papers delivered to the Tenth Anglo-Dutch Historical Conference*, Zutphen: Walburg Press, 1992, pp. 39–49.

Ladero Quesada, M.Á., 'I genovesi a Siviglia e nella sua regione: elementi di permanenza e di radicamento (secoli XIII–XVI)', in Del Treppo, M. (ed.), *Sistema di rapporti internazionali ed élites economiche in Europa (secoli XII–XVII)*, Naples: Liquori Editore, 1994, pp. 211–230.

Lamikiz, X., *Trade and Trust in the Eighteenth-Century Atlantic World: Spanish Merchants and Their Overseas Networks*, Woodbridge: Royal Historical Society, 2010.

Lapeyre, H., *Simón Ruiz et les "asientos" de Philippe II*, Paris: Armand Colin, 1953.

Lindemann, M., *The Merchant Republics. Amsterdam, Antwerp, and Hamburg, 1648–1790*, Cambridge: Cambridge University Press, 2015.

Lobato Franco, I. and Oliva Melgar, J.M., (eds.), *El sistema comercial español en la economía mundial (siglos XVII–XVIII)*, Huelva: Universidad de Huelva, 2013.

Martínez Shaw, C. and Oliva Melgar, J.M., (eds.), *El sistema atlántico español (siglos XVII–XIX)*, Madrid: Marcial Pons, 2005.

Marzagalli, S., ed., *Les Consuls en Méditerranée, agents d'information XVIe–XXe siècle*, Paris: Classiques Garnier, 2015.

Meilink-Roelofsz, M.A.P., 'The Structures of the Trade in Asia in the Sixteenth and Seventeenth centuries. A Critical Appraisal', *Mare Lusolndicum* 4 (1980), pp. 1–43.

Niephaus, H.-T., *Genuas Seehandel von 1746–1848: die Entwicklung der Handelsbeziehungen zur Iberischen Halbinsel, zu West- und Nordeuropa sowie den Überseegebieten*, Köln and Wien: Böhlau, 1975.

North, D., 'Institutions, Transaction Costs, and the Rise of Merchant Empires', in Tracy, J.D. (ed.), *The Political Economy of Merchant Empires. State Power and World Trade 1350–1750*, Cambridge: Cambridge University Press, 1991, pp. 22–40.

O'Brien, P. K., 'European Economic Development: The Contribution of the Periphery', *The Economic History Review* 35 (1982), pp. 1–18.

O'Rourke, K. and Williamson, J., 'When did Globalization Begin?', *European Review of Economic History* 6 no., April (2002), pp. 23–50.

Owens, J.B., *"By My Absolute Royal Authority": Justice and the Castilian Commonwealth at the Beginning of the First Global Age*, Rochester: University of Rochester Press, 2005, p. 246.

―――. 'Dynamic Complexity of Cooperation-Based Self-Organizing Commercial Networks in the First Global Age (DynCoopNet): What's in a Name?', in Crespo Solana, A. and Alonso García, D. (eds.), Special Issue: *Self-organizing Networks and GIS Tools. Cases of Use for the Study of Trading Cooperation (1400–1800)*, *Journal of Knowledge Management, Economics and Information Technology*, 2012, pp. 25–52.

Pardo Molero, J.F. and Lomas Cortés, M., (eds.), *Oficiales reales. Los ministros de la Monarquía Católica (siglos XVI–XVII)*, Valencia: Universidad de Valencia-Red Columnaria, 2012.

Pieper, R., 'Der Mittelmeerraum als Mittler zwischen Orient und Okzident im 16. und 17. Jahrhundert', in Karner S. (ed.), *Wirtschaft und Gesellschaft. Festschrift für Gerald Schöpfer zum 60. Geburtstag*, Graz: Leykam, 2004, pp. 69–85.

Pietschmann, H., 'Imperio y comercio en la formación del Atlántico español', in Lobato Franco, I. and Oliva Melgar, J.M. (eds.), *El sistema comercial español en la economía mundial (siglos XVII–XVIII)*, Huelva: Universidad de Huelva, 2013, pp. 71–95.

Pike, R., *Enterprise and Adventure: the Genoese in Seville and the Opening of the New World*, Ithaca: Cornell University Press, 1966.

Postma, J.M.. *The Dutch in the Atlantic Slave Trade 1600–1815*, Cambridge: Cambridge University Press, 1990.

Poumarède, G., 'Consuls, réseaux consulaires et diplomatie à l'époque moderne', in Sabatini, G. and Volpini, P. (eds.), *Sulla diplomazia in età moderna. Politica, economia, religione*, Milano: Franco Angeli, 2011, pp. 193–218.

Priotti, J.P., *Bilbao et ses marchands au XVIe siècle. Genèse d'une croissance*, Villeneuve d'Ascq: Presses Universitaires du Septentrion, 2004.

Priotti J.-P. and Saupin G., eds., *Le commerce atlantique franco-espagnol. Acteurs, négoces et ports (XVe–XVIIIe siècle)*, Rennes: Presses Universitaires de Rennes, 2008.

Ribeiro, A.S., *Early Modern Trading Networks in Europe: Cooperation and the Case of Simon Ruiz*, London: Routledge, 2015.

Salas Auséns, J.A., 'Pequeños comerciantes extranjeros en la España del siglo XVIII', in Crespo Solana, A. (ed.), *Comunidades transnacionales. Colonias de mercaderes extranjeros en el Mundo Atlántico (1500–1830)*, Madrid: Doce Calles, 2010, pp. 123–142.

Schulte-Beerbühl, M., *The Forgotten Majority: German Merchants in London, Naturalization and Global Trade (1660–1815)*, New York: Berghahn Books, 2014.

Shannon, T.R., *An Introduction to the World-System Perspective*, London: Westview Press, 1989.

Steensgaard, N., 'The Dutch East India Company as an Institutional Innovation", in Aymard, M. (ed.), *Dutch capitalism and world capitalism*, Cambridge: Cambridge University Press, 1982, pp. 235–257.

Subrahmanyam, S., *The Portuguese Empire in Asia, 1500–1700. A Political and Economic History*, London: Longman, 1993.

Trivellato, F., *Familiarity of Strangers: The Sephardic Diaspora, Livorno, and Cross-Cultural Trade in the Early Modern Period*, New Haven and London: Yale University Press, 2009.

———. 'A Republic of Merchants?', in Molho, A. and Ramada Curto, D. (eds.), *Finding Europe: Discourses on Margins, Communities, Images, 13th to 18th Centuries*, Oxford and New York: Berghahn Books, 2007, pp. 133–158.

van den Boogaart, E., Emmer, P., Klein, P. and Zandvliet, K., *La expansión holandesa en el atlántico*, Madrid: Mapfre, 1992.

van den Hoven, B. and Vries, P,. 'Het Hollandse wonder. Handel en politiek in de zeventiende eeuw', *Historisch Tijdschrift*, 1 (1992), pp. 5–21.

Van Leur, J.C., *Indonesian Trade and Society: Essays in Asian Social and Economic History*, The Hague: W. Van Hoeve Ltd., 1955.

Van Young, E., 'Social Networks: A Final Comment', in Böttcher, N., Hausberger, B. and Ibarra, A. (eds.), *Redes y negocios globales en el mundo ibérico, siglos XVI–XVIII*, Madrid: Iberoamericana, 2011, pp. 289–309.

Van Zanden, J.L., *The Rise and Decline of Holland's Economy: Merchant Capitalism and the Labour Market*, Manchester: Manchester University Press, 1993.

Vila Vilar, E., *Los Corzo y los Mañara: Tipos y Arquetipos del mercader con América*, Sevilla: Universidad de Sevilla, 1991.

Wallerstein, I., *The Modern World-System I. Capitalist Agriculture and the Origins of the European World-Economy in the Sixteenth Century,* New York: Academic Press, 1974.

———. *The Modern World-System II: Mercantilism and the Consolidation of the European World-Economy, 1600–1750*, New York: Academic Press, 1980.

Weber, K., *Deutsche Kaufleute im Atlantikhandel 1680–1830: Unternehmen und Familien in Hamburg, Cádiz und Bordeaux*, München: C.H. Beck, 2004.

———. 'La migration huguenote dans le contexte de l'économie atlantique. L'exemple de Hambourg (1680–1800)', in Braun, G. and Lachenicht, S. (eds.), *Les états allemands et les huguenots*, München: Oldenbourg 2007, pp. 125–136.

Weber, K. and Schulte-Beerbühl, M., 'From Westphalia to the Caribbean: Networks of German Textile Merchants in the Eighteenth Century', in Gestrich, A. and Schulte-Beerbühl, M. (eds.), *Cosmopolitan Networks in Commerce and Society: 1660–1914*, London: German Historical Insitute London, 2011, pp. 53–98.

Williamson, J., *Globalization and the Poor Periphery before 1950*, Cambridge: The MIT Press, 2006.

Yun Casalilla, B., ed., *Las redes del Imperio. Élites sociales en la articulación de la Monarquía Hispánica, 1492–1714*, Madrid: Marcial Pons, 2009.

Part I

Merchant networks, early modern long-distance trade and globalisation

Theoretical considerations and historiographical reappraisal

2 Social capital, networks and trust in early modern long-distance trade

A critical appraisal[1]

Xabier Lamikiz

Introduction

In recent years, a growing number of historians have, to varying degrees, drawn on socio-economic theory to analyse and explain the organisation of long-distance trade in the early modern period.[2] Part of this trend has been the picturing of international or global trade as the result of an interconnected web of social networks (and other institutions, both formal and informal) which underpinned that trade. There is no doubt that the use of socio-economic theory plays an enlightening role in explaining merchant collaboration, but in my view this interdisciplinary approach also raises important questions about the historian's job. My concern is threefold. First, there is a great variety of definitions in the literature. When we borrow terminology from the social sciences, too often we either offer no definition of those terms, assuming, for example, that the reader already knows what a social network is; or we put forward our own definitions without paying attention to what other scholars may have written on the matter. Conversely, we incorporate definitions formulated by economists, sociologists, anthropologists or political scientists with little regard to whether we could rephrase and adapt those definitions to our own methodological approaches. In short, there is a clear lack of consistency among historians in relation to definitions.

My second concern has to do with how historians employing socio-economic theory interpret the past. The risk is that we may feel tempted to use the past as a testing ground to demonstrate the validity of certain theories, when in fact our attention should be focused, needless to say, on explaining and understanding the past on its own terms. In my view, theories and analytical tools are useful for the historian as long as they help to explain the past without relegating history to a subsidiary role. In this respect, I fully subscribe to Francesco Boldizzoni's assertion that 'from the point of view of economic history only one thing matters: the compliance of theory to the facts'.[3]

And lastly, should we use socio-economic theory without engaging in, or at least acknowledging the existence of, current debates on precisely the theoretical frameworks we are increasingly resorting to? Economic historians' use of social capital theory is a case in point. There is widespread disagreement as to the essential qualities of social capital among social scientists. Should we not let our readers (mostly other historians) know about this? The problem is that we may choose the view of social capital that best suits our purposes, when in fact there may be alternative views that, if adopted, could point to very different interpretations of the same historical phenomena.

Apart from this brief introduction, this chapter is divided into five sections. In order to set the scene for a subsequent discussion, I first present the so-called agency problem in the context of the early modern long-distance trade. This is a fundamental problem of trade that merchants needed to reduce one way or another, a problem intimately linked to the provision of trust. The second section deals with different attempts by economic historians to systematise the study of trust. This is followed by a discussion about historians' use of social network analysis in order to examine merchant collaboration and the building up of trust. The fourth section focuses on some examples of social capital theory applied to merchants involved in long-distance trade; here, too, the emphasis is on social networks and the creation of personal and institutional trust. The chapter ends with some conclusions.

Long-distance trade and the agency problem

In premodern times, commercial exchanges over long distances posed major problems associated with an array of risks and uncertainties. The long distances in themselves (along with the ensuing delays and coordination problems), hazardous navigations across treacherous seas, cumbersome trade regulations at the ports of origin and destination, poor and slow communications and the unforeseen outbreak of war were among the dangers which could easily turn a promising business venture into a bitter failure or indeed an outright disaster. Of course, risks could be reduced by buying insurance, and many merchants did so. But uncertainties, those economic risks located in the realm of what economists call 'Knightian uncertainty', were a different matter altogether.[4] Their many possible outcomes eluded any attempt at measuring the odds with accuracy, and only measurable risks are insurable. This compelled merchants to resort to strategies other than marine insurance in order to alleviate the perils of uncertainty. The most prevalent uncertainties were associated with market gluts, the recovery of debts and opportunistic behaviour by agents. Sometimes, organising both trade routes and the exchanges along the lines of rigid mercantilist regulations could reduce those uncertainties, although whether those measures actually contributed to the expansion of trade is debatable.[5] Improvements in both the legal framework and the judicial system were also beneficial, and so was the creation and gradual spread of the commercial press. But in the early modern period, developments which had a positive impact on contract enforcement and information flows were relatively infrequent. That is why merchants, in order to reduce uncertainty, needed to obtain the best information available, not only about market conditions but also about the competence and reliability of other merchants. A lot was at stake, for a perceived lack of reliable information was likely to deter traders from engaging in commercial exchanges, which means that for long-distance trade to flourish it was necessary (though not sufficient) to overcome, or at least mitigate, those uncertainties related to agency and imperfect information.

Merchants relied on agents (often not specialised commission agents but merchants or correspondents acting as such, for that fostered reciprocity) to act on their behalf and to obtain information, and were therefore exposed to the so-called agency problem, or in its more explicit phrasing, the principal-agent problem (or dilemma), a concept that is widely used in the social sciences. The agency problem existed because at times the correspondent acting as an agent, by taking advantage of both his distant location and his privileged access to information (a situation called information asymmetry that can lead to conflict of interest or invite moral hazard), could be motivated to act in his own best interest rather than that of the principal.[6]

What did merchants do to reduce what was to a large extent, a problem of personal trust? Economic theory provides different answers to that question. Naturally, it is the historian's job to elucidate whether that logic matches the historical record. For example, forgoing the benefits of division of labour and avoiding agency relations could eliminate the agency problem entirely. From the point of view of economic theory, however, the downside of that strategy is that the merchant would inevitably incur significant opportunity costs arising from the fact he would not be able to engage in other business ventures while travelling with his goods. But whether merchants thought in terms of opportunity costs is another issue, because at times, merchants chose to travel with their goods to markets that were several months' journey away, and this happened even when they had correspondents they could have used in order to skip the long journey. Traders could also reduce exposure to agent misconduct by spreading their risk, that is, by relying on more than one correspondent at the same time. This, however, would increase transaction costs significantly and could, ironically, increase the probability that they would be cheated since there were more people to depend on.[7] Or they could try to exert control over the agent's actions and behaviour by specifying in a contract how he should proceed at all times: the plan for contingencies and what the sanctions would be in case instructions were not satisfactorily followed. But it was precisely because of the difficulty of anticipating and specifying all the possible contingencies that merchants very often preferred to convey general instructions in letters, which in effect were substitutes for agency contracts.[8] After all, one reason to trust an agent was because he had better information.

Another strategy was, of course, to internalise long-distance economic transactions within a partnership (a commenda contract is a good example) where both principal and agent shared profit and risk in a joint venture, or within a hierarchically organised firm that enjoyed monopoly rights over certain regions and trades, such as chartered companies, with agents being employees working under a salary. Notably, early modern chartered companies experimented in high real-wage contracts and other financial incentives to motivate and control their overseas agents and managers.[9]

But perhaps the most important mechanism for coping with the agency problem was to personalise the agency relationship by embedding it in structures of social relations (including, needless to say, family ties). In fact, all the above-mentioned strategies, even chartered companies, exhibited this feature to some degree.[10] This might appear to imply that social relations were sought after because of their potential for economic gain, whereas in fact, the causality could and often did go the other way, with agents being chosen from or through existing social relations and therefore being subject to pre-existing social obligations.[11] It is therefore crucial for historians to take a more holistic approach that also pays attention to non-economic motivations such as sociability, approval, habit, status, obligations and power. It also becomes apparent that the principal-agent problem was addressed within a wider social spectrum that we usually call a social network. Luckily these considerations have not gone unnoticed and are at the heart of some remarkable studies whose arguments and use of theory will provide the focus of this essay.

Since the agency problem revolves around interpersonal trust, in the next section I focus on what historians of early modern long-distance trade have to say on the matter.

Trust

Although it has attracted increasing attention in recent years, trust is still an unconventional subject matter for historians. This is partly because trust is often taken as a self-evident attribute of social life, and partly because it is an elusive, slippery concept to deal with. No historian denies its social and economic significance but few engage with the empirical and theoretical challenges it poses.

Trust was an essential component of pre-modern overseas trade because without it mutually beneficial cooperation would usually be impossible. As Sebouh Aslanian notes, 'trust emerges as an issue because economic transactions in early modern long-distance trade were rarely based on simultaneous exchange'.[12] Unsurprisingly, the significance of trust is repeatedly stressed in early modern trade manuals. From the Englishman Gerrard de Malynes, who in 1622 wrote that 'faith or trust is to be kept between merchants', to his compatriot Wyndham Beawes, who in 1752 wrote that a merchant's first care should be 'the choice of such a correspondent as he can depend on', trade manuals make numerous references to the importance of personal trust.[13] The term itself, trust, was often associated with other related concepts such as confidence, reliability, reputation, dependence, credit, honesty, honour or even faith. This rich terminology echoed ideas of trustworthiness.[14] In short, trust was important because, as historian Craig Muldrew puts it, the early modern economy was 'a system of cultural, as well as material, exchanges in which the central mediating factor was credit or trust'.[15]

But what is trust exactly? Definitions of trust abound among modern scholars. Sociologist Diego Gambetta, for instance, states that 'when we say we trust someone or that someone is trustworthy, we implicitly mean that the probability that he will perform an action that is beneficial ... to us is high enough for us to consider engaging in some form of cooperation with him'.[16] Elsewhere, I note that it is 'an act of faith, based upon personal judgement, but there is no deity involved – only human beings'.[17] Also in the context of long-distance trade, Sebouh Aslanian states that trust is 'the ability of one individual to have confidence that another person "entrusted" with something (e.g. money or fulfilling an important task such as carrying out the instructions in a power of attorney) would not act in a manner detrimental to the entrusting individual'.[18] Tijl Vanneste stresses the importance of combining a rational as well as a social component in order to define what he terms 'commercial trust', because that provides scope for a view of mercantile relationships as being based on individual self-interest, social embeddedness and cultural norms. Thus, for Vanneste, commercial trust is 'the personal valuation of the reputation of another merchant with regard to future behaviour'.[19] On the face of these definitions there does not seem to be much discrepancy as to what trust is. However, things get more complicated when the discussion moves on to the sources, types and levels of trust.

There can be no doubt that throughout the early modern period institutional mechanisms were implemented and improved (such as legal forms of enterprise, notarial systems, written documents, merchant guilds, public law courts and so on) that helped to enforce contracts. And merchants themselves shared norms of conduct, a morality of sorts, which originated from a common commercial culture, helping them to rely on one another.[20] But where does trust ultimately come from? New institutional economics considers institutional arrangements and generalised morality to be the main producers of trust in economic life. By contrast, the new economic sociology, with Granovetter as its leading figure, insists that social relations underlie the creation of trust.[21] It comes as no surprise, then, that historians working on the organisation of long-distance trade are combining both interpretations when attempting to uncover the sinews of merchant collaboration. The problem is that both views are more difficult to reconcile than it would appear.[22]

The above definitions refer primarily to personal or interpersonal trust, which was of paramount importance in the business world that preceded the arrival of the railroad, steamship and telegraph. However, this was not the only type of trust at work, as some economic historians have clearly pointed out. In fact, in the literature, there are numerous taxonomies of trust, elaborated to differing degrees, though the usual problem with distinguishing between types of trust is that they are seldom operational for historical inquiry. This is partly because much of the discussion on trust has centred on its meaning rather than on its functioning. What questions can we ask once trust is defined and deconstructed? The contrast between two recent publications will serve to illustrate this point.

In her book entitled *'Merely for Money'?*, after considering the emotive nature of trust, Sheryllynne Haggerty discusses the distinction between personal trust, institutional trust (also called assurance) and general trust (or confidence).[23] In her words, personal trust is 'an expectation of benign behaviour based on inferences of traits and intentions. It is based on the idea that most people believe, like Adam Smith, that "honesty was the best policy"'.[24] In her taxonomy, personal trust is divided into several types: it can be ascribed (when trust is placed in a person who is believed to have certain inherent features that make them trustworthy) or process-based (which is built from repeated reciprocal exchanges over time). It can also be related to competency, goodwill or a pseudo-contract (where both trading partners uphold universal ethical standards or keep promises, as if a contract were in place). Finally, it can be non-negotiated (the result of non-contractual reciprocal exchanges) or negotiated (which was explicitly bargained for within a one-off process). In contrast, institutional trust means that expectations are based on knowledge of an incentive structure that encourages people to trust each other. But what was this structure made of? 'The business culture of eighteenth-century merchants', Haggerty argues, 'worked as a private-order institution that provided an incentive structure, of which trust was a part. This business culture worked within and alongside other assurance structures such as the law, chartered companies, trade associations and banks'.[25] And finally, at a broader level, merchants had to have trust in the system of commerce in which they participated, which is to say the wider system of mercantilist regulations in which they operated. However, this general trust or confidence came mostly from formal institutions, which renders the distinction between institutional and general trust slightly confusing.

The three types of trust (and their respective subtypes) not only overlapped with one another, they also fluctuated over time. Haggerty identifies each type by employing examples taken from the business correspondence of British merchants operating in the Atlantic in the second half of the eighteenth century, but the utility of this thorough deconstruction of trust is far from clear. In fact, she concludes her discussion by acknowledging the difficulties of assessing where one level of trust ends and another starts. Moreover, their fluctuations seem unobservable. At the heart of those difficulties lies the big question of the transition from a premodern economy where personal trust was particularly important to a modern economy that relies more heavily on impersonal trust. Of course, there were impersonal mechanisms used in the early modern period, but one could hypothesise, for instance, that within the spectrum of personal and impersonal mechanisms that fostered merchant collaboration, a specific period saw a gradual shift towards more reliance on impersonal methods.[26] My point is that we should ask this or similar questions when dissecting the concept of trust. We must try to do more than merely confirm that trust mattered. We must find a way to make both the concept of trust and its deconstruction operational for historical research so that we can use trust to answer specific questions about historical processes.

The second example I would like to discuss is precisely an attempt to make a taxonomy of trust operational by using it to provide an answer to an important question: Did premodern merchant guilds generate social capital and trust that supported economic development?[27] With that aim, Sheilagh Ogilvie makes a double distinction between particularised and generalised trust in persons, and between particularised and generalised trust in institutions. These distinctions suggest that different kinds of trust have very different social and economic consequences. 'Particularized trust depends on specific personal attributes or affiliations of your transaction partner', whereas '[g]eneralized trust, by contrast, is a propensity to enter into transactions with all persons on an equal footing, even with strangers'.[28] Likewise, some institutions foster the development of a generalised trust in impartial institutions that are open to all, whilst others do not. Ogilvie draws upon insights from social capital theory to assert not only that merchant guilds generated particularised trust at best, but also that their experiences raise serious doubts about the tacit assumption of the social capital literature that particularised trust in members of your social network is somehow good for the production of generalised trust in people you do not know.

One may agree or disagree with Ogilvie's take on trust, but there is no doubt that her attempt to provide trust with historical explanatory power deserves careful attention and can inspire other historians to do the same. I will return to Ogilvie's use of social capital theory, of which I am less fond.

Another important question about the concept of trust has to do with how the historian should envision it. Was trusting another merchant a way to overcome uncertainty? Or was placing trust in a colleague merely an expectation? Conceiving trust as a way to overcome uncertainty entails, as political scientist Francisco Herreros notes, a trade-off between trust and information, whereby more information means less reliance on trust.[29] In other words, the better a merchant's information, the less he would need to trust his agents. This would suggest not only that there are substitutes for personal trust, but also that there are varying degrees of it. Moreover, if information is a substitute for trust, then so are formal institutions such as public law courts or notarial systems, because the more efficient they were at enforcing contracts, the less trust a merchant would have to place in his agents.[30] However, if we understand trust as an expectation, this trade-off between personal trust, on the one hand, and information and formal institutions on the other, is to a great extent misleading.[31] Could merchants afford to trust their correspondents only 'a little'? Moreover, we must keep in mind that additional information could also produce distrust. Similar questions can be asked about the role of formal institutions. Did more efficient courts of law serve to dissolve merchants' need for trustworthy correspondents? And if so, when did it happen? Would merchants rely on completely unknown or even dubious agents just because the local authorities were known to be reliable at enforcing contracts?

Interpersonal trust was very important among merchants for conducting long-distance trade, but how was it generated? Usually the emphasis is placed on the first 'F' of what economist Yoram Ben-Porath famously called the F-connection: families, friends and firms.[32] Depicting family as the main supplier of trustworthy associates and agents has become almost a mantra among historians of early modern merchants. But the social life of businessmen also revolved around their friends.[33] This is hardly surprising because for the merchant the world of trade was so broad, and the need to diversify risks so great, that it wasn't feasible to trade only with a handful of merchants. One only needs to have a look at a merchant's letter book to see that the majority of his correspondents were not his relatives. There is, however, an inclination to take trust as an inherent attribute of certain groups that derives mainly from the 'trade diaspora' literature,[34] where scholars have traditionally treated certain ethnic and religious minorities as communities blessed with 'intragroup trust'. This assumption is commonly found in studies of Armenians, Greeks, Jews, Huguenots, Quakers and other successful trade diasporas of the early modern period.[35] In the last few years, however, there have been emphatic attempts to break away from the idea that trust was an inherent attribute of trade diasporas. In this regard, the works of Francesca Trivellato, Sebouh Aslanian and Tijl Vanneste deserve a special mention.[36] In fact, their groundbreaking efforts have two features in common: they use business correspondence as their main primary source, and they rely on either social network analysis (that is the methodical analysis of social networks) or social capital theory (which also places social networks at the centre of analysis) to explain how trust was generated. They do not rely on assumptions or generalisations, but employ concrete examples from actual merchants and their correspondents. From that perspective, it immediately becomes clear that the nature of the principal-agent problem was not only bilateral but also multilateral, for it was embedded in a wider web of social relations. The idea is that by paying close attention to social networks one can study the actual functioning of merchant collaboration in long-distance trade. In the words of Trivellato:

> If we think in terms of social networks, we can narrow the gap between essentialist approaches to trust (I trust you because you are a coreligionist) and assumptions about the equalising effects of legal institutions (I don't trust anyone, but the law will ensure that all the contracts that I sign will be enforced).[37]

This is, no doubt, a persuasive methodological remark, because if we look into who traded with whom and on what grounds, that is, if we carry out a microhistorical examination of the sources, then we should be able to decipher the working of trust at its different levels. Naturally, the social network approach requires, first, to clarify what a network actually is in the context of early modern trade, and, second, to demonstrate the validity of the theoretical arguments put forward with abundant empirical evidence.

Networks

Any contemporary historian working on early modern merchants must embrace the idea that merchants operated through social/merchant/business/trade networks. That is universally accepted. The consequence of this craze for networks is that often the word is, as historian Mike Burkhardt puts it, 'merely used as a metaphor, a trendy term to attract potential readers'.[38] It is fair to say, however, that even as a metaphor, the notion of social networks works quite well: it immediately conveys an idea of collaboration between people, a web of interacting individuals who pursue a common goal. As a result, it has become popular among historians to resort to social network analysis for the reconstruction and examination of cooperation between merchants. In this context, network analysis is, as Vanneste points out, 'a type of economic history that wants to assert the role played by social interaction and cultural background when it comes to trade'.[39] But what is a social network exactly?

According to the *Oxford English Dictionary*, a social network is 'a network of social interactions and personal relationships'.[40] More sophisticated definitions can be found in the social sciences. For network scientists Stanley Wasserman and Katherine Faust, a social network is made of 'a finite set or sets of actors and the relation or relations defined upon them'.[41] For sociologists Joel Podolny and Karen Page, a 'network form of organization' is 'any collection of actors (N ≥ 2) that pursue repeated, enduring exchange relations with one another and, at the same time, lack a legitimate organizational authority to arbitrate and resolve disputes that may arise during the exchange'.[42] These definitions provide a good starting point for the historian but are no more than that. In her latest book, Haggerty discusses a number of definitions provided by social scientists (including the above definition by Podolny and Page) and concludes that none of these suit the context of eighteenth-century Atlantic trade. That is why she puts forward her own definition of business networks: 'a group or groups of people that form associations with the explicit or implicit expectation of mutual long-term economic benefit'.[43] But this definition still doesn't provide all the elements needed to identify a network in the primary sources.

Broadly speaking, historians of premodern merchants agree that networks had to meet some specific criteria. Three basic features stand out: participation was voluntary, there was no formal membership (it was, therefore, an informal association) and participants transferred resources throughout the network in a stable, long-lasting and mutually beneficial manner. But other, additional – and, I should say, equally arbitrary – features are also deemed important in the literature. For example, how many members must a network have to qualify as such? Unlike Podolny and Page, who think there should be at least two actors, those few historians who actually consider this point think there should be at least three. Vanneste, for example, argues that a mercantile network 'is an association between more than two merchants who become engaged in a business relationship that considers insiders and outsiders'.[44] But do all members of a network have to be directly connected to one another? Not according to Burkhardt, for he states that '[a] social network is a group of actors that all are connected to at least two other actors in the group'.[45] By that definition, any community, no matter how big, can be considered a social network.

To define what social networks actually are seems very sensible, but as they conduct social network analysis, historians encounter a problem that often forces them to employ the term in rather vague fashion. That problem, in my view, arises from the exceedingly difficult task of drawing network boundaries. It is reasonable to think that merchants were linked by multiple networks of business ties, as well as other types of social relations, and that these networks often overlapped, which creates significant complications when it comes to studying them. Moreover, merchants' connections consisted of strong as well as weak ties. But was everybody they were in contact with a member of one of their networks? I agree with Haggerty that '[w]e cannot simply say because a group of people know each other that they belong to a network. There has to be something that binds them together, that makes them instrumental'.[46] But how can we identify a network if drawing its specific boundaries seems so difficult? Naturally this calls for drawing artificial borders 'based on our scientific interpretations for research purposes'.[47] It is important to remember that sociologists and anthropologists usually have all the data they need to establish the limits of a network; but early modern historians are not so lucky. In fact, we usually have no option but to make do with incomplete private records that belonged to few merchant houses. This is complicated even further by the fact that networks constitute dynamic patterns that change over time and, therefore, need to be studied from a diachronic as well as a synchronic standpoint. Moreover, when the available source belonged to a particular merchant (which is the case in most studies), there is a clear bias towards seeing him placed at the centre of the networks in which he participated. If we acknowledge all these problems but still consider that the social network analysis approach is worth adopting in full, then we will also have to admit that our work may distort the past more than is recommendable. In other words, one can only hope that, on balance, after weighing up the pros and cons, our understanding of the past will profit from delimiting networks artificially. I would argue that this problem with network boundaries is part of the reason why most historians, myself included, make use of social networks in such a vague manner. Even Trivellato, who claims that she uses the social network analysis approach 'as an analytical tool' rather than 'a mathematical measure', ultimately employs the notion of a social network rather metaphorically and fails to provide a hard and fast definition of it in her influential book.[48] This is no coincidence and stems from the fact that providing a definition calls for clearly delimited examples, which unfortunately, might misconstrue merchants' actual experience.

So an important methodological problem with using social network analysis comes from the fact that a certain volume of consistent data is needed in order to start piecing together social networks. And if we are lucky enough to gather a significant amount of data, then the question arises as to how quantitative our analysis can or should be. This, of course, depends not only on the data at hand but also on the questions we are asking. Quantitative studies dealing with early modern business networks use graph theory in order to examine measurable network properties such as density, size, different centralities, connectedness, power, path length and clustering.[49] But these brave attempts or experiments are too few to show convincingly that applying visual analytics and graph theory can actually tell us something we previously didn't know, or something that couldn't similarly be explained by employing more arcane methods.

Historians working on the creation and maintenance of trust relations are primarily interested in qualitative data about networks. From the literature it is clear that examining mercantile correspondence is the best (though not the only) way to analyse networks in this regard. Here historians prefer to concentrate on case studies rather than widen the scope of their efforts. According to Silvia Marzagalli, for instance, '[t]he most obvious way of studying networks is to analyze the activities carried out by a single firm and its correspondents'.[50] Leos Müller, who analyses the activities of two Stockholm merchant houses, takes that idea one step further and uses merchant letters to study what he calls 'correspondence networks'.[51] Indeed, the connection between networks, trust and epistolary correspondence offers valuable possibilities to the historian, because business letters not only conveyed information that directly affected personal reputations and the perception of trustworthiness; they also show in great detail how merchant collaboration actually happened. And when networks are looked at from the inside it becomes clear that they were not free of problems; they did not always work well and could in fact be detrimental for economic progress.[52] It also becomes clear that merchants required frequent communication, socio-economic incentives and reputation mechanisms in order to cope with the principal-agent problem.

There are other interesting questions regarding networks that need further research. For instance, how personal or impersonal were merchant networks? How did this dichotomy evolve in our period? Was there an appropriate size for a network? Did merchant networks create or overcome trade barriers? Also, when we name networks, are all the terms we employ to accompany them (trade, business, merchant, social and so on) interchangeable? Can we make distinctions between a business network and a trade network? When we refer to merchant networks, for example, we are implying that everyone involved in them was a merchant. However, that was not always the case.

The one characteristic most studies of early modern business networks share is that they adopt a microhistorical standpoint. Merchants are thus seen in conversation with their correspondents and associates, conveying information to one another, demanding payment of debts, voicing approval or disapproval, pondering the viability of seemingly profitable commercial ventures and so on. In essence, they show the importance of sociability as a critical element of commercial exchange. But the full-blown theoretical framework that tries to explain the benefits derived from nurturing sociability is social capital theory. Indeed, it could be said that 'the idea of social capital offers a way of comprehending the operation of networks'.[53]

Social capital

Political scientist Robert Putnam explains with clarity what social capital is: 'Whereas physical capital refers to physical objects and human capital refers to properties of individuals, social capital refers to connections among individuals – social networks and the norms of reciprocity and trustworthiness that arise from them'.[54] And those connections, just as a ship (physical capital) or a merchant's training (human capital), have value, and this value is the direct result of the time and effort invested in nurturing and expanding those connections.

However, although trust and social relations are crucial for the social capital research agenda, neither of them is in itself social capital. As Francisco Herreros puts it, '[s]ocial capital ... is not trust or networks but the obligation of reciprocity that can be derived from relations of trust and the information that can be derived from the participation in social networks'.[55] This means that participation in social networks provides access to resources of social capital in the form of information (which the members of the social network possess and are likely to share with one another) and obligations of reciprocity (which stem from relations of trust).

These definitions may suggest that social capital is a straightforward concept, but that isn't actually the case. For one thing, there is widespread disagreement as to its essential qualities. Perhaps that is the reason why historians seem to be more enthusiastic about social network analysis than about social capital theory. In fact, the concept of social capital is used simply because it is highly evocative of the value of social relations and networks. In those cases, historians are happy to provide a short definition in passing, making no use of social capital theory. For instance, Robin Pearson and David Richardson state that social capital has been a key concept in discussing business networking in the Atlantic world, but they content themselves with a sweeping generalisation as to what it is: 'shared identities based on kinship, family, religious and other forms of association [that] promote trust'.[56] Even more meagre is the definition provided by Leonor Costa, Maria Rocha and Tanya Araujo: 'The contribution of any arrangement to promoting trust may be labelled as social capital'.[57]

There are, nonetheless, historians working on both long-distance merchants and commercial institutions for whom social capital theory offers an adequate explanatory framework. Two recent and remarkable examples are Sebouh Aslanian and Sheilagh Ogilvie, although in my view both historians tend to give priority to theory over the facts. Aslanian defines social capital as '[t]he value generated when individuals join together and invest resources in the formation of ongoing and structured relationships with each other (known as a "social network") that generate collective and individual benefits'.[58] Similarly, Ogilvie defines it as 'a store of value that is generated when a group of people invests in fostering a body of relationships with each other – a social network such as a guild or other cohesive community'.[59] The two definitions are quite similar, but it is important to stress that their notion of social network is somewhat different from the definitions provided by historians using social network analysis, where the emphasis is on specific individuals who established agency relations with specific correspondents. In Ogilvie's case, a merchant guild membership (i.e. a formal institution) is the social network, implying that all the members of the guild somehow shared direct, personal relationships with one another, which they did not. In the case of Aslanian (as with most historians working on trade diasporas) the social network is comprised of all the members of the Julfan-Armenian global diaspora.[60] However, this is not to say that Aslanian and Ogilvie, by somehow adopting a broader view of social networks, are not concerned with network boundaries. Quite the opposite, both their arguments and use of social capital theory rely heavily on well-defined boundaries. There is a reason for this.

Perhaps no social capital theorist has been more influential for historians of merchant collaboration in the early modern period than sociologist James Coleman.[61] His assertion that the presence of two factors or structures –'closure' and 'multiplex relationships' – in a social network contributes greatly to engendering social capital has had a lasting effect upon how historians make sense of social capital. Closure means that the social network must have clearly defined borders, which is to say there can be no doubt who is a member of the network and who is not. This structure, Coleman argues, facilitates, among other things, effective collective sanctioning, information flow and the creation of individual reputations. On the other hand, multiplex relationships refer to dense or multistranded ties between the network members, encompassing different spheres of activity that overlap with one another – economic, social, political, religious and so on. In other words, merchants who are members of a network will generate more social capital if, as well as trading with each other, they also attend the same church, their sons and daughters marry, they share similar political affiliations and so on. Both Aslanian and Ogilvie stress the presence of closure and multiplex relationships in the social networks they study. However, I will argue that they do so somewhat artificially.

Aslanian concentrates on the trading networks of the merchants from the Armenian quarter of Isfahan, known as New Julfa. Julfans were extremely successful in international trade throughout the seventeenth and the first half of the eighteenth century. Their trade diaspora or trade network extended to the main ports and cities of the early modern period, from Western Europe, Russia and the Mediterranean to the Indian Ocean and the remote Canton and Manila. At any given time, the Julfan network included no more than a thousand individuals, including merchants, employees and commenda agents. However, unlike Trivellato and Vanneste, who see the existence of long-distance cross-cultural trade as unequivocal proof that relationships of trust went well beyond ethnic and religious boundaries, Aslanian finds no long-distance agency relations between Julfan and non-Julfan merchants.[62] Nevertheless, this picture of conspicuous intragroup trading does not lead him to conclude that Julfans trusted one another simply because they shared both provenance and cultural background. His interpretation is far more interesting and insightful than that. Among other primary sources, Aslanian examines a collection of 1,700 letters captured by the British in the Indian Ocean in 1748 on board an Armenian ship named *Santa Catharina*. From his analysis of that correspondence he concludes that cooperation and trust between Julfan merchants was never taken as a given. Instead, when it existed, it was the result of a far more complicated process which, according to Aslanian, can be better understood with recourse to social capital theory.

Aslanian points out that social capital is constructed from four elements: a social network, a set of shared norms (either informal or codified), information flows within the social network, and trust and trustworthiness between network members (as a result of the preceding three aspects). From this angle, trust is seen 'as a commodity created by merchants largely through rigorous monitoring of merchant behavior, rewarding individuals upholding high ethical standards, and sanctioning those who break codes of honor and betray their fellow merchants'.[63]

But for this collective mechanism to be effective in long-distance agency relations it was necessary for the Julfan trade network to have a 'peculiar social structure'; in other words, the network needed to be closed and its members needed to have multistranded ties with one another. Once Aslanian incorporates the arguments of Coleman (and Avner Greif) into his work, that peculiar structure comes to be seen as the main reason behind the high levels of social capital and trust within the network.[64] It was, therefore, in the interest of the Julfans to keep their network closed. However, this compliance of theory with facts is to some extent contrived, because even though Aslanian claims not to have found evidence to the contrary, he is no doubt aware that other historians demonstrate that Julfan merchants 'operated in close cooperation with other ethnic groups', and those of standing even 'lent money at respondentia to merchants of other ethnic groups', effectively engaging in long-distance trade with their borrowers.[65] Is Aslanian's use of social capital theory completely invalidated by the fact that the Julfan network was more porous than he suggests? Clearly not, but his example shows that the explanatory power of a theoretical framework may take precedence over historical facts.

In my opinion, Ogilvie's use of social capital theory is far more problematic. She sets out to test (and to debunk) the strong theoretical claim that 'those institutions that generate social capital are superior to those that do not'.[66] To do so she investigates both the social capital generated by merchant guilds and its impact on the medieval and early modern economy (and more generally the role of merchant guilds in the economy). Here too, closure and multiplex relationships are stressed as essential characteristics of the social network (i.e. the guild), so much so that according to Ogilvie, '[m]embers of a merchant guild trusted each other and were willing to transact with each other because of the personal attributes associated with membership in that guild, and because the guild itself penalized deviations from corporate norms'.[67] Crucially, merchant guilds 'did not create a generalized trust in persons, encouraging transactions with strangers. If anything they did the opposite'.[68] However, earlier in her book, in the chapter devoted to principal-agent problems, she also makes a statement which would appear to be at odds with those two quotations: 'the theoretical benefits of merchant guilds as solutions to agency problems were not important in practice – perhaps precisely because of the lost gains from trade involved in limiting one's agency relationships to members of the same social network'.[69]

So transactions were carried out between guild members, but when it came to overseas trade, precisely the sort of exchange that demanded more trust, was it wiser for them to rely on someone else? Ogilvie may well be right that merchant guilds were not solutions to agency problems. In my view, however, the above contradiction stems from her need to portray merchant guilds as firmly closed networks (concentrating more on structure than relationships), because that ultimately allows her to reinforce her view that whatever guilds did, even if it was creating social capital (the wrong kind, of course), was in some way damaging to the economy.

The trouble with social capital theory is that there are, in fact, different theories with varying views of what social capital is and what its different dimensions are. To what extent can these competing views affect historians' interpretations? Based on Ogilvie's example, they can have a big influence. Shouldn't we let our readers know that depending on what our take on social capital is, we may reach different, possibly opposite, conclusions? If we consider that closure – following Coleman's work – is a fundamental feature of a social network, then we may argue, as Ogilvie does, that merchant guilds could hardly benefit the whole economy since the kind of trust they generated (i.e. 'particularized trust' in both persons and institutions, as opposed to 'generalized trust', which is associated with the gradual emergence of impersonal markets and impartial states) was only applicable to and enjoyed by guild members.[70] But if we were to turn instead to Granovetter or Putnam, a sociologist and a political scientist respectively, with their emphasis on the importance of cultivating relationships, however weak, beyond our most immediate circle, then we could safely conclude that the social capital arising from the membership of a merchant guild spread to the rest of society, unless we assume that guild members lived in a social vacuum.[71] Putnam, for instance, argues that '[o]f all dimensions along which forms of social capital vary, perhaps the most important is the distinction between bridging (or inclusive) and bonding (or exclusive)'.[72] 'Bonding social capital' is good for strengthening reciprocity and fostering solidarity, whereas bridging networks are better for 'linkage to external assets and for information diffusion'. Following that distinction, he further asserts that:

> Many groups simultaneously bond along some social dimensions and bridge across others. … In short, bonding and bridging are not 'either-or' categories into which social networks can be neatly divided, but 'more or less' dimensions along which we can compare different forms of social capital.[73]

It would be interesting to see the extent to which the bonding capital fostered by merchant guilds among its members led to the severing of relationships with merchants who were legally excluded from the guild. It would also be interesting to look into whether merchant guilds generated bridging capital. Considering that guild members had no option but to trade with nonmembers, my guess is that merchant guilds, or at least some of them, must have taken measures to favour those relationships. The example of the Bilbao merchant guild or *consulado* in the first half of the eighteenth century, which I have studied in some detail, would suggest precisely that.[74] Thus it would not be far-fetched to argue that even close-knit social networks such as merchant guilds (if they were indeed so close-knit in all cases, which I very much doubt, for members often had competing interests, at least in the case of the Spanish *consulados de comercio*), by both bonding and bridging, could generate some degree of generalised trust.

There are other, alternative theoretical views of social capital that differ substantially from that adopted by Ogilvie. For instance, we could easily conclude that close-knit merchant guilds generated generalised trust if we paid attention to the work of economist Emily Chamlee-Wright who, working through the lens of Austrian capital theory, sees the development of social capital as a process of social learning in which:

> Dispersed and differentiated knowledge can transcend individuals and social networks in forms that are useful to the wider community, such as an over-arching ethos of trust or generalized reciprocity. *People within a community enjoying these norms trust not only people they know personally, but people generally, and in turn, they are trusted by others* [emphasis added].[75]

I am not saying that Chamlee-Wright's and Putnam's views are right and Ogilvie's is wrong. I am simply pointing out that depending on the social capital theory we adopt, or the dimensions that we stress, our interpretation of the past can vary considerably. Ogilvie provides abundant empirical evidence throughout her book, but her arguments against merchant guilds' contribution to the development of generalised trust rely on the application of theory rather than empirical evidence, and her choice of theory happens, rather conveniently, to support her overall idea that, in their eight centuries of existence, merchant guilds were always bad for economic development and that their long survival is explained solely by their ability to redistribute resources to the rich and powerful.

Conclusions

This chapter has tried to raise some questions about historians' views on merchant collaboration in early modern long-distance trade. To set the scene for discussion, the first section has presented merchants' different responses to the so-called principal-agent problem, arguing that this problem is better understood if we acknowledge that merchants' actions were socially and culturally embedded, and therefore also responded to motives other than the purely economic.

The agency problem was, to a large extent, a question of personal trust between merchants. The study of trust, however, has mainly concentrated on the meaning of trust, providing a number of definitions and taxonomies that, in most instances, do not seem to be operational for historical inquiry. To show this general short-coming I have compared two different typologies of trust: one that is purely tax-onomical (Haggerty's) and another that is intended to ask a specific historical question (Ogilvie's) and is therefore operational.

Historians are also resorting to social network analysis in order to examine the sinews of merchant collaboration. However, few historians have opted for analysing networks using quantitative methods and graph theory. The reason for this is not difficult to grasp: the results do not seem to be very promising. Instead, most historians are making a rather vague, I would say metaphorical, use of social networks, which in turn has complicated the task of matching hard and fast definitions of networks with specific historical examples. The problem seems to be that identifying a network requires its boundaries to be delimited, which can only be done artificially and therefore at the risk of being unhistorical.

By contrast, the work of those historians who have resorted to social capital theory depends, to a large extent, on setting up well-defined network boundaries, even though the idea of social network they use is much broader than that conveyed by social network analysis. A social network can be a trade diaspora (Aslanian) or a merchant guild (Ogilvie). But in my view, these attempts have tended either to give priority to theory over primary sources, or have chosen the type of social capital theory that best suits their interests without considering other types which, based on the same empirical evidence, could provide quite different interpretations.

Notes

1 The author is very grateful to Jeremy Baskes, Manuel Llorca-Jaña, Manuel Herrero Sánchez, Klemens Kaps, Jesús María Valdaliso, the members of the Department of Economic History and Institutions of the University of the Basque Country, and the authors of this volume for their invaluable comments and criticisms. Funding for the research was provided by the Spanish Ministry of Economy and Competitiveness through the project HAR 2012–39034–C03–02 (MINECO) and by the Basque University System through the research group IT807–13.

2 Although long-distance trade was considerably smaller than domestic trade in pre-modern times, it was particularly transformative due to both its market-oriented nature and the large profits it could generate. According to Fernand Braudel, long distance trade's 'undisputable superiority' over internal trade 'lay in the concentrations it made possible, which meant it was an unrivalled machine for the rapid reproduction and increase of capital'. In fact, long-distance trade, or 'external trade', was 'an essential factor in the creation of merchant capitalism'; F. Braudel, *Civilization and Capitalism, 15th–18th Century*, vol. 2: *The Wheels of Commerce* (London: Phoenix Press, 1988), p. 408.

3 F. Boldizzoni, *The Poverty of Clio: Resurrecting Economic History* (Princeton, NJ: Princeton University Press, 2011), p. 117.

4 First formulated by American economist Frank Knight in 1921, the distinction between risk and uncertainty is straightforward: risk applies to situations where we do not know the outcome of a given situation, but can accurately measure the odds, which is ultimately the raison d'être of the insurance industry. Uncertainty, in contrast, applies to situations where we cannot set accurate odds simply because we do not have all the information we would need in order to do so. For an interesting discussion of the implications of this distinction in the context of the Atlantic world, see J. Baskes, *Staying Afloat: Risk and Uncertainty in Spanish Atlantic World Trade, 1760–1820* (Stanford: Stanford University Press, 2013), pp. 1–11.

5 Spain's system of annual commercial fleets to Spanish America and the fairs at which the exchanges between Spanish and American merchants were carried out is a good example of risk and uncertainty reduction by means of regulation. See Baskes, *Staying Afloat*, pp. 43–68; X. Lamikiz, 'Flotistas en la Nueva España: diseminación espacial y negocios de los intermediarios del comercio transatlántico, 1670–1702', *Colonial Latin American Review*, 20:1 (2011), pp. 9–33.

6 See S. Ogilvie, *Institutions and European Trade: Merchant Guilds, 1000–1800* (Cambridge: Cambridge University Press, 2011), pp. 315–343

7 Transaction costs are 'the costs of measuring and defining the attributes of the goods and services being exchanged and the costs of enforcing agreements with respect to contracts that are made'; D.C. North, 'Institutions, Transaction Costs and the Rise of Merchant Empires', in J. Tracy (ed.), *The Political Economy of Merchant Empires: State Power and World Trade* (Cambridge: Cambridge University Press, 1991), pp. 22–40, on p. 24.

8 F. Trivellato, *The Familiarity of Strangers: The Sephardic Diaspora, Livorno, and Cross-cultural Trade in the Early Modern Period* (New Haven: Yale University Press, 2009), p. 169.

9 A.M. Carlos and S. Nicholas, '"Giants of An Earlier Capitalism": The Chartered Trading Companies as Modern Multinationals', *Business History Review*, 62:3 (1988), pp. 398–419, on p. 418.

10 A.M. Carlos and S. Nicholas, 'Agency Problems in the Early Chartered Companies: the Case of the Hudson's Bay Company', *Journal of Economic History*, 50:4 (1990), pp. 853–875, on p. 875.

11 As Mark Granovetter points out, 'economic action (like all action) is socially situated, and cannot be explained by individual motives alone; it is embedded in ongoing networks of personal relations rather than carried out by atomized individuals'; M. Granovetter, 'Economic Institutions as Social Constructions: A Framework for Analysis', *Acta Sociologica*, 35 (1992), pp. 3–11, on p. 4.

12 S. Aslanian, *From the Indian Ocean to the Mediterranean: The Global Trade Networks of Armenian Merchants from New Julfa* (Berkeley: University of California Press, 2011), p. 166.

13 X. Lamikiz, *Trade and Trust in the Eighteenth-Century Atlantic World: Spanish Merchants and their Overseas Networks* (Woodbridge: Boydell Press / Royal Historical Society, 2010), pp. 141 and 162.

14 According to philosopher Katherine Hawley, '[t]rust is at the centre of a whole web of concepts: reliability, predictability, expectation, cooperation, goodwill, and – on the dark side – distrust, insincerity, conspiracy, betrayal, and incompetence'; K. Hawley, *Trust: A Very Short Introduction* (Oxford: Oxford University Press, 2012), p. 3.

15 C. Muldrew, *The Economy of Obligation: The Culture of Credit and Social Relations in Early Modern England* (Basingstoke: Macmillan, 1998), p. 4.

16 D. Gambetta, 'Can We Trust Trust?', in D. Gambetta in *Trust: Making and Breaking Cooperative Relations* (Oxford: Basil Blackwell, 1988), pp. 213–237, on p. 217.

17 X. Lamikiz, *Trade and Trust*, p. 9. In the book, I eschew theory almost entirely and, for the most part, take an empirical approach to trust and its role in facilitating commercial as well as social exchanges.

18 S. Aslanian, *From the Indian Ocean*, p. 17.

19 T. Vanneste, *Global Trade and Commercial Networks: Eighteenth-Century Diamond Merchants* (London: Pickering & Chatto, 2011), p. 30.

20 Ibid., p. 32.

21 M. Granovetter, 'Economic Action and Social Structure: The Problem of Embeddedness', *American Journal of Sociology*, 91:3 (1985), pp. 481–510, on p. 491.

22 Granovetter criticises new institutional economics for its emphasis on institutions ('substitutes for trust') as efficient solutions to certain economic problems, because in doing so it provides an 'under-socialised' account of why economic life is not suffused with mistrust and malfeasance. On the other hand, Granovetter argues that there are economists who, while acknowledging the importance of trust, assume it operates in a general, implicit manner, and therefore they offer an 'over-socialised' conception of orderly economic life. Counter to the under- and over-socialised views, '[t]he embeddedness argument stresses instead the role of concrete personal relations and structures (or "networks") of such relations in generating trust and discouraging malfeasance'; Ibid., p. 490.

23 S. Haggerty, *'Merely for Money'? Business Culture in the British Atlantic, 1750–1815* (Liverpool: Liverpool University Press, 2012), pp. 70–95.

24 Ibid., p. 71.

25 Ibid., pp. 71–72.

26 The reverse could also serve as a hypothesis. Silvia Marzagalli, for example, suggests that war was an important turning point in such fluctuations: 'The French Wars [1793–1815] intensified the uncertainty surrounding business choices and forced

merchants to rely more than ever on [personal] trust'; S. Marzagalli, 'Establishing Transatlantic Trade Networks in Time of War: Bordeaux and the United States, 1793–1815', *Business History Review*, 79:4 (2005), pp. 811–844, on p. 812.

27 In fact, the question is part of a larger inquiry into the role of merchant guilds in the medieval and early modern economy; S. Ogilvie, *Institutions and European Trade*.

28 Ibid., pp. 428–429.

29 F. Herreros, *The Problem of Forming Social Capital: Why Trust?* (New York: Palgrave, 2004), p. 8.

30 Institutional arrangements encompassed diverse initiatives. The use of human pawns as a guarantee of slave delivery is a good example; see P.E. Lovejoy and D. Richardson, 'Trust, Pawnship, and Atlantic History: The Institutional Foundations of the Old Calabar Slave Trade', *American Historical Review*, 104:2 (1999), pp. 333–355, on p. 354.

31 F. Herreros makes this point with regard to trust and information. F. Herreros, *The Problem of Forming Social Capital*, p. 8.

32 Y. Ben-Porath, 'The F-Connection: Families, Friends, and Firms and the Organization of Exchange', *Population and Development Review*, 6:1 (1980), pp. 1–30.

33 X. Lamikiz, *Trade and Trust*, pp. 150–153.

34 In his seminal work, Philip Curtin defines trade diasporas as '[t]rade communities of merchants living among aliens in associated networks'; P.J. Curtin, *Cross-Cultural Trade in World History* (Cambridge: Cambridge University Press, 1984), p. 3. In the literature, terms such as entrepreneurial network and diaspora network are usually synonyms for trade diaspora; I. Baghdiantz McCabe, G. Harlaftis and I. P. Minoglou (eds.), *Diaspora Entrepreneurial Networks: Four Centuries of History* (New York: Berg, 2005), p. xviii.

35 This shortcoming of the trade diaspora historiography is aptly discussed in F. Trivellato, *The Familiarity of Strangers*, pp. 10–16.

36 S. Aslanian, *From the Indian Ocean*; F. Trivellato, *The Familiarity of Strangers*; T. Vanneste, *Global Trade*.

37 F. Trivellato, *The Familiarity of Strangers*, p. 163.

38 M. Burkhardt, 'Networks as Social Structures in Late Medieval and Early Modern Towns: A Theoretical Approach to Historical Network Analysis', in A. Caracausi and C. Jeggle (eds.), *Commercial Networks and European Cities, 1400–1800* (London: Pickering & Chatto, 2014), pp. 13–43, on p. 13.

39 T. Vanneste, *Global Trade*, p. 25.

40 www.oxforddictionaries.com/definition/english/social-network. In the 21st century it also is '[a] dedicated website or other application which enables users to communicate with each other by posting information, comments, messages, images, etc.'

41 S. Wasserman and K. Faust, *Social Network Analysis: Methods and Applications* (Cambridge: Cambridge University Press, 1994), p. 20.

42 They further state that '[b]y fostering greater communication than the market does, network forms of organization facilitate greater coordination in the face of changes whose significance cannot be completely conveyed or understood through price signals'; J.M. Podolny and K.L. Page, 'Network Forms of Organization', *Annual Review of Sociology*, 24 (1998), pp. 57–76, on p. 59 and p. 66.

43 S. Haggerty, *'Merely for Money'?*, p. 164.

44 T. Vanneste, *Global Trade*, p. 27.

45 M. Burkhardt, 'Networks as Social Structures', p. 14.

46 S. Haggerty, *'Merely for Money'?*, p. 163.

47 M. Burkhardt, 'Networks as Social Structures', p. 16.

48 F. Trivellato, *The Familiarity of Strangers*, p. 146.

49 See, for example, S. Haggerty and J. Haggerty, 'Visual Analytics of an Eighteenth-Century Business Network', *Enterprise and Society*, 11:1 (2010), pp. 1–25; C. McWaters and Y. Lemarchand, 'Local and Global Merchant Networks: Accounting Across Space and Time', APIRA 2010 Conference paper, Sydney, July 2010.

50 S. Marzagalli, 'Establishing Transatlantic Trade Networks', p. 838.
51 L. Müller, *The Merchant Houses of Stockholm, c. 1640–1800: A Comparative Study of Early Modern Entrepreneurial Behaviour* (Uppsala: S. Academiae Ubsaliensis, 1998), p. 148.
52 D. Hancock, 'The Trouble with Networks: Managing the Scots' Early-Modern Madeira Trade', *Business History Review*, 79:3 (2005), pp. 467–491.
53 A.R. Anderson and S.L. Jack, 'The Articulation of Social Capital in Entrepreneurial Networks: A Glue or a Lubricant?', *Entrepreneurship & Regional Development*, 14 (2002), pp. 193–210, on p. 196.
54 R. Putnam, *Bowling Alone: The Collapse and Revival of American Community* (New York: Simon & Schuster, 2000), p. 19.
55 F. Herreros, *The Problem of Forming Social Capital*, p. 7.
56 R. Pearson and D. Richardson, 'Social Capital, Institutional Innovation and Atlantic Trade before 1800', *Business History*, 50:6 (2008), pp. 765–780, on p. 765.
57 L. Freire Costa, M. Rocha and T. Araujo, 'Social Capital and Economic Performance: Trust and Distrust in Eighteenth-Century Gold Shipments from Brazil', *European Review of Economic History*, 15 (2011), pp. 1–27, on pp. 1–2.
58 S. Aslanian, *From the Indian Ocean*, p. 170.
59 S. Ogilvie, *Institutions and European Trade*, p. 427.
60 Similarly, Daviken Studnicki-Gizbert defines the Portuguese nation's diaspora network in the sixteenth and seventeenth centuries as 'an integrated structure rather than a scattered assortment of individual merchants. This network was extensive, multilateral, and highly interconnected'; D. Studnicki-Gizbert, *A Nation Upon the Ocean Sea: Portugal's Atlantic Diaspora and the Crisis of the Spanish Empire, 1492–1640* (Oxford: Oxford University Press, 2007), p. 97.
61 J. Coleman, 'Social Capital in the Creation of Human Capital', *American Journal of Sociology*, 94:1 (1988), pp. S95–S120.
62 S. Aslanian does not examine cross-cultural trust relations between Julfans and outsiders for two reasons: '(1) the evidence at our disposal suggests that the highest levels of trust in Julfan long-distance trade involved *commenda* partnerships, and most if not all such partnerships were between members of the Julfan community and did not involve outsiders; and (2) in cases involving money lending between Julfans and Indian *sarrafs* in Isfahan, where trust would have been a vital concern, the evidence at hand does not allow us to discuss the matter extensively. This important element of Julfan trade remains to be examined sometime in the future'; S, Aslanian, *From the Indian Ocean*, pp. 168–169.
63 Ibid., p. 17.
64 In fact, Aslanian also incorporates ideas borrowed from the work of economist Avner Greif (on informal institutions, coalitions and collective sanctions among); see A. Greif, 'Reputation and Coalitions in Medieval Trade: Evidence on the Maghribi Traders', *Journal of Economic History*, 49:4 (1989), pp. 857–882. Furthermore, Aslanian also stresses the important role played by additional semiformal and formal legal institutions such as the Julfan Assembly of Merchants (a merchant court that sanctioned commercial disputes) and the Armenian Church and its network of priests that contributed to improving the circulation of information within the network.
65 B. Bhattacharya, 'The "Book of Will" of Petrus Woskan (1680–1751): Some Insights into the Global Commercial Networks of the Armenians in the Indian Ocean', *Journal of Economic and Social History of the Orient*, 51:1 (2008), pp. 67–98, on pp. 82–83. Respondentia is a loan where a ship's cargo is the security, on similar terms to bottomry; that is to say, it combines credit and marine insurance. It was also used by the Julfans to finance Spanish merchants trading between Manila and Acapulco; see A. Baena Zapatero and X. Lamikiz, 'Presencia de una diáspora global: comerciantes armenios y comercio intercultural en Manila, c. 1660–1800', *Revista de Indias*, 74 (2014), pp. 693–722.

66 S. Ogilvie, *Institutions and European Trade*, p. 6.
67 Ibid., p. 430.
68 Ibid.
69 Ibid., p. 321.
70 Ibid., pp. 427–434.
71 R. Putnam, *Bowling Alone*; M. Granovetter, 'The Strength of Weak Ties', *American Journal of Sociology*, 78:6 (1973), pp. 1360–1380.
72 R. Putnam, *Bowling Alone*, p. 22.
73 Ibid., p. 23.
74 X. Lamikiz, *Trade and Trust*, pp. 40–45.
75 E. Chamlee-Wright, 'The Structure of Social Capital: An Austrian Perspective on its Nature and Development', *Review of Political Economy*, 20:1 (2008), pp. 41–58, on p. 48.

Bibliography

Anderson, A.R. and Jack, S.L., 'The Articulation of Social Capital in Entrepreneurial Networks: a Glue or a Lubricant?', *Entrepreneurship & Regional Development*, 14 (2002), pp. 193–210.

Aslanian, S., *From the Indian Ocean to the Mediterranean: The Global Trade Networks of Armenian Merchants from New Julfa*, Berkeley: University of California Press, 2011.

Baena Zapatero, A. and Lamikiz, X., 'Presencia de una diáspora global: comerciantes armenios y comercio intercultural en Manila, c. 1660–1800', *Revista de Indias*, 74:262 (2014), pp. 661–690.

Baghdiantz McCabe, I., Harlaftis, G. and Minoglou, I.P. (eds.), *Diaspora Entrepreneurial Networks: Four Centuries of History*, New York: Berg, 2005.

Baskes, J., *Staying Afloat: Risk and Uncertainty in Spanish Atlantic World Trade, 1760–1820*, Stanford, CA: Stanford University Press, 2013.

Ben-Porath, Y., 'The F-Connection: Families, Friends, and Firms and the Organization of Exchange', *Population and Development Review*, 6:1 (1980), pp. 1–30.

Bhattacharya, B., 'The "Book of Will" of Petrus Woskan (1680–1751): Some Insights into the Global Commercial Networks of the Armenians in the Indian Ocean', *Journal of Economic and Social History of the Orient*, 51:1 (2008), pp. 67–98.

Boldizzoni, F., *The Poverty of Clio: Resurrecting Economic History*, Princeton and Oxford: Princeton University Press, 2011.

Braudel, F., *Civilization and Capitalism, 15th–18th Century. Vol. 2: The Wheels of Commerce*, London: Phoenix Press 1988.

Burkhardt, M., 'Networks as Social Structures in Late Medieval and Early Modern Towns: A Theoretical Approach to Historical Network Analysis', in A. Caracausi and C. Jeggle (eds.), *Commercial Networks and European Cities, 1400–1800*, London: Pickering & Chatto, 2014, pp. 13–43.

Carlos, A.M. and Nicholas, S., '"Giants of An Earlier Capitalism": the Chartered Trading Companies as Modern Multinationals', *Business History Review*, 62:3 (1988), pp. 398–419.

———, 'Agency Problems in the Early Chartered Companies: the Case of the Hudson's Bay Company', *Journal of Economic History*, 50:4 (1990), pp. 853–875.

Chamlee-Wright, E., 'The Structure of Social Capital: An Austrian Perspective on its Nature and Development', *Review of Political Economy*, 20:1 (2008), pp. 41–58.

Coleman, J., 'Social Capital in the Creation of Human Capital', *American Journal of Sociology*, 94:1 (1988), pp. S95–S120.

Curtin, P.J., *Cross-Cultural Trade in World History*, Cambridge: Cambridge University Press, 1984.

Freire Costa, L., Rocha, M. and Araujo T., 'Social Capital and Economic Performance: Trust and Distrust in Eighteenth-Century Gold Shipments from Brazil', *European Review of Economic History*, 15 (2011), pp. 1–27.

Gambetta, D., 'Can We Trust Trust?', in D. Gambetta (ed.), *Trust: Making and Breaking Cooperative Relations*, Oxford: Basil Blackwell, 1988, pp. 213–237.

Granovetter, M., 'Economic Institutions as Social Constructions: A Framework for Analysis', *Acta Sociologica*, 35 (1992), pp. 3–11.

———, 'Economic Action and Social Structure: The Problem of Embeddedness', *American Journal of Sociology*, 91:3 (1985), pp. 481–510.

———, 'The Strength of Weak Ties', *American Journal of Sociology*, 78:6 (1973), pp. 1360–1380.

Grassby, R., *Kinship and Capitalism: Marriage, Family, and Business in the English-Speaking World, 1580–1740*, Cambridge: Cambridge University Press, 2001.

Greif, A., 'Reputation and Coalitions in Medieval Trade: Evidence on the Maghribi Traders', *Journal of Economic History*, 49:4 (1989), pp. 857–882.

Haggerty, S., *'Merely for Money'? Business Culture in the British Atlantic, 1750–1815*, Liverpool: Liverpool University Press, 2012.

Haggerty, S. and Haggerty J., 'Visual Analytics of an Eighteenth-Century Business Network,' *Enterprise and Society*, 11:1 (2010), pp. 1–25.

Hancock, D., 'The Trouble with Networks: Managing the Scots' Early-Modern Madeira Trade', *Business History Review*, 79:3 (2005), pp. 467–491.

Hawley, K., *Trust: A Very Short Introduction*, Oxford: Oxford University Press, 2012.

Herreros, Francisco, *The Problem of Forming Social Capital: Why Trust?*, New York: Palgrave, 2004.

Lamikiz, X., 'Flotistas en la Nueva España: diseminación espacial y negocios de los intermediarios del comercio transatlántico, 1670–1702', *Colonial Latin American Review*, 20:1 (2011), pp. 9–33.

———, *Trade and Trust in the Eighteenth-Century Atlantic World: Spanish Merchants and their Overseas Networks*, Woodbridge: Boydell Press / Royal Historical Society, 2010.

Lovejoy, P.E. and Richardson, D., 'Trust, Pawnship, and Atlantic History: The Institutional Foundations of the Old Calabar Slave Trade', *American Historical Review*, 104:2 (1999), pp. 333–355.

Marzagalli, S., 'Establishing Transatlantic Trade Networks in Time of War: Bordeaux and the United States, 1793–1815', *Business History Review*, 79:4 (2005), pp. 811–844.

McWaters, C. and Lemarchand Y., 'Local and Global Merchant Networks: Accounting Across Space and Time', APIRA 2010 Conference, Sydney, July 2010.

Muldrew, C., *The Economy of Obligation: The Culture of Credit and Social Relations in Early Modern England*, Basingstoke: Macmillan, 1998.

Müller, L., *The Merchant Houses of Stockholm, c. 1640–1800: A Comparative Study of Early Modern Entrepreneurial Behaviour*, Uppsala: S. Academiae Ubsaliensis, 1998.

North, D.C., 'Institutions, Transaction Costs and the Rise of Merchant Empires', in J. Tracy (ed.), *The Political Economy of Merchant Empires: State Power and World Trade*, Cambridge: Cambridge University Press, 1991, pp. 22–40.

Ogilvie, S., *Institutions and European Trade: Merchant Guilds, 1000–1800*, Cambridge: Cambridge University Press, 2011.

Pearson, R. and Richardson, D., 'Social Capital, Institutional Innovation and Atlantic Trade before 1800', *Business History*, 50:6 (2008), pp. 765–780.

Podolny, J.M. and Page, K.L., 'Network Forms of Organization', *Annual Review of Sociology*, 24 (1998), pp. 57–76.

Putnam, R., *Bowling Alone: The Collapse and Revival of American Community*, New York: Simon & Schuster, 2000.

Studnicki-Gizbert, D., *A Nation Upon the Ocean Sea: Portugal's Atlantic Diaspora and the Crisis of the Spanish Empire, 1492–1640*, Oxford: Oxford University Press, 2007.

Trivellato, F., *The Familiarity of Strangers: The Sephardic Diaspora, Livorno, and Cross-cultural Trade in the Early Modern Period*, New Haven: Yale University Press, 2009.

Vanneste, T., *Global Trade and Commercial Networks: Eighteenth-Century Diamond Merchants*, London: Pickering & Chatto, 2011.

Wasserman, S. and Faust, K., *Social Network Analysis: Methods and Applications*, Cambridge: Cambridge University Press, 1994.

3 Understanding networking

Theoretical framework and historical evidence

Montserrat Cachero Vinuesa

Recently, we have witnessed the emergence of network analysis in historical studies. Indeed, the term 'network' can be found in books, journals, articles, international conferences and research projects with increasing frequency. Although network analysis is not a new field of research, its application to the social sciences and the humanities is quite new.[1] Jacob Moreno first used networks to illustrate social relationships in 1934, but a theoretical corpus for social network analysis (SNA) did not emerge until the 1970s.[2] Despite the potential impact of the network approach in social analysis, scholars agree that before 1990 the term was known only to a few academics.[3]

Conversely, since the beginning of the twenty-first century we have entered a new phase that can be termed as the 'network fever'. Molina quantified this trend by using variables such as the number of journals in the field, the degree of the presence of SNA in postgraduate programs and the number of international research projects in which the concept plays a prevalent role.[4] His conclusions reveal that, in the field of sociology, network analysis currently dominates other approaches to social interaction. In Granovetter's words, 'most of human behavior is embedded in interpersonal networks.'[5]

SNA began to be applied in historical analysis even later than in other disciplines, such as anthropology or sociology. Despite its late adoption, the methodology seems to be a good fit for our subject, as shown by the special issue dedicated to 'Network Analysis and History' in the journal *REDES*,[6] and also by the proliferation of academic websites and scientific blogs on historical network analysis such as the *Connected Past* community;[7] the Historical Network Research; and, the Zotero group. Also, funding has followed suit, and an increasing number of research projects which focus on networking in history are being supported, for example The Dynamic Cooperation Networks (DynCoopNet) project, which is sponsored by The European Science Foundation, and ForSeaDiscovery, Forest Resources for Iberian Empires: Ecology and Globalization in the Age of Discovery, which is funded by UNESCO.[8]

However, the novelty of the approach is generating some problems concerning its application to historical studies. One of these 'teething problems' is the application of the term 'network' as a buzzword, devoid of further analytical substance. Several scholars even share the opinion that 'among historians, the term network has been used in a metaphorical sense alone for a long time".'[9] Conversely, other researchers, who became absolutely fascinated by the tool, began to support all their research on data processing software and, on that basis, proceeded to reframe concepts and theoretical models. This can be a very dangerous exercise which often results in empty discourses and confusion. One must always remember that networks are a tool but not the object of analysis.

This apparent confusion has led to some perplexity as to the real nature of networks on a very basic level. More specifically, do we know what networks are? Are they an asset for our discipline? And, if the answer is 'yes', are we exploiting their full potential? This chapter evaluates the possibilities and limitations of SNA for historical analysis, taking into account that networks are not a substitute for historical narrative; indeed, both approaches must be interconnected.[10] According to Düring et al., while the reconstruction of a network and its visualisation will show the potential and limitations of individual behaviour, the examination of the specific actions of said individuals within these structures requires a traditional qualitative approach.

This chapter is organised as follows. The first section is devoted to the definition of networks, including the overall concept and its constitutive elements. The second section explores the foundations of network analysis from a practical point of view, focusing on their application and avoiding mathematical intricacies. The third section analyses the foundations and use of networks. This section also deals with the dark side of networks by highlighting their limitations for historical analysis. The fourth section clarifies some aspects about connectors, networks and the globalisation process. The final section contains the conclusions.

Defining networks

From a mathematical point of view, the definition of networks is quite simple: a set of nodes and the ties that unite them. The nodes – known as dots, agents, actors or points – can be individuals, firms, families, cities, etc. Nodes are the subjects of analysis, and their definition will, consequently, depend on the focus of study. This flexibility, however, does not apply to ties – known as edges, links or arcs – which always refer to relationships. The complexity of social relationships is bewildering, and its rationalization sometimes seems like an impossible mission. The section entitled 'Regarding ties' is devoted to this issue.

Therefore, once the nodes and detected the ties between them are defined, you have a network, because networks are just about that: objects and the interactions between them. According to Molina, 'networks are a pull of relations between a set of elements that allow to the analysis of a specific phenomenon'.[11] Network analysis is neither a paradigm nor a methodology, but rather a way to see reality with a focus on social interaction. Networks allow for more general and flexible analyses, as personal interaction results in ways of organisation that transcend institutions, social groups or economic status.[12] Networks expand, accumulate power, operate in the market, oust competitors and gain privileges, and for this reason we cannot simply remain on the surface of the concept. Instead, we should go one step further and analyse not only networks for themselves, but the way individuals use them and the goals that they achieve. This is the real potential of networks.

About nodes

The first step in every research endeavor should be to wonder about the object of analysis. In network terminology, this is known as selecting the nodes. The researcher has to decide what will and will not be part of the network. This is not an easy task, as one has to draw the boundaries which will contain the field of interest. SNA offers two different techniques to solve the problem: egocentric, or personal networks, and sociocentric, or complete networks.[13] The latter category focuses on a group, while the former begins with an individual. In other words, one should decide whether to analyse the structure of a group and how it interacts with other groups (sociocentric network) or to study the strategies developed by a single individual (egocentric network).[14] Among historians, egocentric networks are more popular, as we have to deal with incomplete information and, therefore, the reconstruction of the social interaction of one person can be easier than the analysis of a whole group. Obviously, these strategies are not exclusive; it is possible to study a person within a group and, for instance, to develop a parallel interest in the relationship of this group with the rest of society.

Sometimes a researcher can be interested in analysing different types of objects. Imagine, for instance, that we are analysing personal messages between intellectuals; our nodes would be the people, and the ties would be the relationships between them. Now, imagine further that the same individuals spend most of their lives writing, not only letters but also books. It would be interesting to relate the persons to the books. By analysing two different kinds of node, people and books, we are producing a bimodal network.[15] This is, in fact, a real project currently underway at Stanford University: *Mapping the Republic of Letters*.[16]

Regarding ties

Once the object of analysis is defined, the next task is to study social interaction. Yet, according to Lemercier, finding interaction patterns can be as difficult as 'finding structure in a mess'.[17] In fact, at this point it is necessary not only to describe but also to define relationships. Why are two or more individuals involved in a mutual relationship? What are they getting out of it? Is there a cost to maintaining the relationship? These are some of the questions we can ask the sources in order to determine which relationships are important enough to be coded and which are not. Obviously, we have to balance research interest and the available information: it is all very well to be ambitious, but we cannot forget that sources always stand as a limitation. In network analysis, one must be very careful and use only reliable information that is supported by the sources: assumptions and intuition will inevitably lead to spurious results.

When working with different relationships, it is useful to label and classify them. The standard categories are family, business, membership and nationality. These are basic, intuitive relationships that pose few problems of definition.[18] Friendship, religious affinity and professional reputation are altogether different kinds of relationships: more complex, less defined and more difficult to detect and measure. The section entitled 'Measurement' proposes some solutions to this problem.

Frequently, the researcher can be interested in analysing not only one but several kinds of relationships: to achieve this, we can use multilevel network analysis. This tool splits the information into different levels and, by overlapping the information, allows for their separate or combined analysis. The preferred degree of analytical complexity can be adapted to the research objectives. According to Lemercier, 'to analyse networks also requires to find patterns at different scales'.[19]

Two of the mathematical properties of ties are of interest for historical analysis: reciprocity and transitivity. Reciprocity is basically concerned with the orientation of relationships.[20] Reciprocity measures whether interactions are one- or two-way affairs. For instance, family links are bilateral by definition: I am related to my father, and my father to me. In business, on the other hand, reciprocity is not always so clear. Figure 3.1 presents data collected from an article published by D. Krackhardt. Both images are flagrantly different. The one on the left illustrates information flows within the company, whereas the one on the right represents relationships of friendship. In the first one, information moves in one direction, along hierarchical lines. One person supplies information to his/her superior, and he/she will, for his/her part, feed it to his/her superior, and so on. Thus, information is moving up the pyramid but is not coming back down. In this case, relationships are one way. When friendship is concerned, however, there are no boundaries and no hierarchies. Lines move in all directions; the center is occupied by the most popular person, who is not necessarily the CEO of the company.

In some research, reciprocity is of little use, but in other cases, it seems to be a crucial factor. M. Düring, in his study about the assistance received by Jewish refugees during World War II, offers an illustrative example. The analysis focuses on the notion of assistance, and it is therefore essential to know the direction in which the economic, social and even emotional support circulated. In the author's own words, his is a 'formal analysis of relations between helpers and recipients of help'.[21]

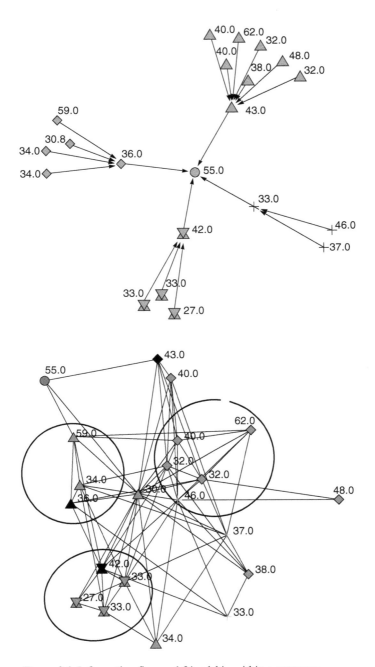

Figure 3.1 Information flow and friendship within a company.

Source: D. Krackhardt 'Assessing the Political Landscape: Structure, Cognition and Power in Organizations', *Administrative Science Quarterly*, 35 (1990), pp. 342–369.

Transitivity, for its part, defines what is connected with what when three or more nodes exist. Figure 3.2 illustrates transitivity with an example. The graphs below contain information about the Welser Company, one of the most relevant commercial firms during the early modern period. With origin in the Middle Ages, the Welser Company had its principal headquarters in Augsburg and branches in more than 13 European cities.[22] The company maintained commercial exchange and connected markets in Europe, Africa, Asia and America. As an example, we will analyse information from four of the company's agents: Bartholomeus V. Welser and Anton Welser, the founders of the company, and the front-line managers at the company's branch in Seville (Hieronimous Sayler and Heinrich Ehinger). The first graph demonstrates that, not surprisingly, all of them are connected.[23] The second image is quite different: it shows information about relatives, and on this occasion only three of them are attached. Indeed, Bartholomeus is related to his brother Anton and to his son-in-law Hieronimous Sayler. Note that Ehinger is isolated and

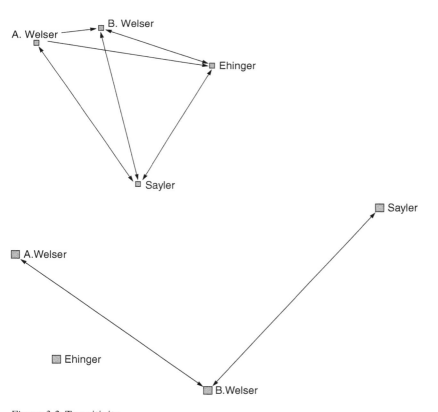

Figure 3.2 Transitivity.

Source: Author's own. Source of the data: J. Friede, *Los Welser en la conquista de Venezuela* (Caracas: Ediciones Edime, 1961).

that between Sayler and the other Welser there is an empty space. In SNA, such empty spaces are termed 'structural holes'.

A structural hole is an empty space between two nodes. This concept has been developed by Ronald Burt. In his book *Structural Holes: The Social Structure of Competition*, Burt articulates a theory of structural holes in which they are defined as discontinuities between exchange relations.[24] The main practical application of this theory concerns the role played by structural holes in brokerage opportunities. Analyzing the flow of information within large companies, the conclusion was reached that there are more entrepreneurial opportunities to broker and control in companies with many structural holes.[25]

The foundations of network analysis

The first step to be taken in order to explore the full potential of network analysis is to define clearly the purpose of our research. It is our responsibility to clarify the question behind research and determine what instruments from SNA's toolbox we are going to use. Quite often, researchers apply arithmetic approaches to the analysis of social relationships without really knowing how or why. The researcher's first task is thus to define exactly what to measure, and the second to verify whether the information available in the sources allows us to do so.

Measurement

There are many ways to approach the strength of ties. From a quantitative point of view, some of them may be regarded as standard, whereas others are dependent on the available sources. The simplest way to approach a relationship is to check if a relationship exists between two or more nodes. Taking the Welser Company as an example, it is possible to interrogate the sources concerning whether Bartholomeus Welser trusted his agent Heinrich Ehinger. If the answer is 'yes', then the variable takes a value of 1, but if the answer is 'no', the value will be 0. This is what econometrists refer to as a 'dummy variable'. J.F. Padgett's analysis of the Florentine elite network structure uses dummy variables to determine who was married to whom.[26]

Perhaps at some point the researcher may be interested in measuring not only the mere existence of a relationship but also its strength. For some social scientists, such as sociologists, assigning a value to a relationship is relatively easy, but for historians this can be a truly difficult task. Obviously, historians have no access to tools such as questionnaires or surveys. The solution to this shortcoming comes from squeezing the sources as much as possible. It is true that some sources are richer than others, a great example of this being testimonies during lawsuits. During previous research, I estimated the strength of a personal relationship through the answers to the following questions: Do you know the defendant? For how many years have you known her/him? The first helps to determine whether a relationship existed between two subjects, and the second is used to assign a value to the link. In this case, the duration of the relationship was used as proxy for its robustness.

Another typical example is the use of contracts, and more specifically, their duration, in order to gauge the strength of the business relationship. For example, A. Polonia et al.[27] attempted a reconstruction of the mercantile network of Simón Ruiz; for this, her team used the number of contracts and the amount of money involved to calculate the relevance of commercial relationships.[28]

Personal messages, such as merchant or migrant letters, are also a first-rate source. They are often full of details and allow any researcher not only to reconstruct personal relationships but also to rank them. Following this approach, J.L. Imízcoz and I. Arroyo Ruiz used eighteenth-century letters to rebuild ego-centered networks with excellent results.[29] Recently, a series of young scholars have made outstanding contributions to the field by using similar information. Ribeiro and Düring, for instance, offer a good example of how to combine historical sources and network analysis to perfection.[30]

Other less common sources are diaries, in which it is possible to find specific information about the subject's personal perception of their relationships, as well as additional information concerning new relationship categories and their duration, intensity, etc. By using such personal chronicles, which covered a period of over five decades, Rosé analysed the reconstruction of aristocratic networks and the composition of French elites surrounding the person of Odo of Cluny, a nobleman and abbot of the Cluny monastery during the tenth century.[31]

Essentially, in our discipline, the measurement of interpersonal relationships is restricted by the nature of the available sources. It is important to know what we are measuring and to extract the maximum possible information from the documents. There is no rule for approaching robustness in relationships, and the estimates will always depend on the kind of information that we have at our disposal.

Visualisation

Graph theory was formulated for the first time in a paper in which Leonhard Paul Euler presented a solution to the problem of the Seven Bridges of Königsberg.[32] Many years later, Jacob Moreno applied this tool to social analysis with a technique called the 'sociogram', which was defined as 'the graphic representation of social interaction'.[33]

Recent advances in the field of information and communications technology (ICT) have facilitated the production of sociograms through the use of specialised software. The most popular among these is UCINET, but other software packages such as NetDraw, Palladio or Sotero have also been used for SNA. More or less sophisticated software can be chosen, depending on the specific needs of the research agenda; for example, Vienna is particularly useful for dynamic networks, and the well-known ARCGIS for placing networks in their geographical context.

Recently, a research team from the universities of Trier and Mainz developed new software (VennMaker) which is specifically suitable for historical network analysis. The strength of this software is that it generates the mathematical data while the user is drawing the graph. Although it is still quite new (launched in 2011), it has already been applied to historical research, with excellent results.[34]

Testing

For those more familiar with SNA, there are two different groups of variables with which to estimate the relative importance of a node within a given network: density and centrality. The first category refers to the degree of interaction in the network as a whole, while the second alludes to the significance of specific actors within the network. The following exercise is useful in order to distinguish between these two groups of variables: imagine that you are in a plane and that you can see the network from above. You can see many lines or just a few: what you are seeing now is density. Density offers a measure of the network from the outside. Imagine now that the plane has already landed and that we are standing inside the network. Now we can look around and observe the relative position of every node: in this case, we are testing centrality.

The calculation of density is quite easy: it is done by dividing the total number of ties by the potential ties. Going back to the example of the Welser Company, let us assume that we have the opportunity to ask all agents who they trust the most within the network; as they all have suspicious dispositions (another assumption), their answers will consist of only one name. The figure below illustrates the information collected during this fictitious survey. As represented in the graph, Anton has faith in his brother Bartholomeus, Bartholomeus is loyal to Sayler, Sayler trusted his partner Ehinger, and Ehinger believed only in Anton Welser. The graph represents a low-density network: all of them are connected, but with a single, unidirectional link. Now, we can compare this information with that provided by the second graph. In this case, we are representing personal and commercial relationships by assigning a value of 0 to those agents with no relation at all, 1 to agents connected by one link, either family or business, and 2 for agents connected by two-way links. The final result is a graph where all are connected (Figure 3.3). It must be kept in mind that more density means more communication and therefore, a higher potential for cooperation.

Occasionally, researchers are interested in the analysis of the role played by agents within networks; for example, figuring out whether there is one or more central agents. This issue directly concerns the centrality value. Centrality can be a way to analyse whether successful agents have many ties and whether those ties are the reason for their success.

The centrality concept is, however, more complex than that of density, and it embraces three different values: degree, closeness and betweenness. Degree is the simplest of these three variables: it can be defined as the number of ties incident upon a node. In personal networks, degree reflects the number of people who can reach an actor directly. Note that this can be a proxy of social influence, as

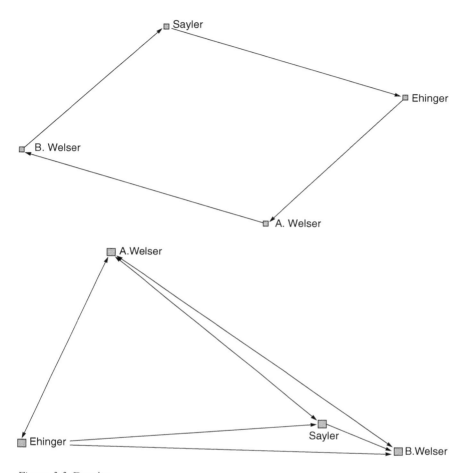

Figure 3.3 Density.

Source: Author's own source of data from J. Favier, *Gold and Spices. The Rise of Commerce in the Middle Ages* (New York: Holmes and Meier Publishers, 1998), and D. Ramos Pérez, 'El negocio negrero de los Welser y sus habilidades monopolistas', *Revista de Historia de América*, 81 (1976), pp. 7–81.

stated by Jackson: 'the more ties an actor has, the more power they (may) have'.[35] Figure 3.3 can also illustrate the degree concept. In the first graph, we can see four lines, whereas the second graph presents six lines; in both cases, the lines represent the total number of connections. Note that ties can be unidirectional or bidirectional, but this issue will have no effect on the calculation of the degree value. Degree values oscillate between 0 and 1, with 1 indicating the maximum degree, when all nodes are connected, and 0 the minimum value when there are no connections at all. In the example below, the degree value is 4/6 for the first graph and 1 for the second.

The other two variables are more complex. Closeness can be defined as the time that it takes for the information to travel from one node to the rest. In other words, how fast can agents reach someone else in the network? More proximity means more power. Betweenness is, for its part, the number of times a node acts as a bridge between other nodes. It measures how important a person is in connecting others. Note that closeness and betweenness are very similar concepts, and a good way to distinguish between them is by keeping in mind that closeness is about distance whereas betweenness is about bridging points. In other words, closeness is about control of information, and betweenness about the degree of autonomy of actors within the network.

The following figure should help to clarify the differences between closeness and betweenness. The figure is based on the frequency of letter-exchange among different agents of the Welser Company in 1530. In order to simplify Figure 3.4, personal information has been omitted, and only origin and destination are given.

Information from America was channeled via Seville. If one of the agents from the Augsburg headquarters wanted to send instructions to the agents in Santa Marta, he had to do it through Seville's branch. Seville, sitting in the middle of the network, was one step away from Augsburg, Venezuela and Santo Domingo, but two steps away from Santa Marta. In consequence, if anyone wanted to reach Santa Marta he had to go through Seville, even if Santo Domingo was closer. Thus, regarding Santa Marta, Seville has a higher betweenness value, but in terms of closeness Santo Domingo and Venezuela are better choices.

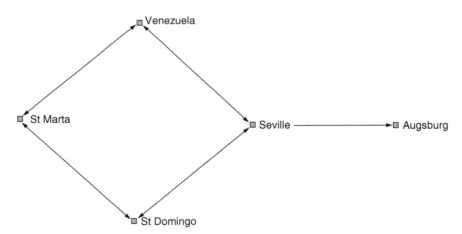

Figure 3.4 Closeness and betweenness.

Source: Author's own. Source of data: 'Francisco y Martín de Orduña, hermanos, vecinos de la ciudad de Sevilla, con Bartolomé y Antonio Belzar y Compañía de Alemanes, sobre ajuste de cuentas, 1533–1539', *Archivo General de Indias, Sección Justicia*, 717, N. 1, R. 1, fols. 113–125.

What lies behind networks?

At this stage, it should be clear that networks are the structures that shape social relationships. By analysing these structures, we can test how social interaction works. However, we are only scratching the surface of the matter, and we should dig deeper, reach inside relationships and explain which forces are responsible for the emergence of these structures. In other words, our aim is to explain what leads individuals to interact and what they gain from this interaction. Research is not complete unless it identifies the forces that outline the social structure. As Sheilagh Ogilvie pointed out, only a few studies recognise the features underlying social interaction or examine the effect of such structures on society or the economy in general.[36]

Although social relationships are extremely varied in nature, all of them are based on the same element: trust. The *Oxford Dictionary* defines trust as a 'firm belief in the reliability, truth or ability of someone or something'.[37] In network analysis, trust is the glue of social connections. Trust can be personal or impersonal, the result of face-to-face relationships or second-hand information. Trust arises from kinship, religious affinity, neighbourly relations and nationality. Trust can be the result of a long business relationship or an excellent professional reputation.

In the analysis of specific examples, trust is a key factor that needs to be analysed. The historical record must be asked a series of crucial questions about the foundations of social interaction. Were relationships long or short? Were they stable? Did actors maintain relationships over long periods of time or interrupt them after a while and, if so, how easily did they break them up? Can we represent the evolution of relationships? Answers will be different from one case to the next, but they are essential for a full understanding of the real nature of networks.

Networks: what are they for?

From the arguments above, it is obvious that building and maintaining networks is a costly strategy. Hence, why do people bother getting involved in such structures? Why does social interaction adopt this shape? The answer is quite simple: individuals assume this cost because they will reap the benefits at a later stage. Thus, the final result of personal relationships has been labeled 'social capital'.

According to Coleman and Putnam et al., social capital is the value generated when agents exert themselves to create relationships with one other, aiming to obtain benefits in the long run.[38] Generally, economic historians reduce the concept to net income in terms of money, wealth or business opportunities, but this form of capital can also be used for social and political purposes. The information circulating through a network can be used to gain political power, concessions and social promotion. We must remember that the most relevant agents are not those who control the money or the goods but rather the information. Those who possess information have the ability to anticipate.

In historical analysis, the sources can again provide evidence about the quality and quantity of information traveling throughout networks. Personal letters, diaries, notary deeds and court testimonies are rich sources for knowing who had access to news, as well as for the comparison of the information handled by different agents within the network.

Apart from information, networked social structures also have other benefits. According to J.S. Coleman, social networks foster the adoption of shared norms and help to overcome obstacles to collective action. Shared norms, in turn, promote trust, which reduces transaction and enforcement costs. In fact, these principles are commonly part of the toolbox of political, religious and economic organisations, as they are an effective means of controlling a group and discouraging opportunistic behaviour.

A final outcome of networking is collective action. Collective action has often been identified with different forms of group punishment; yet, the concept also embraces other phenomena, such as the management of common resources, collective bargaining and government control. Collective action is a well-known concept for historians. While in the past agents relied on social networks and defined themselves as part of a community, current society is driven by individualism and depends on the market and the state.

In conclusion, network analysis is much more than a methodological approach: it is a far-reaching way to describe, measure and represent social interaction. Network analysis is about analyzing the forces that generate this interaction and describing the final outcome of the resulting relationships. In other words, networks not only describe who is connected to whom but also the reasons for these connections.

The limitations of network analysis

Despite all of its advantages, network analysis also has a dark side. It is obvious that the application of network tools is limited by information and, as historians know well, information is not perfect, and even that generated today is imperfect, and historical data is by nature fragmentary and incomplete. This is precisely what makes our discipline so challenging and dynamic: every single day one can find a piece of information that may change conventional wisdom. History is not what has been written, it is about what scholars are writing right now and will write in the near future.

An additional obstacle is the necessary level of abstraction when using modeling. The purpose of a model is to represent reality and, in a very simple way, analyse it and interpret it. Models, by definition, are simplifications, abstraction or idealisations, which can be a source of interpretive error. On the other hand, mathematical models must remain simple because if the model is too complex it will lose its explanatory power. This is a fine balance to negotiate, as going beyond mere description involves additional problems of measurement and modeling.

Finally, I must briefly mention the use and abuse of mathematics. We all know that mathematics is an exact discipline; in comparison, social systems are chaotic and inexact, so the application of equations and mathematical calculation can lead to spurious results. Mathematicians and historians are currently working together to solve this problem through the application of the principle of fuzzy logic to social systems.[39] Still, this remains a largely unexplored field, and for the moment, it is important to decide the degree of mathematical sophistication that should be applied to each specific piece of research.

Connectors, networks and the globalisation process

The concept of connectors is a recent attempt to emphasise the role played by merchants, sailors, emigrants and other voyagers who sailed across the ocean and became channels of communication between two different worlds.[40] Indeed, the Atlantic was a space of contact and exchange from very different perspectives. Geography became more complex and the world expanded. Over the course of more than a century, the idea of America was constantly getting bigger, as the information about every expedition reached Europe and changed the perception of the New World.

New social possibilities appeared. For most people, America was an opportunity to scale the social ladder and reinvent themselves. Emigrants called their beloved(s) to join them in the colonies, and, suddenly, marriage markets in the New World emerged as an attractive possibility for an important proportion of European females.[41]

From an economic perspective, the Atlantic meant large-scale trade, investment and potential profits. Every vessel was full of valuable information about prices, products, qualities and markets. Trade patterns changed, new commercial instruments were developed and European luxury consumption and demand were deeply affected.

The huge increase in circulation at all levels enlarged the scale of international exchange dramatically, and it is in this commerce involving products, ideas, news and technology that the role of individuals acting as connectors becomes key and the application of network analysis a useful tool. SNA has created the possibility of measuring, representing and testing the exchange of goods and economic factors on both sides of the Atlantic.

Some scholars even describe the American phenomenon as opening a first globalisation. Was the discovery of America the beginning of a globalisation process? This question has shaken academia and been the subject of heated debates and controversial answers.

To globalise or not to globalise

One of the top debates in Atlantic history revolves around the question: 'when did globalisation begin?' According to some historians, such as Frank or Bentley, the process started as early as 1492, right after the discovery of America.[42] These scholars highlight the universal importance of these events and the opening of enormous regions to international commerce. According to André Gunder Frank, the new territories and their potential were an extraordinary stimulus for worldwide agricultural and industrial specialisation.[43]

However, economic historians Jeffrey Williamson and Kevin O'Rourke opened Pandora's box by claiming that globalisation was the result of industrialisation, and, therefore, it cannot be said to have occurred before the nineteenth century.[44] They state that before the Industrial Revolution there was not an international commodity market, but that this comprised only national markets separated by strong barriers and high transport costs.

The in-depth analysis of both positions results in the conclusion that there is little ground for the debate, which is based on a misunderstanding. Scholars are simply using the same term to refer to two different things. From a strictly economic point of view, globalisation is a process of commodity market integration, which also involves international factor mobility. The concept may seem very narrow, but it is also accurate: starting with differentiated national markets, the process becomes visible in the progressive dissolution of boundaries and the creation of a new international market.

Historians, however, apply a more general concept of globalisation visible through a significant intensification in the process of exchange; thus, the process becomes visible in the increase of international trade volume and technology transfers,[45] the transformation of consumption patterns, and the densification of trade routes. The definition is, indeed, very broad, and it incorporates not only economic but also social and cultural factors. It is very clear that such a process had already taken place when the Old and the New Worlds came together, but also that it does not amount to economic globalisation; more accurately, the phenomenon should be addressed as internationalisation.

Putting it simply, globalisation is the phenomenon that leads to the construction of an international market by lowering barriers and improving transport. The economic definition of globalisation involves three different aspects: commodities, barriers and transport systems. Regarding the first aspect, most historians know that Atlantic trade was based on luxury goods and not on commodities.[46] Of course, this is only true for imports. European exports are a very different issue: the top five include olive oil, wine and even cereals, three basic components of the Mediterranean diet.

Concerning barriers, historical evidence is very clear. In the Atlantic, trade barriers did not decline but actually increased. Specific new taxes, for example, were created for commercial transactions with the Spanish colonies. This is the case with the *Almojarifazgo de Indias* or the *Averia*, two very different taxes which were, nevertheless, tailor-made for trade with the New World.[47] It is commonly accepted that the Spanish monopoly in America was not really a monopoly from an economic point of view, but rather an apparatus designed to raise revenue via taxation.

Finally, the issue of the development of the transport system and the reduction of freight costs is more controversial. The period that followed the discovery of America was one of vast improvement in shipbuilding and navigation technologies, resulting in a very significant reduction in shipping costs. The statement by K. O'Rourke and J. Williamson about the slight reduction of freight costs in Atlantic trade in the sixteenth century is supported by little evidence. They use Hamilton's classic data for the trade in dried codfish between Andalusia and Valencia to argue that progress in navigation during the sixteenth and the seventeenth centuries had no effect on freight costs. It seems nonsense to extrapolate trading conditions among Spanish ports to the Atlantic trade.

Conclusions

Social Network Analysis captures the complexity of history and allows for testing at two different levels: the group and the individual. From a group perspective, it is possible to measure crucial variables, such as cohesion and structural holes. Besides, the network approach creates the possibility of testing the quality of the information circulating by comparing pieces of information from every actor, at the beginning and at the end of the chain.

Regarding individuals, we can test for their position, their relevance within the group, the number and quality of their connections, and their dependence on others. We can also measure the significance of actors acting as free-riders and as group members. In the field of Atlantic history, this is especially important; when individuals take up the role of connectors, network analysis gives us the opportunity to represent, measure and analyse the exchange of products, ideas, news and technology.

The potential of network analysis for the historical sciences has been realised only recently, but it is already producing excellent results in the form of papers, books, research projects and PhD dissertations. Additionally, computer engineers are developing new specific software for historical network analysis. These programs capture the complexity of our discipline, incorporating time and geographical space into the analysis.

Notwithstanding these achievements, there is still a long way to go. Computer tools need to be improved and network values applied but without losing touch with common sense. We should not forget that networks are a means and not an end: only sources can decide if network analysis is a source of good or evil for our topic.

Notes

1 For further information about the history of Social Network Analysis, see L. Freeman, *The Development of Social Network Analysis: A Study in the Sociology of Science* (Vancouver: Empirical Press, 2004).
2 Social network analysis: henceforth, SNA.
3 For this debate, see D.M. Crovi Druetta, M.A. López Cruz and R. López González, *Redes Sociales: Análisis y Aplicaciones* (Mexico D.F.: Universidad Autónoma de México y Plaza Valdés, 2009).
4 See J.L. Molina, *El Análisis de Redes Sociales: Una Introducción* (Barcelona: Editorial Bellaterra, 2001), pp. 71–73.

5 See M. Granovetter, 'Economic Actions and Social Structure: The Problem of Embeddedness,' *American Journal of Sociology*, 91 (1985), pp. 481–510, on p. 504.
6 This special issue can be found at http://revista-redes.rediris.es/indicevol21.htm.
7 This research community hosts a successful international conference and produces several publications. In only four years, the project has been sponsored by different research centers and institutions such as the Oxford University Press. See http://connectedpast.net/. Research groups with a similar objective are the Zotero group (https://www.zotero.org/) and the Historical Network Research (http://historicalnetworkresearch.org/).
8 For further information on this project, see http://forseadiscovery.cchs.csic.es/.
9 See the homepage of http://historicalnetworkresearch.org/.
10 See M. Düring and M. Stark, 'Historical network Analysis', in G. Barnett and J.G. Golson (eds.), *Encyclopedia of Social Networks* (London: Sage, 2011), pp. 1543–1545. See also M. Schenegg, 'Strategien und Strukturen. Herausforderungen der qualitativen und quantitativen Netzwerkforschung', in M. Gamper, and L. Reschke (eds.), *Knoten und Kanten. Soziale Netzwerkanalyse in Wirtschafts- und Migrationsforschung* (Bielefeld: Verlag, 2010), pp. 55–75.
11 J.L. Molina, *El Análisis de Redes Sociales*, p. 36.
12 C. Lemercier, 'Formal Methods in History: Why and How?', *HAL Working Paper Series* (2011). Available at https://halshs.archives-ouvertes.fr/halshs-00521527v2/document.
13 For further information on egocentric and sociocentric network, see C. McCarty and J.L. Molina, 'Social Network Analysis', in R.H. Bernard and C.C. Gravlee (eds.), *Handbook of Methods in Cultural Anthropology* (Lanham: Rowman & Littlefield, 2014), pp. 631–657.
14 J.M. Imizcoz and L. Arroyo Ruiz, 'Redes sociales y correspondencia epistolar: Del análisis cualitativo de las relaciones personales a la reconstrucción de las redes ego-centradas', *REDES-Revista hispana para el análisis de redes sociales*, 21: 3 (2011), pp. 98–138, on p. 99.
15 When three or more different objects are being analysed, we should use the term 'multimodal".
16 Early results from the project are available at http://republicofletters.stanford.edu/index.html.
17 C. Lemercier, 'Formal Methods in History', p. 2.
18 Despite being commonly used, the term 'nationality' is rather ambiguous regarding the early modern period; in fact, scholars refer to nationality not only as a geographical origin but also to designate a merchant community. In this regard see T. Herzog, *Defining Nations: Immigrants and Citizens in Early Modern Spain and Spanish America* (New Haven: Yale University Press, 2003). Indeed, it is quite difficult to determine what a nation is and whether a given individual belongs to it. In some types of documents, for example contracts, individuals generally express their origin and declare their affiliation to a nation. See M. Cachero, *Should We Trust? Explaining Trade Expansion in Early Modern Spain, Seville 1500–1600* (PhD dissertation presented at the European University Institute, Florence, 2010).
19 C. Lemercier, 'Introducción ¿En qué punto se encuentra el análisis de redes en la Historia?', *REDES-Revista hispana para el análisis de redes sociales*, 21:3 (2011), pp. 1–12, on p. 3.
20 This property also has been referred to as "symmetry". See J.F. Padgett 'Matrimonio y estructura de la élite de la Florencia Renacentista, 1282–1500', *REDES-Revista hispana para el análisis de redes sociales*, 21:3 (2011), pp. 42–70, on pp. 51–54.
21 This study is the subject of a PhD dissertation, which will be published this year in book form. A presentation is available at http://martenduering.com/projects/covert-networks-during-the-holocaust/.
22 J. Friede, *Los Welser en la conquista de Venezuela* (Caracas: Edime, 1961).

23 The position represents the strength of the relationship.
24 See R.S. Burt, *Structural Holes*.
25 For a review of the relevant literature, see R.S. Burt, J.E. Janotta and J.T. Mahoney, 'Personality correlates of structural holes', *Social Networks*, 20 (1998), pp. 63–87, on pp. 63–66.
26 See J.F. Padgett 'Matrimonio y Estructura de la Élite de la Florencia Renacentista'.
27 A. Polonia, S. Pinto and A.S. Ribeiro, *Trade Networks in the First Global Age. The case study of Simon Ruiz Company: Visualization Methods and Spatial Projections* (2014), unpublished, available at www.academia.edu/7658353/Trade_networks_in_the_First_Global_Age._The_case_study_of_Simon_Ruiz_Company_visualization_methods_and_spatial_projections.
28 Also, see M. Cachero, *Should We Trust?*, for more examples of the use of contracts as proxies for the robustness of commercial links.
29 J.L. Imízcoz and I. Arroyo Ruiz, 'Redes sociales y correspondencia epistolar'.
30 A.S. Ribeiro, *Early Modern Trading Networks in Europe: Cooperation and the Case of Simon Ruiz* (London: Routledge, 2015); M. Düring, *Verdeckte soziale Netzwerke im Nationalsozialismus. Berliner Hilfsnetzwerke für verfolgte Juden.* (Berlin: De Gruyter, 2015).
31 I. Rosé, 'Construire une société seigneuriale. Itinéraire et ecclésiologie de l'abbé Odon de Cluny (fin du IXe-milieu du Xe siècle)', *Collection d'études médiévales de Nice*, 8 (2012).
32 This famous paper was published in 1736. See N. Biggs, E. Lloyd and R. Wilson, *Graph Theory, 1736–1936* (Oxford: Oxford University Press, 1986).
33 See J.L. Moreno, *Who Shall Survive?* (New York: Beacon House, 1934), p. 15.
34 For additional information on VennMaker, see M. Düring, 'VennMaker para historiadores: Fuentes, redes sociales y programas informáticos', *REDES-Revista hispana para el análisis de redes sociales*, 21:3 (2011), pp. 388–420. The software is available online and a trial version can be downloaded from www.vennmaker.com/testversion-und-bestellmoeglichkeit?lang=en.
35 M. O. Jackson, *Social and Economic Networks* (Princeton: Princeton University Press, 2008), p. 35.
36 S. Ogilvie, 'Social Capital, Social Networks and History', Working Paper Faculty of Economics, University of Cambridge, (2000), pp. 1–3. Available at www.academia.edu/2782117/Social_Capital_Social_Networks_and_History_-_2000_-_Working_Paper.
37 Definition available at www.oxforddictionaries.com/es/definicion/learner/trust.
38 J.S. Coleman, 'Social Capital in the Creation of Human Capital', *American Journal of Sociology*, 94:Supplement (1989), pp. 95–120; R.D. Putnam, R. Leonardi and R.Y. Nanetti, *Making Democracy Work: Civic Traditions in Modern Italy* (Princeton: Princeton University Press, 1993).
39 For additional information on this issue, see J. Owens and E.A. Coppola, 'Fuzzy Set Theory (or Fuzzy Logic) to Represent the Messy Data of Complex Human (and other) Systems'. White paper available at www.academia.edu/1100044/Fuzzy_Set_Theory_or_Fuzzy_Logic_to_Represent_the_Messy_Data_of_Complex_Human_and_other_Systems.
40 The use of the term 'connectors' for referring to merchant networks was used for the first time in M. Herrero Sánchez and I. Pérez Tostado 'Conectores del Mundo Atlántico' in *Irlanda y el Atlántico Ibérico* (Valencia: Albatros, 2010), pp. 307–322.
41 For additional data about this process, see P. Boyd-Bowman, 'Patterns of Spanish Migration to the Indies until 1600', *The Hispanic American Historical Review*, 56:4 (1976), pp. 580–604 ; A. Eiras Roel, *La emigración española a ultramar, 1492–1914* (Madrid: Asociación de Historia Moderna, Editorial Tabapress, 1991).
42 See A.G. Frank, *ReOrient: Global Economy in the Asian Age* (Berkeley: University of California Press, 1998); J.H. Bentley, 'AHR Forum-Cross-Cultural Interaction and Periodization in World History', *American Historical Review*, 101 (1996),

pp. 749–770. Several researchers claim that globalisation began even before 1492. For instance, J.L. Abu-Lughod, *Before European Hegemony: The World System A.D. 1250–1350* (Oxford: Oxford University Press, 1991) locates the beginning of the process after the Pax Mongolica, in the transition between the thirteenth and the fourteenth centuries. Also A.G. Frank and B.K. Gills, *The World Systems: Five Hundred or Five Thousands?* (London and New York: Routledge, 1994) place the beginnings of globalisation 5,000 years ago.

43 See A.G. Frank, *ReOrient*, p. 52.
44 See K. O'Rourke and J. Williamson, *Globalization and History: The Evolution of a Nineteenth-Century Atlantic Economy* (Cambridge: MIT Press, 2000); K. O'Rourke and J. Williamson, 'When Did Globalisation Begin?', *European Review of Economic History*, 6 (2002a), pp. 23–50; K. O'Rourke and J. Williamson, 'After Columbus: Explaining Europe's Overseas Trade Boom, 1500–1800', *Journal of Economic History*, 62 (2002b), pp. 417–456.
45 Trade volume can be a very tricky proxy, as a boost can be the consequence of an increment in population, land or technology.
46 According to L. García Fuentes, *El Comercio Español con América, 1650–1700* (Seville: Escuela de Estudios Hispano Americanos, 1980), the top five products imported from Spanish America in the sixteenth and the seventeenth centuries were dyeing materials, silver, leather, sugar and cocoa.
47 The *Almojarifazgo* was the classic royal tariff for trading with the colonies, and the *Avería* was a tax raised to force merchants to contribute to the maintenance of the fleet system. See A. García-Baquero González, *La Carrera de Indias: Suma de Contratación y Océano de Negocios* (Seville: Algaida, 1992).

Bibliography

Bentley, J.H., 'AHR Forum-Cross-Cultural Interaction and Periodization in World History', *American Historical Review*, 101 (1996), pp. 749–770.

Biggs, N., Lloyd, E. and Wilson, R., *Graph Theory, 1736–1936,* Oxford: Oxford University Press, 1986.

Boyd-Bowman, P., 'Patterns of Spanish Migration to the Indies until 1600', *The Hispanic American Historical Review*, 56:4 (1976), pp. 580–604.

Burt, R.S., *Structural Holes: The Social Structure of Competition*, Cambridge: Harvard University Press, 1992.

Burt, R.S., Jannotta, J.E. and Mahoney, J.T., 'Personality correlates of structural holes', *Social Networks*, 20 (1998), pp. 63–87.

Cachero Vinuesa, M., *Should We Trust? Explaining Trade Expansion in Early Modern Spain, Seville 1500–1600* (PhD Dissertation defended at the European University Institute, Florence, 2010).

———, 'Redes mercantiles en los inicios del comercio atlántico. Sevilla entre Europa y América, 1520–1525', in Böttcher, N., Hausberger, B. and Ibarra, A. (eds.), *Redes y Negocios Globales en el Mundo Ibérico, siglos XVI–XVIII*, Mexico D. F.: El Colegio de México, Iberoamericana, Vertvuert, 2011, pp. 25–52.

Coleman, J.S., 'Social Capital in the Creation of Human Capital', *American Journal of Sociology*, 94:Supplement (1989), pp. 95–120.

Crovi Druetta, D.M., López Cruz, M.A. and López González, R. (eds.), *Redes Sociales: Análisis y Aplicaciones*, México D. F.: Universidad Autónoma de México y Plaza y Valdés, 2009.

Düring, M., *Verdeckte soziale Netzwerke im Nationalsozialismus. Berliner Hilfsnetzwerke für verfolgte Juden*, Berlin: De Gruyter, 2015.

———, 'From Hermeneutics to Data to Networks: Data Extraction and Network Visualization of Historical Sources', *The Programming Historians*, (2015), available at http://programminghistorian.org/lessons/creating-network-diagrams-from-historical-sources

————, 'VennMaker para historiadores: Fuentes, redes sociales y programas informáticos', *REDES-Revista hispana para el análisis de redes sociales*, 21:3 (2011), pp. 388–420.

Düring, M. and Stark, M., 'Historical Network Analysis', in Barnett, G. and Golson, J.G. (eds.), *Encyclopedia of Social Networks*, London: Sage, 2011, pp. 1543–1545.

Eiras Roel, A., *La emigración española a ultramar, 1492–1914*, Madrid: Asociación de Historia Moderna, Editorial Tabapress, 1991.

Frank, A.G., *ReOrient: Global Economy in the Asian Age*, Berkeley: University of California Press, 1998.

Freeman, L., *The Development of Social Network Analysis: A Study in the Sociology of Science*, Vancouver: Empirical Press, 2004.

Friede, J., *Los Welser en la conquista de Venezuela*, Caracas: Edime, 1961.

García-Baquero González, A., *La Carrera de Indias: Suma de Contratación y Océano de Negocios*, Sevilla: Algaida, 1992.

García Fuentes, L., *El Comercio Español con América, 1650–1700*, Seville: Escuela de Estudios Hispano Americanos, 1980.

Granovetter, M., 'Economic Actions and Social Structure: The Problem of Embeddedness', *American Journal of Sociology*, 91 (1985), pp. 481–510.

Imizcoz, J.M. and Arroyo Ruiz, L., 'Redes sociales y correspondencia epistolar: Del análisis cualitativo de las relaciones personales a la reconstrucción de las redes ego-centradas', *REDES-Revista Hispana para el Análisis de Redes Sociales*, 21: 3 (2011), pp. 98–138.

Jackson, M.O., *Social and Economic Networks*, Princeton: Princeton University Press, 2008.

Krackhardt, D., 'Assessing the Political Landscape: Structure, Cognition and Power in Organizations', *Administrative Science Quarterly*, 35 (1990), pp. 342–369.

Lemercier, C., 'Formal Methods in History: Why and How?', *HAL Working Paper Series*, (2011), https://halshs.archives-ouvertes.fr/halshs-00521527v2/document.

McCarty, C. and Molina, J.L., 'Social Network Analysis', in Bernard, R.H. and Gravlee, C.C. (eds.), *Handbook of Methods in Cultural Anthropology*, Lanham: Rowman & Littlefield, 2014, pp. 631–657.

Molina, J.L., *El Análisis de Redes Sociales: Una Introducción*, Barcelona: Editorial Bellaterra, 2001.

Moreno, J.L., *Who Shall Survive?* New York: Beacon House, 1943.

Ogilvie, S., 'Social Capital, Social Networks and History', Working Paper, Faculty of Economics, Cambridge (2000). www.academia.edu/2782117/Social_Capital_Social_Networks_and_History_-_2000_-_Working_Paper.

O'Rourke, K. and Williamson, J., 'When Did Globalization Begin?', *European Review of Economic History*, 6 (2002a), pp. 23–50.

————, 'After Columbus: Explaining Europe's Overseas Trade Boom, 1500–1800', *Journal of Economic History*, 62 (2002b), pp. 417–456.

————, *Globalization and History: The Evolution of a Nineteenth-Century Atlantic Economy*, Cambridge: MIT Press, 2000.

Owens, J. and Coppola, E.A., 'Fuzzy Set Theory (or Fuzzy Logic) to Represent the Messy Data of Complex Human (and other) Systems', White Paper, U.S. National Science Foundation, www.academia.edu/1100044/Fuzzy_Set_Theory_or_Fuzzy_Logic_to_Represent_the_Messy_Data_of_Complex_Human_and_other_Systems.

Padgett, J.F., 'Matrimonio y Estructura de la Élite de la Florencia Renacentista, 1282–1500', *REDES-Revista Hispana para el Análisis de Redes Sociales*, 21: 3 (2011), pp. 42–70.

Polonia, A., Pinto, S. and Ribeiro, A.S., *Trade Networks in the First Global Age. The case study of Simon Ruiz Company: Visualization Methods and Spatial Projections*, (2014), unpublished, www.academia.edu/7658353/Trade_networks_in_the_First_Global_Age._The_case_study_of_Simon_Ruiz_Company_visualization_methods_and_spatial_projections.

Putnam, R.D., Leonardi R. and Nanetti, R.Y., *Making Democracy Work: Civic Traditions in Modern Italy*, Princeton: Princeton University Press, 1993.

Ribeiro, A.S., *Early Modern Trading Networks in Europe: Cooperation and the Case of Simon Ruiz*, London: Routledge, 2015.

Rosé, I., *Construire une Société Seigneuriale. Itinéraire et Ecclésiologie de l'abbé Odon de Cluny (fin du IXe-Milieu du Xe Siècle)*, Collection d'études Médiévales de Nice 8 (2012).

Schnegg, M., 'Strategien und Strukturen. Herausforderungen der qualitativen und quantitativen Netzwerkforschung', in Gamper, M. and Reschke, L. (eds.), *Knoten und Kanten. Soziale Netzwerkanalyse in Wirtschafts- und Migrationsforschung* (Bielefeld: Verlag, 2010), pp. 55–75.

4 Merchants and the beating of a butterfly's wings

From local to global in the transfer of economic behaviour models in the eighteenth century

Ana Crespo Solana

Self-organised commercial networks in the global history of trade

In July 1716, Philippe Couturier, a merchant of French origin, but a naturalised resident of Amsterdam, described perhaps the best form of trust-based mercantile cooperation: 'the manufactures, invoices and products sent from Amsterdam to Cádiz to be shipped to the West Indies were always to be sent in the name of Spanish merchants and this was something which was not just necessary, but mandatory, as otherwise, the efforts of a great many people in a long chain of work from the Oostzee (Baltic ports), the Indies, the ports of the Levant and Spain would be broken by the greed [sic]' of the officials who confiscated the goods which were not traded according to the law.[1] This behaviour, which is evidence of the classic paradigm of the use of a *testaferro* (front man) in Spanish colonial trade, also serves as indisputable proof that socio-economic relationships within this system were driven by 'network reciprocity'. These must have involved, spatially and temporally, mechanisms for expanding the network, including new associates, and seeking out potential allies with the aim of ensuring profitable business dealings and the guaranteed survival of the networks themselves. But one thing that can be proved when visualising this relationship model is that if there is anything that characterises cooperation in the early modern period, it is, in fact, dispersal.

Mercantile behaviour in the first global age has been approached from different perspectives. While Anglo-American and Northern European specialists have taken much from British neo-liberal theory of the seventeenth and eighteenth centuries, the academic world of the Iberian Peninsula has drawn on traditional Roman law when it comes to describing these socio-economic behaviours, and hence, the merchants themselves. The qualitative and representational analysis, in which network studies contribute to both perspectives is becoming widespread now, again emphasising the global dynamic of interactions, in evidence from the fifteenth century, revealed by studying mercantile networks in global trade.[2] In recent years, as a result of research carried out as part of a collaborative international project, a group of historians, including myself, have opted to adopt the concept of a 'self-organizing network' to define the behaviour of the agents that made up such mercantile networks.[3] A shared vision of *self-organised commercial networks* from the perspective of global history is yet to emerge, although there have already been some papers by specialists who are following the same theoretical and methodological path.[4]

The term 'self-organised' or 'self-organising network' refers to an interdisciplinary theory. However, we historians have utilised the concept accepted in economics and the biology of evolution, which offers this definition: 'complex and flexible nuclei which form integrated, evolutionary networks in the historical framework corresponding to the centuries of the early modern period, through traders, producers, communities and government officials'. These have also been defined as 'flexible commercial networks of international scope and based on family or business relationships'. Self-organization was a way of life that involved cooperative phenomena within the scope of the social dilemma.[5] Heylighen described the particular features of this type of analysis in multi-agent systems: 'The system tends to self-organise, in the sense that local interactions eventually produce global coordination and synergy. The resulting structure can, in many cases, be modelled as a network, with stabilized interactions functioning as links connecting the agents. Such complex, self-organized networks typically exhibit the properties of clustering, being scale-free, and forming a small world'.[6]

The concept of self-organizing networks shifts the analysis of mercantile agents in the first global age to a transnational framework of migration and the formation of regional economic systems. While Fujita and Krugman established the types of forces responsible for moulding the spatial structure of an economy based on the combination of territorial restrictions and agents' capacity to concentrate their business in certain spaces,[7] transnational theories argue that the international movement of people, goods and ideas created new global cultures, as well as new social and political identity-forming spaces. The two paradigms, between spatial geography and economic history, are not contradictory and are closely related.[8] From a historical and social perspective, this *self-organising* created and defined new behavioural spaces, referring to how space and the economy may be determined by human behaviour, while also shaping the economic phenomena of spatial integration. This perspective links history to sociological ideas which argue that society and individuals are not separate realities and interact with one another.[9] This sense can be carried over to the study of economic exchange. Understanding how small alterations in socio-economic behaviour within the families of local merchants may or may not bring about changes in nonlinear systems and produce a butterfly effect in the rapid increase of and forms of behaviour in trade networks in linked spaces, even if said spaces are geographically distant. After years spent analysing Dutch and Flemish merchants in eighteenth-century Cádiz, it is possible to establish a representation of these behavioural mechanisms in databases and networks, offering concrete descriptions of the extent of the networks at a social and spatial level from the perspective of local subsidiary operations and how the theory of *network reciprocity* and *group augmentation* fits here.

Local community and corporate framework

The historiography of mercantile communities has been based on socio-institutional studies, primarily *consulados* (merchant guilds), and the analysis of relations between merchants and political powers.[10] Nevertheless, microeconomic studies of individual trading families and companies have provided the majority of our knowledge of foreign communities. There always remain certain aspects which have yet to be explored in depth as historical studies become increasingly more interdisciplinary within the framework of the spatial humanities and their emerging methodologies. Additionally, despite the dynamics of social actors within the networks, modern historiography continues to employ strict compartmentalization in the majority of cases. It is not possible to conduct a study by focusing solely on the élite, or by isolating economic issues from political and social matters. If there is one thing that characterises this 'small world', it was the densification of networks and interaction between different social classes. The case analysed by Picazo Muntaner in his study of Spanish networks in the Philippines during the seventeenth century provides evidence of how merchants and government officials or colonial authorities developed extensive collaborative networks, most of them invisible. These were established to engage in clandestine trade, creating a real dynamic of struggles and feuds to obtain as much power as possible in both the administrative and commercial arenas.[11] This type of analysis makes it possible to detect the presence of well-documented dynamics involving competition to place trusted men in the most profitable public posts, and to enable these contacts, now well positioned, to provide other members of the network with greater security to ship unregistered merchandise, engage in smuggling or carry out other activities alongside their legal business.

One benefit could be the analysis of these communities from the perspective of their function as links between production and consumption. There are some studies which make mention of this relationship. Although they focus heavily on western Andalusia, they underscore the important connection between commercial activity and the arrival of American silver in Europe with the development of European capitalism. However, it should also be noted that these studies have been produced from a macroeconomic perspective, which has undoubtedly influenced how studies on colonial trade have been carried out.[12] Bustos Rodríguez stresses that, in the absence of studies on domestic trade within Andalusia, there are very few clues as to how mercantile agents functioned when removing regional products, primarily agricultural, which constituted the *tercio de frutos* (the third of all shipments to Spanish America reserved as the 'fruits of the land'), or local textiles, always exceeded by foreign goods.[13]

Mercantile agents played an undisputed role in the flow of trade. Basically, they were warehousers of products and capital (hard cash), which linked them directly to consumption and finances. They were also shipping agents. Their role could not be separated from the characteristics of the sociocultural integration of many of these social communities. As history has demonstrated, the mechanisms deriving from or generated by facilitating and managing this integration constitute a key element in our understanding of the symbolic interactionism of mercantile networks and groups in early modern Spain.[14] All of the merchant communities had one common denominator: the presence of travelling agents who moved around and sailed with their goods. This explains the long-term transitory nature of many of the members of the foreign communities. These merchants expanded their own business dealings, while at the same time becoming part of a social world built by other traders.[15]

The key to understanding the strategies used by mercantile networks to evolve in space and time is cooperation. Studies on cooperation have lately attracted a great deal of interest and in the case of human societies, our lack of knowledge about what exactly it is and why it occurs is striking. Noë, director of the most ambitious interdisciplinary research programme on cooperation in recent years, states that: 'Cooperation, sometimes disguised as "reciprocal altruism", "mutualim", "symbiosis", "reciprocity" or "trading", is a central focus of inquiry in many scientific disciplines such as anthropology, biology, economics, political science, psychology, sociology, history, artificial intelligence and robotics'. What these all have in common is that they explore 'cooperative interactions'.[16] In short, we have interdisciplinary papers which provide an answer to the question of how cooperation strategies were established and developed by merchants in the early modern period: the studies on the Villena Cartel and smuggling in Spain under Philip II; the trade of the Flemish nation in Cádiz in the eighteenth century; 'private trading' on voyages of the East Indian Company (EIC) between 1601 and 1833 and smuggling of Chinese tea in the mid-eighteenth century.[17]

The case of Low Countries merchants is paradigmatic, making up a nonminority group in a mercantile society relatively adapted to a space limited by the sea and maritime activities. Divided between the Flemish nation, and to a much lesser extent, the Dutch *consulado* (maritime consulate), their socio-economic and even political behaviour was influenced by their activities in the Indies trade, primarily through the fleet to New Spain and the connection between the Baltic, Northern European, French Atlantic coast, Mediterranean and Iberian Peninsula markets via the maritime routes of the Straatvaart (Levant trade). Beginning in the 1720s, Low Countries participation in *Registro* (Register) ships increased. They worked for trading companies, interacting with other merchants and institutions. They formed an identified group and some were associated with each other in some way or worked together in circles with regular customers and associates, which also involved other local agents.[18] It was very common for traders to tend to associate with each other in different ways and manners via various undertakings and business dealings, depending on the different business opportunities they identified. Business interactions are thus known and visible, constituting a firm or trade name which can be analysed through historical documents. Apart from the private trading companies, clearly defined in a paper by Carrasco González,[19] there were also other forms of mercantile cooperation. These have been represented in relational form in the following prototype taken from the 'CrespoDynCoopNet Data collection' database (Figure 4.1).

Generally, the majority of these traders were grouped around private companies or other forms of mercantile cooperation. They were quite different from those that formed part of the large monopolies. In fact, there are few references to such

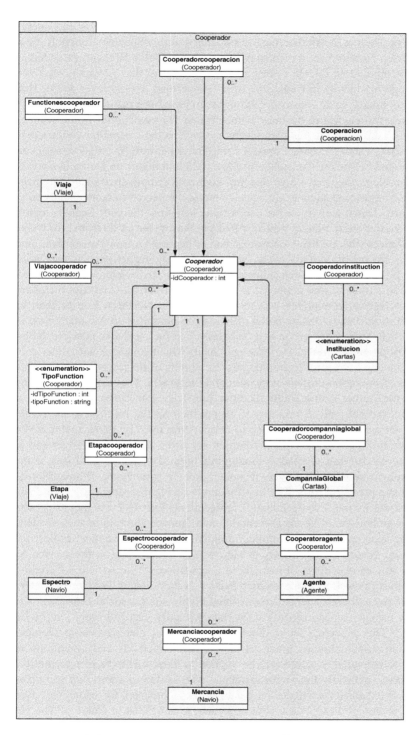

Figure 4.1 Relational model of mercantile cooperation.[20]

involvement among the Flemish community in Cádiz. There is one interesting case in which a Dutch merchant is associated with a Spanish monopoly. In 1753, Federico Timmerman, a merchant from Aalst, in Dutch Brabant, extended a loan in the amount of 23,833 reales and 3 cuartillos to the *Compañía de Granada* through his factors in Cádiz, the firm Timmerman, Hasenclever & Co. But this did not appear to be common.[21] It may even have been that these merchants were reluctant to engage in business with some of the monopolies established by the Spanish crown in the eighteenth century, such as the *Compañía Guipuzcoana de Caracas*, which the Dutch opposed. In fact, a petition by an anonymous author presented before the Consulado in May 1728 laid blame on Dutch businesses for the problems they had – both this new company and private traders that wished to charter registered ships to Caracas – despite the decree to reduce taxes on cacao imports. Dutch activity in the cocoa trade benefited the very Spanish merchants who viewed the market as well supplied, purchasing the cacao from Low Countries consignees who, on many occasions, had re-exported it from Amsterdam. In other words, the majority of this cacao came from smuggling activities in the Caribbean Sea. Equipping a registered ship solely to carry cacao to Spain was very expensive for Cádiz traders, who preferred to purchase it from Low Countries merchants.[22]

Interest in monopolies was more common in Northern Europe than in the south. In his study on the model of British communities in Atlantic cities, David Hancock defined this group as a 'subclass'.[23] In fact, it is also possible to observe a prosopographic model for these merchants which coincides with other community models. This profile emphasises the actions of these traders as demarcating areas of operation of their associates and customers. They engaged in a range of activities rather than a single lucrative job. They sometimes constituted a small group, but not really a minority if we put their spatial location in the context in a given city. Although the types of cooperation used by these agents varied, as shown in Figure 4.1, the most common activities were holding silver and goods in deposit, serving as a factor, smuggling, bills of exchange and loans, including maritime risk. This might vary depending on the community, although we do not yet have precise details. The key functions of Flemish and Dutch merchants in Cádiz during the seventeenth and eighteenth centuries were acting as consignees and warehousers of goods and capital, and this was the root of their tendency to set up local subsidiary operations.[24] English merchants created an endless variety of joint ventures, investments of various kinds, including in the service sector. This was another form of mercantile cooperation within society.[25] Certain communities (as well as Genoese merchants and the French) had similar patterns of functions and their agents demonstrated highly similar social behaviour. Among these groups, we can identify what Hancock calls 'fast followers', in the British case.[26] This concept, used to describe opportunistic merchants who adopted new or somewhat unknown practices and imitated methods and operations which they found suitable, could also be applied to those members of mercantile communities, generally long-term residents, who settled in a port city to implement market expansion strategies on behalf of the companies for which they worked. One example of this is the case of Leonardo van Aalst, a native of The Hague, who temporarily settled in Cádiz in 1737 to expand the businesses of several

Northern European firms, acknowledging that he had commissions from 'others' and those for which he had to find a market.[27]

In truth, they were not great businessmen or bankers and at times, they physically came from the social periphery of their city of origin. They were people who adapted their actions to the opportunities that presented themselves, which was also a reason for their transmigratory patterns and regular travel. They would often gather around an individual whose influence and social position made him beneficial for business, and who became the main nucleus of a given network. By following routes, it is possible to observe how the networks moved products, people and information. In theory, these were maintained by the reputation and trust built up among them, but this could vary, producing changes within the network. Despite the fact that the role of cooperation cannot be understood without interpersonal trust, the problem is more complex, involving actions of reciprocity and 'group augmentation' strategies.[28] In a given society, group augmentation occurs when a group of individuals find themselves in a position to increase the size of their group and their territory. This theoretical meaning has been used in sociology and evolutionary biology to understand the need for cooperation in social and natural systems.[29] This expansion must be selective, as the presence of more individuals within the network must always enhance the survival of the original members of that network. In historical and sociological terms, this can translate into an aristocratisation or elitisation of the longest established groups already linked by blood ties and institutional commitments. This 'group selection' will undoubtedly have an effect on the trust and reputation of the group's individuals. Roitman provides evidence of this in his study on the 'Portuguese Nation' in Amsterdam (Sephardic traders), where she analyses the emergence of new cooperative networks beyond a simple centre of action.[30] The idea of group selection can clearly be seen in the competition among mercantile groups of different nationalities in Cádiz. This form of cooperation can also be seen in smuggling and illegal trade networks, as I have demonstrated in an article.[31] When a smuggler or a merchant made illicit use of legal supplies, he was convicted of wrongdoing and had to pay a fine, but the fine did not stop the behaviour because it was considered no more than a business cost, much like banks are paying now for their illegal trades and manipulation of global interest rates.

Using the data model created to analyse a large quantity of information distributed in layers relating to merchants, ships and cooperation, it is possible to establish that the main characteristic of networks of Spanish merchants in the seventeenth and eighteenth centuries was that they made up a 'small world' of global interactions.[32] Theories on complex systems define this 'small world' as a network with many nodes (see Figure 4.2) and dense and relatively independent subgraphs. This is a nonlinear complex system, a theory applicable to various fields of research, including history.[33] A preliminary representation of one of these networks of merchants produced using data from the local prototype of the 'CrespoDynCoopNet Data collection' database, including all the information available on mercantile agents, offers a view of this 'small world'. It can be represented as seen in Figure 4.2.

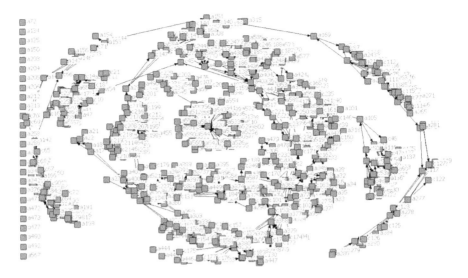

Figure 4.2 Atlantic mercantile network model with merchant data (1650–1760).

Source: *Crespo DynCoopNet Data collection database.* CSIC Digital Repository.

This extensive network encompasses a large number of social networks with more than 100 nodes. These networks are made up of individuals or groups of individuals with patterns of contact or interaction among them. They may occasionally also include institutions as subnetworks that incorporate other groups of individuals. It is not possible to establish a connection in the analysis between the actions of individual actors and forms of behaviour for the system as a whole in this nonlinear and highly distributed system. In other words, the behaviour of the network cannot be explained by the total sum of the partial actions of its constituent parts. This is to say, if we consider the state of the system at its starting point based on given initial conditions and follow its evolution over time, the final result is quite a bit different from anticipated. These mercantile networks are characterised by the properties of centrality, which refers to the position of the nodes in the networks, and centralization, understood as the structure of a network as a whole. At the same time, these ideas are based on the concepts of degree, brokering and proximity, apart from the density that all networks possess. Degree refers to the number of links which a social agent has in the network; brokering means that a social agent is placed between two other agents in the network; and proximity is the distance between an agent and the rest of the network. As has been pointed out by Hausberger, Ibarra and Böttcher, this is important for analysing the concept of network and its functionality, as well as its value for describing the association among agents and institutions.[34] However, there is something more than this, as the manner in which the network evolves will have an impact on the system as a whole. Thus, a complex network is defined as a network in which there are many parts interacting with each other, the aspect to which the adjective 'complex' refers. It does not mean that the system is complicated. Each part has its own internal structure and is responsible for performing a specific function. What happens to one part of the system affects the entire system in an extremely nonlinear manner, displaying – and this is very significant in mercantile networks of the early modern period – emergent behaviours.

Networks and behavioural space

We have seen that *self-organised networks* is a broad concept, but one which is focused on the view of human behaviour as a factor which shapes history and the construction of space. This is true both from a geographic-physical perspective and as 'behavioural space', closely related to the idea of 'mental maps'[35] in the discipline of history and the perception of 'social space' which they produce.[36] There are three underlying problems with understanding the network as a behavioural space. One is the actual definition of community and network, which I have discussed; another is the meaning of the idea of connection and the role of these communities in making up economic spaces. A community was a key microsociety for the formation of certain networks of associates and relations, but also the connections and contact among them and an entire range of local agents, forming a spatial network which generally expanded beyond local boundaries. The result was that although some of these communities were not numerous (as in the Dutch case), in terms of their influence on the spatial structure of the economy, they formed true 'hubs' among empires.[37]

In historical analysis it is possible to develop a spatial representation according to the geographical knowledge of historical spatial concepts based on the theories of Ernst Carrier (1874–1945), a philosopher of the Marburg school, who described the 'three spaces'.[38] This historical-spatial representation can be divided between behavioural, observational and geographical space.[39]

According to Wachowicz et al., 'the Observational Space contains the classes that conceptualise the observations of the three-dimensional filled in space. Observations are measurement values at every point in space, based on some measurement scale, which can be quantitative or qualitative. Besides, observations are always marked by some degree of uncertainty, which depends on the type of historical sources. On the other hand, Geographical Space is the fundamental conceptual framework where we are able to compare and quantify objects, their sizes and shapes in relation to the landscape. Finally, the Behavioural Space consists of individuals, groups and organisations that maintain relations through intentional (cooperative) activities based upon a more or less common set of rules, norms and values and act within the boundaries of the institutions that are derived from it. An important difference between behavioural and observational spaces is that the latter has been mostly described in geographic terms while the first has not.' The spatial representation can be implemented in Protégé software, and it has been applied[40] to examining the evolution of cooperation among merchants and between merchants and other groups in the 'CrespoDynCoopNet Data collection' and the information about maritime routes, ships and merchants. The results are illustrated in Figure 4.3.

A visualization of a spatial network made up by the port cities which comprised the business dealings of the Low Countries communities on the western Atlantic coast links us to a number of cities between which commercial traffic of differing intensity developed. The following networked representation was made using the local prototype of the 'Crespo DynCoopNet data collection' database, which is currently being expanded with information on the number of ships (many of them located shipwrecks which are also currently the subject of archaeological exploration) and commercial ports of call.[41] See Figure 4.4.

In these maps of finance, trade and distribution of consumer goods, producers and buyers are dispersed in space. For this reason, a large part of the efforts made by agents in their commercial activity involved trying to cover this space. Transport and communications were among the main factors of spatial integration. Many businesses and trading companies worked to place these tools close to producers and buyers. As a result, improvements in maritime transport over the centuries were among the causes of economic development[42]. On the spatial map

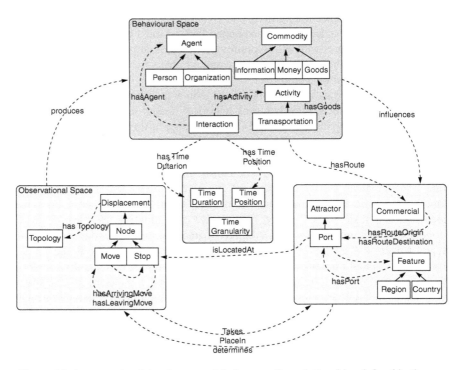

Figure 4.3 An example of the classes and their respective relationships defined in the spatial representation implemented in Protégé software.

Source: Wachowicz et al. (2008), Appendix in Crespo Solana (2000).

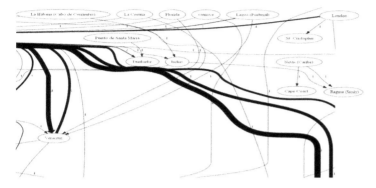

Figure 4.4 Port spatial network of Low Countries merchants in Cádiz, 1670–1748 (detail).
Source: Crespo DynCoopNet Data Collection. Figure by Roberto Maestre.

of market integration, those firms which require intensive and frequent interactions with their customers positioned themselves close to demand.

These forms of spatial integration established a behavioural space in which agents had to develop certain mechanisms of network reciprocity in order to supply the interdependencies within the network. If local subsidiary operations were based on the ability of a given trading house to maintain the same associates, relations and friends, surviving over long spaces of time,[43] these mechanisms, traditionally inspiring the well-known theory of trust, generated the characteristic network reciprocity.

Spatial networks and human cooperation: network reciprocity

Studies have demonstrated that the personal relationships which knit together foreign merchants in Seville and Cádiz extended to the Americas and other European regions, especially the Mediterranean and the north as far as the Baltic Sea. The majority of them established strong businesses around ego-centred networks.[44] For this type of analysis, we do not always find the required information in documentary sources. Generally speaking, historians are required to locate a certain type of information in the documentary sources which would provide data about the activity and role of communities in spatial integration: how they influenced changes in supply and demand or traffic flows through control of routes, and how trade networks influenced markets and their interaction. These data do not necessarily always need to be quantitative. What would be more valuable is qualitative data offering the possibility of analysing the evolutionary processes between systems over time: analysis of different networks that formed around a given 'social environment' in order to see the modes of spatial organization of the collaborative networks and spot cases of competition and collaboration, and to define models of cooperation alongside their visualisation. Those places where organic or community behaviours which lent cohesion and corporatism to mercantile colonies were experienced – such as guilds, religious relationships or common devotions – and were also where greater social mechanisms of cooperation developed.

In mercantile networks, it is possible to see how as their organization to cooperate or compete among themselves developed, structural holes were created. This concept, used by sociologist Martin Nowaks, is appropriate to the study of the historical emergence of new behavioural models in human society. In my study of the Flemish and Dutch community in Cádiz, I have been able to determine how these mercantile networks were able to locate a structural hole in which to develop or produce a new mechanism for the social and economic survival of the community. This phenomenon occurs depending on the space and on a sequence of events, which are essential if we want to represent the data in a geographic information system. Generally speaking, though it is still too early to answer many of the questions about how the forms of cooperation and other social and economic mechanisms within the framework of these structural holes in human behaviour emerged, it is possible to consider whether the models of cooperation among agents influenced the spatial organisation of trade networks, the levels of risk in businesses, the exercise of power and the division of labour and to what extent. For example, it was common for a foreign merchant to obtain profits from a city's tax or customs revenue in order to assist those from his nation to establish relationships – sometimes family ties through the marriage of children or siblings with local elites, or through 'patronage' – thus gaining socio-institutional privileges and financial benefits supported by his professional colleagues and fellow community members. Another example are the profits obtained from customs duties and provincial and local taxes, which were often gained as a result of their work as moneylenders to the tax collectors (tax farmers) who also belonged to the same network as the merchant. There are a number of documented cases in which tax collectors were robbed of these by nonpayment or delays in loans and liens which would lead to public auction of the same. Clearly, the inclusion of these tax collectors in the networks of foreign merchants constituted an example of group augmentation, which in the vast majority of cases, led to the expansion of the main merchant's network. One example is the case of the purchase of the 'Nueva Alcabala' (1 per cent tax on sale and exchange of goods) and the 4 per cent paid for goods, clothing and merchandise to the *Real Aduana de Cádiz* (Cádiz Royal Customs House) by Pedro de Grotte in 1713, thus benefitting the other members of his network due to an unsatisfied loan of the Ponce de León family, to whose entailed estate this right to customs duties belonged.[45] A similar case is the position of measurer at the *Alhóndiga de Sevilla* (Seville Wheat Market) held by Nicolás Snellincq in 1723, which belonged to his grandchildren and which he bought at auction for 28,000 vellon ducats. The *Audiencia de Sevilla* granted him this purchase in perpetuity.[46]

Complementary to the conclusions of the trust theory, the idea of reciprocity has an even greater impact on the network's ability to increase the number of nodes and agents, extend itself in time and space, produce temporal stability in business circles and seek out profitable associates as part of a suitable group-selection strategy. It is in this network of contacts where it is possible to identify the different models of agents and the various types of cooperation through which emergent behavioural mechanisms spread. The ability to maintain associates who are potentially profitable from a social and economic perspective even underlies the trader's wishes when it came to establishing a will or 'final wishes'.[47] Reciprocity also provided opportunities to acquire the capacity for knowledge transfer.[48] This network reciprocity produced a number of economic and social strategies. Social reciprocity is also taken into consideration in certain cases: for example, merchants would sometimes store the belongings of colleagues or associates in cases of absence, bankruptcy, death or business travel.[49]

Merchants had many reasons to collaborate with one another. Among the factors contributing to collaboration among merchants may have been language. Flemish merchants collaborated with the Dutch, but this was not true of the Walloons, who appeared to prefer the French. Notarial contracts reflect these transcultural relationships, especially charter contracts, powers of attorney and commercial loans. They reveal two aspects which refer to local operations within the network: trust and reciprocity. What becomes clear in this analysis is that these negotiations are the opportunity for new roles to emerge which derive from the type of cooperation itself, as local subsidiary operations meant that the members involved would establish economic and social 'indebtedness' practices. For example, many commission agents and factors came to the city with employment contracts, as in the case of some merchants from Amsterdam. When the company or individual merchant arrived as an agent or commission agent in the service of firms began to achieve a certain degree of success, and their business was divided amongst several branches of the city's mercantile economy, their firm, to some extent, could not be considered a subsidiary operation any longer and its trade name could become the head of a newly established clan resident in Cádiz. The firm no longer had a company at its core and began to revolve around a family, with its corresponding branches of associates, relations and friends. Nonetheless, these 'new' independent merchants could not survive in the city without the acceptance of the other economic clans in the community and even the mercantile society in general. Their business was involved in the local economy and needed to create ties between the interests of the original and local firms. This was the case, for example, of the Van Hemert family, which despite gaining their independence as *cargadores de Indias*, after acting as commission agents and factors for many years, continued to serve their former parent company associates in Amsterdam, the firm of Philipe Couturier.[50]

Traditionally, issues relating to interdependence among agents have been explained by the concept of 'trust', a very significant theory in the analysis of socio-economic exchange, defined as 'confident positive expectations regarding another's conduct'.[51] But this type of analysis of networks demonstrates that cooperation as simple direct reciprocity is no longer as surprising or interesting when we analyse large merchant communities which overflow the bounds of behavioural space and physical space. Study of relationships between the Flemish nation and other Low Countries merchants within the 'nation' demonstrates that cooperation emerged from indirect reciprocity, known as network reciprocity, which emphasises even more the idea of reputation.[52] What is more, this type of cooperation reinforces cooperation within the networks of the first global age.

In the case of the colonial trade of Cádiz, it was made up of factors of production which could move around in space: technical knowledge, ships and capital. In these open economies, political and bureaucratic power was channelled in support of mobile producers and creating a climate of investment in which free factors of production could prosper. But in this context, there is a difference between market and economic space. While the market is the centre of exchange and the place in which the space is structured, economic space varies depending on the elements that make up the activities of the networks. It also changes over time. Economic space was 'a distance which generated costs and the minimization of these costs gave rise to the creation of a theory of optimum location for production activities'. As a result, for centuries, transport and maritime trade constituted the main driving forces behind a region's growth.

In the case of Low Countries merchants in Cádiz, network reciprocity and interaction with shipping routes can be described as follows: the strategy of the merchant firms of the Flemish community in Cádiz can be compared to that developed by other groups of the same nationality settled in other geographical areas of Europe, such as the Baltic and the Mediterranean.[53] The interrelated group of mercantile and financial activities was carried out, generally, within a characteristic legal framework: the trading companies. This institutional framework closely paralleled the way in which the networks of agencies and maritime routes were connected. For that reason, the existence of a trading house gave internal cohesion to the company itself. In addition, its organization was very similar to that of a firm of agents. Their dynamics and evolution, although revealing some fluctuations at times, demonstrated great long-term stability. The centralization and spreading of networks made the flow of capital and its storage in the cities possible. Mercantile practices and methods used in such activities did not evolve significantly over time. Deposits of money, payment of commissions, currency exchange, insurance and the different occupations related to maritime transport were some of the key aspects on which the organizational system of these companies was based. Two fundamental pillars, i.e. the *goederenhandel* or *warenhandel* (trade of goods) and the deposit of money in the cities were two intrinsically related aspects. Their importance in relation to the American market lay in their capacity to store goods in bulk that were to be shipped aboard the fleets of New Spain and in the *Registro* ships that regularly set sail heading both for other ports in the area around the Caribbean Sea and for the mainland. The reason for the credit deposits was to maintain the trade of goods, since the bulk of them were brought by the fleet of the *Societëit van de Levantse Handel* (Society for Mediterranean Trade of Amsterdam and Middelburg), founded in June 1625 and with an important trading post in Cádiz from the time of the Twelve Years' Truce. It was agreed that merchants and freighters in both Amsterdam and Cádiz should pay a series of taxes to guarantee the legality of this trade. This Oriental convoy began to arrive in Cádiz on an annual basis and rather regularly up to at least 1734, with the aim of linking up with the Spanish fleets and galleons. They arrived regularly in those months when the Spanish ships were due to depart, generally separate. Whereas many continued their journey around eastern Spain and the Mediterranean, further Dutch ships, having previously changed their name, were included in the fleets going to America. In this endeavour, Dutch and Flemish merchants relied, in most cases, on collaboration from officials at the Casa de la Contratación in Cadiz. They were very frequently linked with them, as well as with other local figures, by business or personal interests.[54]

A specific case: merchant and consignee Juan Baptista de Roo

Transactions involved in this route represented opportunities for merchants that developed a range of strategies for expanding their businesses alongside and in symbiosis with the business of the Indies fleet, without doing too much that broke Spanish laws. It is also true that if we analyse the personal networks of some Flemish merchants associated with the Levant fleet and with Indies business, we find that these businesses incorporated the cooperation of local agents, independent merchants, Spanish officials and even those responsible for local taxes. We will be looking at the network which formed around the Dutch merchant Juan Baptista de Roo, who acted as a consignee for the Cádiz company Levantse Handel, including himself as a citizen of the Flemish nation despite his northern origins. As Roo served various firms from Rotterdam and Amsterdam, this caused suspicion among some native merchants, who referred to him as 'a native of Brabant or Fleming, Jan Baptista de Roo'.[55] He had a small network, but with interconnected nodes that linked him to the Flemish elite and local administrators and officials. He was not the main agent in this network, but other agents positioned in higher social and economic strata served as his intermediaries and protectors of his business dealings. As a consignee for the Dutch trade with the Levant, he received commissions in his name which actually belonged to other agents. Perhaps this behaviour and type of network were common among merchants who were long-term residents abroad, and they may have had an influence on their becoming fully integrated into the city where they traded, by marriage or another social commitment to other groups of citizens. However, Juan Baptista de Roo was the son of an Amsterdam merchant who had settled in the city, marrying a daughter of the Hercq & Vandentrille business clan. Juan Baptista was the steward of the Flemish nation in 1738. Since 1715, he had been part of his father's company, Roo, Hercq & Vandentrille, one of the city's richest and most active Flemish firms.[56] As a young Flemish merchant, he got his start in business in the shadow of his progenitors during the 1710s, protected by the prestigious Hercq & Vandentrille clan. However, he married a Cádiz woman, Juana Grosso y Gómez, who was not only part of the mercantile world, but from a family with ties to the Spanish navy. From 1750 to 1760, he continued to act as shipping agent for the *Societëit van de Levantse Handel*, an activity he carried out as part of a network of associates and allies, both local and of different nationalities, settled in various port cities in which he engaged in his family business dealings. The complexity of the network during this period indicates that Juan Baptista de Roo was a 'secondary' agent, not a member of the socio-institutional élite of Cádiz, but a key worker in the businesses of others. He stored and handled capital and goods dispatched to him from Amsterdam, Rotterdam and Zandaam, ports of the Sociedad para el comercio de Levante, where there were firms that shipped products to Cádiz. De Roo was in correspondence with the *boekhouder* (bookkeeper) Jan Bilderbercq. Other ports were Hamburg (with Bastián Krijgman, his associate there), the ports of the *Oostzee* (Baltic ports), Genoa (where another Dutch merchant, Jan Jacob de Beer, acted as his consignee), Ghent (through native merchants Baldovino Gasnman and Domingo de Courchelle, who were also married to his two sisters), and in Spain, Málaga, La Coruña, San Sebastián and El Ferrol. These numerous business transactions were also carried out under the auspices of relations between the Hercq y Vandentrille family, De Roo's protectors, and a number of agents in the navy and Spanish institutions: Joseph de Santmanat (deputy general of the region, member of the *Cámara de Castilla* and military and civil governor of Cádiz) and Juan José Navarro (captain general). De Roo also had good relations in 1767 with the Dutch consul in Cádiz, Jan Willem Nagel, who had previously been consul of Málaga in 1744, and who in some manner concealed certain types of irregular business that Roo conducted between the ports of northern Spain, Genoa and Cádiz. From time to time, these raised suspicions among Spanish authorities (Roo was always saved by the good relations between the family of his mother, Juana Catalina Hercq, and the Hercq y Vandentrille clan, including the aforementioned Santmanat and Navarro).[57]

What types of activities were carried out in relation to these businesses? The merchant's function as a holder of money and goods was essential. It was also an appropriate way to check his effectiveness as a consignee at the port. Ships loaded with goods freighted by a Low Countries firm arrived at the destination port where the consignee – the merchant's agent – stored the merchandise. In subsequent months, such merchandise was sold and redistributed. The agent kept the accounts for the business at the port, as well as holding money in trust on behalf of a third party, to be spent according to his associate's instructions. The accounts were fully settled upon explicit instructions from the supplier of the goods or at certain important moments in the lives of the associates, such as a wedding, death, signing of a contract, etc. Some types of documents, such as inventories from bankruptcies, transfers, contracts, etc., illustrate how deposits of money and payment to suppliers were made.

Further to the great diversity of services related to the sailing and arrival of the fleets in port, one of the most interesting subjects is private loans. The gradual increase in the use of *Registro* ships instead of the old fleets and galleons lead to an increase in this type of involvement, whereby insurance and marine risk (bottomry loan) became the most usual ways of obtaining financing. Some Flemings who owned ships sailing as part of large convoys or fleets, as well as some owners of cargoes freighted on the ships, requested loans to obtain risk contracts. They were paid in currency minted in the Americas upon returning to port and almost every transaction was supervised by a Spanish agent or *testaferro*. In many confirmed cases, the capital came from transactions carried out between Cádiz-based Flemings acting as bankers and Dutch traders involved in the routes of the Straatvaart.[58]

Conclusions

One characteristic that defines the networks of the early modern period is that they display a corporate framework inherited from traditional models of human behaviour which are not incompatible with operating within a network. The network is made up of strong ties and weak ties where junctions and chaos occur. Encounters between social actors produce innovation and the emergence of new types of cooperation that gave rise to new roles and new relational types, establishing a wide range of social hierarchies and dependencies. In general terms, the main characteristics of network reciprocity, related to trust and group augmentation, were improvement and integration. As a result of these circumstances, filled with a valuable historical narrative, the networks of the merchants of the first global age left a legacy in those places where they settled, as well as contributing to the building of port infrastructure and local institutions. Their small local businesses had the impact of large-scale business and the majority of them operated as wholesale traders. Many of these agents conducted their business in circles revolving around certain key agents who were always businessmen (financiers and wholesale traders) or employees of institutions. They were able to achieve a certain social status through trade deals and social opportunism: religion, good family, cultural level, patronage and social protection, etc. This behaviour is repeated in the majority of mercantile communities established in different maritime and port areas. These merchants were concerned to increase their social status and create a new and better world for themselves. As a result, they practised group augmentation strategies which led to other social behaviours. Underneath it all, it is possible to see how network reciprocity and group augmentation are the real strategies used by these merchants.

In short, analysis of these networks cannot be defined by an analysis of their influence on the historical structuring of territories. In fact, economic specialization is dependent on space, implying a need for spatial analysis. We must analyse how the networks controlled and integrated regional economies through this map of nodal points and globally analyse their influence and their political and economic pressure groups. This perspective is being introduced in the new comparative analyses of the mercantile empires, which have already produced some results, such as the most recent paper on global Dutch networks.[59] The key to commercial success, 'integration', is based on or characterised by a wide range of activities which had to be organised or carried out simultaneously in a chain of business dealings that involved agency and deployment of a selection of associates and potential allies with the aim of consolidating the support of local institutions and officials. The activities generated through agency, local subsidiary operations and chains of business dealings financed the businesses, while the merchants and their allies became users of the socio-economic assets generated in society, as well as supplying funds to third parties.

Lastly, I consider it possible to offer a response to the question of to what extent the expansion of networks influenced the emergence of new functions and new types of cooperation in the mercantile world of the first global age. There are many unresolved questions concerning how the forms of cooperation and other social and economic mechanisms emerged. However, the main question is: *Are these cooperation-based networks an example of self-organizing networks capable of producing qualitative system change?* It confirms that in the spatial-temporal evolution of the mercantile networks of the first global age lies the genesis of innovative behaviours that developed under the protection of the territorial expansion of these very networks. This occurred in a dispersed manner, yet was concentrated in local nodes, with different levels in terms of the types of agents and an atmosphere of local and global cooperation and competition.

Notes

1 Stadsarchief Amsterdam (StA) (former Gemeente Archief), notariele archiven, 5821A/556, Amsterdam, 14 de julio de 1716.

2 D. Ringrose, *Expansion and Global Interaction, 1200–1700* (San Diego: University of California; New York: Addison Wesley Longman, 2001). This investigation has been made in the project: GlobalNet, MICINN (HAR2011-27694).

3 DynCoopNet Project. See scientific results in: A. Crespo Solana and D. Alonso García (coords.), 'Self-organizing Networks and GIS Tools. Cases of Use for the Study of Trading Cooperation (1400–1800)', *Journal of Knowledge Management, Economics and Information Technology*, special issue, June (2012).

4 R. Mukherjee, ed., 'Oceans Connect'. *Reflections on Water Worlds Across Time and Space* (Delhi: Primus Book, 2013); J.B. Owens, 'Towards a Geographically-Integrated History, Connected World History: Employing Geographic Information Systems (GIS)', *History Compass*, 5 (6) (2007), pp. 2014–2040.

5 A. Crespo Solana, 'Introducción' and Schulte-Beerbühl, M. 'Merchant Empires: Mercaderes Hamburgueses en Londres y sus redes de comercio internacional (1660–1815)', in A. Crespo Solana, (coord.), *Comunidades transnacionales. Colonias de mercaderes extranjeros en el Mundo Atlántico (1500–1830)* (Madrid: Doce Calles, 2010), pp. 15–29 and 103–123.

6 F. Heylighen, 'Complexity and Self-Organization', M.J. Bates and M. Niles Maack (eds.), *Encyclopedia of Library and Information Sciences* (London: Routledge, 2008), pp. 1–20.

7 M. Fujita, P. Krugman and A.J. Venables, *The Spatial Economy: Cities, Regions, and International Trade* (Cambridge: The MIT Press, 1999).

8 L. Basch, N. Glick Schiller and S. Szanton Blanc, *Nations Bounded. Transnational projects, Postcolonial Predicaments and Deterritorialized Nation-States* (The Netherlands: Gordon and Breach Science Publishers, 1994).

9 C.W. Mills, *La imaginación sociológica*, 1961, quoted in: J.L. Álvaro Estramiana (ed.), *Fundamentos sociales del comportamiento humano* (Barcelona: Editorial UOC, 2003), pp. 23–24.

10 M. Herrero Sánchez, 'La red consular europea y la diplomacia mercantil en la edad moderna', in J.J. Iglesias, R.M. Pérez García and M.F. Fernández Chaves (eds.), *Comercio y Cultura en la Edad Moderna* (Sevilla: Editorial Universidad de Sevilla, 2015), pp. 121–151.

11 A. Picazo Muntaner, 'Rivalidades en las redes de poder de Manila: el golpe contra el gobernador Diego de Salcedo', *El Futuro del Pasado: revista electrónica de historia*, 4 (2013), pp. 375–388.

12 Bustos Rodríguez, M., 'Comercio y comerciantes en la Andalucía del Antiguo Régimen: estado de la cuestión y perspectivas', *Obradoiro de Historia Moderna*, no 17 (2008), pp. 43–76.

13 J. Everaert, *De internationale en koloniale handel der Vlaamse firma's te Cadiz, 1670–1700* (Brugges: De Tempel, 1973); M. Bustos Rodríguez, 'Hacer de la necesidad virtud: el comercio textil de la Andalucía Atlántica con América en el siglo XVIII', *Estudis*, 36 (2010), pp. 87–130; A. González Enciso, 'El comercio en la España interior en la época moderna', *Obradoiro de Historia Moderna*, no. 17 (2008), pp. 15–42.

14 H. Blumer, *El Interaccionismo simbólico, perspectiva y método* (Barcelona: Hora D.L., 1982).

15 A. Crespo Solana, 'Diasporas and the Integration of Merchant Colonies: Flemish and Dutch Network in Early Modern Spain', *Le Verger – bouquet V*, janvier 2014.

16 R. Noë, Introduction to *The Evolution of Cooperation and Trading*, ESF EUROCORES programme, (Strasbourg: European Science Foundation, 2011).

17 J.B. Owens, *'By My Absolute Royal Authority'. Justice and the Castilian Commonwealth at the Beginning of the First Global Age* (New York: University of Rochester Press, 2005); A. Crespo Solana, 'Dutch Merchant Networks and the Trade with the Hispanic Port Cities in the Atlantic (1648–1778)', in N. Böttcher, B. Hausberger and A. Ibarra, (coords.), *Redes y negocios globales en el mundo ibérico, siglos XVI–XVIII* (México: Iberoamericana Vervuert, El Colegio de México, 2011), pp. 107–143; E. Erickson and P. Bearman, 'Routes into Networks: The Structure of English Trade in the East Indies, 1601–1833', 2004, *Working Papers, Institute for Social and Economic Research and Policy* (ISERP Working Papers, 04–07) (http://hdl.handle.net/10022/AC:P:969, accessed 3 January 2014); W. Ashworth, *Customs and Excise: Trade, Production and Consumption in England, 1640–1845* (Oxford: Oxford University Press, 2003), pp. 176–8; A.E.C. McCants, 'Exotic Goods, Popular Consumption, and the Standard of Living: Thinking about Globalization in the Early Modern World', *Journal of World History*, 18, 4 (2007), pp. 433–462.

18 A. Crespo Solana, 'Dutch Merchant Networks', pp. 107–143.

19 A, Carrasco González, *Comerciantes y casas de negocios en Cádiz, 1650–1700* (Cádiz: Universidad de Cádiz, 1997).

20 CrespoDynCoopNet Data Collections http://hdl.handle.net/10261/28394 (accessed January 2014).

21 Archivo Histórico Provincial de Cádiz (AHPC) Protocolos notariales, 15/3630, fols. 919 y v. Cádiz, 18 diciembre de 1753. Préstamo de la compañía Timmerman, Hasenclever y co a Juan Alvárez como representante en Cádiz de la Real Compañía de Granada.

22 Archivo General de Indias de Sevilla (AGI) Arribadas, 12, Memorial del cacao, 11 de mayo de 1728.

23 D. Hancok, *Citizens of the World: London Merchants and the Integration of the British Atlantic Community, 1735–1785* (Cambridge: Cambridge University Press, 1997).

24 A. Crespo Solana, 'Dutch Merchant Networks', pp. 110–140.

25 M.N. García Fernández, *Comunidad extranjera y puerto privilegiado: Los británicos en Cádiz durante el siglo XVIII* (Cádiz: Universidad de Cádiz, 2005), p. 138.

26 D. Hancock, *Citizens*, pp. 45–63.

27 AHPC, Protocolos notariales, 9/1600, Cádiz, enero 1737.

28 R. Court, 'Januensis Ergo Mercator: Trust and Enforcement in the Business Correspondence of the Brignole family', *The Sixteenth Century Journal*, 35:4 (2004), pp. 987–1003; J.B. Owens, 'Social Networks of Milanese Merchants in Sixteenth-Century Castile', in R. Mukherjee, ed., *Networks in the First Global Age, 1400–1800* (Delhi: Primus Book, 2011), pp. 159–183.

102   *Ana Crespo Solana*

29 See J. Korb and J. Heinze, 'The Ecology of Social Life: A Synthesis', in J. Korb and J. Heinze (eds.), *Ecology of Social Evolution* (Berlin, Heidelberg: Springer Verlag, 2008), pp. 245–260.
30 J.V. Roitma, *The Same but Different? Intercultural Trade and the Sephardim (1595–1640)* (Leiden: Brill, 2011).
31 A. Crespo Solana, 'Dutch Merchants Networks', pp. 143–160; A. Crespo Solana, 'A Network-Based Merchant Empire', in G. Oostindie and J.V. Roitman (coords.), *Dutch Atlantic Connection: Linking Empires, Bridging Borders, 1680–1800* (Leiden: Brill, 2014), pp. 139–158.
32 Data model explained in: E. Pérez Asensio, I. del Bosque Gonzalez, R. Maestre Martinez, J.M. Sánchez-Crespo Camacho and A. Crespo Solana, 'Modelling and Implementation of a Spatio-Temporal Historic GIS', in A. Crespo Solana and D. Alonso García (coords.), *Self-Organizing Networks and GIS Tools. Cases of Use for the Study of Trading Coopeation (1400–1800)*; *Journal of Knowledge Management, Economics and Information Technology* (June 2012), pp.145–190.
33 Owens, J.B. 'Towards a geographically-integrated, connected world history: employing Geographic Information Systems (GIS)', *History Compass*, 5 (6) (2007), pp. 2014–2040.
34 N. Böttcher, B. Hausberger and I. Ibarra (coords.), Introdución, p. 14.
35 R. Pieper and P. Schmidt (eds.), Introduction to *Latin American and the Atlantic World/El Mundo Atlántico y América Latina, Essays in Honor of Horst Pietschmann* (Köln: Böhlau Verlag, 2005).
36 F.W. Boal and D.N. Livingstone (eds.), *The Behavioral Environment. Essays in Reflection, Application and Re-Evaluation* (London and New York: Routledge, 1989).
37 J.B. Owens, 'Towards a Geographically-Integrated, Connected World History: Employing Geographic Information Systems (GIS)', p. 2020.
38 M. Wachowicz, D. Orellana, A. Crespo Solana, J.B. Owens and M.A. Bernabé, 'A Spatial Representation for Reasoning about the Atlantic Commercial Routes of the 18th Century', *Paper presented in 33rd annual conference program of the Social Science History Association, Session: Contributory GIS For Historical Research*, Miami, October 23–26, 2008.
39 Ibid.
40 A. Crespo Solana, *El comercio marítimo entre Amsterdam y Cádiz (1713–1778)* (Madrid: Banco de España, no. 40, 2000).
41 CrespoDynCoopNet Data Collections, http://hdl.handle.net/10261/28394 (accessed January 2014).
42 W. Kasper, 'Economía Espacial', pp. 46–49. M.A. Scheifler, *Economía y Espacio. Un análisis de las pautas de asentamiento espacial de las actividades económicas* (Bilbao: Universidad del Pais Vasco, 1991).
43 J.W. Veluwenkamp, *Ondernemersgedrag op de Hollandse stapelmarkt in the tijd van de Republiek. De Amsterdamse handelsfirma Jan Isaac de Neufville & comp. 1730–1764* (Meppel: Krips Repro, 1981).
44 R. Pieper and P. Lesiak, 'Redes mercantiles entre el Atlántico y el Mediterráneo en los inicios de la Guerra de los 30 Años', A. Ibarra and G. de Valle Pavón (coords.), *Redes sociales e instituciones comerciales en el imperio español, siglos XVII al XIX* (México: Instituto Mora, 2007), pp. 19–39.
45 AHPC, p.n, 9/1576, fols. 591 y ss. Cádiz, 21 de julio de 1713.
46 AHPC, p.n, 5/996, fols. 10–11v, Cádiz, 12 enero de 1723. Snellincq granted Benito Berbruggen, another Fleming from Seville,, the authority to perform the duties of the post and collect the gains.
47 AHPC, Protocolos notariales, 5/1001, Última voluntad de Gerardo Beumer, Cádiz, 1728.
48 S. Wasserman and K. Faust, *Social Network Analysis, Methods and Application* (Cambridge: Cambridge University Press, 1997).
49 AHPC, Protocolos notariales, 9/1581, fols. 74 y v. Cádiz, 22 de febrero de 1718. Jorge Balde, factor in Cádiz for the Amsterdam company Viuda e hijo de Juan de Balde,

received notification from the executor of his brother and partner in Cádiz, Jorge Balde, that the latter had left 12 paintings owned by him of the *Life of the Lord* with Flanders pine frames at the house of the merchant Flora Hercq.

50 StA, notariele archiven, 5821A/556, Amsterdam, 14 de julio de 1716. Letter of Philippe Couturier, kooplieden in Amsterdam.

51 R.J. Lewicki, D.J. McAllister and R.J. Bies, 'Trust and Distrust: New Relationships and Realities', *Academy of Management Review*, 23 (1998), pp. 438–458. P. Dasgupta, 'Trust and Cooperation Among Economic Agents', *Philosophical Transaction of the Royal Society*, B 364 (2009), pp. 3301–3309, doi:10.1098/rstb.2009.0123.

52 K. Sigmund, *The Calculus of Selfishness* (Princeton: Princeton University Press, 2010).

53 M.C.A.E. Engels, *Merchants, Interlopers, Seamen and Corsairs. The "Flemish" Community in Livorno and Genoa (1615–1635)* (Hilversum: Verloren, 1997); J.W. Veluwenkamp, *Archangel. Nederlandse ondernemers in Rusland, 1550–1785* (Amsterdam: Uitgeverij Balans, 2000).

54 A. Crespo Solana, *Comercio marítimo*, pp. 32–36; J.I. Israel, 'The Phases of the Dutch Straatvaart (1590–1713): A Chapter in the Economic History of the Mediterranean', *Tijdschrift loor Zeegeschiedenis*, 99 (1986), pp. 189–212; K. Heeringa, *Bronnen tot de Geschiedenis van den Levantschen Handel, 1661–1726*, vol. 2, ('S Gravenhague: Martines Nijhoff, 1917); J.G. Nanninga (ed.), *Bronnen tot de Geschiedenis van den Levantschen handel, 1727–1765* ('S Gravenhague: Martines Nijhoff, 1952).

55 Nationaal Archief, Archief van de Directie van de Levantse Handel en de Navigatie in de Middellandse Zee (1614), 1625–1826 (1828), 173, II, Letter in Cádiz, 22 December 1767.

56 AHPC. P.n. 5354; 2/372, fol. 5; Notaría 16, 3765, fols. 140–142.

57 NA, Archief van de Levantse Handel, 173 II; AHPC, p.n. 3763–3771.

58 Loan between Livino B. Van den Broeck and Francisco Wulff, en 1748. A.H.P.C, P.N, 23/5338, fols. 73–74v. Data and information about Dutch trade with America: J. Postma and V. Enthoven (eds.), *Riches from Atlantic Commerce: Dutch Transatlantic Trade and Shipping, 1585–1817* (Leiden: Brill, 2003).

59 G. Oostindie and J.V. Roitman, eds., *Dutch Atlantic Connection*.

Bibliography

Álvaro Estramiana, J.L. (ed.), *Fundamentos sociales del comportamiento humano*, Barcelona: Editorial UOC, 2003.

Ashworth, W., *Customs and Excise: Trade, Production and Consumption in England, 1640–1845*, Oxford: Oxford University Press, 2003.

Basch, L., Glick Schiller, N. and Szanton Blanc, S., *Nations Bounded. Transnational Projects, Postcolonial Predicaments and Deterritorialized Nation-States*, London: Gordon and Breach Science Publishers, 1994.

Blumer, H., *El Interaccionismo simbólico, perspectiva y método*, Barcelona: Hora D.L., 1982).

Boal, F.W. and Livingstone, D.N. (eds.), *The Behavioral Environment. Essays in Reflection, Application and Re-Evaluation*, London and New York: Routledge, 1989.

Bustos Rodríguez, M. 'Hacer de la necesidad virtud: el comercio textil de la Andalucía Atlántica con América en el siglo XVIII', *Estudis*, 36 (2010), pp. 87–130.

———, 'Comercio y comerciantes en la Andalucía del Antiguo Régimen: estado de la cuestión y perspectivas', *Obradoiro de Historia Moderna*, no. 17 (2008), pp. 43–76.

Carrasco González, G., *Comerciantes y casas de negocios en Cádiz, 1650–1700*, Cádiz: Universidad de Cádiz, 1997.

Court, R.J., 'Ergo Mercator: Trust and Enforcement in the Business Correspondence of the Brignole family', *The Sixteenth Century Journal*, vol. 35, 4 (2004), pp. 987–1003.

Crespo Solana, A. (coord.), *Comunidades transnacionales. Colonias de mercaderes extranjeros en el Mundo Atlántico (1500–1830)*, Madrid: Doce Calles, 2010.

————, 'A Network-Based Merchant Empire', in Oostindie, G. and Roitman, J.V. (coords.), *Dutch Atlantic Connection: Linking Empires, Bridging Borders, 1680–1800*, Leiden: Brill, 2014, pp. 139–158.

————, 'Diasporas and the Integration of Merchant Colonies: Flemish and Dutch Network in Early Modern Spain', *Le Verger – bouquet V*, janvier 2014.

————, *El comercio marítimo entre Amsterdam y Cádiz (1713–1778)*, Madrid: Banco de España, no. 40, 2000.

————, 'Dutch Merchant Networks and the Trade with the Hispanic Port Cities in the Atlantic (1648–1778)', Böttcher, N., Hausberger, B. and Ibarra, A. (coords.), *Redes y negocios globales en el mundo ibérico, siglos XVI–XVIII*, México: Iberoamericana Vervuert, El Colegio de México, 2011, pp. 107–143.

Crespo Solana, A. and Alonso García, D. (coords.), 'Self-organizing Networks and GIS tools. Cases of Use for the Study of Trading Cooperation (1400–1800).' *Journal of Knowledge Management, Economics and Information Technology*, special issue, June (2012).

Engels, M-Ch., *Merchants, Interlopers, Seamen and Corsairs. The 'Flemish' Community in Livorno and Genoa (1615–1635)*, Hilversum: Verloren, 1997.

Erickson, E. and Bearman, P., 'Routes into Networks: The Structure of English Trade in the East Indies, 1601–1833', *Working Papers, Institute for Social and Economic Research and Policy* (ISERP Working Papers, 04–07), 2004, http://hdl.handle.net/10022/AC:P:969, (accessed 3 January 2014).

Everaert, J., *De internationale en koloniale handel der Vlaamse firma's te Cadiz, 1670–1700*, Brugges: De Tempel, 1973.

Fujita, M., Krugman, P. and Venables, A.J., *The Spatial Economy: Cities, Regions, and International Trade*, Cambridge: MIT Press, 1999.

García Fernández, M.N., *Comunidad extranjera y puerto privilegiado: Los británicos en Cádiz durante el siglo XVIII*, Cádiz: Universidad de Cádiz, 2005.

González Enciso, A., 'El comercio en la España interior en la época moderna', *Obradoiro de Historia Moderna*, no. 17 (2008), pp. 15–42.

Hancock, D. *Citizens of the World: London Merchants and the Integration of the British Atlantic Community, 1735–1785*, Cambridge: Cambridge University Press, 1997.

Heeringa, K., *Bronnen tot de Geschiedenis van de Levantschen Handel: Tweede Deel 1661–1726*, vol. 2., 'S Gravenhague: Martinus Nijhoff, 1917.

Herrero Sánchez, M., 'La red consular europea y la diplomacia mercantil en la edad moderna', in Iglesias, J.J., Pérez García, R.M. and Fernández Chaves, M.F. (eds.), *Comercio y Cultura en la Edad Moderna*, Sevilla: Editorial Universidad de Sevilla, 2015, pp. 121–151.

Heylighen, F., 'Complexity and Self-Organization', in Bates, M.J. and Nyles Maack, M., (eds.), *Encyclopedia of Library and Information Sciences* (London: Routledge, 2008), pp. 1–20.

Israel, J.I. 'The Phases of the Dutch Straatvaart (1590–1713): A Chapter in the Economic History of the Mediterranean', *Tijdschrift loor Zeegeschiedenis*, 99 (1986), pp. 189–212.

Karl, S., *The Calculus of Selfishness*, Princeton: Princeton University Press, 2010.

Kasper, W., 'Economía espacial', in Henderson, D.R. (dir.), *Enciclopedia Fortune de Economía*, Barcelona: Ediciones Folio, 1999, pp. 46–49.

Korb, J. and Heinze, J. (eds.), 'The Ecology of Social Life: A Synthesis', in *Ecology of Social Evolution*, Berlin, Heidelberg: Springer–Verlag, 2008, pp. 245–260.

Lewicki, R.J., McAllister, D.J. and Bies, R.J., 'Trust and Distrust: New Relationships and Realities', *Academy of Management Review*, 23 (1998), pp. 438–458.

McCants, A.E.C., 'Exotic Goods, Popular Consumption, and the Standard of Living: Thinking about Globalization in the Early Modern World', *Journal of World History*, 18:4 (2007), pp. 433–462.

Mills, C.W., *La imaginación sociológica*, Mexico City: Fondo de Cultura Económica 1961.

Mukherjee, R. ed., *Oceans Connect. Reflections on Water Worlds Across Time and Space*, Delhi: Primus Book, 2013.

Nanninga, J.G. (ed.), *Bronnen tot de Geschiedenis van den Levantschen handel, 1727–1765*, Nederland: 'S Gravenhague, La Haya, 1952.

Noë, R., Introduction to *The Evolution of Cooperation and Trading*, ESF EUROCORES programme, Strasbourg: ESF, 2011.

Owens, J.B., *"By My Absolute Royal Authority": Justice and the Castilian Commonwealth at the Beginning of the First Global Age*, New York: University of Rochester Press, 2005.

———, 'Social Networks of Milanese Merchants in Sixteenth-Century Castile', in Mukherjee, R. (ed.), *Networks in the First Global Age, 1400–1800*, Delhi: Primus Book, 2011, pp. 159–183.

———, 'Towards a Geographically-integrated, Connected World History: Employing Geographic Information Systems (GIS)', *History Compass*, 5 (6) (2007), pp. 2014–2040.

Partha D., 'Trust and Cooperation Among Economic Agents', *Philosophical Transaction of the Royal Society*, B 364 (2009), pp. 3301–3309, doi:10.1098/rstb.2009.0123.

Pérez Asensio, E., Bosque, I., del Maestre, R., Sánchez-Crespo Camacho, J.M. and Crespo Solana, A., 'Modelling and Implementation of a Spatio-Temporal Historic GIS', in Crespo Solana, A. and Alonso García, D. (coords.), 'Self-Organizing Networks and GIS Tools. Cases of Use for the Study of Trading Cooperation (1400–1800)', *Journal of Knowledge Management, Economics and Information Technology* (June 2012), pp. 145–190.

Picazo Muntaner, A., 'Rivalidades en las redes de poder de Manila: el golpe contra el gobernador Diego de Salcedo', *El Futuro del Pasado: revista electrónica de historia*, 4 (2013), pp. 375–388.

Pieper, R. and Schmidt, P. (eds.), Introduction to *Latin American and the Atlantic World/ El Mundo Atlántico y América Latina, Essays in honor of Horst Pietschmann*, Köln: Böhlau Verlag, 2005.

Pieper R. and Lesiak, P., 'Redes Mercantiles entre el Atlántico y el Mediterráneo en los Inicios de la Guerra de los 30 Años', in Ibarra, A. and de Valle Pavón, G. (coords.), *Redes sociales e instituciones comerciales en el imperio español, siglos XVII al XIX*, México: Instituto Mora, 2007, pp. 19–39.

Postma, J. and Enthoven, V. (eds.), *Riches from Atlantic Commerce: Dutch Transatlantic Trade and Shipping, 1585–1817*, Leiden: Brill, 2003.

Ringrose, D., *Expansion and Global Interaction, 1200–1700*, San Diego: University of California; New York: Addison Wesley Longman, 2001.

Roitma, J.V., *The same but different? Intercultural Trade and the Sephardim (1595–1640)*, Leiden: Brill, 2011.

Scheifler, M.A., *Economía y Espacio. Un análisis de las pautas de asentamiento espacial de las actividades económicas*. Bilbao: Editorial de la Universidad del País Vasco, 1991.

Veluwenkamp, J.W. *Ondernemersgedrag op de Hollandse stapelmarkt in de tijd van de Republiek. De Amsterdamse handelsfirma Jan Isaac de Neufville & comp. 1730–1764*, Groningen: RijksUniversiteit Groningen, 1981.

———, *Archangel. Nederlandse ondernemers in Rusland, 1550–1785*, Amsterdam: Uitgeverij Balans, 2000.

Wachowicz, M., Orellana, D., Crespo Solana, A., Owens, J.B. and Bernabé, M.A., 'A Spatial Representation for Reasoning about the Atlantic Commercial Routes of the 18th Century', *Paper presented in 33rd annual conference program of the Social Science History Association, Session: Contributory GIS for Historical Research*, Miami, October 23–26, 2008.

Wasserman, S. and Faust, K., *Social Network Analysis, Methods and Application*, Cambridge: Cambridge University Press, 1997.

Part II

The social composition of networks

Cultural identities versus transnationality

5 Adaptive strategies

French and Flemish merchant communities in Seville as connectors of European and American markets (1570–1650)

Eberhard Crailsheim

At the beginning of the so-called European expansion in the fifteenth century, southern European navigators explored the Atlantic. When they encountered the closest Atlantic islands, some daring merchants saw their agricultural potential and started to exploit them. At the peak of the European discovery of the Atlantic, when Europeans discovered the American continent, it was southern Europeans who led the way, especially the Genoese and some individuals from the Iberian Peninsula. It was only in the sixteenth century that explorers, sailors, and merchants from north-western Europe also ventured to travel these waters in significant numbers. Owing to the Iberian head start, the English, French and Dutch/Flemish states could, at first, neither compete in the founding of colonies nor offer their merchants the same opportunities. Consequently, many merchants from these north-western shores, not willing to abstain from the new American market, proceeded along alternative routes. They saw their chance either by conducting pirate raids along Spanish trading routes or by smuggling in America with the help of natives and Castilians. A third option was to access America legally through connections with Castilian merchants at the central trading hub of the Spanish Empire: Seville.

From very early on, Seville was the only Spanish port for American trade.[1] Situated about 80 km inland, it was protected from enemy attacks from the sea but was still well connected with the Atlantic via the Guadalquivir River. In 1503, following the Portuguese model, the *Casa de la Contratación* (House of Trade) was established, and it was given authority over American trade. In 1543, a consulate was founded as a corporate association for all merchants engaged in the American trade, and whose main role was to defend their interests. In general, only Castilians were allowed to trade with America and become members of this body, which excluded the crowns of Aragón and Portugal on the Iberian Peninsula (Portugal was united under the Spanish king between 1580 and 1640, but maintained its own very different colonial system), as well as all other foreigners. If north-western Europeans wanted to trade legally with Spanish America, they had to do so from Seville and they had to do so indirectly, through Castilian merchants.[2]

As early as the late Middle Ages, Seville was an attractive city for merchants,[3] but it was only with the discovery of the rich silver mines in the viceroyalties of

Peru (Potosí) and New Spain (Zacatecas) in the 1540s that the city was almost overrun by foreign merchants. By then, Seville was the heart of the early modern Atlantic economy, and foreign merchants set its rhythm. At least that was/is the judgment of both contemporary seventeenth-century analysts (*arbitristas*), such as Sancho de Moncada,[4] and twenty-first-century historians such as Stanley and Barbara Stein or Antonio Domínguez Ortiz.[5] The heyday of foreigners in Seville was arguably between around 1580 and 1640, when the plague hit the city. Indeed, an examination of the largest business concerns engaged with Seville's colonial trade in 1640 indicates that 55 per cent belonged to merchants of foreign origin (first-, second-, or sometimes third-generation immigrants in Seville), while only about 45 per cent at most were Castilian.[6] The penetration of Seville's merchant society by foreigners and the subsequent entanglement of both groups, seems to have been acute.

This chapter focuses on the protagonists of the European Atlantic trade who connected the Americas with the north-western European market. The two key nations (in the sense of a corporative mercantile organisation of people of common origin and language) in Seville regarding this connection were the Flemish and the French. This chapter investigates their specific commercial and social behaviour and their private and business networks. It will discuss the institutional consolidation of the two merchant colonies in Seville as well as their various assimilation patterns, while also examining the size of both communities, their marriage policies, business preferences and susceptibility to political events. Finally, it will assess collective commercial and social strategies based on cultural factors such as homophily, trust and shared mental models.

The Flemish nation

Merchants from the Netherlands, which since 1522 had been part of the Spanish Crown, can be located in Seville as early as the middle of the sixteenth century.[7] At the beginning of the Eighty Years' War, in 1568, the population of the northern regions of the Netherlands, where Protestantism had spread, revolted against the Spanish government and in 1581 declared their independence (the 'Dutch'). The inhabitants of the southern regions, however, remained Catholic and loyal to Spain (the 'Flemings'). The war that followed raged until 1648 and had a military as well as an economic dimension. It brought enormous suffering and deprivation, devastation and mass migration and it caused a strong transformation of the economic structures. A prominent event of this war was the siege of Antwerp between 1584 and 1585, which was to have serious consequences. Antwerp, buzzing with trade and acting as the residence of a large number of rich merchants, was the north's dominant commercial harbour. The exhausting siege, the subsequent sack and the politics of the victorious Spanish armies drove many merchants away. The Protestants fled to the north, whereas many Catholics headed south. Before 1585, only about a dozen Flemish merchants lived in Seville. Afterwards, however, their number soared to about 200 and this rose even further until the end of the century.[8]

A sample of 1,700 notarial documents from Seville yields a total 'census' of 1,106 foreign merchants in the city. The sample covers about three to four months (first half of the year) of four different years (1580, 1600, 1620 and 1640), mainly from the notary offices V, XII, XVI and XXIV.[9] Differentiating between foreigner and native in the seventeenth century is difficult, because, as T. Herzog states, first it depended of the situation, and second there existed categories in between 'foreigner' and 'native'.[10] For this study, foreigners are considered those who are not born in Castile, as well as those born in Castile but with foreign parents (these so-called *jenízaros* were officially considered Castilians but frequently faced grave bureaucratic hindrances).[11] Focusing on the origin of the merchants, moreover, naturalised merchants (equal rights as Castilians) and those with the status of a citizen (equal rights and obligation in the municipality as fellow citizens) are also considered foreigners.[12] A clear differentiation between the merchants based on their origin is a difficult task and it is hard to tell a Dutchmen from a Fleming if he deliberately stated to be from Flanders – something that happened frequently during the Eighty Years' War.[13] Therefore, the identification of the origin of the foreigners is based on the indication in the respective files as well as using the data provided in the naturalisation files of the *Archivo General de Indias* (AGI);[14] in addition, secondary sources were consulted.[15]

Overall, 37 per cent of the merchants of the sample, the largest group, were Flemish (including 24 Dutchmen). In close second place were the Portuguese, with 25 per cent, followed by the Genoese (17 per cent), the French (9 per cent), the British (5 per cent), other Italians (4 per cent) and the Germans (3 per cent). The isolation of the data corresponding to four selected years (1580, 1600, 1620 and 1640) makes the trend self-evident: over time, the proportion of Flemish in Seville's foreign colony rose from 30 per cent in 1580 and 27 per cent in 1600, to 42 and 40 per cent, respectively, in 1620 and 1640.[16]

The devastation of the war in the Netherlands, the close political relations between Spain and Flanders and the commercial attraction of the American market encouraged many Flemish merchants to send their sons or other young relatives to Seville to learn the trade and, eventually, become the representatives of their commercial houses there. In the early seventeenth century, these apprenticeships were in such demand that the 'host' merchants could charge up to 1,000 pesos per apprentice.[17]

Dutchmen and Flemings were different only in terms of religion and political affiliation. Hence, due to their obvious similarities, for example in their appearance and language, one could expect that Flemish merchants in Seville had to struggle with the mistrust and even the hostility of the locals. However, this does not seem to have been the case, and the integration of the Flemish into Seville's society was quite successful. They avoided living in separate quarters but had their houses in various parts of the city. For their servants, they did not only employ their countrymen but Spaniards as well, and they also adopted the custom of buying slaves, which was not common in the Netherlands. They invested parts of their fortune in the city and its hinterland, building houses, running pensions and hostels, and cultivating vineyards, olive groves and pastures. For the transmission of their property, they adopted the Spanish institution of the *mayorazgo* (i.e. primogeniture), primarily as a way to keep their landed property undivided.[18]

Religion was one of the key causes for the war in the Netherlands, and it was also a critical issue in Seville. In the 1560s, many Flemings were persecuted by the Inquisition for not attending religious services and for their lack of religiosity. Toward the end of the century, however, the situation had changed and the Flemings were demonstrating their faith in a variety of ways. They founded the religious brotherhood (*cofradía*) of San Andrés, which had its own chapel, and created charitable foundations; for example, a hospital. In addition, they maintained a hospice, an asylum and their own archive – all of which was funded through a levy on their trade. The brotherhood of San Andrés can be seen as a tool for the mutual social, financial and spiritual assistance of the Flemish community in Seville, but at the same time, it also facilitated the integration of the Flemings into Spanish society. The Flemings willingly paid for expensive funerals according to local customs, donated generously to the local clergy and arranged requiem masses for the deceased. Rich merchants even founded their own chapels and many Flemings gave their children to the convents or joined the local church, in which they held important offices.[19] Moreover, the Flemings not only displayed their loyalty to the Catholic Church but also to the Spanish Crown. They contributed to the cost of the Spanish army and raised their own company of infantry. Many young Flemings from Seville became officers of the Spanish army;[20] for example, Diego Sirman[21] and Melchor de Haze.[22] In general, it can be pointed out, on one hand, that the Flemings formed some sort of micro-society which strengthened the internal cohesion, helped to maintain Flemish networks and contributed to the success of the Flemish merchants in Seville,[23] and on the other, they gradually integrated into the Spanish society of the city, establishing strong connections with local elites.[24]

Whereas the first generation of Flemings in Seville were mainly interested in furthering their commercial careers, their progeny – already integrated into the local society – eagerly pursued aristocratic titles (*hidalguía*)[25] – for example, Don Luis Clut, Don Diego Sirman and Francisco Helman[26] – and public offices in the city council, the Inquisition and the orders of Santiago and Calatrava. Some even became pre-eminent artistic and cultural patrons, such as Nicolas Antonio Nicolas.[27] For many Flemish merchants, the wealth accumulated through risky trade transactions was only a stepping stone to the social recognition of their family and the integration of their children into the higher ranks of Sevilian society. Their final goal was to accumulate land and titles of nobility with their attached social and commercial advantages, especially social privileges, political power and tax exemptions.[28]

In 1611, the Flemish community in Seville founded its own consulate, which emerged as an offshoot of the brotherhood of San Andrés. While the 'nation' was a proper elitist corporative mercantile organisation of Flemish and Dutch merchants who were residents and citizens of Seville, the consulate was an administrative institution that rather supervised and supported the activities of transient

Flemings and Dutchmen in the city.[29] The consul received an annual salary of 400 ducats from the Spanish king (being the Count of Flanders at that time). The consul represented the interests of the members of the consulate before the local authorities and settled conflicts between one another. Even though the consulate was officially responsible for the 'German and Flemish nation,' it was the Flemish merchants who dictated its rules and controlled the key offices, especially the position of the consul.[30]

Taking a closer look at the residences of a sample of 314 Flemings who feature in the aforementioned notarial records (offices V, XII, XVI and XXIV), 214 (68 per cent) were residents (including citizens) of Seville or lived in Lower Andalusia (the lowlands of the Guadalquivir valley). This means that almost one-third of the Flemings who feature in the notarial files did not reside permanently in Lower Andalusia.[31] Among the two-thirds that did, some had settled and integrated into local society after successfully seeking their fortune in the city; others resided for just a short while in the city and then moved on; others settled down in Seville but left many years later, without having integrated. Still, the records reveal a certain continuity of family names: many of those who appear in 1600 re-emerge in 1620 (15 per cent), and several of the names featured in 1620 are also attested in 1640 (11 per cent). Overall, in 1580, 1600 and 1620, almost two-thirds of the Flemings on record had their more or less long-term residence in Lower Andalusia, while the remaining third came only briefly to Seville or simply sent a representative while they remained in Antwerp and other places in Flanders. In 1640, the percentage of Flemings living permanently in Lower Andalusia had risen to 75 per cent.

The French nation

In the fifteenth century, Seville was only a port of call for French merchants on their way to the more interesting Mediterranean ports. In the sixteenth century, however, many French merchants established their trading houses in Lower Andalusia, and Seville became the most important French commercial outpost in Spain.[32] The number of Frenchmen grew significantly, a trend that was to continue during the following century.[33] The French formed the largest foreign community in Spain, where they pursued all sorts of occupations,[34] and even though A. Domínguez Ortiz states that during the seventeenth century almost none of the wealthy businessmen that came to Spain did so with the intention of settling down there permanently,[35] many French merchants in Seville became enormously rich. Most of them came from Vitré, Saint-Malo, Bayonne, Rouen, Bordeaux and Nantes[36] and took up residence in Lower Andalusia.[37] In 1580, the records show 27 French merchants in Sanlúcar de Barrameda, at the mouth of Seville's estuary,[38] and in the following years their numbers grew even further (the effects of political changes on the French merchant community in Seville will be addressed later).[39] In 1620, 65 members of the French community in Seville addressed a letter to the Spanish king, and, in 1625,[40] 11 merchants from Seville and 12 from Cadiz wrote a petition to the French ambassador.[41] These numbers indicate that a number of Frenchmen lived permanently in Lower Andalusia during the period under consideration. The aforementioned sample of 1,106 foreigners in Seville (1570 to 1650) includes 87 Frenchmen, around 9 per cent of the total, in fourth place after the Flemish, the Portuguese, and the Genoese. Between 1580 and 1600, they grew from around 6 to 7 per cent in 1580 to around 14 per cent in 1620. In 1640, their number had dropped and they amounted to only around 4 per cent of the foreign community.

The French consulate emerged much earlier than the Flemish one, and the first French consul was appointed as early as 1578.[42] Whereas the Flemish consul, as a subject of the Spanish Crown, was appointed by the Spanish monarch, the French consul was chosen by the French king. The role of the French consul was to represent the local French nation, acting as a spokesman for his co-nationals before the local authorities, and to judge quarrels between French subjects.[43] In 1604, plans were launched to establish a general consul for the whole of Andalusia, but this project was never realised.[44] In the seventeenth century, the French consuls in Seville had a pleasant lifestyle, not unlike those of high Crown officials and the upper Castilian nobility.[45] For the accommodation of their compatriots, the French nation owned and managed fifteen hostels in Sanlúcar de Barrameda in the early seventeenth century, more than the Flemish or the English. In addition, the French nation had the right to levy a special tax on French ships in order to maintain their own charitable foundation, the brotherhood of Saint Louis.[46] Even though the Frenchmen in Lower Andalusia did not have their own military unit like the Flemings, they also engaged in military services for the Spanish king, for example by joining the Flemish company from Cadiz.[47] The wealthy French merchant, Antonio de Sandier, for example, held the position of infantry captain.[48]

Of the 87 verified Frenchmen in the records between 1570 and 1650, 50 lived permanently in Lower Andalusia (57 per cent). While that percentage was still low in 1600 (39 per cent), in 1620 it had risen to 55 per cent, and in 1640 to 90 per cent.[49] By 1640, most of the Frenchmen featured in the investigated notary records were long-term residents. About 30 per cent of them were already in the records from 1620, which is strong evidence for continuity. In this regard, the French present much more variation (between 39 and 90 per cent) than the Flemish (between around 65 and 75 per cent). Volatility was, therefore, much more significant among the Frenchmen, whereas the Flemings were a more permanent element of Sevilian society.

The orientation of private networks

On a technical level, networks are composed of nodes and edges. In social networks, nodes are, generally, people, and edges are the relationships between them.[50] Whereas in commercial networks, these relationships consist, for instance, of sales, credit obligations and other agreements between business partners, private networks are based on kinship and friendship connections. Owing to the lack of family archives pertaining to the merchants under examination, the only available source for the reconstruction of their private networks is the official documentation left by some of them in the Archivo General de Indias.[51] These files include information about those rich foreign merchants in Seville who applied for a letter of naturalisation.[52] Between 1570 and 1650, 313 foreigners applied for naturalisation; 76 among them were Flemings and 25 Frenchmen. The letter of naturalisation gave the owner the right to participate directly in the American trade without having to resort to a Castilian intermediary. The requisites for naturalisation were to be able to certify more than 10 years of residency in the Kingdom of Castile (in 1608, this was extended to 20 years), to possess a certain amount of property and to be married to a Castilian woman. The latter, especially, should have guaranteed the social integration of foreigners.[53]

The merchants' applications provide much detail about the marriage strategies of wealthy French and Flemish merchants. The daughters of foreigners who were born in Castile were, according to the *ius solis*, considered Castilians.[54] They were known as *jenízaras* and played an important role in the establishment of family networks in Seville.[55] Marriage to a *jenízara* was a valid option for those who applied for naturalisation. Of the Flemings, 54 per cent wed Castilian women for whom no foreign ancestry could be attested, while the remaining 46 per cent married *jenízaras* of Flemish descent. Of the French, 64 per cent married Castilian women and 36 per cent married *jenízaras*. Yet, not all of the *jenízaras* who married Frenchmen were of French descent; in fact, only half of them (18 per cent) had French parents, while the other half had Flemish ancestors.

For both nations, ties to their compatriots were important, and often private and business connections were very closely interwoven. The family Antiñaque is a good example: the Frenchman Pedro de Antiñaque, who had probably come to Seville from Salers in the Auvergne in 1569, and his wife Beatris Castro had five children. Three of his daughters wed foreign merchants: the Frenchman Pedro de la Farxa married Antonia de Antiñaque (before 1619), his compatriot Pedro de Alogue married Beatris de Casto de Antiñaque (1631) and the Genoese Juan Ayrolo married Maria de Antiñaque (before 1621); all three were eminent merchants in Seville. When Pedro de la Farxa died, he gave power of attorney and tutelage over his children to his wife but also to his compatriot and brother-in-law Pedro de Alogue. In addition, he gave the same power to two more of his co-nationals, the merchants Jacques Bules and Alberto Juan Treguarte. All of these merchants had been granted letters of naturalisation and did business with one other and with other merchants in Flanders. They can be considered the richest and most powerful French merchants in Seville (their trade volume in 1635 amounted to 631,947 ducats).[56] Similar cases can be found among the Flemish merchants, who also had both commercial and personal relationships with their compatriots.[57]

The lists of witnesses attached to the merchants' applications for naturalisation are another indicator of the social behaviour of foreign merchants in Seville and an important piece of evidence for the reconstruction of their social networks. Since each of these witnesses testified on behalf of the foreign merchant, it can be assumed that they were on good terms. Concerning the Flemish merchants, most foreign witnesses were Flemings or were of Flemish descent (i.e. *jenízaros*), followed at a distance by French and Italian witnesses. Of the French applicants, on the other hand, it was not their compatriots who were chosen most often as witnesses – not one single French witness could, in fact, be found – but the Flemish, who once more appear as the most common witnesses.[58]

Companies and family business

The data extracted from the notarial and commercial archives gives an accurate picture of the structure of the companies on which the merchants based their commercial relationships.[59] In most cases, all members belonged to the same nation. The Flemings were especially keen on channeling their business through long-term partnerships. During the period under consideration, they founded 26 companies in which only Flemish partners were involved. Most of these companies were active in 1620 and dealt with textiles. Often, larger companies specialised in a specific product, such as indigo, ginger, and, in particular, linen. Of the Flemish companies, eighteen can be considered family companies of different types. The brothers Pedro, Francisco and Nicolas Monel, who were of Flemish descent, for instance, traded and smuggled merchandise between Europe and America and worked together as brokers and middlemen for compatriots and wealthy French merchants who had no direct access to the rich American trade.[60] Other renowned examples of companies constituted by siblings in 1620 were the De Neves,[61] the Sirmans[62] and the Cluts.[63] A father-son structure can be shown for the Corbetes and the Arnaos (1600),[64] as well as in the Antonios[65] and the Coniques (1620).[66] More complex family connections were incorporated into the company structure with the Bibiens[67] and the Lemaires; members of the Lemaires resided in Seville and traded between the city, Holland, Zeeland and London.[68]

French merchants, on the other hand, were more reluctant to create long-term companies. Six French companies have been found, four of which were also family-based, for example the company created by the brothers Jorge and Carlos de Bues,[69] and that created by the cousins Jaques and Pedro Soming, both of whom were active in 1600.[70] The firm created by the brothers Antonio and Francisco de Sandier was, for its part, active in 1620.[71] Finally, the company founded by the brothers Niculas and Alonso Magon was active in 1640.[72] Aside from these 'national' companies, other companies in which several nations combined also existed. These were less common, but often also the largest, for example the company created by the Frenchman Guillermo Guillu and the Flemings Miguel Galle and Juan Tolinque in 1620. For at least seven years, this company was an active commercial link between the American and European markets, primarily dealing with indigo and ginger.[73] Overall, a few key observations are as follows: first, companies were most often created by members of the same nation; secondly, the family company was the predominant model; and thirdly, all companies whose members came from more than one foreign nation had some Flemish involvement.

The orientation of commercial networks

Once the composition of French and Flemish private networks and business companies is clear, the orientation of their commercial networks also becomes much more accessible. In the notarial records for the 4 years under investigation (1580, 1600, 1620 and 1640), 1,059 documents attest to some form of foreign involvement, resulting in a network of 3,488 nodes. Within these nodes, a sub-network emerges which contains all of the existing 314 Flemish nodes and the individuals connected to them, which adds up to 943 nodes.[74] Within this Flemish network (over the years), the prevailing non-Spanish business partners were other Flemings. In 1620, in fact, more than every third node (the ratio is 1:2.6) was of Flemish origin. The second most common nationality, however, changed: in 1580, it was the English, in 1600 the Italian, in 1620 the French and in 1640 the Portuguese.

The French network, for its part, was considerably smaller. It contained only 349 nodes, 87 of which were French. It was mostly made up of and dominated by non-compatriots. In the years 1600 and 1640,[75] the Flemings were the most numerous nodes in French networks. Only in 1620 did Frenchmen, instead of the Flemings, control French networks. In that year, the number of Frenchmen was the highest on record (56). In terms of percentage, French nodes amounted to 3.9 per cent of all nodes in 1620, compared to 2.0 per cent in 1600 and 1.5 per cent in 1640. In 1620, one in four of the businessmen included in French networks was a Frenchman (ratio 1:3.8). The following section will examine in detail what conclusions can be drawn from these figures.

Synthesis of results

The examination of the private and commercial connections of the members of these two nations has given us an interesting insight into their social strategies. Historiography has long emphasised that merchants tend to do business with people of the same origin, language, religion, family, etc.[76] Sociology has labelled this phenomenon 'homophily'. The homophily principle structures all kinds of networks including family, friendship and business. According to this principle, 'a contact between similar people occurs at a higher rate than among dissimilar people' ('similarity breeds connection').[77] Moreover, ties between similar individuals last longer than between non-similar parties.[78] Essentially, communication runs more easily between similar people, thus facilitating negotiation, than between people who are very different from one another. The underlying basis of this principle lies, among other factors (e.g. language), in the shared mental models that exist between similar individuals, such as common moral beliefs, worldviews, customs, expectations, etc.[79] Shared common values curtail complexity in human interaction because they allow for the assumption of actions and reactions. In other words, communication among similar individuals with shared mental models fosters trust and creates the conditions for social advancement. Thereby, communication can be established very quickly and businesses can proceed with low transaction costs.[80]

The strongly cohesive Flemish nation in Seville is a showcase of this homophily principle. Not only did the Flemish not segregate themselves from the local Castilians, but they were, in fact, well assimilated into Sevillian society; that notwithstanding, they displayed strong ties of solidarity with one another. If they did not marry into the old Castilian families, they married Flemish *jenízaras*, and their legal witnesses before the Casa la Contratación were always Flemish and Spanish. Furthermore, on a commercial level they also preferred dealing with their compatriots, founded many Flemish-only companies, and preferred entering into commercial partnerships with other Flemings.

The French, on the other hand, exhibited totally different behaviour – although they can still be considered homophilic. Frenchmen stayed and tried to assimilate into Sevillian society too; for example, by founding institutions and religious organisations as well as supporting the Spanish king militarily, but not to the same extent as the Flemish. More Frenchmen married Castilian women, but the number of them marrying French *jenízaras* was much lower. The gap was filled by *jenízaras* of Flemish descent. Regarding witnesses, the situation was even more striking: no French witnesses testified on behalf of French applicants, but many Flemings did. On a commercial level, Flemings were predominant in the business networks in which the French participated, and 1620 is the only year in which the French had more links with their compatriots. This situation raises a number of questions, which I shall try to address in the following paragraphs by way of conclusion.

Why did so many French merchants seek private and commercial links with the Flemings?

During the whole period under consideration, the French community in Seville was smaller than the Flemish. Overall, Flemings accounted for 9 per cent of the city's commercial population. Flemish nodes amounted to 2.6 per cent of the total in 1580, 7.3 per cent in 1600, 11.9 per cent in 1620 and 10.0 per cent in 1640. The French, for their part, barely accounted for 0.6 per cent in 1580, 2.0 per cent in 1600, 3.9 per cent in 1620 and 1.5 per cent in 1640 (an aggregate total of 2.5 per cent) (Table 5.1).

Furthermore, Flemish commercial networks (9.3 per cent of all nodes in 1580, 26 per cent in 1600, 31 per cent in 1620 and 34 per cent in 1640) were always larger than French ones (1.4 per cent, 7.3 per cent, 15.0 per cent and 9.5 per cent) (Table 5.2).

Hence, the size of the Flemish merchant community in Lower Andalusia and its disposition to settle and establish social networks enabled Flemish merchants to build networks which were dominated by their own co-nationals, whom they presumably trusted the most.

French networks, on the other hand, were never so extensive, thus forcing French merchants to resort to other nations to maintain their networks. While,

Table 5.1 Proportion of Flemish and French individuals from the 3,488 nodes mentioned in the documents under examination[a].

	1580	1600	1620	1640
Flemings (total 314)	2.6	7.3	11.9	10.0
French (total 87)	0.6	2.0	3.9	1.5

a The total size of the networks in each year are 1580: 503 nodes; 1600: 895 nodes; 1620: 1,438 nodes; 1640: 652 nodes. In Archivo de Protocolos de Sevilla (APS) 1607, 2607, 3494, 3607, 3697, 6979, 7420, 7421, 7496, 7497, 9390, 9983, 9984, 10060, 10996, 16714, 16715, 16766, 16867, 16869, 16870, 16969, 16979, 17869, 18484.

Table 5.2 Proportion of Flemish and French networks (for annual numbers and sources, see the footnote in Table 5.1).

	1580	1600	1620	1640
Flemings	9.3	26	31	34
French	1.4	7.3	15	9.5

naturally, Castilians played a key role in French networks (also in Flemish ones), they were not of much help regarding the north-western European market, where only the Flemings were capable of supporting the French merchants, which may be the reason French merchants tended to approach the Flemish nation on a private as well as a commercial level.

Why was 1620, when Frenchmen dominated their commercial networks, different?

In 1620, there was a larger proportion of Frenchmen in all networks; nearly one in four nodes in French networks was a Frenchman, and the French networks were larger than ever, accounting for 15 per cent of the total nodes (the French nodes alone accounted for 3.9 per cent, cf. Table 5.1). In 1620, for the first and only time, Frenchmen were more numerous in the French networks than Flemings. It can be concluded that as soon as the French nation was large enough, French merchants immediately took the lead in their business networks. Homophily between Frenchmen was, it seems, higher than between Frenchmen and Flemings. However, Flemings were still the strongest commercial link between north-western Europe and Lower Andalusia, so they still held a prominent position in the French networks, second only to the French.

Why were there so few Frenchmen in French networks in 1640?

In 1635, Louis XIII declared war on Philip III. Immediately, both states confiscated what had suddenly become enemy property, and all trade between France and Spain was officially prohibited. After a while, some restrictions were loosened.

However, until the signing of the Treaty of the Pyrenees in 1659, Frenchmen found it very difficult to trade between Lower Andalusia and France.[81] The French presence in Seville in 1620 and 1640 is revealing of the consequences of the conflict. Whereas 1620 saw French activities in the city peak, in 1640 only a few Frenchmen remained. Most had decided to move elsewhere with their business. French nodes dropped a significant 62 per cent (from 3.9 per cent to 1.5 per cent of total nodes). Remarkably, during the same period the size of the French networks diminished at a slower pace, shrinking by only 37 per cent (from 15 per cent to 9.5 per cent of all nodes). That means that in 1640 a relatively small number of Frenchmen were still able to maintain a relatively large business network. Whereas in 1620 one in four nodes in French networks was a Frenchmen (ratio 1:3.8), in 1640 it was only one in six (ratio 1:6.2).

Who were the merchants who stayed in Lower Andalusia despite the war?

Only ten individuals of French descent can be verified in the records corresponding to 1640. All of them, except for one merchant, who lived in Saint-Malo, were well integrated into the social and commercial life of Lower Andalusia. At least five of them were members of the Consulate of Indies, at least six had received a letter of naturalisation before 1635 and at least seven participated in the American trade. When the war broke out between France and Spain, 1,466,813 ducats were confiscated from Frenchmen in Spain. Five of the merchants who were present in Seville in 1640 lost 631,947 ducats on that occasion, which means that their goods amounted to 43 per cent of all confiscated goods in Spain. These merchants were Pedro de la Farxa, Pedro de Alogue, Lanfran David, Alberto Juan Treguarte and Jaques Bules, who were all well integrated into local society. Most of the less-wealthy and less-integrated French merchants had left town before their goods could be seized, having been warned of the upcoming conflict. All five wealthy merchants who stayed were in possession of a letter of naturalisation. Therefore, it is conceivable that those who stayed trusted the power of their letters of naturalisation to keep them from harm – naturalisations in theory guaranteed the holder access to all Castilian and American trade. After the five merchants saw themselves stripped of their property and privileges, they appealed against the confiscation. A year later, King Philip IV promised to return the lost property, acknowledging their naturalisations and permitting them to continue with their trade in Seville. However, the thankful merchants had to donate the sum of 140,000 ducats to the royal treasury and struggled to be recognised again as naturalised Castilians, in a process that lasted several years.[82]

How did the war affect the conduct of the Frenchmen in Lower Andalusia?

The war had multiple consequences for the French in Lower Andalusia. First, most of them left the region and only the most integrated ones remained.

Second, the remaining merchants struggled to get back on their feet, as many of their compatriots had left, thus forcing them to resort systematically to the Flemings to keep their businesses going. Homophily or not, with only ten Frenchmen a French-based network was not possible. Finally, the character of their trade also seems to have changed. Whereas in 1620 the French in Seville generally engaged in the import of French products, in 1640 their preferred field of activity was the financial sector, and they acted as financiers, especially for other merchants who specialised in the American trade. There were certainly sound reasons for this shift from the trade of goods to the credit business. One of them was definitely the difficulty to maintain the old trade relations with France, especially because of the trade restrictions.

Final remarks

As they were exposed to a dynamic and sometimes hostile environment, merchant communities abroad had to adapt and be capable of responding to changing conditions. The example of the Flemish nation in Seville between 1570 and 1650 stresses the importance of the phenomenon of homophily in such exile groups, and confirms the principle that similarity breeds connection. This holds true for all of the investigated Flemish and also the French networks in 1620. However, in order to fully understand the behaviour of merchant colonies abroad, many more factors must be taken into consideration. The case of the French in 1600, for example, highlights the importance of numbers. When the size of the French nation was too small to build up stable and self-sustaining business networks, alternative strategies emerged. In this case, the French connected with the larger (and similarly oriented) Flemish network, which offered them many commercial advantages. In 1620, when the number of Frenchmen in Seville had grown, the French focused on their own compatriots, which was fully in line with the homophily principle. Therefore, the French nation in Lower Andalusia remained flexible and capable of reacting to the changing social and commercial environment. Moreover, the French colony also adapted its strategies to the shifting political situations. Having lost many members owing to the economic disruptions brought about by the war, in 1640, the French network in Seville became Flemish-dominated once more. In addition, their business strategies changed as the old connections to France became unreachable. In conclusion, the concept of homophily is a powerful tool for revealing aspects of the behaviour of 'national' communities in foreign environments, but in order to understand the full variety of actions and the multiple strategies that were open to each individual agent, many more factors must be taken into consideration.

Notes

1 E. Trueba, *Sevilla maritima (siglo XVI)* (Seville: Padilla Libros, 1990), pp. 19–41; H. Kellenbenz, 'Die Einwohnerschaft der Stadt Cadiz um 1535 und ihre Fremdenkolonie', *Spanische Forschungen der Görresgesellschaft*, 1st ser., 20 (1962),

pp. 79–102, on p. 80; P.E. Perez-Mallaina, 'Auge y decadencia del puerto de Sevilla como cabecera de las rutas indianas', *Caravelle*, 69 (1997), pp. 15–39; F. Morales Padrón, *Historia de Sevilla: La Ciudad del Quinientos* (Seville: Universidad de Sevilla, 1989), pp. 177–181;. A. Dominguez Ortiz, *Historia de Sevilla: La Sevilla del siglo XVII* (Seville: Universidad de Sevilla, 2006); idem, *Orto y ocaso de Sevilla* (Seville: Universidad de Sevilla, 1991).

2 A. Acosta Rodríguez, A.L. González Rodríguez and E. Vila Vilar (eds.), *La Casa de la Contratación y la navegación entre España y las Indias* (Seville: Universidad de Sevilla, CSIC, 2003); R.S. Smith, *The Spanish Guild Merchant. A History of the Consulado, 1250–1700* (New York: Octagon, 1972).

3 E. Otte Sander, *Sevilla, siglo XVI: Materiales para su historia económica* (Seville: Centro de Estudios Andaluces, 2008), pp. 129–130; idem, 'El comercio exterior andaluz a fines de la edad media', *Hacienda y comercio. Actas del II coloquio de Historia Medieval Andaluza* (Seville: Diputación provincial de Sevilla, 1982), pp. 193–240; idem and A.M. Bernal Rodríguez, *Sevilla y sus mercaderes a fines de la Edad Media* (Seville: Fundación el Monte, Vicerrectorado de Relaciones Institucionales y Extensión Cultural et al., 1996); M.A. Ladero Quesada, *La ciudad medieval (1248–1492)* (Seville: Universidad de Sevilla, 1989); M. Greene, 'Beyond the Northern Invasion: The Mediterranean in the Seventeenth Century', *Past and Present* 174 (2002), pp. 42–71.

4 M.L. Martínez de Salinas Alonso, 'Contribución al estudio sobre los arbitristas. Nuevos arbitrios para las Indias a principios del siglo XVII', *Revista de Indias*, 50:188 (1990), pp. 161–169.

5 S.J. Stein and B.H. Stein, *Silver, Trade, and War. Spain and America in the Making of Early Modern Europe* (Baltimore and London: Johns Hopkins University Press, 2000), pp. 15–16, 82; A. Domínguez Ortiz, 'Los extranjeros en la vida española durante el siglo XVII', in idem (ed.), *Los extranjeros en la vida española durante el siglo XVII y otros artículos* (Seville: Diputación de Sevilla Area de Cultura y Ecología, 1996), pp. 17–182.

6 J. Gil-Bermejo García, 'Mercaderes sevillanos II. Una relación de 1640', *Archivo Hispalense*, 188 (1978), pp. 25–52; E. Crailsheim, 'Extranjeros entre dos mundos. Una aproximación proporcional a las colonias de mercaderes extranjeros en Sevilla, 1570–1650', *Jahrbuch für Geschichte Lateinamerikas/Anuario de Historia de America Latina*, 48 (2011), pp. 179–202, on p. 200.

7 E. Otte Sander, *Sevilla, siglo XVI*, p. 284.

8 E. Stols, 'La colonía flamenca de Sevilla y el comercio de los Paises Bajos españoles en la primera mitad del siglo XVII', *Anuario de Historia Económica y Social*, 2:1 (1969), pp. 363–381, on pp. 364–365, 380; idem, 'Les marchands flamands dans la Péninsule Ibérique à la fin du seizième siècle et pendant la première moitié du dix-sixième siècle', in H. Kellenbenz (ed.), *Fremde Kaufleute auf der Iberischen Halbinsel* (Cologne and Vienna: Böhlau Verlag, 1970), pp. 226–238, on p. 226. E. Otte Sander questions this enormous increase in their numbers (E. Otte Sander, *Sevilla, siglo XVI*, p. 284), but the sources confirm the numbers supplied by E. Stols.

9 The selection of the offices resulted from the search for foreign merchants, based on recommendations of local experts such as E. Vila Vilar.

10 T. Herzog, 'Naturales y extranjeros. Sobre la construcción de categorías en el mundo hispánico', in Cuadernos de historia moderna. Anejos 10. Los Extranjeros y la Nación en España y la América Española (2011), pp. 21–31.

11 M. García Mauriño Mundi, *La pugna entre el Consulado de Cádiz y los jenízaros por las exportaciones a Indias (1720–1765)* (Seville: Universidad de Sevilla, 1999), pp. 43–44; cf. also the Recopilación de las Leyes de Indias, ley 27, título 27, libro 9.

12 A. Crespo Solana, *Mercaderes atlánticos. Redes del comercio flamenco y holandés entre Europa y el Caribe* (Córdoba: Universidad de Córdoba, 2009), p. 133.

13 A. Crespo Solana, *Mercaderes atlánticos*, pp. 136–137.

14 AGI Contratación 50A, 50B, 51A, 596A, 596B.

15 Such as E. Stols, *De Spaanse Brabanders of de Handelsbetrekkingen der Zuidelijke Nederlanden met de Iberische Wereld 1598–1648* (Brussels: Palais de Academiën, 1971); A. Girard, *Le commerce français à Séville et Cadix au temps des Habsbourg. Contribution à l'étude du commerce étranger en Espagne aux XVIe et XVIIe siècles* (Paris: E. de Boccard, 1932); or E. Vila Vilar, *Los Corzo y los Mañara: Tipos y arquetipos del mercader con Indias* (Seville: EEHA, 1991). Thereby, it can be hoped to minimise the margin of error.

16 Archivo de Protocolos de Sevilla (APS) legajos 1607, 2607, 3494, 3607, 3697, 6979, 7420, 7421, 7496, 7497, 9390, 9983, 9984, 10060, 10996, 16714, 16715, 16766, 16867, 16869, 16870, 16969, 16979, 17869, 18484. The calculations presented in this paper, if not otherwise indicated, are based on these sources. Additional support for my conclusions can be found in Archivo General de Indias (AGI) Contratación 50A, 50B, 51A, 596A, 596B. Cf. Crailsheim, 'Extranjeros entre dos mundos', pp. 185–187.

17 E. Stols, 'La colonía flamenca de Sevilla y el comercio de los Paises Bajos españoles en la primera mitad del siglo XVII', *Anuario de Historia Económica y Social*, 2:1 (1969), pp. 363–381; idem, 'Les marchands flamands dans la Péninsule Ibérique à la fin du seizième siècle et pendant la première moitié du dix-sixième siècle', in H. Kellenbenz (ed.), *Fremde Kaufleute auf der Iberischen Halbinsel* (Cologne and Vienna: Böhlau Verlag, 1970), pp. 226–238.

18 E. Stols, 'La colonía flamenca', p. 367; M. Moret, *Aspects de la société marchande de Séville au début du XVIIe siècle* (Paris: Marcel Rivière et Cie., 1967), pp. 49, 51; cf. also A.d.C. Viña Brito, 'Los flamencos en Canarias en el siglo XVI. ¿Una comunidad extranjera? Especificidades en la isla de La Palma', *Revista de Historia Canaria*, 194 (2012), pp. 161–192.

19 E. Stols, 'La colonía flamenca', pp. 367–368. In 1611, the 97 richest German and Flemish merchants signed a document for the aid of charitable foundations. M. Moret, *Aspects de la société marchande*, p. 54; A. Crespo Solana, 'Nación extranjera y cofradía de mercaderes. El rostro piadoso de la integración social', in M.B. Villar García and P. Pezzi Cristóbal (eds.), *Los extranjeros en la España Moderna. Actas del I Coloquio Internacional, celebrado en Málaga del 28 al 30 de noviembre de 2002* (Malaga: Universidad de Málaga, 2003), vol. 2, pp. 175–187.

20 E. Stols, 'La colonía flamenca', pp. 367–368.

21 E. Stols, *De Spaanse Brabanders*, vol. 2, p. 61.

22 AGI Contratación 50B and 51A, s.f.; R. Baetens, *De nazomer van Antwerpens welvaart. De diaspora en het handelshuis De Groote tijdens de eerste helft der 17de eeuw* (Brussels: Gemeentekrediet van België, 1976), vol. 1, pp. 151–154.

23 A. Crespo Solana, 'Elementos de transnacionalidad en el comercio flamenco-holandés en Europa y la Monarquía hispánica', in *Cuadernos de historia moderna. Anejos 10. Los Extranjeros y la Nación en España y la América española* (2011), pp. 55–76, p. 63.

24 J. García Bernal and M. Gamero Rojas, 'Las corporaciones de nación en la Sevilla moderna. fundaciones, redes asistenciales y formas de sociabilidad', in B. José García García, Ó. Recio Morales (ed.), *Las corporaciones de nación en la monarquía hispánica. Identidad, patronazgo y redes de sociabilidad* (Madrid: Fundación Carlos de Amberes 2014), pp. 347–388.

25 E. Stols, 'La colonía flamenco', pp. 367–368.

26 E. Stols, 'Les marchands flamands dans la Péninsule Ibérique', pp. 231–232; idem, *De Spaanse Brabanders*, vol. 2, p. 35.

27 E. Vila Vilar, 'Los europeos en el comercio Americano. Sevilla como plataforma', in R. Pieper and P. Schmidt (eds.), *Latin America and the Atlantic World / El mundo atlántico y América Latina (1500–1850). Essays in Honor of Horst Pietschmann* (Cologne and Vienna: Böhlau Verlag, 2005), pp. 279–296, on p. 294.

28 R. Pike, *Aristocrats and Traders. Sevillian Society in the Sixteenth Century* (Ithaca and London: Cornell University Press, 1972), pp. 99–100.

29 A. Crespo Solana, *Mercaderes atlánticos*, pp. 134–135.
30 E. Stols, *De Spaanse Brabanders*, vol. 1, pp. 80–93; M. Moret, *Aspects de la société marchande*, pp. 53–58; A. Crespo Solana, *Entre Cádiz y los Países Bajos. Una comunidad mercantil en la ciudad de la ilustración* (Cadiz: Fundación Municipal de Cultura del Ayuntamiento de Cádiz, 2001), pp. 177–179; cf. also idem, 'Nación extranjera'; idem, 'Las comunidades mercantiles y el mantenimiento de los sistemas comerciales de España, Flandes y la República holandesa, 1648–1750', in M. Herrero Sánchez and A. Crespo Solana (eds.), *España y las 17 provincias de los Países Bajos. Una revisión historiográfica (XVI–XVIII)* (Córdoba: Universidad de Córdoba, 2002), pp. 443–468; M. Aglietti, M. Herrero Sánchez and F. Zamorra Rodríguez (eds.), *Los cónsules de extranjeros en la Edad Moderna y principios de la Edad Contemporánea* (Aranjuez: Doce Calles, 2013).
31 A permanent residence in Lower Andalusia can be assumed when the Flemish or French immigrant has received a letter of naturalisation, when he is referred to as a citizen or resident of an Andalusian town, or when he appears in more than one of the sample years.
32 A. Domínguez Ortiz, 'Los extranjeros en la vida española', p. 75. Cf J.-Ph.; J. Priotti, 'Plata Americana, costes de transacción y mutaciones socio-económicas en el atlántico hispano-bretón (1570–1635)', in I. Lobato Franco and J.M. Oliva Melgar (eds.), *El sistema comercial español en la economía mundial (siglos XVII–XVIII)* (Huelva: Universidad de Huelva, 2013), pp. 97–125.
33 A. Girard, *Le commerce français à Séville et Cadix au temps des Habsbourg* (Paris: E. de Boccard, 1932), pp. 50, 538, 547; H. Kellenbenz, 'Fremde Kaufleute auf der Iberischen Halbinsel vom 15. Jahrhundert bis zum Ende des 16. Jahrhunderts', in idem (ed.), *Fremde Kaufleute*, pp. 265–376, on p. 299.
34 In Spain, as in Seville, French communities were dominated by rich merchants, who formed the strongest group in political and economic terms, but not the most numerous. Small traders, wage earners, and seamen were far more numerous. The French nation in Spain was a large and heterogeneous group, which in 1626 amounted to about 200,000 individuals. A. Girard, *Le commerce français*, pp. 558–572.
35 A. Domínguez Ortiz, 'Los extranjeros en la vida española', pp. 75–76.
36 A. Girard, *Le commerce français*, pp. 44–45, 547; F. Mauro, 'Les marchands du Midi de la France et la Péninsule Ibérique aux XVe et XVIe siècles', in Kellenbenz (ed.), *Fremde Kaufleute*, pp. 100–117, on p. 129; for Vitré, cf. H. Lapeyre, *Une famille de marchands. Les Ruiz* (Paris: A. Colin, 1955), p. 395.
37 A. Girard, *Le commerce français*, pp. 558–572.
38 E. Lorenzo Sanz, *Comercio de España con América en la época de Felipe II* (Valladolid: Diputación Provincial de Valladolid, 1986), vol. 1, p. 89.
39 A. Girard, *Le commerce français*, pp. 44–45, 547.
40 E. Lorenzo Sanz, *Comercio de España*, vol. 1, pp. 91–92.
41 A. Girard, *Le commerce français*, pp. 538, 545–549, 566; Kellenbenz, 'Fremde Kaufleute auf der Iberischen Halbinsel', p. 299; D. Ortiz, 'Los extranjeros en la vida española', p. 77; cf. M. Bustos Rodríguez, *Cádiz en el sistema Atlántico* (Seville: Silex, 2005), p. 140.
42 A. Girard, *Le commerce français*, p. 51.
43 N. Steensgaard, 'Consuls and Nations in the Levant from 1570 to 1650', in S. Subrahmanyam (ed.), *Merchant Networks in the Early Modern World* (Aldershot: Variorum, 1996), pp. 179–221, on pp. 180–181; A. Girard, *Le commerce français*, pp. 90–91, 579–589; Lorenzo Sanz, *Comercio de España*, p. 89.
44 M. Moret, *Aspects de la société marchande*, pp. 57–58.
45 A. Girard, *Le commerce français*, p. 579.
46 M. Moret, *Aspects de la société marchande*, pp. 49, 54.
47 H. Sánchez de Sopranis, 'Las naciones extranjeras en Cádiz durante el siglo XVII', *Estudios de Historia Social de España*, 4:2 (1960), pp. 639–677, on pp. 647, 654.

48 AGI Contratación 50B, s.f.; cf. E. Vila Vilar, 'Una amplia nómina de los hombres de comercio Sevillano del S. XVII', *Minervae baeticae: Boletín de la Real academia Sevillana de Buenas Letras*, 30 (2002), pp. 139–191; E. Lorenzo Sanz, *Comercio de España*, vol. 1, p. 91.

49 In 1580, all three Frenchmen in the Seville records were permanent residents in Seville. One of them, the consul of the French nation Manuel de Bues, even received a letter of naturalization.

50 D. Jansen, *Einführung in die Netzwerkanalyse. Grundlagen, Methoden, Forschungsbeispiele* (Opladen: Leske+Budrich, 2003); M. Emirbayer and J. Goodwin, 'Network Analysis, Culture, and the Problem of Agency', *American Journal of Sociology*, 99:6 (1994), pp. 1411–1454.

51 AGI Contratación 50A, 50B, 51A, 596A, 596B.

52 Three hundred and thirteen foreigners applied for naturalization between 1570 and 1650; 76 among them were Flemings and 25 Frenchmen.

53 AGI Contratación 50B, s.f.; cf. *Recopilación de las Leyes de Indias*, ley 31–32, título 27, libro 9.

54 T. Herzog, *Defining Nations. Immigrants and citizens in early modern Spain and Spanish America* (New Haven and London: Yale University Press, 2003), p. 11.

55 J.M. Díaz Blanco and N. Maillard Álvarez, '¿Una intimidad supeditada a la ley? Las estrategias matrimoniales de los cargadores a indias extranjeros en Sevilla (siglos XVI–XVII)', *Nuevo Mundo Mundos Nuevos*, (2008), (Colloques), URL: http://nuevomundo.revues.org/28453 (30.6.2015).

56 Archivo General de Simancas (AGS) C.S. 168, s.f.; AGI Contratación 50B, 596B, s.f.; E.Vila Vilar, 'Una amplia nómina'; E. Crailsheim, 'Les marchands français à Séville (1580–1650). Les examples de Pedro de la Farxa, Lanfran David et Pedro de Alogue', in J.-Ph. Priotti and G. Saupin (eds.), *Le commerce atlantique franco-espagnol – Acteurs, négoces et ports (XVe–XVIIIe siècle)* (Rennes: Presses Universitaires de Rennes, 2008), pp. 233–248.

57 E. Crailsheim, 'Behind the Atlantic Expansion. Flemish Trade Connections of Seville in 1620', *Research in Maritime History* 42, in M. Fusaro and A. Polónia (ed.), *Maritime History as Global History*, (2010), pp. 21–46.

58 In that regard, the fact that the Flemings were part of the Spanish composite monarchy, and hence subjects of the Spanish king (while the French were not), should not be forgotten, as their testimony was possibly rated higher.

59 A. García-Baquero González, *La Carrera de Indias. Suma de la contratación y océano de negocios* (Seville: Algaids, 1992), pp. 239–245.

60 E. Stols, *De Spaanse Brabanders*, Vol. 2, p. 2; AGI Contratación 5318, N. 1, R. 42, ff. 1r–33r; AGI Contratación 5340, N. 13, ff. 1r–3v; AGI Contratación 5358, N. 32, ff. 1r–33r; AGI Contratación 5378, N. 13, ff. 1r–4v (all from the PARES database http://pares.mcu.es/). APS 3607, ff. 141r–142r; APS 10060, ff. 315r–316r.

61 APS 16869; Vila Vilar, 'Una amplia nómina', p. 169.

62 APS 16869.

63 APS 3607.

64 APS 9984.

65 APS 16896 and 16870; cf. Vila Vilar, "Los europeos en el comercio americano".

66 APS 10060.

67 APS 16896 and 16870; APS 3607, ff. 267r–270v, 822v–825r; APS 16869, ff. 935r–938v; APS 16870, ff. 183r–185v.

68 E. Crailsheim, 'Behind the Atlantic Expansion', pp. 30–35.

69 APS 16766, ff. 378–380.

70 APS 16766, f. 156v; Vila Vilar, 'Una amplia nómina', p. 180.

71 AGI Contratación 5318, N. 1, R. 42, ff. 1r–33r [PARES]. A. Vidal Ortega and E. Vila Vilar, "El comercio lanero y el comercio trasatlántico. Écija en la encrucijada", in *Écija y el Nuevo Mundo: Actas del VI Congreso de Historia* (Écija: Ayuntamiento de

Écija, 2002), pp. 57–67, on pp. 59–67; cf. also Vila Vilar, "Los europeos en el comercio Americano", pp. 292–294.

72 AGI Contratación 50B, s.f.; APS 7497, ff. 61–63, 145–146.

73 APS 16869, ff. 995r–996r; a similar document without signatures: APS 16869, ff. 940r–941r; AGI Contratación 816, Autos entre partes: N. 17 [PARES].

74 The Flemish network for each year includes, roughly, all nodes (individuals) also mentioned in each document – that is, everyone who was in any way connected to the Flemings.

75 In the year 1580, the most common nodes in French networks were Italians – the sample is, however, rather small and barely representative.

76 M.D. Ramos Medina, 'El origen de una élite negociante en Madrid: los mercaderes de lonja franceses en el siglo XVII', *Espacio, Tiemo y Forma*, 14:4 (2001), pp. 349–375, on p. 373; idem, 'Algunas sagas comerciales francesas en el Madrid de la segunda mitad del seiscientos', *Espacio, Tiemo y Forma*, 12.4 (1999), pp. 223–247, on p. 225.

77 M.L. McPherson, M. Smith-Lovin and J.M. Cook, 'Birds of a Feather. Homophily in Social Networks", *Annual Review of Sociology*, 27 (2001), pp. 415–444, on pp. 415–416.

78 M.L. McPherson, M. Smith-Lovin and J.M. Cook, 'Birds of a Feather', pp. 415.

79 D.C. North and AT. Denzau, 'Shared Mental Models. Ideologies and Institutions', *Kyklos*, 47:1 (1994), pp. 3–31, on p. 4.

80 N. Luhmann, *Vertrauen. Ein Mechanismus der Reduktion sozialer Komplexität* (Stuttgart: Lucius & Lucius, 2000).

81 Á. Alloza Aparicio, 'El comercio francés en España y Portugal. La represalia de 1635', in C. Martínez Shaw and J. Ma. Oliva Melgar (eds.), *El sistema atlántico español (siglos XVII–XIX)* (Madrid: Marcial Pons Historia, 2005), pp. 127–161; Y.-M. Bercé, *La naissance dramatique de l'absolutisme 1598–1661* (Paris: Seuil, 1992), pp. 143–164; A. Girard, *Le commerce français*, pp. 82–83, 130, 473, 508–531; cf. J. I. Israel, "El comercio de los judíos sefardíes de Amsterdam con los conversos de Madrid a través del suroeste francés", in J. Contreras (ed.), *Familia, religión y negocio. El sefardismo en las relaciones entre el mundo ibérico y los Países Bajos en la Edad Moderna* (Madrid: Fundación Carlos Amberes, 2003), pp. 373–391; for Saint-Maló, cf. A. Lespagnol, *Messieurs de Saint-Malo: une élite négociante au temps de Louis XIV* (Saint-Malo: l'Ancre de Marine, 1991); J. Bottin, 'Réflexions sur un modèle de croissance commerciale: Saint-Malo et ses négociants à l'époque de Louis XIV", *Revue d'histoire moderne et contemporaine*, 42:1 (1995), pp. 142–150; for the Canary Islands, cf. F. Morales Padrón, *El comercio canario-americano. Siglos XVI, XVII, XVIII* (Seville: EEHA, 1955), pp. 279ff.; A.D. Brito González, *Los extranjeros en las Canarias Orientales en el siglo XVII* (Las Palmas de Gran Canaria: Ediciones del Cabildo de Gran Canaria, 2002), pp. 100–107.

82 AGI Contratación 50B, s.f.; AGS C.S. 168; Alloza Aparicio, 'El comercio francés', p. 144; P. Collado Villalta, 'El embargo de bienes de los portugueses en la flota de Tierra Firme de 1641', *Anuario de Estudios Americanos*, 36 (1979), pp. 169–207, on pp. 171–173; cf. M. Herrero Sánchez, 'La política de embargos y el contrabando de productos de lujo en Madrid (1635–1673). Sociedad cortesana y dependencia de los mercados internacionales', *Hispania: Revista española de historia*, 201 (1999), pp. 171–191, on p. 190.

Bibliography

Acosta Rodríguez, A., González Rodríguez, A.L. and Vila Vilar, E. eds., *La Casa de la Contratación y la navegación entre España y las Indias*, Seville: Universidad de Sevilla, CSIC, 2003.

Aglietti, M., Herrero Sánchez, M. and F. Zamorra Rodríguez, F., eds., *Los cónsules de extranjeros en la Edad Moderna y principios de la Edad Contemporánea*, Aranjuez: Doce Calles, 2013.

Alloza Aparicio, Á., 'El comercio francés en España y Portugal. La represalia de 1635', in Martínez Shaw, C. and Oliva Melgar, J.Ma., eds., *El sistema atlántico español (siglos XVII–XIX)*, Madrid: Marcial Pons Historia, 2005, pp. 127–161.

Baetens, R., *De nazomer van Antwerpens welvaart. De diaspora en het handelshuis De Groote tijdens de eerste helft der 17de eeuw*, Brussels: Gemeentekrediet van België, 1976.

Bercé, Y.-M., *La naissance dramatique de l'absolutisme 1598–1661*, Paris: Seuil, 1992.

Bottin, J., 'Réflexions sur un modèle de croissance commerciale: Saint-Malo et ses négociants à l'époque de Louis XIV', *Revue d'histoire moderne et contemporaine*, 42:1, 1995, pp. 142–150.

Brito González, A.D., *Los extranjeros en las Canarias Orientales en el siglo XVII*, Las Palmas de Gran Canaria: Ediciones del Cabildo de Gran Canaria, 2002.

Bustos Rodríguez, M., *Cádiz en el sistema Atlántico*, Seville: Silex, 2005.

Collado Villalta, P., 'El embargo de bienes de los portugueses en la flota de Tierra Firme de 1641', *Anuario de Estudios Americanos*, 36, 1979, pp. 169–207.

Crailsheim, E., 'Les marchands français à Séville (1580–1650). Les examples de Pedro de la Farxa, Lanfran David et Pedro de Alogue', in Priotti, J.-Ph. and G. Saupin, G., eds., *Le commerce atlantique franco-espagnol – Acteurs, négoces et ports (XVe–XVIIIe siècle)*, Rennes: Presses Universitaires de Rennes, 2008, pp. 233–248.

———. 'Behind the Atlantic Expansion. Flemish Trade Connections of Seville in 1620', *Research in Maritime History, 42, Maritime History as Global History*, Fusaro M. and Polónia, A., eds., 2010, pp. 21–46.

———. 'Extranjeros entre dos mundos. Una aproximación proporcional a las colonias de mercaderes extranjeros en Sevilla, 1570–1650', *Jahrbuch für Geschichte Lateinamerikas/ Anuario de Historia de America Latina*, 48, 2011, pp. 179–202.

Crespo Solana, A., *Entre Cádiz y los Países Bajos: Una comunidad mercantil en la ciudad de la ilustración*, Cadiz: Fundación Municipal de Cultura del Ayuntamiento de Cádiz, 2001.

———. 'Las comunidades mercantiles y el mantenimiento de los sistemas comerciales de España, Flandes y la República holandesa, 1648–1750', in Herrero Sánchez, M. and Ana Crespo Solana, A., eds., *España y las 17 provincias de los Países Bajos. Una revisión historiográfica (XVI–XVIII)*, Córdoba: Universidad de Córdoba, 2002, pp. 443–468.

———. 'Nación extranjera y cofradía de mercaderes. El rostro piadoso de la integración social', in Villar García, M.B. and Pezzi Cristóbal, P., eds., *Los extranjeros en la España Moderna. Actas del I Coloquio Internacional, celebrado en Málaga del 28 al 30 de noviembre de 2002*, Malaga: Universidad de Málaga, 2003, vol. 2, pp. 175–187.

Díaz Blanco, J.M. and Maillard Álvarez, N., '¿Una intimidad supeditada a la ley? Las estrategias matrimoniales de los cargadores a indias extranjeros en Sevilla (siglos XVI–XVII)', *Nuevo Mundo Mundos Nuevos* 2008 (Colloques), URL: http://nuevomundo.revues.org/28453 (30.6.2015).

Dominguez Ortiz, A., *Historia de Sevilla: La Sevilla del siglo XVII*, Seville: Universidad de Sevilla, 2006.

———. *Orto y ocaso de Sevilla*, Seville: Universidad de Sevilla, 1991.

———. 'Los extranjeros en la vida española durante el siglo XVII', *Los extranjeros en la vida española durante el siglo XVII y otros artículos*, Seville: Diputación de Sevilla Area de Cultura y Ecología, 1996, pp. 17–182.

Emirbayer, M. and Goodwin, J., 'Network Analysis, Culture, and the Problem of Agency', *American Journal of Sociology*, 99:6, 1994, pp. 1411–1454.

García-Baquero González, A., *La Carrera de Indias. Suma de la contratación y océano de negocios*, Seville: Algaids, 1992.

Gil-Bermejo García, J., 'Mercaderes sevillanos II. Una relación de 1640', *Archivo Hispalense*, 188, 1978, pp. 25–52.

Girard, A., *Le commerce français à Séville et Cadix au temps des Habsbourg*, Paris: E. de Boccard, 1932.

128   *Eberhard Crailsheim*

Greene, M., 'Beyond the Northern Invasion: The Mediterranean in the Seventeenth Century', *Past and Present*, 174, 2002, pp. 42–71.
Herrero Sánchez, M., 'La política de embargos y el contrabando de productos de lujo en Madrid (1635–1673). Sociedad cortesana y dependencia de los mercados internacionales', *Hispania: Revista española de historia*, 201, 1999, pp. 171–191.
Herzog, T., *Defining Nations. Immigrants and citizens in early modern Spain and Spanish America*, New Haven and London: Yale University Press, 2003.
Israel, J.I., 'El comercio de los judíos sefardíes de Amsterdam con los conversos de Madrid a través del suroeste francés', in Contreras, J., ed., *Familia, religión y negocio. El sefardismo en las relaciones entre el mundo ibérico y los Países Bajos en la Edad Moderna*, Madrid: Fundación Carlos Amberes, 2003, pp. 373–391.
Jansen, D., *Einführung in die Netzwerkanalyse. Grundlagen, Methoden, Forschungsbeispiele*, Opladen: Leske + Budrich, 2003.
Kellenbenz, H., 'Die Einwohnerschaft der Stadt Cadiz um 1535 und ihre Fremdenkolonie', *Spanische Forschungen der Görresgesellschaft*, 1st ser., 20, 1962, pp. 79–102.
———. 'Fremde Kaufleute auf der Iberischen Halbinsel vom 15. Jahrhundert bis zum Ende des 16. Jahrhunderts', *Fremde Kaufleute auf der Iberischen Halbinsel*, Cologne and Vienna: Böhlau Verlag, 1970, pp. 265–376.
Kellenbenz, H. ed., *Fremde Kaufleute auf der Iberischen Halbinsel*, Cologne and Vienna: Böhlau Verlag, 1970.
Ladero Quesada, M.A., *La ciudad medieval (1248–1492)*, Seville: Universidad de Sevilla, 1989.
Lapeyre, H., *Une famille de marchands. Les Ruiz*, Paris: A. Colin, 1955.
Lespagnol, A., *Messieurs de Saint-Malo: une élite négociante au temps de Louis XIV*, Saint-Malo: l'Ancre de Marine, 1991.
Lorenzo Sanz, E., *Comercio de España con América en la época de Felipe II*, Valladolid: Diputación Provincial de Valladolid, 1986.
Luhmann, N., *Vertrauen. Ein Mechanismus der Reduktion sozialer Komplexität*, Stuttgart: Lucius & Lucius, 2000.
Martínez de Salinas Alonso, M.L., 'Contribución al estudio sobre los arbitristas. Nuevos arbitrios para las Indias a principios del siglo XVII', *Revista de Indias*, 50:188, 1990, pp. 161–169.
McPherson, M., Smith-Lovin, L. and Cook, J.M., 'Birds of a Feather. Homophily in Social Networks', *Annual Review of Sociology*, 27, 2001, pp. 415–444.
Morales Padrón, F., *El comercio canario-americano. Siglos XVI, XVII, XVIII*, Seville: EEHA, 1955.
———. *Historia de Sevilla: La Ciudad del Quinientos*, Seville: Universidad de Sevilla, 1989.
Moret, M., *Aspects de la société marchande de Séville au début du XVIIe siècle*, Paris: Marcel Rivière et Cie., 1967.
North, D.C. and Denzau, A.T., 'Shared Mental Models. Ideologies and Institutions', *Kyklos*, 47:1, 1994, pp. 3–31.
Otte Sander, E., *Sevilla, siglo XVI: Materiales para su historia económica*, Seville: Centro de Estudios Andaluces, 2008, pp. 129–130.
———. 'El comercio exterior andaluz a fines de la edad media', in *Hacienda y comercio. Actas del II coloquio de Historia Medieval Andaluza*, Seville: Diputación provincial de Sevilla, 1982, pp. 193–240.
Otte Sander, E. and Bernal Rodríguez, A.M., *Sevilla y sus mercaderes a fines de la Edad Media*, Seville: Fundación el Monte, Vicerrectorado de Relaciones Institucionales y Extensión Cultural y Ayuntamiento de Sevilla, 1996.
Perez-Mallaina, P.E., 'Auge y decadencia del puerto de Sevilla como cabecera de las rutas indianas', *Caravelle*, 69, 1997, pp. 15–39.
Pike, R., *Aristocrats and Traders. Sevillian Society in the Sixteenth Century*, Ithaca and London: Cornell University Press, 1972.

Priotti, J.-Ph., 'Plata Americana, costes de transacción y mutaciones socio-económicas en el atlántico hispano-bretón (1570−1635)', in Lobato Franco, I. and Oliva Melgar, J.M., eds., *El sistema comercial español en la economía mundial (siglos XVII−XVIII)*, Huelva: Universidad de Huelva, 2013, pp. 97−125.

Ramos Medina, M.D., 'Algunas sagas comerciales francesas en el Madrid de la segunda mitad del seiscientos', *Espacio, Tiemo y Forma*, 12.4 (1999), pp. 223–247, on p. 225.

————. 'El origen de una élite negociante en Madrid: los mercaderes de lonja franceses en el siglo XVII', *Espacio, Tiemo y Forma*, 14:4, 2001, pp. 349–375.

Sánchez de Sopranis, H., 'Las naciones extrangeras en Cádiz durante el siglo XVII', *Estudios de Historia Social de España*, 4:2, 1960, pp. 639–677.

Smith, R.S., *The Spanish Guild Merchant. A History of the Consulado, 1250–1700*, New York: Octagon, 1972.

Steensgaard, N., 'Consuls and Nations in the Levant from 1570 to 1650', in Subrahmanyam, S., ed., *Merchant Networks in the Early Modern World*, Aldershot: Variorum, 1996, pp. 179–221.

Stein, St.J. and Stein, B.H., *Silver, Trade, and War. Spain and America in the Making of Early Modern Europe*, Baltimore and London: Johns Hopkins University Press, 2000.

Stols, E., 'La colonía flamenca de Sevilla y el comercio de los Paises Bajos españoles en la primera mitad del siglo XVII', *Anuario de Historia Económica y Social*, 2:1, 1969, pp. 363–381.

————. 'Les marchands flamands dans la Péninsule Ibérique à la fin du seizième siècle et pendant la première moitié du dix-sixième siècle', in Kellenbenz, H. ed., *Fremde Kaufleute auf der Iberischen Halbinsel*, Cologne and Vienna: Böhlau Verlag, 1970, pp. 226–238.

————. *De Spaanse Brabanders of de Handelsbetrekkingen der Zuidelijke Nederlanden met de Iberische Wereld 1598−1648*, Brussels: Palais de Academiën, 1971.

Trueba, E., *Sevilla maritima (siglo XVI)*, Seville: Padilla Libros, 1990.

Vidal Ortega, A. and Vila Vilar, E., 'El comercio lanero y el comercio trasatlántico. Écija en la encrucijada', *Écija y el Nuevo Mundo: Actas del VI Congreso de Historia*, Écija: Ayuntamiento de Écija, 2002.

Vila Vilar, E., 'Una amplia nómina de los hombres de comercio Sevillano del S. XVII', *Minervae baeticae: Boletín de la Real academia Sevillana de Buenas Letras*, 30, 2002, pp. 139–191.

————. 'Los europeos en el comercio Americano. Sevilla como plataforma', in Pieper, R. and Schmidt, P., eds., *Latin America and the Atlantic World/El mundo atlántico y América Latina (1500–1850). Essays in Honor of Horst Pietschmann*, Cologne and Vienna: Böhlau Verlag, 2005, pp. 279–296.

Viña Brito, C., 'Los flamencos en Canarias en el siglo XVI. ¿Una comunidad extranjera? Especificidades en la isla de La Palma', *Revista de Historia Canaria*, 194, 2012, pp. 161–192.

6 Agents of globalisation

An approximation to Santi Federighi's commercial network, c. 1620–1643

José L. Gasch-Tomás

Introduction

From 1594 to 1606 the Florentine Francesco Carletti made a voyage around the world which took him from Europe to India and across to Nagasaki, the Philippines and Macao. He wrote the following about his stay in the viceroyalty of New Spain: 'Acapulco is the capital of the province of New Spain, where we disembarked and stayed several days [...] A great quantity of money is taken here to buy merchandise which are made in the provinces [i.e. The Philippine Islands], especially wool cloths and silk sheets which are made with silk from China, from where two or three ships arrived at this port with merchandise from that kingdom which are transported to Mexico throughout the route of the Philippines [...] To Mexico City arrived all which is carried by the fleets from Spain to Veracruz, which is the port at the north wind (*tramuntana*). This port is far away from Mexico City more than 240 miles, so that Mexico City is in the middle of two seas, the North Sea and the South Sea'.[1] Carletti's words reflect a reality – around 1600, that New Spain was among the few places in the world that commercially connected several continents (the Americas, Asia, Europe and Africa).

Jan de Vries divided the concept of globalisation in the early modern period in two terms.[2] The first term is 'hard' globalisation, which is the definition given by economic historians such as William O'Rourke and Jeffrey G. Williamson, who understand globalisation as a process of convergence of markets at the international level, which can be quantitatively evaluated by assessing the global convergence of prices and salaries.[3] The second is 'soft' globalisation, which is defined as the existence of transcontinental contact and trade 'on a scale that generated deep and lasting impacts on all trading partners' from the sixteenth century onwards.[4] Whether we understand globalisation in its 'hard' sense or in its 'soft' sense, trading networks were its agents during the early modern era. Because of its wide territory, the Spanish empire was an excellent framework to test how trading networks were agents of globalisation.[5] Merchants who had international business in the Spanish empire used extensive networks to avoid risks, transfer information, monitor dealings and, in doing so, lower transaction costs in commercial operations, which over time reduced prices and opened the way for international markets to converge ('hard' globalisation).[6] The way to do so was by using formal institutions that penalised actions contrary to agreements or by enforcing trust with collective sanctions based on anthropological ties such as family and reputation within those networks. Both Spanish and foreign merchants who lived in Spanish *entrepôts* used these two systems.[7] Furthermore, they connected markets and territories which were disconnected before the sixteenth century ('soft' globalisation), which laid the basis for the convergence of markets. Trans-'national' communities who lived in American and European cities and ports formed networks that entangled markets and territories in the Atlantic and beyond, which allowed places such as the Caribbean Sea to become privileged areas in the articulation of global commercial routes.[8] By addressing a case study, that of the commercial network of the wholesaler Santi Federighi who lived in Mexico City during the first half of the seventeenth century, this chapter is meant to illustrate how Mexican merchants connected commercial systems that were thousands of miles distant from each other in the seventeenth century.

Santi Federighi, also called Stefantoni Federighi in some documents, was a member of one of the most powerful merchant families of the Hispanic Atlantic during the late sixteenth and seventeenth centuries. His grandfather emigrated from Tuscany to Seville in the second half of the sixteenth century in search of, like many others at the time, the treasures of the West Indies trade. In Seville, the Federighi family merged with two other Italian families, the Fantoni and the Bucarelli families, forming one of the richest merchant firms that operated in the Hispanic Atlantic.[9] The head of the family in New Spain was Santi Federighi, who amassed a fortune from his commercial businesses during the 1620s and 1630s. He died in 1643.[10]

Santi Federighi concentrated his capital on cochineal trade, but he also was a money lender and invested in the Philippine trade via the so-called Manila galleons. The trans-'national' character of Federighi was given not only by his Italian origins (notwithstanding the fact that he was born in Seville), but also by his capacity to manage a network comprised of dozens of merchants that spanned from Southeast Asia to Europe (Castile and Italy). To what extent did Santi Federighi's network have influence across different commercial systems? How did Santi Federighi manage to connect the Philippines, New Spain and Europe, and to organise the movement of merchandise and goods between different world regions in the first half of the seventeenth century? The answers to these queries will show the way in which the trading network of a Sevillian merchant of Italian origins who lived in Mexico City contributed to the creation global markets in the early modern era. I will specifically focus on three international markets in which Federighi invested: silver, cochineal and the Manila Galleon trade.

This chapter compiles the initial results of an ongoing research project I am developing on the role of great Mexican traders in the internationalisation of the New Spanish economy during the seventeenth century. The project is based on various documents, such as private letters and business letters, and so forth, that belonged to Santi Federighi. Furthermore, the project is based on merchandise reports, which usually accompanied the business letters that merchants sent to each other, and collected lists of traded goods.

The business of silver

The economic significance of silver mining in international trade and the New Spanish economy is well known. Mining was central to colonial Mexican commerce because silver provided a stable medium of exchange in the viceroyalty. It was the conduit through which the economy of the richest Iberians and Creoles, which was based on capital investment in international trade, agriculture and urban real estate, worked.[11] Furthermore, silver became a basis for internationalisation of trade in the Atlantic World and Asia. New Spain became one of the main silver-producing regions in the world in the sixteenth century. Global webs of trade centred on the mercantile activities of traders who lived in silver mining areas, such as Peru, Japan and New Spain itself.[12]

In New Spain, silver production was in the hands of mine owners who lived in cities such as Zacatecas and Aguascalientes, which were among the most productive silver mines of the viceroyalty. They owned silver mines and contracted miners from the subaltern (indigenous) populations and sold silver to mine 'refiners' (*refinadores*), i.e., businessmen in charge of silver processing. Bar silver was then sold to wholesalers who exported silver away from the viceroyalty or sold it to mints such as that of Mexico City. This circuit enabled silver to end up feeding global trade. During the seventeenth century silver production was possible because both mine owners and 'refiners' were backed by the credit of traders from principal cities, especially Mexico City, or by the credit of *alcaldes mayores* (district governors), who might also have been financed by main traders from Mexico City.[13]

Santi Federighi's commercial activities are a paradigm of the way in which Mexican wholesalers participated in silver mining: he provided merchants of mining cities with merchandise and credit and also purchased refined silver bars to finance his regional and international commercial activities. It seems that Federighi mostly invested in the mines of Zacatecas, which were the biggest silver mines of New Spain, more than in other minor mines, such as Aguascalientes. The letters of the brokers and commercial agents of Federighi in Zacatecas reflect his *modus operandi* regarding silver mining. He not only purchased silver in great quantities from mine owners, 'refiners' and other merchants from Zacatecas, but also sold merchandise such as European cloth (*ruán de Castilla*), canvas and slaves through their agents and peddlers, who informed him about the situation of the market for these products in Zacatecas.[14] Most of his operations in Zacatecas consisted of crediting mine owners. Nevertheless, Federighi usually had problems collecting debts from the mine owners of Zacatecas even in economic conjunctures marked by mining expansion, such as in the 1620s. For instance, business letters dated in 1624 show that most Federighi's debtors in Zacatecas had cash-flow problems.[15] More than just problems of trust, it likely reflects the delicate economic situation in which mine owners, whose capital was usually based on short-term loans with high interest, permanently lived.

The financing of and investment in silver production lubricated Federighi's commercial operations in and out of the viceroyalty of New Spain. Silver was the lifeblood of his network, which spanned from the Philippines to Europe and included Asian cities such as Manila, New Spanish cities such as Antequera de Oaxaca, Puebla de los Ángeles, Aguascalientes and Zacatecas among others, Lima in Peru, Havana in the Caribbean, and Seville in Europe. Figure 6.1 uses UCINET (Netdraw) software to depict the ego-network of Santi Fedeighi, who is at the very centre of the graph. The network includes the different commercial agents, brokers and partners with whom Federighi kept contact from c. 1620 to his death in 1643. He had commercial contacts distributed right across the Spanish empire. Most of them lived in the Americas, especially in New Spanish cities where he concentrated his investments. However, the business that Federighi had with some of the main New Spanish cities was based on products which had an international market. This was the case of cochineal dye.

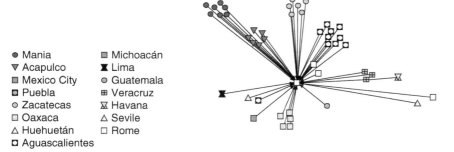

● Mania   ▣ Michoacán
▼ Acapulco   ✖ Lima
▣ Mexico City   ◉ Guatemala
▱ Puebla   ⊞ Veracruz
◎ Zacatecas   ⊠ Havana
▢ Oaxaca   △ Sevile
△ Huehuetán   ▢ Rome
▱ Aguascalientes

Figure 6.1 Ego-network of Santi Federighi (c. 1620–1643). Each figure represents a merchant or commercial agent.

Source: AGN, *Indiferente Virreinal* (sections *Consulado*, *Filipinas* and *Industria y Comercio*).

Santi Federighi's cochineal trade

From the sixteenth to the eighteenth century, cochineal became, after silver, the most important New Spanish export. Of all the dyes produced in the Americas and used in Europe, cochineal was the most in demand. No other dye (not even indigo or Campeche wood) was so much appreciated by European royalty, nobility and churches than the intense crimson one produced from cochineal. Textile industries demanded more and more red dyes during the sixteenth century as the taste for strong red dresses escalated among European elites. Cochineal produced in the Americas, most especially in the area of Oaxaca, which got the monopoly to produce this dye, was to fit European demand. According to Carlos Marichal, the production of New Spanish cochineal was essentially a European demand-driven process. Castile then became one of the most important re-exportation markets of cochineal for the rest of Europe, especially Italy and the United Provinces.[16]

Wholesalers from Mexico City played a key role in the production and internationalisation of the cochineal trade during the early modern era, but they were far from being the only agents. The system of production of cochineal was based on the *repartimiento* system, which lasted until 1787. According to historiography, the indigenous population, local officers such as district governors (*alcaldes mayores*), and local merchants were, besides wholesale merchants, involved in such a system. Wholesale merchants from big cities such as Mexico City received funds from Veracruz merchants, who provided local merchants from Oaxaca with money. Oaxaca merchants then lent those resources to *alcaldes mayores* who governed the so-called 'Indian communities' (*repúblicas de indios*). These district governors financed indigenous families of cochineal-producing towns, who had to repay them in the form of cochineal at a fixed price, much lower than that of market prices, of course, when it was harvested. Governors shipped the final product to Veracruz merchants. This is how literature on the topic has explained the way in which cochineal was produced and traded in New Spain during the early modern era.[17] The main commercial strategies used by Iberian merchants in the Atlantic World during the early modern era are well documented.[18] The case of Santi Federighi, who became one of the most prominent dealers in cochineal in his epoch, sheds light on the way in which New Spanish merchants managed cochineal business during the first half of the seventeenth century.

Santi Federighi had three systems through which he invested in the cochineal trade, which were based on three types of intermediaries who managed his businesses in Oaxaca. First, he had brokers in several cities of Oaxaca. He not only had contact with merchants from the main city of Oaxaca (Antequera) who invested in the cochineal *repartimiento* and provided him with cargos of dye.[19] Furthermore, Federighi had brokers and agents in other minor towns of the region such as Teococouilco. These brokers and agents from minor towns bought cochineal on behalf of Federighi and also repeatedly sent him information about the state of the market. Data on the fluctuations of prices, which depended highly on factors as varied as the arrivals and departures of Atlantic fleets, the climate, to that of the problems with debt collection, were among the most common information on the cochineal market sent to Federighi from his agents in Antequera and the different towns of Oaxaca.[20]

Second, Federighi also had agents who were travelling instead of having a seat in a specific place from where they collected information. This was the case, for instance, of Jacinto Barbosa, an agent who wrote in his letters to Federighi how he constantly moved around the viceroyalty – between Acapulco, Oaxaca and Veracruz. This constant movement of some of Federighi's agents allowed him to have fresh information with a more flexible perspective, as these agents got his information across the viceroyalty. As mentioned above, prices of cochineal, similar to other products, not only depended on the crop but also depended highly on the time schedules of fleets, which is to say the availability of overseas transport as a means to send the product to international markets. For this reason, a delay in the fleet arriving in or departing from Veracruz might have catastrophic consequences due to oversupply, especially for merchants who had a great stock of cochineal ready to be sold as the prices would drop the next year. A travelling agent like

Jacinto Barbosa who had information from different areas of the viceroyalty gave timely intelligence to Federighi on these and other market circumstances.[21]

Third, Santi Federighi not only received information about the market of cochineal directly from his partners, brokers and agents in Oaxaca, but also indirectly from people who seem to have been very close to him but did not live in Oaxaca. For instance, he received information about the market of cochineal from Pedro de Miranda. De Miranda did not live in Oaxaca, but in Puebla de los Ángeles, which had been also capital of a cochineal-producing area during the sixteenth century and was located halfway between Mexico City and Oaxaca. Pedro de Miranda was not only a priest and Federighi's own chaplain, which is to say a person he could trust, but also a person who had his own interest in the cochineal market and also disposed of a great knowledge on the performance of the cochineal market. For instance, Pedro de Miranda, who obtained information from his own informants, transmitted messages to Federighi about which district governors and local merchants from Oaxaca could offer him better business terms, and also about possible strategies to hoard cochineal and, in doing so, control prices.[22] In summary, getting information from third parties was also a more flexible way to get information on the market situation, like in the case of travelling agents, and also to compare information: in other words it was a way to guarantee that his agents in Oaxaca deserved his trust.

Finally, it seems from Santi Federighi's case that Veracruz merchants did not have the credit and investor role in cochineal dye that the literature has pointed out, at least during the first half of the seventeenth century. Federighi's letters show that the merchants from Veracruz acted more as brokers between the merchants from Mexico City and those from Seville and Cadiz than as investors in cochineal. 'Yesterday I received six boxes of cochineal dye that Fernando Ortiz, resident in Oaxaca, sends in your behalf' (*Ayer rresevi seis caxones de grana que Fernando Ortiz vezino de Oaxaca ynvia por quenta de V*[uestra] *M*[erced]). This note was sent by Pedro de Vertiz from Veracruz to Santi Federighi in 1641.[23] Federighi's documents are full of similar notes which indicate that the Veracruz merchants linked to him did not credit his investments in cochineal but only managed the re-exportation of cochineal from Oaxaca to Seville.[24] The main addressee in Seville of Santi Federighi's shipments of cochineal was his partner and brother-in-law Antonio Maria Bucarelli.[25] On occasions, merchants from Veracruz even acted as brokers of Federighi for the management of his business in cochineal in Oaxaca by directly negotiating with local merchants and district governors of Oaxaca in behalf of Federighi, but not as his credit provider.[26]

Commercial networks across the Manila Galleon trade route

In 1565, Spanish soldiers initiated the conquest of the Philippine Islands. That very year an expedition commanded by Miguel López de Legazpi and Andrés de Urdaneta, who had departed from New Spain, found their way back to the

American continent. Until then several Spanish expeditions stopped over at the Philippines (the archipelago was named in honour to the prince Philip, later Philip II, by Ruy López de Villalobos in 1542) en route to Asia, but they did not find how to come back to the Americas across the Pacific Ocean. Only when López de Legazpi and Urdaneta's expedition found the Kuroshio ocean current, which moves north-eastward from eastern China and the Philippines to North America and then south-westward from North America to the Philippines, could the Spaniards start the conquest of the Philippine archipelago. In 1565, they founded the city of Cebu on the island of the same name, and in 1571, Manila on the western coast of Luzon. The Spaniards expected to find a land full of spices. However, few spices were produced in the Philippines, especially on the main island, Luzon. Only Mindanao produced notable quantities of cinnamon. The few galleons that crossed the Pacific bound for New Spain in the years immediately after 1565 only carried small quantities of cinnamon, fruits of the islands and textiles produced by Tagalog populations.[27]

Despite the initial disappointment, Spaniards settled in the Philippines, which became a General Captaincy (*Capitanía General*) administratively integrated into the viceroyalty of New Spain. The Philippines were conceived as a military and strategic point in Southeast Asia by the Hispanic crown. Furthermore, in the late sixteenth century, when both European and Spanish American merchants on the one hand, and Chinese merchants on the other, started moving to Manila, it also became an international *entrepôt* in which Mexican merchants had strong economic interests.[28] The commercial system developed by the Europeans in Southeast Asia was based on three commercial trading webs, which interacted with each other. The first was that of the English East India Company (EIC), which had two key ports in Bantam and Surat. The second web was that of the Dutch *Vereenigde Oost-Indische Compagnie* (VOC), whose hub ports in the seventeenth century were Batavia, Ceylon, Melaka, Nagasaki and Taiwan, among others.[29] The third commercial web was that of the Hispanic monarchy, which had only one main port, Cavite in Manila, and was characterised by a certain peculiarity. Unlike the English and Dutch commercial webs in the Asia-Pacific area, the Spanish commercial web around Manila had a remarkable shortcoming: Manila merchants could not trade directly with any other port of the area but only with 'foreign' merchants, mainly Portuguese, Chinese, Dutch and English, who moved to Cavite to do business with them. This situation made the Philippine trade highly dependent on the dynamics and interests of networks whose focus was far from Manila.[30] The Spanish commercial web around Manila was the network in which Mexican merchants such as Santi Federighi were integrated through investment in the Manila galleons.

The main commercial operations that took place in Manila were the exchange of American silver for Asian-manufactured goods such as Chinese silk and porcelain. Merchants who immigrated to Manila from the Americas and Europe acted as agents of Mexican wholesalers. They sold American silver to Chinese merchants living in Manila and also to Dutch, English and Portuguese merchants who operated, many times illegally, in the port of Cavite. In exchange these agents received Asian goods which they annually loaded in the Manila galleons on consignment to the wholesalers of Mexico City via Acapulco – for climatic reasons the Manila galleons only sailed once annually from Acapulco to Manila and then from Manila to Acapulco. However, in the late sixteenth and early seventeenth century the market of Asian goods was still in formation in the Spanish empire. For the first time in Spanish history, the purchase and consumption of Asian manufactures went beyond royal families and the wealthiest nobles, especially in New Spain, where bureaucrats, artisans and other middle-class elites chose Chinese silk and other Asian products among their preferred fabric and goods of their material culture. In Castile, the process was slower, but the presence of Asian goods grew during the first half of the seventeenth century as the circulation of Asian goods from the Americas to Castile increased during that period due to the expansion of trade of the Manila galleons and growing demand for Asian goods in Iberia.[31]

In this context of shaping a new market, merchant networks of Mexican traders played a role in the expansion of taste for Chinese porcelain and silk in the Americas and Iberia. Santi Federighi was among those who intervened in and was a protagonist of market formation for Asian goods in the Spanish empire. Mexico City's wholesalers, like Federighi, were financial investors in the Manila Galleon trade. They provided merchants of Manila with resources. Furthermore, Mexican merchants invested in Manila's trade through two types of systems. The first system was based on the establishment of partnerships with merchants of Manila. In doing so, two or more partners from Manila and Mexico City supplied the same quantity of capital or its equivalent in work, and the surplus derived from the commercial operations in the Manila galleons was proportionally distributed. The second system was having commercial agents who lived temporarily or permanently in Manila. These agents might be either brokers who occasionally travelled to Manila to do business on behalf of their payer in Mexico City, or 'permanent' commercial agents (*encomenderos*) who lived in Manila, where they had their own businesses, managed Mexican merchants' investments in the Manila Galleon Trade Route, shipped merchandise to Acapulco and received a fixed salary or a commission depending on the success of the transactions from the merchants of Mexico.[32] Santi Federighi used this latter system. He had an *encomendero* who lived in Manila who exchanged silver for Asian goods on behalf of Federighi and received a commission for every annual transaction.

Santi Federighi's *encomendero* was Ascanio Guazzoni, and his origins were, like Federighi's origins, Florentine. The fact that Guazzoni was of Florentine origin reflects that in long-distance and risky operations such as those of the Manila Galleon Trade Route, Santi Federighi trusted people with whom he shared geographic and cultural origins.[33] Not by chance, for transactions across the other long-distance route of the New Spanish trade which was the trans-Atlantic route, Federighi also drew on anthropological resources such as 'national' and family ties to operate exports and imports, as he had his own brother-in-law, Antonio Maria Bucarelli, who was also of Tuscan origin and his main partner in Iberia. It seems that trust based on family and political identities was the preferred method of rich New Spanish merchants like Santi Federighi to guarantee trust in commercial operations of long-distance trade, including the Manila Galleon Trade Route.[34]

Nonetheless, Santi Federighi's involvement in trans-Pacific trade did not finish in the Philippines, but rather Manila and the Pacific Ocean were only the beginning of a series of new transactions. Once silver was exchanged for Asian goods in Manila, which were then shipped to Acapulco, the products were distributed in the viceroyalty of New Spain and beyond. Here there are also some lessons on the way in which Mexican merchants' networks globally operated to be taken from Federighi's case. Unlike the case of cochineal, of which the cargos were usually managed by agents and brokers from Oaxaca, it seems that Federighi himself managed the dispatches of Chinese porcelain and the rest of Asian goods from his house and warehouses of Mexico City. Federighi received the cargos from Acapulco once the Manila galleons arrived in New Spain around January.[35] He re-exported a part of the cargos to Seville.[36] He shipped another part of Chinese cargos to elites of New Spain who were close to him. For instance, Federighi usually dispatched boxes of Chinese merchandise to Andrés Fernández de Miranda, who lived in Puebla de los Ángeles.[37] On occasion, when the goods to be dispatched were textiles, they had been previously dyed in Mexico City. This is what happened with Pedro de Vergara Gaviria, who lived in Carrión (Atlixco) near Puebla, to whom Federighi consigned a piece of cloth from China after making sure it had been dyed, like Vergara Gaviria had asked.[38] In some other cases people from Puebla travelled themselves to Mexico City to buy Asian products in the warehouse of Santi Federighi.[39] By managing the dispatches instead of entrusting them to commercial agents, Santi Federighi contributed to shape a market of Asian goods, which by 1600 was still very limited in the Spanish empire.

Conclusions

Santi Federighi was an agent of globalisation in the seventeenth century. His Italian origins, the fact that he extended a commercial network from the Americas to Iberia and created his own network operating from the Philippines to Europe, and the way in which he connected several commercial systems of the world, made him a paradigm of the New World which was being born in the sixteenth and seventeenth century.

Santi Federighi's business concentrated on one of the most productive economic sectors of the viceroyalty of New Spain, the production and export of cochineal. He did not contract Indians to plant nopal and harvest cochineal. Indeed, he likely never had the need to travel southward to Oaxaca, nor had he the need to receive the cargos of cochineal in Mexico City where he lived, as the product was sent directly to Veracruz to be exported to Seville by his own chain of agents. However, Federighi was a driving force in the internationalisation of this booming dye. He provided merchants from Oaxaca and district governors in charge of the *repartimiento system* with resources and credit, and also provided the means for the product to be shipped to Iberia across the Atlantic, from which he obtained large profits. In other words, the bulk of the capital invested in operations related to the production and exportation of cochineal, which guaranteed that the scarlet dye arrived at and was distributed across Europe, was provided by merchants like Santi Federighi.

Furthermore, Santi Federighi took the risk of investing in the profitable but unsafe trade of the Manila Galleon traffic. The annual cycle on which the Manila Galleon trade depended on the constant dangers surrounding the galleons, which required considerable expense such as marine insurance and the investment of great quantities of money. Santi Federighi did it. In this way he and his network contributed to the circulation of products, i.e. Asian goods such as Chinese silk and porcelain, which were relatively new among segments of the population beyond monarchs, nobles and prelates, and propelled and satisfied a rising demand for such products in New Spain and Iberia.

Last but not least, silver production was also among the interests of Federighi's operations. He financed silver mining from which he increased the benefits for his commercial house. Furthermore, through his operations in mines like Zacatecas, Federighi could buy silver which he then sold to mints or re-exported to Europe. But more importantly, silver was the good that allowed exchanges within New Spain on the one hand, and between New Spain and the Philippines and Iberia on the other. In this way silver became the fuel which allowed the machinery of Federighi's network to run and connect different trading systems.

Santi Federighi deployed all sorts of mechanisms to enforce his commercial operations. His business in cochineal and its implication in long-distance markets such as the trans-Pacific and trans-Atlantic trade reflect it. He turned to family ties to make sure that long-distance trade, which by definition was riskier than short-distance operations, took place in secure conditions. However, given the impossibility to constantly rely on such a safe mechanism owing to the difficulty of having relatives and fellow countrymen distributed all over the viceroyalty, he launched other mechanisms which are visible in his operations in cochineal trade. For his operations in Oaxaca, he counted on travelling agents who moved over the viceroyalty to send him fresh information, and also third parties who had good knowledge of the cochineal market and informed him about the conditions of markets and merchants who might offer him better conditions to contract.

Beyond the figure of Santi Federighi, this case depicts a far-reaching economic reality: the role of merchants of European origins who settled in the Americas, whose networks became conduits of commercial interaction that impacted on trading partners from different continents and established the base for a global market. It is hard to prove the existence of any process of market convergence on the international level as early as the first half of the seventeenth century, but it is worth pointing out that the commercial activities of American merchants such as Santi Federighi were a necessary precondition for later global market convergence. For this reason, the study of the performance of Santi Federighi's network contributes to a better understanding not only of the seventeenth-century economic history of New Spain, which is one of the most unknown periods of the American colonial history in comparison to the sixteenth and the eighteenth centuries, but also the way, in a context of economic risk and uncertainty, in which high transaction costs and the difficulty of avoiding cheating in commercial operations, a reduced group of American networks were able to connect regional markets separated from each other by oceans. The later development of international markets and the progressive reduction of transaction costs, which were laid on the commercial activities of merchants like Federighi, ended up shaping a truly global, integrated market.

Notes

1 Carletti, F., *Mi viaje alrededor del mundo (1594–1606)* (Madrid: Noray, 2014), pp. 71–74. Obviously, Carletti made a mistake in defining Acapulco as the capital of the 'province' (i.e. viceroyalty) of New Spain, which was Mexico City.
2 De Vries, J., 'The limits of globalization in the early modern world', *Economic History Review*, 63(3), 2009, pp. 1–24.
3 O'Rourke, K. and Williamson, J.G., 'When did globalization begin?', *European Review of Economic History*, 6, 2002, pp. 23–50.
4 Flynn, D.O. and Giráldez, A., 'Path dependence, time lags and the birth of globalisation: A critique of O' Rourke and Williamson', *European Review of Economic History*, 8, 2004, p. 83.
5 A recent and excellent example is Böttcher, N., Hausberger, B. and Ibarra, A., eds., *Redes y negocios globales en el mundo ibérico, siglos XVI–XVIII* (Madrid: Iberoamericana, 2011).
6 Menard, R.R., 'Transport costs and long-range trade, 1300–1800: Was there a European 'transport revolution' in the early modern era?', in Tracy, J.D. (ed.), *Political Economy of Merchant Empires* (Cambridge: Cambridge University Press, 1991), pp. 228–275. O'Rourke and Williamson's work has produced a prolific debate based on empirical studies of prices on the convergence of international markets from the seventeenth to the nineteenth century.
7 Cachero Vinuesa, M., 'Redes mercantiles en los inicios del comercio atlántico. Sevilla entre Europa y América', in Böttcher, N., Hausberger, B. and Ibarra, A. (eds.), *Redes y negocios globales* (Madrid: Iberoamericana, 2011), pp. 25–51. More details on theoretical assumptions to study networks as mechanisms to reduce transaction costs can be seen in chapters by Xavier Lamikiz and Montserrat Cachero Vinuesa.
8 Crespo Solana, A. (ed.), *Comunidades transnacionales. Colonias de mercaderes extranjeros en el mundo atlántico (1500–1830)* (Madrid: Doce Calles, 2010); Crespo Solana, A., 'The wider world: Spatial expansion and integration in the Hispanic Atlantic, 16th to 18th centuries', in Crespo Solana, A. (ed.), *Spatio-Temporal Narratives. Historical GIS and the Study of Global Trading Networks (1500–1800)* (Cambridge: Cambridge Scholars Publishing, 2014).
9 See more information about the Fantoni family, and more generally about the comercial connections between Tuscany and Andalusia, in Iglesias Rodríguez, J.J., *El árbol de Sinople Familia y patrimonio entre Andalucía y Toscana en la Edad Moderna* (Sevilla: Universidad de Sevilla, 2008).
10 Núñez Roldán, F., 'Tres Familias Florentinas en Sevilla: Federighi, Fantoni y Bucarelli (1570–1625)', *Presencia Italiana en Andalucía. Actas del III Coloquio Hispano-Italiano* (Sevilla: CSIC, 1989), pp. 23–50; Hoberman, L.S., *Mexico's Merchant Elite, 1590–1660. Silver, State, and Society* (Durham, NC: Duke University Press, 1991), p. 41.
11 This contrasts with the economy of the subaltern populations of New Spain, which continued using grains of cacao as in pre-Hispanic times because of the lack of copper coins: Romano, R., *Moneda, pseudomonedas y circulación monetaria en las economías de México* (México, D. F.: Fondo de Cultura Económica, 1998).

12 TePaske, J.J., *A New World of Gold and Silver* (Leiden: Brill, 2010); Gasch-Tomás, J.L., 'La contribución de los galeones de Manila a las alteraciones de precios del maíz en Nueva España, c. 1550–1650', in Bernabeu Albert, S., Mena García, C. and José Luque Azcona, E.M. (eds.), *Filipinas y el Pacífico: nuevas miradas, nuevas reflexiones Sevilla* (Sevilla: Universidad de Sevilla, Servicio de Publicaciones, forthcoming).

13 Romano, R. *Mecanismos y elementos del sistema económico colonial americano, siglos XVI–XVIII* (México, D. F.: Fondo de Cultura Económica, 2004), pp. 363–364; Hoberman, L.S., 'El crédito colonial y el sector minero en el siglo XVII: aportación del mercader de plata a la economía colonial', in López-Cano, M.P. and del Valle Pavón, G. (eds.), *El crédito en Nueva España* (México, D. F.: Instituto de Investigaciones Dr. José María Luis Mora, 1998), pp. 61–82.

14 Letters dated 9 April, 12 July, and 27 November 1624: Archivo General de la Nación (henceforth AGN), Indiferente Virreinal, caja-exp.: 5602-001. Consulado.

15 Letters dated 12 July, 17 September and 18 September, 1624: AGN, Indiferente Virreinal, caja-exp.: 5602-001.

16 Marichal, C. 'Mexican cochineal and European demand for luxury dye, 1550–1850', in Aram, B. and Yun-Casalilla, B. (eds.), *Global Goods and the Spanish Empire, 1492–1824: Circulation, Resistance, and Diversity* (London: Palgrave, 2014), pp. 201–204; Lee, R., 'American Cochineal in European Commerce, 1526–1625', *Journal of Modern History*, 23 (1951), pp. 205–224.

17 Sánchez, C.C., Suárez, S., Suárez, M. and Bosa, S., 'Evolución de la producción y el comercio mundial de la grana cochinilla, siglos XVI–XIX', *Revista de Indias*, LXVI, 237 (2006), pp. 479–480; Marichal, C., 'Mexican Cochineal', pp. 208–210; Baskes, J., 'Institutions and Cross-cultural Trade: *Repartimiento* Credit and Indigenous Production of Cochineal in Eighteenth-Century Oaxaca', *The Journal of Economic History*, 65, 1, (2005), pp. 186–210.

18 See a summary in Lamikiz, X., *Trade and Trust in the Eighteenth-Century Atlantic World* (London: The Royal Historical Society, 2010), pp. 1–22.

19 Letter of Carlos de Covarrubias from Oaxaca on 14th June, 1630: AGN, Indiferente Virreinal, caja-exp.: 5651-017. Consulado, pp. 175–176.

20 AGN, Indiferente Virreinal, caja-exp.: 5651-017. Consulado, pp. 140–141.

21 AGN, Indiferente Virreinal, caja-exp.: 6015-023. Consulado.

22 Letter on 2 April, 1624: AGN, Indiferente Virreinal, caja-exp.: 5602-001. Consulado. Other examples in AGN, Indiferente Virreinal, caja-exp.: 5602-001. Consulado; AGN, Indiferente Virreinal, caja-exp.: 5651-017. Consulado; AGN, Indiferente Virreinal, caja-exp.: 5651-017. Consulado.

23 Letter on 19 March, 1641: AGN, Indiferente Virreinal, caja-exp.: 6015-023. Consulado, p. 17.

24 Letter on 15 June, 1629: AGN, Indiferente Virreinal, caja-exp.: 5651-017. Consulado, pp. 179–180; Letter on 25th June, 1629: AGN, Indiferente Virreinal, caja-exp.: 5651-017. Consulado, pp. 186–187; Letter on 9 July, 1629: AGN, Indiferente Virreinal, caja-exp.: 5651-017. Consulado, pp. 197–198.

25 Letters on 21 February and 31 May, 1627, and on 18 April, 1634: AGN, Indiferente Virreinal, caja-exp.: 5651-017. Consulado; AGN, Indiferente Virreinal, caja-exp.: 5602-001. Consulado.

26 This was the case of the aforementioned Pedro de Vertiz and also Lucián Espinel. Letter 25th April, 1627: AGN, Indiferente Virreinal, caja-exp.: 5651-017. Consulado, pp. 129–130; Letter 16 June, 1629: AGN, Indiferente Virreinal, caja-exp.: 5651-017. Consulado, p. 185.

27 Schurtz, W.L., *El Galeón de Manila*. Madrid: Ediciones de Cultura Hispánica, 1992; Phelan, J.L., *The Hispanization of the Philippines: Spanish Aims and Filipino Responses, 1565–1700* (Madison: University of Wisconsin Press, 2010).

28 Álvarez, L.A., 'Don Quijote en el Pacífico: la construcción del proyecto español en Asia, 1591–1606', *Revista de Historia Económica – Journal of Iberian and Latin America Economic History*, 23 (2005), pp. 241–273.
29 Gaastra, F.S., 'The Dutch East India Company in National and International Perspective', in Haudrère, P. (ed.), *Les flottes des Companies des Indes* (Vincennes: Service historiques de la Marine, 1996), pp. 299–317.
30 Muntaner, A.P. 'Mapping and Visualization of Commercial Networks in the Pacific Ocean during the 17th Century', in Crespo Solana, A. (ed), *Spatio-Temporal Narratives. Historical GIS and the Study of Global Trading Networks (1500–1800)* (Cambridge: Cambridge Scholars Publishing, 2014), pp. 228–241. Another commercial web, not included in this explanation, was that of the Chinese merchants, who operated between Canton-Macao and Manila.
31 More details about this process of formation of a market for Asian goods in the Spanish empire in Gasch-Tomás, J.L., 'Globalisation, Market Formation and Commoditisation in the Spanish Empire. Consumer Demand for Asian Goods in Mexico City and Seville, c. 1571–1630', *Revista de Historia Económica – Journal of Iberian and Latin America Economic History*, 32(2), (2014), pp. 189–221; Gasch-Tomás, J.L., 'Asian Silk, Porcelain and Material Culture in the Definition of Mexican and Andalusian Elites, c. 1565–1630', in Aram, B. and Yun-Casalilla, B. (eds.), *Global Goods and the Spanish Empire, 1492–1824: Circulation, Resistance, and Diversity* (London: Palgrave, 2014), pp. 153–173.
32 Yuste López, C., 'De la libre contratación a las restricciones de la *permission*. La andadura de los comerciantes de México en los giros iniciales con Manila, 1580–1610', in Bernabéu Albert, S. and Martínez Shaw, C. (eds.), *Un océano de seda y plata: el universo económico del Galeón de Manila* (Sevilla: CSIC, 2013), pp. 85–106.
33 Here the term 'national' must be understood as belonging to the same *imagined community*: Anderson, B.R., *Imagined Communities. Reflections On the Origin and Spread of Nationalism* (London: Verso, 1991).
34 Nonetheless, in the late 1630s Ascanio Guazzoni went into a series of catastrophic commercial operations which ended up in his bankruptcy, for which Santi Federighi had to resort to other commercial agents in Manila to manage his businesses there: Gasch-Tomás, J.L., *Global trade, circulation and consumption of Asian goods in the Atlantic World. The Manila Galleons and the Social Elites of Mexico and Seville (1580–1640)*, PhD thesis (Florence: European University Institute, 2012), pp. 138–144.
35 Federighi's documents are full of papers with notes of merchandise shipped from his agents in Acapulco to him: AGN, Indiferente Virreinal, caja-exp.: 5845-077. Consulado, p. 8; AGN, Indiferente Virreinal, caja-exp.: 5887-014, Industria y Comercio, pp. 9–11.
36 Letter of Lucián Espinel from Veracruz on 15th January, 1627: AGN, Indiferente Virreinal, caja-exp.: 5651-017. Consulado. Letter of Antonio Maria Bucarelli on 21st February, 1627: AGN, Indiferente Virreinal, caja-exp.: 5651-017. Consulado.
37 Letter on 1st May and 14th June, 1627: AGN, Indiferente Virreinal, caja-exp.: 5651-017. Consulado; AGN, Indiferente Virreinal, caja-exp.: 5651-017. Consulado.
38 Letter on 16 March 1628: AGN, Indiferente Virreinal, caja-exp. 3269-002. Consulado.
39 This was what Juan Francisco de Meneses from Puebla did in 1627: AGN, Indiferente Virreinal, caja-exp.: 5651-017. Consulado, pp. 151–152.

Bibliography

Alonso Álvarez, L., 'Don Quijote en el Pacífico: la construcción del proyecto español en Asia, 1591–1606', *Revista de Historia Económica – Journal of Iberian and Latin America Economic History*, 23, 2005, pp. 241–273.

Anderson, B.R., *Imagined Communities. Reflections on the Origin and Spread of Nationalism*, London: Verso, 1991.

Baskes, J., 'Institutions and Cross-cultural Trade: *Repartimiento* Credit and Indigenous Production of Cochineal in Eighteenth-Century Oaxaca', *The Journal of Economic History*, 65, 1, 2005, pp. 186–210.

Böttcher, N., Hausberger, B. and Ibarra, A. (eds.), *Redes y negocios globales en el mundo ibérico, siglos XVI–XVIII*, Madrid: Iberoamericana, 2011.

Cachero Vinuesa, M., 'Redes mercantiles en los inicios del comercio atlántico. Sevilla entre Europa y América', in Böttcher, N., Hausberger, B. and Ibarra, A. (eds.), *Redes y negocios globales*, Iberoamericana: Madrid, pp. 25–51.

Carletti, F., *Mi viaje alrededor del mundo (1594–1606)*, Madrid: Noray, 2014.

Crespo Solana, A. (ed.), *Comunidades transnacionales. Colonias de mercaderes extranjeros en el mundo atlántico (1500–1830)*, Madrid: Doce Calles, 2010.

———, 'The wider world: Spatial expansion and integration in the Hispanic Atlantic, 16th to 18th centuries', in Crespo Solana, A. (ed.), *Spatio-Temporal Narratives. Historical GIS and the Study of Global Trading Networks (1500–1800)*, Cambridge: Cambridge Scholars Publishing, 2014, pp. 1–44.

De Vries, J., 'The Limits of Globalization in the Early Modern World', *Economic History Review*, 63 (3) (2009), pp. 1–24.

Flynn, D.O. and Giráldez, A., 'Path Dependence, Time Lags and the Birth of Globalisation: A Critique of O'Rourke and Williamson', *European Review of Economic History*, 8 (2004), pp. 81–108.

Gaastra, F.S., 'The Dutch East India Company in National and International Perspective', in Haudrère, P. (ed.), *Les flottes des Companies des Indes*, Vincennes: Service historiques de la Marine, 1996, pp. 299–317.

Gasch-Tomás, J.L., 'Global Trade, Circulation and Consumption of Asian Goods in the Atlantic World. The Manila Galleons and the Social Elites of Mexico and Seville (1580–1640), PhD thesis, Florence: European University Institute, 2012.

———, 'Globalisation, Market Formation and Commoditisation in the Spanish Empire. Consumer Demand for Asian Goods in Mexico City and Seville, c. 1571–1630', *Revista de Historia Económica – Journal of Iberian and Latin America Economic History*, 32(2), (2014), pp. 189–221.

———, 'Asian Silk, Porcelain and Material Culture in the Definition of Mexican and Andalusian Elites, c. 1565–1630', in Aram, B. and Yun-Casalilla, B. (eds.), *Global Goods and the Spanish Empire, 1492–1824: Circulation, Resistance, and Diversity*, London: Palgrave, 2014, pp. 153–173.

———, 'La contribución de los galeones de Manila a las alteraciones de precios del maíz en Nueva España, c. 1550–1650', in Bernabeu Albert, S., Mena García, C. and José Luque Azcona, E. (eds.), *Filipinas y el Pacífico: nuevas miradas, nuevas reflexiones Sevilla*, Sevilla: Universidad de Sevilla, Servicio de Publicaciones (forthcoming).

Hoberman, L.S., *Mexico's Merchant Elite, 1590–1660. Silver, State, and Society*, Durham: Duke University Press, 1991.

———, 'El crédito colonial y el sector minero en el siglo XVII: aportación del mercader de plata a la economía colonial', in del Pilar López-Cano, M. and del Valle Pavón, G. (eds.), *El crédito en Nueva España*, Mexico, D. F.: Instituto de Investigaciones Dr. José María Luis Mora, 1998, pp. 61–82.

Iglesias, R. and Juan, J., *El árbol de Sinople Familia y patrimonio entre Andalucía y Toscana en la Edad Moderna*, Sevilla: Universidad de Sevilla, 2008.

Lamikiz, X., *Trade and Trust in the Eighteenth-Century Atlantic World*, London: The Royal Historical Society, 2010.

Lee, R., 'American Cochineal in European Commerce, 1526–1625', *Journal of Modern History*, (1951), pp. 205–224.

Marichal, C., 'Mexican Cochineal and European Demand for Luxury Dye, 1550–1850', in Aram, B. and Yun-Casalilla, B. (eds.), *Global Goods and the Spanish Empire, 1492–1824: Circulation, Resistance, and Diversity*, London: Palgrave, 2014, pp. 197–215.

Menard, R.R., 'Transport Costs and Long-range Trade, 1300–1800: Was there a European "Transport Revolution" in the Early Modern Era?', in Tracy, J.D. (ed.), *Political Economy of Merchant Empires*, Cambridge: Cambridge University Press, 1991, pp. 228–275.

Muntaner, A.P., 'Mapping and Visualization of Commercial Networks in the Pacific Ocean During the 17th Century', in Crespo Solana, A. (ed.), *Spatio-Temporal Narratives. Historical GIS and the Study of Global Trading Networks (1500–1800)*, Cambridge: Cambridge Scholars Publishing, 2014, pp. 228–241.

Núñez Roldán, F., 'Tres Familias Florentinas en Sevilla: Federighi, Fantoni y Bucarelli (1570–1625)', in *Presencia Italiana en Andalucía. Actas del III Coloquio Hispano-Italiano*, Sevilla: CSIC, 1989, pp. 23–50.

O'Rourke, K., and Williamson, J.G., 'When did globalization begin?', *European Review of Economic History*, 6, 2002, pp. 23–50.

Phelan, J.L., *The Hispanization of the Philippines: Spanish Aims and Filipino Responses, 1565–1700*, Madison: University of Wisconsin Press, 2010.

Romano, R., *Moneda, pseudomonedas y circulación monetaria en las economías de Mexico*, México, D. F.: Fondo de Cultura Económica, 1998.

———, *Mecanismos y elementos del sistema económico colonial americano, siglos XVI–XVIII*, México, D. F.: Fondo de Cultura Económica, 2004.

Schurtz, W.L., *El Galeón de Manila*, Madrid: Ediciones de Cultura Hispánica, 1992.

Suárez Bosa, M. and Sánchez Silva, C., 'Evolución de la producción y el comercio mundial de la grana cochinilla, siglos XVI–XIX', *Revista de Indias*, LXVI, 237, (2006), pp. 474–489.

TePaske, J.J., *A New World of Gold and Silver*, Leiden: Brill, 2010.

Yuste López, C., 'De la libre contratación a las restricciones de la *permission*. La andadura de los comerciantes de México en los giros iniciales con Manila, 1580–1610', in Bernabéu Albert, S. and Martínez Shaw, C. (eds.), *Un océano de seda y plata: el universo económico del Galeón de Manila*, Sevilla: CSIC, 2013, pp. 85–106.

Primary sources

Archivo General de la Nación (México City), *Indiferente Virreinal*, sections *Consulado, Filipinas* and *Industria y Comercio*.

7 Nations? What nations? Business in the shaping of international trade networks

Seville in the eighteenth century

Manuel F. Fernández Chaves and
Mercedes Gamero Rojas

Introduction

During recent years, there has been significant progress in the study of foreign residents in the Hispanic monarchy, especially in the field of social and economic history, which has benefitted greatly from a study trend that focuses on merchants as the key factor in the operation of foreign communities.[1] The activities of foreign residents, either in the commercial sector or the army, have been the subject of a large number of works based on the ideas of 'nation' or of the foreigners' nationality as Flemish, English or French naturals; for example, those who have made a key contribution to our knowledge of mercantile colonies, as well as of Spanish and Atlantic economy and history. New works which emerged in the wake of this intense historiographical activity have stressed other issues, such as the role played by foreigners in the formation and control of the Spanish domestic market,[2] or their naturalisation as the king's subjects,[3] which has resulted in a new and productive research field, both in Spain and abroad.[4]

Similarly, the number of studies on the participation of these foreigners in 'national' corporations (hospitals, brotherhoods, colleges), which articulated their integration into their host cities, is also growing.[5] Although they appeared for the first time towards the end of Philip II's reign, despite being linked with previous European and Iberian traditions, these corporations did not reach their prime until the seventeenth century; they provided the related national group with cohesion, a sense of belonging and identity for its members and their activities, even if these corporations did not necessarily include all members of the community or if their members were often a mixed bag.[6] Membership was voluntary, but it was frequently considered crucial for the safeguarding of business transactions in a foreign country.[7]

Thus, foreign 'nations' were a sort of 'professional college' for merchants, which, to a lesser extent, were also open to other professionals and non-'nationals'. Membership was, therefore, essentially administrative in nature, not unlike nationality in the present day, and was related to certain rights and duties, for example the election of consuls and *jueces conservadores* (special judges with jurisdiction over foreign residents),[8] which was often a lengthy process.[9] Membership was voluntary, and members and groups could thus enter and leave the corporation at their will.

For example, the Dutch, who had belonged to the Flemish nation in Seville since its creation, were by the late seventeenth century, operating with their own consuls and were among the wealthiest and most enterprising colonies in the city. The allied declaration of war against Louis XIV in 1702 put them in a difficult position, and many resumed their role as members of the Flemish nation. Their family names, which had become progressively 'Castilianised', facilitated these camouflage operations; for instance, Pedro Monteoro (a natural of Schagen, Holland), dropped his former surname, Goutsbergh, for the Spanish version, 'which is the same name Monteoro which was and is my name'.[10] The Irish in Seville never constituted a nation, but rather played an ambiguous game as Catholics and, in some cases, as subjects of the British monarchy.[11] Their national corporation, the Sociedad de San Patricio, was constituted only at a very late date.[12]

At any rate, regardless of their national origin and geopolitical considerations, merchants always shared a common interest: that trade could proceed with as few restrictions as possible. For this reason, we may say that they belonged to the 'nation of trade', the interests of which may or may not coincide with those of the rest of society and their respective governments, for which trade restrictions were a useful geopolitical tool. For this reason, government-appointed consuls were not always 'in synch' with their 'nations'.[13]

It must be taken into consideration that families, which were one of the key factors in the emergence and reproduction of mercantile houses in the Modern period, were often 'transnational' in nature. Occasionally, this led members of families to break national solidarity, either by entering into marriage with naturals of the country in which they operated or by drawing up matrimonial alliances with members of other merchant 'nations'. These alliances aimed to achieve economic advancement but also other social gains which were not necessarily related to trade. This 'transnational' attitude was not restricted to marriage alliances but also extended to the economic sphere – the consolidation of trade partnerships, the opening of new markets or both – and was to a large extent dependent on the evolution of international commerce and politics. Moreover, families were not closed entities, but, as some works have pointed out, the relationships between their members not only contributed to internal cohesion, commercial trust and networking[14] but were also open to people from outside the 'national' group. For this reason, business transactions, kinship relations and friendship could exist between people of different origins, and even 'family' businesses could be 'multinational'.

In addition, the different role played by kinship, inter-family relationships and the notions, which are so highly-regarded by the modern scholars, of 'network' and 'trust' in different commercial communities[15] must be taken into account, along with the religious factor, which was an additional element of cohesion in some mercantile communities, for instance the Irish Jacobites.

Trust and solidarity among merchants, regardless of nationality of origin, manifested itself through both legal and illegal transactions. When conditions required it, contraband became rife, and underground cooperation networks proliferated in harbour cities. The last third of the seventeenth century is a good example: Louis

XIV's expansionist policies and the subsequent boycotts and restrictions set up against French exports caused the emergence and growth, for example in Cádiz in 1689, of a network of dummy-firms, renamed companies, false account books, churches and convents used as warehouses, corrupt local officials and incapacitated anti-contraband courts.[16]

However, solidarity could also be expressed by legal means, especially during war-ridden or post-war periods which were dominated by uncertainty, when merchants joined to confront together the new scenarios thus created. In this way, on 10 January 1702, a group of 33 'businessmen and residents in Seville' of different nationalities (British, Dutch, Flemish, Italian and German), who were represented by the Dutch Pedro Monteoro and the French Miguel Lemaistre, resident in Puerto de Santa María, filed a statement to stress the *bona fides* that had always characterised their relationship, and without which business would be impossible:

> the style and practice of merchants is that monetary fines imposed for the non-fulfilment of commitments and agreements reached by said men of business are indeed paid ... in order to ensure that the good faith between merchants is preserved, because otherwise contracts and agreements would never be kept with enormous prejudice to the merchants, who are thus especially asked to meet exactly all their obligations so as not to open the door to fraud and theft, which would be to the great detriment of commerce, the preservation of which depends on integrity and good faith, and so we declare.[17]

The signatories, as aforementioned, came from all major trading nations. It must be noted that the British community was still almost intact, before the majority of their members returned to England in the first steps of the Spanish War of Succession (see Table 7.1).

A similar event took place in 1764. The deputies and members of the Spanish, French, Flemish and Irish nations in Seville met in order to create a common fund

Table 7.1 Signatories of the agreement to preserve the bona fides in payments and debts.

Flemish and German nation	Alexandro Carlos de Licht, Juan Thormohlen, Enrique Lepin, Livino Theri, Diego de Hanon, Pedro Francisco Willetens, Daniel Vernimen, Gil Huneus, José Francisco Adriaensens, Luis Manteau, Domingo van Peene, Adrián de Brucq, Carlos Davalos, Lorenzo Dorques and Enrique de Bocq
British nation	Thomas Wynmars, Francisco Aycarte, Enrique Wayte, Thomas Salmon, Thomas Hopkins, Thomas Bate, Juan Bate, Ricardo Malcher and Enrique Sander
French nation	Nicolás and Enrique de Lange and Cornelio Couturier
Italian nation	Luis Paganeli, Rafael Bini and Bartolome Ginori

Source: AHPSe, PNS, leg. 5159, f. 13, 10-I-1702.

with which to face the legal costs associated with the lawsuits that were at the time being fought against the urban guilds (see Table 7.2); 4 per cent of all commercial transactions were to be put aside for this purpose.[18] A significant proportion of Seville-based Spanish wholesale traders was represented in this association. Most members, either Spanish or otherwise, had no officially registered investment in American trade (although they participated in it in one way or another). Only a few of the foreign members represented by this association were also members of their own 'national' associations.

These examples show that national solidarity was only one factor in bringing these merchants together; business solidarity, regardless of nationality, was in itself a crucial cohesive element, as Ana Crespo Solana pointed out:

Table 7.2 Signatories of the agreement to create a common fund for paying lawsuits costs.

Spanish nation	Deputies: Antonio Aguirre, Francisco Javier Carazas, Luis Cerero, Juan Antonio Herreros, José de Mier y Noriega Members: Pedro Arnay, Fuentes y Barrera, Pedro Bascó, José Antonio Cabezón, Manuel del Castillo e Hijo, Francisco Manuel Coello, José Cotiella, Juan Manuel Díaz, Miguel Echalaz, Antonio Elías y Hermano Cª., Juan García de Torres, Cristóbal García, José Timoteo García, Juan Gómez Dozal, José Antonio Gómez, Pedro González de la Rubia, José de Juaniz Echalaz, Nicolás Leone, Santiago Llagos, Juan and Santiago Manfredi, Santiago Meabe Arruzabialde, Manuel Prudencio de Molviedro, Juan Moro, Juan Miguel de Ochoa, Ignacio de la Oreja, Manuel Paulín de la Barrera, Manuel Paulín, José Pérez de Baños, José del Rey, Tomás Rioja, Manuel Rodríguez Benito, Juan José Rodríguez de Pedroso el menor, Juan Manuel Rodríguez, Francisco Ruiz Toranzo, Manuel Ruiz, Nicolás Sánchez de Aguilera, Gaspar de Sologuren, Juan Tejera, Manuel de la Tejera, Domingo ¿Torresurer?, Domingo Antonio Urruchi, José Salvador Valverde, Luis Vargas, Juan Bautista Villarino, Juan Manuel Vivero
French nation	Pedro Behic (deputy), Antonio Arboré, Hermanos Bernede and Co Cª, Pedro Castaign, Miguel Charles, Jacobo Nicolás Molini, Pratmeur Dubernad and Co., José Sonnet
Flemish nation	Nicolás Constantino Keerse (deputy), José Livino Adriansens, Juan Antonio Blommaert, Juan Dherve, Jacobo Nicolás Dierexens and Co., Juan de Domens, Luis Antonio Havet y Maestre, Juan José Jansens, Francisco Keyser, Livino Ignacio Leirens and Co., Juan Antonio Lommaert, José Manteau, Luis José Manteau, Vicente Naquens, Felipe Sergeant, Francisco Tumier, Agustín van Hee, Juan Bautista van Rethergen, Jacobo van der Meulen, Viuda de Gand e Hijo, Norberto Vernimen, Juan Whitt
Irish nation	Juan Galbally (deputy), Tomas Butler, Guillermo Darwin, Ricardo Dumphy, Patricio Harper, Tomás Macores, Pedro Merry, Pablo Shee, White & Plunkett

Source: AHPSe, PNS, leg. 3802, f. 423 y ss.

Many studies ... describe the emergence of new forms of cooperation and competition among economic agents and how merchants developed mechanisms for trade and cooperation. Commerce in the first global age was characterized by high rates of smuggling. This was not possible without cooperation and close relationships between agents who on most occasions lived very far apart from each other ... these agents formed an oligopoly and almost always previously had or had developed ties of kinship through marriage or patronage by means of various mechanisms of symbiosis and integration ... trust and reputation were crucial.[19]

The Irish and Flemish communities and Atlantic trade in Seville during the eighteenth century

In Seville, as well as in other harbours on the Iberian Peninsula, the Irish maintained an ambiguous relationship with their British nationality, which they invoked whenever it suited their commercial interests, despite their Catholicism and/or Jacobitism.[20] The conditions created by the Spanish War of Succession and the departure of many British merchants contributed to this, and the Irish merchants made the most of the change of dynasty in Spain[21] to take the 'big leap ahead' that Recio Morales, among others, has described.[22] In addition, the Irish showed no qualms in interacting with other mercantile communities, such as the French and the Flemish. The Irish, therefore, always oscillated between their English connection and their Catholicism, which they used in order to gain prerogatives in Spain.[23] Eventually, the Irish ended up specialising in their role as middlemen between the British and merchants from other nations.

The Irish constructed this mediating role progressively, following their successive migration waves from Ireland. These began in the 1640s, encouraged by Strafford's policies first and then by Cromwell's plantations. The Battle of the Boyne and the Treaty of Limerick in 1689 triggered the mass migration of Catholic and Jacobite Irish, especially to Flanders and France, where they enlisted as mariners, soldiers and merchants.[24]

The Irish born in exile were linked by group solidarity, but they also created economic ties with the local population, which allowed them to channel their double identity towards previously unexplored spaces, such as the Iberian Atlantic. They used their networks based in France and took advantage of the strong economic and geopolitical strength of France, as pointed out by L.M. Cullen.[25]

The French merchant communities cannot be viewed in isolation; both their growth and decline were intimately associated with the evolution of an Irish merchant network not only in Spain and the West Indies but elsewhere, and the complex financial relations between its members were cleared through a community in London which waxed and waned in step with the network at large.[26]

As already noted, the Irish exiles did not totally cut their ties with Ireland or England,[27] and over time they built networks, which were notably transnational in nature, of economic and social connections. Transnationality was an essential feature of business life in modern Europe, and must always be taken into consideration in the analysis of the role played by 'mercantile nations' in commercial hubs.[28] With the beginning of the Spanish War of Succession, many of these Irish families were ready to step forward and occupy the commercial spaces that the war had created in Spain and its colonies, and, as we shall see, many of the Irish merchants who participated in this commercial race were, in fact, based in France and Flanders, where the Irish had been forging their mixed identity since the seventeenth century. This identity was further enhanced by their presence in Spain and its overseas colonies. The large Irish community in cities such as Ostend, Bruges and, to a lesser extent, Ghent encouraged the cooperation of the Irish based in France and facilitated their penetration of the Spanish market; the incorporation of the Spanish Low Countries into Charles VI's crown in 1713 did not disrupt these connections. If anything, they became more intense, in what is one of the most interesting outcomes of the Spanish War of Succession; the Irish advancement in Spain cannot be divorced from their commercial base in France and the Low Countries. This is, for example, the case with the Carew of Ostend/ Bruges, Matthew Prossert and his relationship with the family of Endimion Porter (who had a commercial house in Cádiz), and Dominicus Linch,[29] whose family had very strong links with the commercial networks in Cádiz and Seville, and who even held municipal offices in the latter.[30] For his part, Thomas Ray was a very important Ostend-based merchant and a representative of his compatriots in Bruges during the 1700s. From 1715 onwards, Ray maintained intense commercial links with Spain, sending his partner in Dunkirk, Edward Gough, to Cádiz and transacting with other Irish there, for example Richard Hore and Patrick White, who created their own commercial dynasties in Andalusia.[31] Both Ray and his apprentice John Gould traded in France with Irish and American leather, smuggled Asian products (provided by the Ostend Company) into the British islands, and speculated with wheat sent to Spain and Tuscany in the 1720s and 1730s, among many more business deals involving the Iberian peninsula. In order to achieve this, they relied upon the Archdeacon family, Prosser & Porter Company in Flanders and Cádiz and the rise of Lorenzo Ley, as well as on the solid Carew, Langton & Co.[32]

The French cities of Nantes,[33] Saint-Malo[34] and Dunkirk,[35] regions such as Brittany[36] and the Aquitanian harbours of Bordeaux and La Rochelle, among others,[37] were the training ground for these Irish merchants who, as well as taking part in some of the transactions carried out from these harbours in the eighteenth century, for example in the Antillean trade, intermingled with French and Flemish commercial dynasties. Morlaix does not seem to have been as important for the Seville-based Irish as it was for the Flemish, but some connections existed.[38] The presence of the Irish was also very significant in Flanders, especially in Ostend and Bruges,[39] as well as in Ghent.[40] At the same time, the strong position of some

Irish in Rotterdam, for example the Archdeacon family, which was also present in Dunkirk, Bruges, Cádiz and London, was a springboard for trade with the French colonies during the eighteenth century. Via Sint Eustatius, the Irish supplied the French Antilles with beef and other Irish products, sailing under a Dutch flag and in cooperation with some French-Irish, such as the Kavanaghs, or Irish firms, such as that of the French from Galway,[41] who were also present in Cádiz and Seville.

Among the Irish in Seville, the French city of Lille appears as a significant referent. For instance, the Irishman Bartolomé Morrogh, son of Thomas Morrogh and Elena Gould, was in partnership with members of the Lille-based Livert family. Two members of this family, Francisco and Pedro, were appointed executors of his will, along with the Irish and fellow-businessmen Jorge Waters, resident of Cádiz, and Felipe Nagle, resident of Seville.[42] In the early eighteenth century, Morrogh cashed some bills of exchange, which were issued by the Madrid-based Cafreri and Faini, in the name of the firm Livert & Morrogh.[43] It is likely that Morrogh arrived in Andalusia with Luis Livert, who before 1700 had been in partnership with the Dutch Luis Leghez, in Cádiz.[44] In 1700, Morrogh married the French Juana Luisa Desreumaux, who died in childbirth shortly after in El Puerto de Santa María, and in 1709 he married the Dunkirk-born (to a French father and an Irish mother) Ana Gabriela Farvacques.[45] Due to his close links with France, he was unsurprisingly appointed deputy of the French nation in Seville, which was based in the Chapel of San Luis in the Convent of San Francisco.[46] During his absences, his business was entrusted to French merchants with no Irish ancestry, for instance the Breton Pablo Bocage, partner of his fellow Breton Pedro Dutramble, who in 1711 owed Morrogh some money for a series of bills of exchange issued in Paris.[47] Therefore, we can suggest that the French and the Irish had a close trust-based relationship, in many cases because the Irish had been raised on French soil. In another example, Miguel de Basse, a Frenchman, was the executor of the last will of the Irishwoman Margarita Walsh, widow of the Frenchman Juan Treyver, in 1728.[48] The relationship between the Irish and the French was so close that even an Englishman such as Guillermo Darwin found it convenient to marry a French wife, the Sevillian (but of French parents) María Marsellaque; after becoming a widower, he married the Irishwoman Elena Conry in 1739.[49]

Carlos Morphy, an Irishman raised in Lille, son of Lille-born María Margarita Petipaz and the Irishman Juan Morphy, worked in 1713 in Francisco Linch's (another Irishman) Sevillian house. His brother, Juan, was a canon in Bruges, where their mother had died the previous year.[50] The same pattern is repeated in Nantes. Matías Shee, resident in Seville, stated in his last will, dated 1749, that he was the son of the Irishman Matías Shee and the Frenchwoman Margarita Doude, and that Nantes was his birthplace. He was the cashier of the Seville-based Irish firm Grand & Dunphy. He also declared that part of his father's inheritance was entrusted to the Irishman Patricio Archer, who was a resident of Nantes.[51] Nantes was also the birthplace of Juan Stalpert, who was married to the Irishwoman Justina Lorenza Plunkett, *vecina* of Madrid but resident of Seville in 1732.[52]

French and Flemish ports, in short, were the background for the commercial community that connected the British Isles with the Spanish Monarchy and its American colonies. Thus, when the Irish arrived in force to form commercial communities in the eighteenth century, they were preceded by at least two generations of exiles in France or Flanders (exiles who, in any case, had not totally lost touch with Ireland and London). It is important to stress this, because the names entered in the censuses preserved in Cádiz from the 1770s onwards correspond mostly to immigrants who had arrived directly from Ireland (especially from Waterford), and it must be remembered that these immigrants had the support of those who were exiled more than half a century earlier.[53] Their 'acquired transnationality' made them ideal middlemen for other merchants (French, Flemish and British). For example, in 1750, the Cádiz-based French firm of Siochan and Boyetet hired the services of the Seville-based Irish company of White & Plunkett in order to arrange the shipment of 50 oil casks to Amsterdam on board James McDonnell's British vessel.[54] In 1732, the Irishman Pedro Carpinter, resident in Lyon, sent a letter to Giraud Colomb & Co. in Cádiz, asking them to pay 375 *doblones* to Patricio Conry, in Seville, with the guarantee of the firm Sarsfield & Glatar.[55] These merchants were Irish who were naturalised French in Nantes in 1672, and they intermingled with the high local bourgeoisie. A generation later, during the Spanish War of Succession, Jacques Sarsfield moved to Cádiz, although he later returned to Nantes.[56] This family was also present in Ostend, where they worked in partnership with Thomas Ray in his transactions with Spain and other countries.[57]

The Irish also operated as middlemen for merchants from other countries from Holland, especially Rotterdam, where there was a substantial Irish community; for example, Grand Dunphy & Co. in 1747 acted as the intermediaries of the Dutchman Juan Witt for the collection, in instalments, of the debt of Amsterdam-based Abraham Scheremberg and of Johan Pieters van Carn, who was from Elberfeld (in the Holy Roman Empire).[58] At the same time, Witt was, alongside the Irishmen Pedro Merry and Tomás Macores, the executor of Juana Keating, mother-in-law of the Englishman and *vecino* of Seville, Guillermo Darwin.[59] Darwin was English, but he always worked with the Irish, and in 1741 he acted as the executor of Miguel Coleman for the resolution of his business deals and the liquidation of his property in Holland, where Darwin was heading that year. In addition, Coleman left Darwin 37,000 *reales de plata* (rsp.) in his last will.[60]

By taking advantage of the competitive freight prices of the Dutch, the Irish living in lower Andalusia were becoming a key factor in the commercial transactions between Spain and Holland and the proto-industrial areas of the Rhineland.[61] For example, in 1732, the Irish company of Oliver French and José Rice received 2,300 pesos from the Madrid-based Álvaro de Aguirre & Co. in two bills of exchange issued in Cádiz by the Dutch company Antonio van Vaes & Co[62]; in 1774, Pedro and Gerardo Merry received a shipment of ribbon from

Elberfeld;[63] in 1780, Pablo Shee received different textiles in two Dutch vessels shipped by the Ghent-based merchant Guillermo Goetsials (Gottschalk) (incidentally, during the transfer of the cargo to another vessel, which was bound for Seville, in Sanlucar, the Dutch vessels ran aground)[64]; in 1757, White, Harper & Co. declared the arrival of eight barrels of nails from Amsterdam aboard the galley *Juana Margarita*, which was captained by Obbe Sehagen, and eight more aboard the vessel *Amistad*;[65] and lastly, the Irishman Tomas Butler specialised in supplying cargoes of fruit and salt for these ships' return trip,[66] while negotiating the debts of other Irish such as José Darwin (son of Guillermo Darwin) through bills of exchange issued in England and received by Smiah & Payne, in Cádiz, who executed them through Hore, van Halen & Co.,[67] which was co-owned by an Irishman and a Dutchman. Some Dutch, such as Jacobo Constantino Keerse, also acted as middlemen between Irish traders. In 1750, Keerse represented the Sanlúcar-based Bernardo Fallon in a claim against the Irishman Miguel Morphy, who was a skipper, for a cargo of wheat and broad beans from Topsham, Cornwall.[68] The Dutch and the Irish often worked together in bringing wheat imports. For instance, in 1737 Tomás Macores acted as the representative of another Irishman, José Blanco, during the arrival of 2,549 bushels of 'red English' wheat, at 32 *reales* per bushel.[69]

In addition to cooperating with the Irish, the Dutch in Seville also worked alongside the French colony in the city, forming partnerships primarily in order to share maritime risks,[70] (see Table 7.3) for example in the wool-export trade (see Table 7.4). While the former opened the Dutch market to the latter, the French acted as capitalists and entrepreneurs, reducing the costs of the Seville-based Dutch sharing the cost of maritime insurances and participating in the cargo. This also made sense given the intermittent state of war between France, England and Spain, as it was always convenient that one of the members of the partnership could intervene if the vessel were taken by a ship of his own nationality.[71]

Something similar occurred with cargo insurance, where cooperation and risk-sharing was very common. García-Baquero demonstrated that, on the America-Cádiz route, wholesale lending was concentrated in a few hands.[72] On other routes, however, risks seem to have been more spread out, at least in the documented cases. In 1693, a vessel sailing under a Dutch flag between Smyrna and Cádiz, where the cargo was to be delivered to Frederique Mandt (a resident of Seville), was insured for 24,495 rsp. by a number of merchants of different origin. In 1694, Samuel Houblon (GB), resident in Seville, and Tomás Costa (SP), resident in Cádiz, insured a trip between Cádiz and London for 66,000 rsp. Finally, Bartolomé Morrogh insured a cargo travelling between Nantes and Martinique for 26,800 rsp; all of his insurers lived in Seville, except for Jacob de la Fontaine, who lived in Amsterdam. These examples make clear that the Dutch, Flemish and the Irish developed a strong transnational trade, where the routes, agents and the networks roots where spread over different 'national' spaces,[73] and is possible to find examples of cooperation and concurrence between Dutch and other merchants such the English in other contexts.[74]

Table 7.3 Some common freights of 'Sevillian' traders.

Year	Ship origin	Route	Name	Captain	Merchants	Cargo
1708	Danish	Sanlúcar–'North'	Lanquesont	Enrique Brandt	Juan Bautista Clarebout, caballero de Calatrava (FL), Gil Huneus (FL) and Luis Manteau (FL), Bartolomé Morrogh (GB), Miguel Lemaestre (FR), Juan Mallen (SP), Noberto Vernimen (FL) and Luis Doye and Co (FL), Gil Huneus (FL), Luis Manteau (FL), Domingo Van Peene (FL) and Lorenzo Dorcques (HRE), Pedro Dutramble (FR) and Pablo Bocage (FR), Enrique de Lange (FR), Pedro Monteoro (NE), Juan Bautista Clarebout (FL)	Wool
1709	Swedish	Spain–Amsterdam	Kalmar's Castle	Matias Martens	Juan Bautista Clarebout caballero de calatrava (FL), Juan Havet (FL), Ignacio Leyrens (FL), Juan Jacobs (FL), Enrique de Lange & Co., (FR), Gil Huneus (FL), Juan Manteau (FL), Lorenzo Dorques (HRE), Pedro Monteoro (NE), Juan Antonio Maestre (FL), Francisco van Craywincquel (FL), Pedro Jacobs (FL), Pedro Jacobs (FL), Juan Silvestre Fernández (SP)	Wool, eau-de-vie, olive oil, olives
1710	Basque (Vizcaya)	London–Cádiz	San Francisco and Santo Domingo	Juan de Aliaga	Livert & Morrogh (FR/GB), Havet, Leirens & Jacobs (FL), Van der Wilde & Cardon (FL/FR), Jacobo Malcampo (FL), Gaspar Malcampo (FL), Esteban Malcampo (FL).	Unknown

(continued)

Year	Ship origin	Route	Name	Captain	Merchants	Cargo
1711	Basque	London-Cádiz	San Antonio de Padua	Juan de Escarza (Portugalete)	Gaspar Malcampo (FL), Juan Bautista Clarebout (FL), Miguel Lemaistre (FR), Juan Bautista van der Wilde (FL) and Pedro Cardon (FR), Jacobo Malcampo (FL), Habe Leirens y Jacobs (FL), Juan Felix Clarebout (FL), Luis Doye (FR), Norberto Vernimen (FL). *In Cádiz:* Saolpartt Romet and Co. (?), Juan B. Coppenole, Carlos Rusel, Guillermo Maze (IR), Enrique Storm, Luis Mays y Cª.	Unknown
1726	Dutch	-	El Huérfano		Livino Braquelman (FL), Luis Doye (FL) Miguel Carreño (SP), Diego Pérez de Baños (SP), Marcos Pringle (IR)	Merchandise
1727	Dutch	-	San Antonio de Padua		Norberto Vernimen (FL), Livino Braquelman (FL) Joues & Debasse (FR) Miguel Debasse (FR)	Wool
1788	Dutch	-	La Margarita Constancia		Antonio de Sologuren, Bern. Tobías, Antonio Elías and Co. Torrijos y Zaldívar, D. Juan Antonio de Aspergorta, Melchor García, Juan de Noreña (all SP) Deputies for collecting the value of the damages, Juan Michielsens (FL), Norberto Vernimen (FL).	Merchandise

Source: AHPSe, PNS, leg. 5167, fols 33, 259; leg. 5170, fol. 33r; leg. 5173, fol. 366; leg. 5174, fol. 151r; leg. 5189, fol. 330; leg. 5190, fol. 567; leg. 13181, w.fol.

Table 7.4 Main wool exporters from Seville in 1734.

Wool exports—Seville, 1734	Wool Arrobas	rv, mrs
Luis Doye (FL)	5,0761.5	9,206.25
Gil Huneus and Luis Manteau (FL)	11,043	2,002.30
Miguel Maestre (FL)	26,693.75	4,841.17
Leirens, Jacobs and Co. (FL)	8,774.5	1,591.15
Norberto Vernimen (FL)	55,258.75	10,022.14
Miguel de Basse (FR)	3,499.5	634.24
Francisco Cardon (FR)	655.5	118.30
Juan B. Vanderwilde y Cª. (FL)	2,901.75	526.10
Francisco Craybinquel (FL)	16,756.75	3,039.7
Lorenzo Dorcques (HRE)	1,883.5	341.18
Daniel O'Brien (IR)	1,143	207.10
Francisco Bizeul (FR)	11,666	2,101.9
Enrique de Lange o sus hermanos (FR)	7,851.25	1,424
Pedro Reynaud and D. Carlos Marín (FR/SP)	1,945.75	352.30
Pedro de Prado (FR)	12,770.25	2,316.6
Juan B. Plateboet (FL)	2,855.75	517.12
Simón de Olazabal (SP)	20,091.5	3,626.13
Francisco de Iturbe (SP)	3,570.75	647.21
Juan Bautista Lepin (HRE)	126.5	22.32
TOTAL	240,249.25	43,532,323

Source: AHPSe, PNS, leg. 5197, fol. 246. [Amounts expressed in *reales de vellón* (rv) and *maravedies de vellón* (mrs)].

As Table 7.5 shows, the Dutch were particularly active in the insurance business, followed by the Irish and some Spanish and French. In the wool trade, the Dutch again played a major role, followed by the French, who were also very active in this sector. In 1734, the Dutch exported 175,046 aerobe of wool, while the other nations combined barely reached 65,203.5 aerobe.

Table 7.5 Collective insurances assigned in Seville.

Year	Insurer	*rsp*
1693	Jacob de la Fontaine (NE)	5,000
	Enrique Lepin (Holy Roman Empire; HRE)	10,000
	Pedro Pelarte (FL)	2,060
	Juan Hopkins (GB)	1,240
	Martín Amiano Sastizábal (SP)	6,195
1694	Enrique Lepin (HRE)	5,000
	Diego Maestre (FL)	5,000
	Juan Thormolen (HRE)	4,000
	Pedro Pelarte (FL)	4,000
	Bartolomé Ginori (Genoa)	10,000
	Rafael Bini (Genoa)	3,000
	Juan Bautista and Esteban Malcampo (FL)	7,000
	Martín Amiano Sastizábal (SP)	20,000
	Antonio Zulaica (SP)	5,000
	Abraham Neuyen (NE)	3,000
1710	Gaspar Malcampo (FL)	1,600
	Jacobo Malcampo (FL)	4,000
	Gil Huneus and Juan Manteau (FL)	3,200
	José Maestre (FL)	3,200
	José Havet (FL)	-
	Jorge Jacobs and Livino Leirens (FL)	3,200
	Norberto Vernimen y Luis Doye (FL)	1,600
	Pedro Monteoro (NE)	2,000
	Lorenzo Dorques (HRE)	1,600
	Francisco Bizeul (FR)	1,600
	Bernardo Antonio Elizarry (SP)	1,600

Source: AHPSe, PNS, leg. 5147, fols 264, 273, 274, 275, 276. leg. 5148, fols 421–424, 442–448, 558. leg. 5174, fol. 224. (Amounts expressed in *reales de plata*.)

Conclusions

Between the final decades of the seventeenth century and the first 60 years of the eighteenth century, the Irish community flourished in Seville and in other cities in Lower Andalusia and Malaga. This community had close links with the European Atlantic façade and the British Isles. Members of this community played an important role as mediators between different political, economic and religious spheres in the traditional Flemish community in Seville and Cádiz which they joined, which had strong ties with the American colonies and, of course, the North Atlantic and Holland. Neither the Flemish nor the Irish had their own state, but while the latter did not organise themselves as a 'nation' until very late, the former was one of the earliest and most prestigious nations in the whole of the Spanish Monarchy. The Flemish were a key factor, if not *the* key factor, in the formation of Grafe's and Irigoin's 'stakeholder empire'.[75] In addition, their activities were the springboard for other merchant groups, especially the French and the English, for whom 'national' was a flexible and not always necessary or convenient instrument because routes, transactions, cooperation, trust and stability could be achieved outside national institutions; fostering economic activity and the aperture of new markets was always prioritised over national considerations.

Notes

1   A. Domínguez Ortiz's pioneering work, *Los extranjeros en la vida española durante el siglo XVII y otros artículos* (Sevilla: Diputación de Sevilla, 1996) was followed by the publication of a large number of books and articles. Congresses have played an especially important role in bringing specialists together and in widening the scope of research results. See, for example, M.B. Villar García and P. Pezzi Cristóbal (dirs), *Los extranjeros en la España Moderna, Actas del I Coloquio Internacional* (Málaga: Universidad de Málaga, 2003); A. Crespo Solana (ed.), *Comunidades transnacionales. Colonias de mercaderes extranjeros en el Mundo Atlántico (1500–1830)* (Madrid: Doce Calles, 2010); I. Pérez Tostado and E. García Hernán (eds.), *Irlanda y el Atlántico Ibérico. Movilidad, participación e intercambio cultural (1580–1823)* (Valencia: Albatros ediciones, 2010); M. Herrero Sánchez et al. (eds.), *Génova y la Monarquía Hispánica (1528–1713)* (Génova: Società ligure di storia patria, 2011); B.J. García García and Ó. Recio Morales (eds.), *Las corporaciones de nación en la Monarquía Hispánica (1580–1750). Identidad, patronazgo y redes de sociabilidad* (Madrid: Fundación Carlos de Amberes, 2014); B. Yun Casalilla (ed.), *Las redes del imperio. Élites sociales en la articulación de la Monarquía Hispánica, 1492–1714* (Madrid: Marcial Pons, 2009). Also, J.J. Iglesias Rodríguez, R.M. Pérez García and M.F. Fernández Chaves (eds.), *Comercio y cultura en la Edad Moderna. Actas de la XIII Reunión Científica de la Fundación Española de Historia Moderna* (Sevilla: Universidad de Sevilla, 2015), among many others. For a complementary and suggestive point of view, see J.J. Ruiz Ibáñez and I. Pérez Tostado (eds.), *Los exiliados del rey de España* (Madrid: Fondo de Cultura Económica, 2015).

2   G. Pérez Sarrión, *La península comercial. Mercado, redes sociales y Estado en España en el siglo XVIII* (Madrid: Marcial Pons, 2012). For another point of view, see R. Grafe, *Distant Tyranny. Markets, power and backwardness in Spain, 1650–1800* (New Jersey: Princeton University Press, 2012).

3 Again, A. Domínguez Ortiz studied this issue in 'Las concesiones de naturalezas', in *Estudios americanistas* (Madrid: Real Academia de la Historia, 1998), pp. 117–134; or 'Documentos sobre mercaderes flamencos establecidos en Sevilla a comienzos del siglo XVIII', in J.A. Casquero Fernández (ed.), *Homenaje a Antonio Matilla Tascón* (Zamora: Diputación de Zamora, 2002), pp. 151–160, and was followed by many others. See also T. Herzog, *Defining Nations: Immigrants and Citizens in Early Modern Spain and Spanish America* (New Haven and London: Yale University Press, 2003).

4 The pace of publication is so fast that recently published overviews are quickly becoming obsolete. See M.B. Villar García, 'Los extranjeros en la España Moderna: la expansión de un campo historiográfico a partir de la obra de Domínguez Ortiz', in J.L. Castellano Castellano and M.L. López-Guadalupe Muñoz (eds.), *Homenaje a Antonio Domínguez Ortiz* (Granada: Universidad de Granada, 2008), vol. II, pp. 859–872; Ó. Recio Morales, 'Los extranjeros y la historiografía modernista', *Cuadernos de Historia Moderna. Anejos*, X (2011), pp. 33–51; idem, 'Redes sociales y espacios de poder de la naciones en la Monarquía Hispánica. Un estado de la cuestión', in Ó. Recio Morales (ed.), *Redes de nación y espacios de poder. La comunidad irlandesa en España y la América española, 1600–1825* (Valencia: Albatros, 2012), pp. 37–53; M. Bustos Rodríguez, 'Comercio y comerciantes en la Andalucía del Antiguo Régimen: Estado de la cuestión y perspectivas', *Obradoiro de Historia Moderna*, 17 (2008), pp. 43–76.

5 Ó. Recio Morales, 'Redes sociales y espacios de poder', pp. 37–53.

6 B.J. García García, 'La Real Diputación de San Andrés de los Flamencos. Formas de patronazgo e identidad en el siglo XVII', in B.J. García García and Ó. Recio Morales, (eds.), *Las corporaciones de nación en la Monarquía Hispánica (1580–1750). Identidad, patronazgo y redes de sociabilidad* (Madrid: Fundación Carlos de Amberes, 2014), pp. 59–107, on pp. 59–60.

7 See the conclusions about the Flemish merchant community, in A. Crespo Solana's 'El concepto de ciudadanía y la idea de nación según la comunidad flamenca de la Monarquía Hispánica', in B.J. Garcia García and Ó. Recio Morales (eds.), *Las corporaciones de nación*, pp. 389–411.

8 A. Crespo Solana, 'El juez conservador ¿Una alternativa al cónsul de la nación?' in M. Aglietti, M. Herrero Sánchez and F. Zamora Rodríguez (eds.), *Los cónsules de extranjeros en la Edad Moderna y principios de la Edad Contemporánea* (Madrid: Doce Calles, 2013), pp. 23–34.

9 For an excellent example, see J.M. Díaz Blanco, 'La construcción de una institución comercial: el consulado de las naciones flamenca y alemana en la Sevilla moderna', *Revista de Historia Moderna, Anales de la Universidad de Alicante*, 33 (2015), pp. 123–145. Also along the same lines, B.J. García García, 'La Nación Flamenca en la corte española y el Real Hospital de San Andrés ante la crisis sucesoria (1606–1706)', in A. Álvarez, Ó. Alvariño, B.J. García García and V. León Sanz (eds.), *La pérdida de Europa. La guerra de Sucesión por la Monarquía de España* (Madrid: Fundación Carlos de Amberes, Ministerio de Cultura, 2007), pp. 379–442; also, B.J. García García, 'La real Diputación', pp. 59–107.

10 Archivo Histórico Provincial de Sevilla, Protocolos Notariales de Sevilla (hereafter, AHPSe PNS), leg. 5148, f. 290.

11 This attitude, however, could occasionally lead to some problems and the scorn of the British community, for example in Cádiz and Seville. For which, see M.G. Carrasco, 'La factoría británica de Cádiz a mediados del siglo XVIII: organización y labor asistencial', in M.G. Villar García and P. Pezzi Cristóbal (eds.), *Los extranjeros en la España moderna* (Málaga: Universidad de Málaga, 2003), pp. 255–265; M.F. Fernández Chaves and M. Gamero Rojas, 'El Reino de Sevilla como escenario del ascenso del poder social y económico de los extranjeros en el siglo XVIII: el caso irlandés', in Ó. Recio Morales (ed.), *Redes de nación y espacios de poder* (Valencia: Albatros, 2012), pp. 191–217.

12 M.F. Fernández Chaves and M. Gamero Rojas, 'Hacer del dinero riqueza: estrategias de ascenso económico y asentamiento de los comerciantes irlandeses en la Sevilla del siglo XVIII', in I. Pérez Tostado and E. García Hernán (eds.), *Irlanda y el Atlántico Ibérico. Movilidad, participación e intercambio cultural (1580–1823)* (Valencia: Albatros ediciones, 2010), pp. 1–22.

13 V. Montojo Montojo, 'Crecimiento mercantil y desarrollo corporativo en España: los Consulados extraterritoriales extranjeros (ss. XVI–XVII)', *Anuario de Historia del Derecho Español*, 62 (1992), pp. 47–66; F.J. Zamora Rodríguez, '"Dar el cordero en guarda al lobo" Control hispánico sobre los consulados de extranjeros durante el siglo XVII e inicios del siglo XVIII', *Tiempos Modernos*, 30 (2015/1), pp. 1–20.

14 S. Haggerty, *The British-Atlantic Trading Community, 1760–1810* (Boston and Leiden: Brill, 2009); F. Trivellato, 'Sephardic Merchants in the Early Modern Atlantic and Beyond. Toward a Comparative Historical Approach to Business Cooperation', in R.L. Kagan and Philip D. Morgan (eds.), *Atlantic Diasporas: Jews, Conversos and Crypto-Jews in the Age of Mercantilism, 1500–1800* (Baltimore: Johns Hopkins University Press, 2009), pp. 99–120.

15 See M.G. Carrasco González, *Comerciantes y casas de negocios en Cádiz, 1650–1700* (Cádiz: Universidad de Cádiz, 1997), pp. 52–59; X. Lamikiz, *Trade and Trust in the Eighteenth Century Atlantic World: Spanish Merchants and their Overseas Networks* (Woodbridge: Royal Historical Society, 2010); J. Baskes, *Staying Afloat. Risk and Uncertainty in Spanish Atlantic World Trade, 1760–1820* (Stanford: Stanford University Press, 2013).

16 Á. Alloza Aparicio, 'La tesorería de las haciendas del contrabando, 1647–1697', in C. Martínez Shaw and M. Alfonso Mola (eds.), *España en el comercio marítimo internacional (siglos XVII–XIX). Quince estudios* (Madrid: UNED, 2009), pp. 111–141.

17 AHPSe, PNS, leg. 5159, fol. 13, 10-I-1702.

18 These temporary and very specific associations of traders created in order to preserve mercantile interests were very common and had a long tradition. For the city of Seville, see, for instance, E. Otte, 'Los mercaderes transatlánticos bajo Carlos V', *Anuario de Estudios Americanos*, 47 (1990), pp. 95–121.

19 A. Crespo Solana, 'The Formation of a Social Hispanic Atlantic Space and the Integration of Merchant Communities Following the Treaties of Utrecht', *Culture & History Digital Journal*, 3:1 (2014), pp. 1–12, on p. 5.

20 Ó. Recio Morales, 'Irish Emigré Group Strategies of Survival, Adaptation and Integration in Seventeenth and Eighteenth Century Spain', in T. O'Connor and M.A. Lyons, (eds.), *Irish Communities in Early Modern Europe* (Dublin: Four Courts Press, 2006), pp. 240–266. Also, idem, 'Identity and Loyalty: Irish Traders in Seventeenth Century Iberia', in D. Dickson, J. Parmentier and J. Ohlmeyer (eds.), *Irish and Scottish Mercantile Networks in Europe and Overseas in the Seventeenth and Eighteenth Centuries* (Gent: Academia Press, 2007), pp. 197–210. More recently, see C. O'Scea, 'Special Privileges for the Irish in the Kingdom of Castile (1601–1680): Modern Myth or Contemporary Reality?', in D. Worthington (ed.), *British and Irish Emigrants and Exiles in Europe, 1603–1688* (Leiden and Boston: Brill, 2010), pp. 107–124.

21 The case of the Bermingham/Macores family is in this regard paradigmatic; see F. Chaves and G. Rojas, 'El Reino de Sevilla', pp. 191–217. See also, M.G. Carrasco, 'La factoría británica', P. Fernández Pérez, *El rostro familiar de la metrópoli. Redes de parentesco y lazos mercantiles en Cádiz, 1700–1812* (Madrid: Siglo XXI, 1997).

22 Ó. Recio Morales, 'Conectores de imperios: la figura del comerciante irlandés en España y en el mundo atlántico del siglo XVIII', in Crespo Solana (ed.), *Comunidades transnacionales*, pp. 313–336. This fact was pointed out by J.O. McLachlan, *Trade and Peace with Old Spain, 1667–1750. A Study of the Influence of Commerce on Anglo-Spanish Diplomacy in the First Half of the Eighteenth Century* (New York: Octagon Books, 1974).

23 Ó. Recio Morales, 'Identity and Loyalty'; C. O'Scea, 'Special Privileges'. For the Irish presence in Spain and their political activity, see Ó. Recio Morales (ed.), *Ireland and the Spanish Empire* (Dublin: Four Court Press, 2010), especially pp. 167–234 and pp. 257–269.

24 G. Chausinand-Nogaret, 'Une elite insulaire au service de l'Europe: les Jacobites au XVIIIe siècle', *Annales ESC*, 5 (1973), pp. 1097–1122.

25 É. Ó Ciosáin, 'Hidden by 1688 and After: Irish Catholic Migration to France, 1590–1685', in D. Worthington (ed.), *British and Irish Emigrants and Exiles in Europe, 1603–1688* (Leiden and Boston: Brill, 2010), pp. 125–138. Also, idem, 'A Hundred Years of Irish Migration to France, 1590–1688', in T. O'Connor (ed.), *The Irish in Europe* (Dublin: Four Court Press, 2001), pp. 125–138.

26 L.M. Cullen, 'The Irish merchant communities of Bordeaux, La Rochelle and Cognac in the Eighteenth Century', in L.M. Cullen and P. Butel (eds.), *Négoce, et industrie en France et en Irlande au XVIIIe et XIXe Siècles* (Bordeaux: CNRS, 1980), pp. 51–63, on p. 51.

27 S. Talbott, 'Such Unjustifiable Practices? Irish Trade, Settlement and Society in France, 1688–1715', *The Economic History Review*, 67:2 (2014), pp. 556–577.

28 About this issue, see A. Crespo Solana, 'Elementos de transnacionalidad en el comercio flamenco-holandés en Europa y la Monarquía Hispánica', *Cuadernos de Historia Moderna*, X (2011), pp. 55–76. In addition, the state often made use of these transnational networks; see K. Kaps, 'Entre el servicio estatal y los negocios transnacionales: el caso de Paolo Greppi, cónsul imperial en Cádiz (1774–1791)', in M. Aglietti, M.D. Herrero Sánchez and F. Zamora Rodríguez (eds.), *Los cónsules de extranjeros*, pp. 225–235.

29 J. Parmentier, 'The Irish Connection: The Irish Merchant Community in Ostend and Bruges During the Late Seventeenth and Eighteenth Centuries', *Eighteenth-Century Ireland*, 20 (2005), pp. 32–54, on pp. 40–45.

30 F.J. Campese Gallego, *Los comuneros sevillanos del siglo XVIII. Estudio social, prosoprográfico y genealógico* (Sevilla: Fabiola de Publicaciones, 2004).

31 P. Fernández Pérez, *El rostro familiar, passim*.

32 J. Parmentier, 'The Irish Connection', pp. 38–43, 46–47. One of these firms sent Flemish textiles to Cádiz, where they were sold in exchange for silver *reales*, which were then exchanged for commodities in Surat, commodities which eventually had to be sold back to Flanders; ibid, pp. 42–43. For Ley and Langton, ibid, 46–7, and for L. Ley and R. Hore, and Carew, Langton and Co. in Cádiz, see P. Fernández Pérez, *El rostro familiar*. Archdeacons were also present, along with the White/Blanco, in the port of Huelva; see J.L. Gozálvez Escobar, 'Comerciantes irlandeses en la Huelva del siglo XVIII', in A. García-Baquero González (ed.), *La burguesía de negocios en la Andalucía de la Ilustración* (Cádiz: Diputación de Cádiz, 1991), pp. 271–292.

33 G. Saupin, 'Les réseaux commerciaux des irlandais de Nantes sous le Règne de Louis XIV', in Dickson, Parmentier and Ohlmeyer (eds.), *Irish and Scottish mercantile networks*, pp. 115–146. Talbott, 'Such unjustifiable practices?'.

34 M.A. Lyons, 'The Emergence of an Irish Community in Saint-Malo, 1550–1710', in O'Connor (ed.), *The Irish in Europe*, pp. 107–126.

35 C. Pfister, 'Dunkerque et l'Irlande. 1690–1790', in D. Dickson, J. Parmentier and J. Ohlmeyer (eds.), *Irish and Scottish mercantile networks*, pp. 93–114.

36 E. Ó Ciosáin, 'Les irlandais en Bretagne 1603–1780: "invasion", accueil, intégration', in C. Laurent and H. Davis (eds.), *Irlande et Bretagne. Vingt siècles d'Histoire* (Rennes: Terre de Brume Éditions, 1994), pp. 153–166.

37 L.M. Cullen, 'The Irish Merchant Communities of Bordeaux', pp. 51–63.

38 F. Nagle *vecino* in San Salvador parish, received from Marcos Crenes Brough, resident of Morlaix, eight *tercios* of *creas* brought in the ship 'La Esperanza' captain Martin Maes, AHPSE, PNS, leg. 5167, f. 422, 13-III-1706.

39 J. Parmentier, 'The Sweets of Commerce: the Hennessys of Ostend and Their Network in the Eighteenth Century', in D. Dickson, J. Parmentier and J. Ohlmeyer (eds.), *Irish and Scottish Mercantile Networks*, pp. 67–91. Also, idem, 'The Irish Connection'.

40 For instance, we find D. Felipe Juan Fernando José de Power (Son of John Power), *vecino* of Ghent and resident in Seville, giving a power of attorney to Agustín Valcke, probably of Flemish nationality, *vecino* of Seville AHPSe, PNS, leg. 3787, f. 101r, 10-IV-1748.

41 T.M. Truxes, 'Dutch-Irish Cooperation in the Mid-Eighteenth-Century Wartime Atlantic', *Early American Studies*, 10:2 (2012), pp. 303–334, on pp. 322–323. Likewise, John Archdeacon also distributed Irish products provided by other Irish merchants, for instance Matthew Prosser, resident of Bruges. The French were very active and widely represented in southern Spanish ports, despite their weak position with regard to the Waterford merchants, according to L.M. Cullen, 'Galway Merchants in the Outside World, 1650–1800', in L.M. Cullen (ed.), *Economy, Trade and Irish Merchants at Home and Abroad, 1600–1988* (Dublin: Four Courts Press, 2012), pp. 165–192, on pp. 188–189. We know that some Irish merchants used false papers to pass off British ships as Dutch in the voyage from the Canary Islands to Jamaica in 1740; see J. Parmentier, 'The Irish Connection', pp. 36, 43.

42 AHPSe, PNS, leg. 5170, f. 9r, 10-I-1708.

43 AHPSe, PNS, leg. 5167, f. 464r, 16-IV-1706, f. 484r, 23-III-1706, f. 491r, 21-III-1706, f. 543r y f. 544r, 20-IV-1706. The amounts involved were 171, 200, 266 ½, 512 ½, and 205 *doblones*, but only the first of these bills, paid by the Sevillian merchants Rafael Bino and Luis Pagareli, was for his benefit. The third bill was owed to Guillermo Mace, another Irish trader.

44 Archivo Histórico Provincial de Cádiz, Protocolos Notariales de Cádiz, leg. 871, f. 533r, 4-IX-1700. Leghez was appointed to be the legal executor of his last will and testament.

45 AHPSe, PNS, legs. 5170, f. 9r, 10-I-1708, y 3777, f. 294r, 1709.

46 AHPSe, PNS, leg. 5178, f. 908, 26-XI-1715.

47 AHPSe, PNS, legs. 5170, f. 517r, 28-VI-1708 y 5174, f. 149, 3-III-1711, for 270 *doblones*.

48 AHPSe, PNS, leg. 5191, f. 676r.

49 AHPSe, PNS, leg. 3808, f. 981r, 22-XII-1770.

50 AHPSe, PNS, leg. 6413, f. 52. Carlos gave his brother power of attorney in order to receive his mother's inheritance.

51 AHPSe, PNS, leg. 3787, f. 517r.

52 AHPSe, PNS, leg. 5195, f. 235r, 19-IV-1732. After she became a widow, Justina gave power of attorney to Juan Guehlagh, merchant and resident in La Fosse, Nantes, for the management of her husband's estate in the city.

53 For these censuses, see M.C. Lario de Oñate, *La colonia mercantil británica e irlandesa en Cádiz a finales del siglo XVIII* (Cádiz: Universidad de Cádiz, 2000). Also, eadem, 'The Irish traders of Eighteenth-Century Cádiz', in D. Dickson, J. Parmentier and J. Ohlmeyer (eds.), *Irish and Scottish Mercantile Networks*, pp. 211–230.

54 AHPSe, PNS, leg. 3788, f. 145, 12-V-1750.

55 AHPSe, PNS, leg. 5195, f. 273r, 25-IV-1732.

56 G. Saupin, 'Les réseaux commerciaux des irlandais', pp. 131–32.

57 J. Parmentier, 'The Irish Connection', pp. 41, 45–46.

58 AHPSe, PNS, leg. 3785, f. 3 y 4, 4-I-1746. These debts amounted to 6,333 rsp in the first case and 12,151 rsp in the second. Payment to Scheremberg in AHPSe, PNS, leg. 3786, f. 19r, 13-I-1747, and partial payment to van Carn in the same file, f. 20r.

59 AHPSe, PNS, leg. 3786, f. 262, 20-V-1747.

60 AHPSe, PNS, leg. 3783, f. 525r and 531r., 22 and 23-XII-1741.

61 In this, they exploited the traditional commercial relationship between Cádiz and Flanders; see A. Crespo Solana, 'Dutch Mercantile Networks', pp. 123–124, 129–130.

62 AHPSe, PNS, leg. 5195, f. 232r, 19-IV-1732.

63 AHPSe, PNS, leg. 3812, f. 209, a barrel containing 1,172 dozen 'balduque' ribbons and 130 dozen thread ribbons, loaded in Amsterdam aboard the Dutch vessel *Recht Door Zee*.

64 AHPSe, PNS, leg. 3815, f. 96. The cargo was composed of 2 'frangotes' of white twine, 2 pieces of linen and 2 half pieces of 'Holanda batista' (sic), loaded in Ostend aboard the Dutch ship 'Posta del Mar', which was insured in Amsterdam against all risks for 2,280 florins. Also, the cargo included 3 'frangotes' of raw twine loaded in Ostend aboard the Dutch ship 'El gusto del mar', which was insured between Amsterdam and Seville for 1,800 florins.

65 AHPSe, PNS, leg. 3795, f. 107, 1-III-1757.

66 AHPSe, PNS, leg. 6446, f. 445, 449, 699r. The fruit was sent to Ostend, where Butler had an agent, Juan Goul, who had to work to preserve the company's interest because the ship's skipper, Simon Plats, had loaded so much salt that there was no room for the amount of fruit stipulated by Carew & Langton, who were Irish traders in Cádiz. It was very common for Dutch ships to carry salt, as well as Andalusian agricultural products, on their return trip from Spain. See A. Crespo Solana, *Mercaderes atlánticos*, p. 123.

67 AHPSe, PNS, leg. 6465, f. 699r-v, bills of exchange dating to 6 November and 16 December 1766.

68 AHPSe, PNS, leg. 3788, f. 554r.

69 AHPSe, PNS, leg. 5200, f. 108, 15-II-1738.

70 For maritime insurance, see J. Pons Pons, 'El seguro marítimo en España (1650–1800)', *Hispania. Revista Española de Historia*, 67:225 (2006), pp. 271–294; M.G. Carrasco González, 'El negocio de los seguros marítimos en Cádiz a finales del siglo XVIII', *Hispania. Revista española de Historia*, 59:201 (1999), pp. 269–304; A.M. Bernal, *La Financiación de la Carrera de Indias (1492–1824) Dinero y crédito en el comercio colonial español con América* (Madrid: Tabapress, 1993); Ó.Cruz Barney, *El riesgo en el comercio Hispano-Indiano: préstamos y seguros marítimos durante los siglos XVI a XIX* (México: UNAM, 1998); M.D. Herrero Gil, *El mundo de los negocios en Indias. Las familias Álvarez Campana y Llano San Ginés en el Cádiz del siglo XVIII* (Madrid: CSIC, 2013); J. Baskes, *Staying afloat. Risk and Uncertainty in Spanish Atlantic World Trade, 1760–1820* (Stanford: Stanford University Press, 2013), pp. 179–273.

71 For example, Christian Francisco Livert, from Lille, and the Dutchman Luis Doye were entrusted with the recovery of a cargo taken by French privateers in 1708.

72 A. García-Baquero González, 'Préstamo e inversión financiera en el Cádiz de la Carrera de Indias: el riesgo marítimo en las flotas de 1765 y 1768', in A. García-Baquero González (ed.), *Comercio y burguesía mercantil en el Cádiz de la Carrera de Indias* (Cádiz: Diputación de Cádiz, 1989), pp. 137–155.

73 A. Crespo Solana, '¿Redes de dependencia inter-imperial? Aproximaciones teóricas a la funcionalidad de los agentes de comercio en la expansión de las sociedades mercantiles', in I. Pérez Tostado and E. García Hernán (eds.), *Irlanda y el Atlántico Ibérico. Movilidad, participación e intercambio cultural (1580–1823)* (Valencia: Albatros ediciones, 2010), pp. 35–50; A. Crespo Solana, 'Elementos de transnacionalidad'. See also, A. Crespo Solana, 'Geostrategy of a System? Merchant Societies and Exchange Networks as Connection Centres in the Spanish Atlantic Trade in the First Global Age', in R. Mukherjee (ed.), *Networks in the First Global Age, 1400–1800* (Kundli, Haryana: Indian Research Council, Primus Books, 2011), pp. 11–32. About the Spanish Monarchy as a transnational space, see A. García-Baquero González, 'Los extranjeros en el tráfico con Indias: entre el rechazo legal y la tolerancia funcional', in M.B. Villar García and P. Pezzi Cristóbal (eds.), *I Coloquio Internacional. Los extranjeros en la España moderna* (Málaga: Universidad de Málaga, 2003), vol. I, pp. 73–99; M. Herrero Sánchez and I. Pérez Tostado (eds.), 'Conectores del mundo atlántico: los irlandeses en

la red comercial internacional de los Grillo y Lomelin', in I. Pérez Tostado, E. García Hernán (eds.), *Irlanda y el Atlántico Ibérico. Movilidad, participación e intercambio cultural (1580–1823)* (Valencia: Albatros ediciones, 2010), pp. 307–321. In general, see the works published in A. Caracausi and C. Jeggle (eds.), *Commercial Networks and European Cities, 1400–1800* (London: Pickering & Chatto, 2014).

74 D. Ormrod, *The Rise of Commercial Empires. England and the Netherlands in the Age of Mercantilism, 1650–1770* (Cambridge: Cambridge University Press, 2003).

75 R. Grafe and A. Irigoin, 'A Stakeholder Empire: The Political Economy of Spanish Imperial Rule in America', *Economic History Review*, 65:2 (2012), pp. 609–651.

Bibliography

Alloza Aparicio, Á., 'La tesorería de las haciendas del contrabando, 1647–1697', in C. Martínez Shaw and M. Alfonso Mola (eds.), *España en el comercio marítimo internacional (siglos XVII–XIX). Quince estudios*, Madrid: UNED, 2009, pp. 111–141.

Baskes, J., *Staying Afloat. Risk and Uncertainty in Spanish Atlantic World Trade, 1760–1820*, Stanford: Stanford University Press, 2013.

Bernal, A.M., *La Financiación de la Carrera de Indias (1492–1824), Dinero y crédito en el comercio colonial español con América*, Madrid: Tabapress, 1993.

Bustos Rodríguez, M., 'Comercio y comerciantes en la Andalucía del Antiguo Régimen: Estado de la cuestión y perspectivas', *Obradoiro de Historia Moderna*, 17 (2008), pp. 43–76.

Campese Gallego, F.J., *Los comuneros sevillanos del siglo XVIII. Estudio social, prosopográfico y genealógico*, Sevilla: Fabiola de Publicaciones, 2004.

Caracausi, A., C. Jeggle (eds.), *Commercial Networks and European Cities, 1400–1800*, London: Pickering & Chatto, 2014.

Carrasco González, M.G., *Comerciantes y casas de negocios en Cádiz, 1650–1700*, Cádiz: Universidad de Cádiz, 1997.

———. 'El negocio de los seguros marítimos en Cádiz a finales del siglo XVIII', *Hispania. Revista española de Historia*, 59:201 (1999), pp. 269–304.

———. 'La factoría británica de Cádiz a mediados del siglo XVIII', in M.B. Villar García and P. Pezzi Cristóbal (eds.), *Los extranjeros en la España Moderna, Actas del I Coloquio Internacional*, Málaga: Universidad de Málaga, 2003, vol. 1, pp. 255–265.

Chausinand-Nogaret, G., 'Une elite insulaire au service de l'Europe: les Jacobites au XVIIIe siècle', *Annales ESC*, 5 (1973), pp. 1097–1122.

Crespo Solana, A. (ed.), *Comunidades transnacionales. Colonias de mercaderes extranjeros en el Mundo Atlántico (1500–1830)*, Madrid: Doce Calles, 2010.

———. '¿Redes de dependencia inter-imperial? Aproximaciones teóricas a la funcionalidad de los agentes de comercio en la expansión de las sociedades mercantiles', in Pérez Tostado, I. and García Hernán, E. (eds.), *Irlanda y el Atlántico Ibérico. Movilidad, participación e intercambio cultural (1580–1823)*, Valencia: Albatros ediciones, 2010, pp. 35–50.

———. 'Elementos de transnacionalidad en el comercio flamenco-holandés en Europa y la Monarquía Hispánica', *Cuadernos de Historia Moderna*, X (2011), pp. 55–76.

———. 'Geostrategy of a System? Merchant Societies and Exchange Networks as Connection Centres in the Spanish Atlantic Trade in the First Global Age', in R. Mukherjee (ed.), *Networks in the First Global Age, 1400–1800*, Kundli, Haryana: Indian Research Council, Primus Books, 2011, pp. 11–32.

———. 'El juez conservador ¿Una alternativa al cónsul de la nación?', in Aglietti, M. Herrero Sánchez, M. and Zamora Rodríguez, F. (eds.), *Los cónsules de extranjeros en la Edad Moderna y principios de la Edad Contemporánea*, Madrid: Doce Calles, 2013, pp. 23–34.

————. 'El concepto de ciudadanía y la idea de nación según la comunidad flamenca de la Monarquía Hispánica', in García García, B.J. and Recio Morales, Ó. (eds.), *Las corporaciones de nación en la Monarquía Hispánica (1580–1750)*. *Identidad, patronazgo y redes de sociabilidad*, Madrid: Fundación Carlos de Amberes, 2014, pp. 389–411.

————. 'The Formation of a Social Hispanic Atlantic Space and the Integration of Merchant Communities Following the Treaties of Utrecht', *Culture & History Digital Journal*, 3:1 (2014), pp. 1–12.

Cruz Barney, Ó., *El riesgo en el comercio Hispano-Indiano: préstamos y seguros marítimos surante los siglos XVI a XIX*, México: UNAM, 1998.

Cullen, L.M., 'The Irish Merchant Communities of Bordeaux, La Rochelle and Cognac in the Eighteenth Century', in Cullen, L.M. and Butel, P. (eds.), *Négoce, et industrie en France et en Irlande au XVIIIe et XIXe Siècles*, Bordeaux: CNRS, 1980, pp. 51–63.

Cullen, L.M., (ed.), 'Galway Merchants in the Outside World, 1650–1800', *Economy, trade and Irish Merchants at Home and Abroad, 1600–1988*, Dublin: Four Courts Press, 2012, pp. 165–192.

Díaz Blanco, J.M., 'La construcción de una institución comercial: el consulado de las naciones flamenca y alemana en la Sevilla moderna', *Revista de Historia Moderna. Anales de la Universidad de Alicante*, 33 (2015), pp. 123–145.

Domínguez Ortiz, A., *Los extranjeros en la vida española durante el siglo XVII y otros artículos*, Sevilla: Diputación de Sevilla, 1996.

————. 'Las concesiones de naturalezas', *Estudios americanistas*, Madrid: Real Academia de la Historia, 1998, pp. 117–134.

————. 'Documentos sobre mercaderes flamencos establecidos en Sevilla a comienzos del siglo XVIII', in Casquero Fernández, J.A. (ed.), *Homenaje a Antonio Matilla Tascón*, Zamora: Diputación de Zamora, 2002, pp. 151–160.

Fernández Chaves, M.F. and Gamero Rojas, M., 'Hacer del dinero riqueza: estrategias de ascenso económico y asentamiento de los comerciantes irlandeses en la Sevilla del siglo XVIII', in Pérez Tostado, I. and García Hernán, E. (eds.), *Irlanda y el Atlántico Ibérico. Movilidad, participación e intercambio cultural (1580–1823)*, Valencia: Albatros Ediciones, 2010, pp. 1–22.

————. 'El Reino de Sevilla como escenario del ascenso del poder social y económico de los extranjeros en el siglo XVIII: el caso irlandés', in Recio Morales, Ó. (ed.), *Redes de nación y espacios de poder. La comunidad irlandesa en España y la América española, 1600–1825*, Valencia: Albatros, 2012, pp. 191–217.

Fernández Pérez, P., *El rostro familiar de la metrópoli. Redes de parentesco y lazos mercantiles en Cádiz, 1700–1812*, Madrid: Siglo XXI, 1997.

García-Baquero González, A., 'Préstamo e inversión financiera en el Cádiz de la Carrera de Indias: el riesgo marítimo en las flotas de 1765 y 1768', in García-Baquero González, A. (ed.), *Comercio y burguesía mercantil en el Cádiz de la Carrera de Indias*, Cádiz: Diputación de Cádiz, 1989, pp. 137–155.

————. 'Los extranjeros en el tráfico con Indias: entre el rechazo legal y la tolerancia funcional', in Villar García, M.B. and Pezzi Cristóbal, P. (eds.), *I Coloquio Internacional. Las corporaciones de nación en la Monarquía Hispánica (1580–1750). Identidad, patronazgo y redes de sociabilidad*, Madrid: Fundación Carlos de Amberes, 2014.

García García, B.J., 'La Nación Flamenca en la corte española y el Real Hospital de San Andrés ante la crisis sucesoria (1606–1706)', in Álvarez Ossorio Alvariño, A., García García, B.J. and León Sanz, V. (eds.), *La pérdida de Europa. La guerra de Sucesión por la Monarquía de España*, Madrid: Fundación Carlos de Amberes, Ministerio de Cultura, 2007, pp. 379–442.

García García, B.J., 'La Real Diputación de San Andrés de los Flamencos. Formas de patronazgo e identidad en el siglo XVII', in García García, B.J. and Recio Morales, Ó. (eds.), *Las corporaciones de nación en la Monarquía Hispánica (1580–1750). Identidad, patronazgo y redes de sociabilidad*, Madrid: Fundación Carlos de Amberes, 2014, pp. 59–107.

García García B.J. and Recio Morales, Ó. (eds.), *Las corporaciones de nación en la Monarquía Hispánica (1580–1750). Identidad, patronazgo y redes de sociabilidad*, Madrid: Fundación Carlos de Amberes, 2014.

Gozálvez Escobar, J.L., 'Comerciantes irlandeses en la Huelva del siglo XVIII', in García-Baquero González, A. (ed.), *La burguesía de negocios en la Andalucía de la Ilustración*, Cádiz: Diputación de Cádiz, 1991, pp. 271–292.

Grafe, R., *Distant Tyranny. Markets, Power and Backwardness in Spain, 1650–1800*, New Jersey: Princeton University Press, 2012.

Grafe, R. and. Irigoin, A., 'A Stakeholder Empire: The Political Economy of Spanish Imperial Rule in America', *Economic History Review*, 65:2 (2012), pp. 609–651.

Haggerty, S., *The British-Atlantic Trading Community, 1760–1810*, Boston and Leiden: Brill, 2009.

Herrero Gil, M.D., *El mundo de los negocios en Indias. Las familias Álvarez Campana y Llano San Ginés en el Cádiz del siglo XVIII*, Madrid: CSIC, 2013.

Herrero Sánchez M. et al., (ed.) *Génova y la Monarquía Hispánica (1528–1713)*, Génova: Società ligure di storia patria, 2011.

Herrero Sánchez, M. and Pérez Tostado, I., 'Conectores del mundo atlántico: los irlandeses en la red comercial internacional de los Grillo y Lomelin', in Pérez Tostado, I. and García Hernán, E. (eds.), *Irlanda y el Atlántico Ibérico. Movilidad, participación e intercambio cultural (1580–1823)*, Valencia: Albatros Ediciones, 2010, pp. 307–321.

Herzog, T. *Defining Nations: Immigrants and Citizens in Early Modern Spain and Spanish America*, New Haven and London: Yale University Press, 2003.

———. *Vecinos y extranjeros. Hacerse español en la Edad Moderna*, Madrid: Alianza, 2006.

Iglesias Rodríguez, J.J., Pérez García, R.M. and Fernández Chaves, M.F. (eds.), *Comercio y cultura en la Edad Moderna. Actas de la XIII Reunión Científica de la Fundación Española de Historia Moderna*, Sevilla: Universidad de Sevilla, 2015.

Kaps, K., 'Entre el servicio estatal y los negocios transnacionales: el caso de Paolo Greppi, cónsul imperial en Cádiz (1774–1791)', in Aglietti, M., Herrero Sánchez, M. and Zamora Rodríguez, M. (eds.), *Los cónsules de extranjeros*, Madrid: Doce Calles, 2013, pp. 225–235.

Lamikiz, X., *Trade and Trust in the Eighteenth Century Atlantic World: Spanish Merchants and their Overseas Networks*, Woodbridge: Royal Historical Society, 2010.

Lario de Oñate, M.C., *La colonia mercantil británica e irlandesa en Cádiz a finales del siglo XVIII*, Cádiz: Universidad de Cádiz, 2000.

———. 'The Irish Traders of Eighteenth-century Cádiz', in Dickson, D., Parmentier, J. and Ohlmeyer, J. (eds.), *Irish and Scottish Mercantile Networks in Europe and Overseas in the Seventeenth and Eighteenth Centuries*, Gent: Academia Press, 2007, pp. 211–230.

Lyons, M.A., 'The Emergence of an Irish Community in Saint-Malo, 1550–1710', in T. O'Connor (ed.), *The Irish in Europe*, Dublin: Four Court Press, 2001, pp. 107–126.

McLachlan, J.O., *Trade and Peace with Old Spain, 1667–1750. A Study of the Influence of Commerce on Anglo-Spanish Diplomacy in the First Half of the Eighteenth Century*, New York: Octagon Books, 1974.

Montojo Montojo, V., 'Crecimiento mercantil y desarrollo corporativo en España: los Consulados extraterritoriales extranjeros (ss. XVI–XVII)', *Anuario de Historia del Derecho Español*, 62 (1992), pp. 47–66.

Ó Ciosáin, É., 'Les irlandais en Bretagne 1603–1780: "invasion", accueil, intégration', in Laurent, C. and Davis, H. (eds.), *Irlande et Bretagne. Vingt siècles d'Histoire*, Rennes: Terre de Brume Éditions, 1994, pp. 153–166.

———. 'A Hundred Years of Irish Migration to France, 1590–1688', in O'Connor, T. (ed.), *The Irish in Europe*, Dublin: Four Court Press, 2001, pp. 125–138.

———. 'Hidden by 1688 and After: Irish Catholic Migration to France, 1590–1685', in Worthington, D. (ed.), *British and Irish Emigrants and Exiles in Europe, 1603–1688*, Leiden and Boston: Brill, 2010), pp. 125–138.

Ormrod, D., *The Rise of Comercial Empires. England and the Netherlands in the Age of Mercantilism, 1650–1770*, Cambridge: Cambridge University Press, 2003.

O'Scea, C., 'Special Privileges for the Irish in the Kingdom of Castile (1601–1680): Modern Myth or Contemporary Reality?', in Worthington, D. (ed.), *British and Irish Emigrants and Exiles in Europe, 1603–1688*, Leiden and Boston: Brill, 2010, pp. 107–124.

Otte, E., 'Los mercaderes transatlánticos bajo Carlos V', *Anuario de Estudios Americanos*, 47 (1990), pp. 95–121.

Parmentier, J. 'The Irish Connection: The Irish Merchant Community in Ostend and Bruges During the Late Seventeenth and Eighteenth Centuries', *Eighteenth-Century Ireland*, 20 (2005), pp. 32–54.

————. 'The Sweets of Commerce: The Hennessys of Ostend and their Network in the Eighteenth Century', in Dickson, D., Parmentier, J. and Ohlmeyer, J. (eds.), *Irish and Scottish Mercantile Networks in Europe and Overseas in the Seventeenth and Eighteenth Centuries*, Gent: Academia Press, 2007, pp. 67–91.

Pérez Sarrión, G., *La península comercial. Mercado, redes sociales y Estado en España en el siglo XVIII*, Madrid: Marcial Pons, 2012.

Pérez Tostado, I. and García Hernán, E. (eds.), *Irlanda y el Atlántico Ibérico. Movilidad, participación e intercambio cultural (1580–1823)*, Valencia: Albatros ediciones, 2010.

Pfister, C., 'Dunkerque et l'Irlande. 1690–1790', in Dickson, D., Parmentier, J. and Ohlmeyer, J. (eds.), *Irish and Scottish Mercantile Networks in Europe and Overseas in the Seventeenth and Eighteenth Centuries*, Gent: Academia Press, 2007, pp. 93–114.

Pons Pons, J., 'El seguro marítimo en España (1650–1800)', *Hispania. Revista Española de Historia*, 67:225 (2006), pp. 271–294.

Recio Morales, Ó., 'Irish Emigré Group Strategies of Survival, Adaptation and Integration in Seventeenth and Eighteenth Century Spain', in O'Connor, T. and Lyons, M.A. (eds.), *Irish Communities in Early Modern Europe*, Dublin: Four Courts Press, 2006, pp. 240–266.

————. 'Identity and Loyalty: Irish Traders in Seventeenth Century Iberia', in Dickson, D., Parmentier, J. and Ohlmeyer, J. (eds.), *Irish and Scottish Mercantile Networks in Europe and Overseas in the Seventeenth and Eighteenth Centuries*, Gent: Academia Press, 2007, pp. 197–210.

————. *Ireland and the Spanish Empire*, Dublin: Four Court Press, 2010.

————. 'Conectores de imperios: la figura del comerciante irlandés en España y en el mundo atlántico del siglo XVIII', in Crespo Solana, A. (ed.), *Comunidades transnacionales. Colonias de mercaderes extranjeros en el Mundo Atlántico (1500–1830)*, Madrid: Doce Calles, 2010, pp. 313–336.

————. 'Los extranjeros y la historiografía modernista', *Cuadernos de Historia Moderna. Anejos*, X (2011), pp. 33–51.

Recio Morales, Ó. (ed.), 'Redes sociales y espacios de poder de la naciones en la Monarquía Hispánica. Un estado de la cuestión', *Redes de nación y espacios de poder. La comunidad irlandesa en España y la América española, 1600–1825*, Valencia: Albatros ediciones, 2012, pp. 37–53.

Ruiz Ibáñez J.J. and Pérez Tostado, I. (eds.), *Los exiliados del rey de España*, Madrid: Fondo de Cultura Económica, 2015.

Saupin, G., 'Les réseaux commerciaux des irlandais de Nantes sous le Règne de Louis XIV', in Dickson, D. Parmentier, J. and Ohlmeyer, J. (eds.), *Irish and Scottish Mercantile Networks in Europe and Overseas in the Seventeenth and Eighteenth Centuries*, Gent: Academia Press, 2007, pp. 115–146.

Talbott, S., 'Such Unjustifiable Practices? Irish Trade, Settlement and Society in France, 1688–1715', *The Economic History Review*, 67:2 (2014), pp. 556–577.

Trivellato, F., 'Sephardic Merchants in the Early Modern Atlantic and Beyond. Toward a Comparative Historical Approach to Business Cooperation', in Kagan, R.L. and Morgan, P.D. (eds.), *Atlantic Diasporas: Jews, Conversos and Crypto-Jews in the Age of Mercantilism, 1500–1800*, Baltimore: Johns Hopkins University Press, 2009, pp. 99–120.

Truxes, T.M., 'Dutch-Irish Cooperation in the Mid-Eighteenth-Century Wartime Atlantic', *Early American Studies*, 10:2 (2012), pp. 303–334.

Villar García, M.B. and Pezzi Cristóbal, P. (eds.), *Los extranjeros en la España Moderna, Actas del I Coloquio Internacional*, Málaga: Universidad de Málaga, 2003.

Villar García, M.B., 'Los extranjeros en la España Moderna: la expansión de un campo historiográfico a partir de la obra de Domínguez Ortiz', in Castellano Castellano, J.L. and López-Guadalupe Muñoz, M.L. (eds.), *Homenaje a Antonio Domínguez Ortiz*, Granada: Universidad de Granada, 2008, vol. II, pp. 859–872.

Yun Casalilla, B., *Las redes del imperio. Élites sociales en la articulación de la Monarquía Hispánica, 1492–1714*, Madrid: Marcial Pons, 2009.

Zamora Rodríguez, F.J., '"Dar el cordero en guarda al lobo". Control hispánico sobre los consulados de extranjeros durante el siglo XVII e inicios del siglo XVIII', *Tiempos Modernos*, 30 (2015/1), pp. 1–20.

Part III

Connecting spaces

Networks and systems, merchants
and political economies

8 Interconnecting trade regions

International networks of German merchants in the eighteenth century

Margrit Schulte Beerbühl

Introduction

Between the sixteenth century and the end of the Napoleonic Wars, radical changes affected empires and trade routes. The pace of these changes accelerated in the eighteenth century, as constant warfare led to the emergence of new centres of power on the European mainland and to the rise of Britain as the dominant industrial and commercial power worldwide. At the same time, migration and trade drew links between distant, and hitherto little connected, regions of the world.

A number of recent publications have emphasized the fundamental role played by early modern trade networks in the emergence of a modern world economy. Family, trust, reputation, and flexibility have been highlighted as significant factors in overcoming the uncertainty and risk of long-distance trade.

The rise of the early modern global economy has been primarily associated with European colonisation, particularly on the part of Spain, France and, above all, Britain. However, the establishment of international trading networks was not restricted to the colonial powers. From a very early period smaller states also contributed to the expansion of European trade beyond the confines of national, regional and even continental borders. Already in the sixteenth century powerful merchant houses, such as the Fuggers or the Welsers, from Augsburg, expanded their commercial activities to the New World.[1] Following the decline of these merchant families, and the dissolution of the Hanseatic League, the contribution German merchants made to shaping the commercial landscape of Europe seemed to have diminished significantly.

From the 1660s onwards, however, German merchants began to assert their presence in the leading European commercial and port cities of Europe and to establish new long-distance networks. It will be shown that, although the old German Reich was split into a multitude of small states and possessed few colonies and even then only temporarily, it was able to participate in the emerging world economy, and to contribute to the interconnection of colonial empires and peripheral areas alike into a worldwide network.

Studies of merchant networks tend to implicitly consider spatial factors in order to account for their geographical scope, but equal attention is rarely paid to their densification, their shifting, oscillating geographies and the long-term interconnection of independent spatial networks. New approaches borrowed from migration history, leading to notions of step and chain migration; the history of diaspora communities; and the examination of social interaction between merchants of different nationalities and ethnicities, may contribute to a better understanding of the expansion and survival of these networks, some of which remained active for over one-and-a-half centuries. From a long-term perspective, these approaches help to reveal the means by which networks overcame the many trade restrictions posed by mercantilist policies and warfare.

The expansion of trade led to a reorganization of space and of the way in which it was experienced. Recent debates on the concept of 'spatial turn' have highlighted that people act both within and upon space, implying that knowledge and experience will have an impact on the perception of space itself.[2] Along with migration and transportation of goods, channels of information opened up thus carrying news and customs over distances. They had a significant impact on social relationships, not only locally but across distances contributing to new form of communitarisation

In the first part of this chapter, I outline the expansion of German merchant networks from the hinterland to the north German port cities, and the patterns of mobility which contributed to the merging of separate networks. I then turn to the mobility and settlement patterns caused by the migration of Hanseatic German merchants to leading port cities, which were the gateways to the non-European world. These are treated separately for analytical purposes only, as merchant families migrating to any of the main continental ports could of course relocate again. After looking at mobility patterns from a spatial perspective, I offer a brief examination of the changing structure of communication practices and social relations that engendered a European and cosmopolitan commercial elite; this will be essential in understanding the resilience of commercial networks in a war-ridden age full of interruptions to trade. In the second part I shall turn to the challenges posed to trade by the French Revolutionary and Napoleonic Wars and the means by which merchants sought to bypass them.

Spanning a commercial network across the European mainland and beyond

During the period under review, German linen was one of the most important export commodities worldwide, being much sought after in the New World (that is, in the British, Spanish and Portuguese colonies) as well as in Africa. It has been said that 'Germany paid for its colonial goods with linen'.[3] These textiles were manufactured in Silesia, Saxony and the northwestern regions of Germany between the Bergisches Land and Hanover. Low wages and prices gave German products a competitive edge.

Around the turn of the eighteenth century one of the main customers for German linen was Britain. In 1701, 76.3 per cent of all linen imported to Britain came from the German States.[4] The demand for German textiles predominantly came from the English overseas colonies,[5] where slaves and poor whites needed cheap and light linen.[6] At the beginning of the century more than 90 per cent of all cloth imported from Germany was re-exported to the colonies.[7] Furthermore, Silesian and western German fabric found its way to Africa and, via the British Caribbean dominions, to the Spanish American colonies.[8]

Demand for linen fabrics in the British colonies declined during the eighteenth century after the British government decided to build a competitive linen industry in Scotland and Ireland. In the last quarter of the century this was rapidly replaced by the new cotton industry. In the Spanish and Portuguese colonies, demand for linen fabrics persisted until about the 1830s. Towards the end of the eighteenth century, approximately half of the Silesian linen at a value of about eight to ten million Taler was exported to Spain and Spanish America.[9] Linen from the north-western regions of Germany was well-known in the New World (under such names as Osnabrughs, Ozenbrigs, Rosas de Westphalia and Tecklenburghs), where it enjoyed a good reputation for its quality and price.

The question thus arises: how did this linen find its way to these distant markets? After all, German traders could not rely on powerful trading companies like the Dutch or British East and West India Companies.

Due to the large number of small bishoprics and dukedoms into which north-western Germany was divided, industrial activity was from the start heavily dependent on exports. Indeed, from the days of the Hanseatic League, merchant families sent young members abroad to explore new market opportunities, a tradition that has survived until today.

From the mid-seventeenth century onwards, a process of step and chain migration of young family members and other relations to the port cities of Hamburg, Bremen, Amsterdam and London can be perceived. London soon became the preferred destination, as the British capital provided a ready-made infrastructure for global trade.

Thus, the offspring of merchant families based in small towns such as Elberfeld (which is today a part of Wuppertal in the Ruhr Valley) in the Dukedom of Berg and Hamm or Herford, in Westphalia, left their family homes to seek their fortunes elsewhere. For example, the Teschemacher family of Elberfeld, had ten children, six male and four female; of the six sons, four left their hometown between the 1660s and 1680s, one to settle in Bremen and three in London. Similarly, of the eight sons of the Zurhorst family from Hamm, two went to London, two to Amsterdam and one to St. Petersburg, while another one died when still young and the remaining one stayed at home to take over his father's business.

This process of step and chain migration continued for more than a century. Between 1660 and 1791, fourteen young merchants left Elberfeld to establish themselves as linen merchants in London. From Herford, a similarly high number left their hometown to settle in Bremen and London along with other young merchants from the nearby towns of Brunswick, Osnabrück and Bielefeld.

A similar step and chain migration originated from Silesia and Saxony starting slightly later, that is, at the turn of the eighteenth century and lasted until its end. At least twelve Silesian merchants settled in London. These figures only comprise those migrants who acquired a British nationality. Due to the lack of sources, the number of non-naturalised immigrant merchants is hard to estimate, but surviving private records suggest that their number at least matched that of naturalised merchants, and was probably much higher. In addition, we must also take into consideration those merchants who stayed in London for a couple of years only.[10]

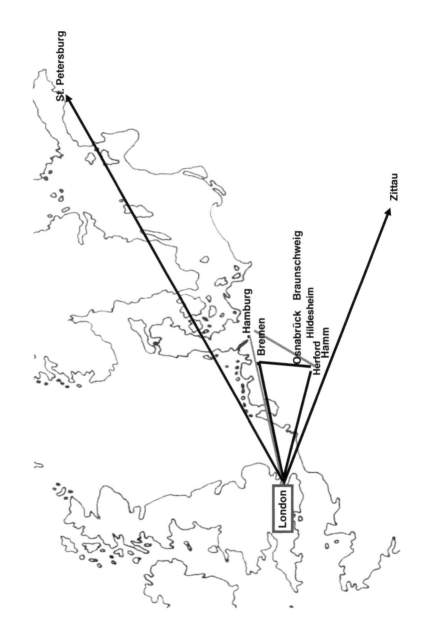

Map 8.1 Migration pattern of merchants from the northwestern region.

The pattern of migration was not unidirectional. Return-migration or transmigration was an integral part of it. Remigration did not necessarily mean returning to the migrant's hometown but could crystallise in onward migration, for example, via London to Silesia and Saxony or even to Portugal, Italy and other regions. Thus, migrants interconnected the German hinterland with the main ports on the North Sea, London, St. Petersburg and other places.

Among the Herford immigrants, for example, several members of the Pritzler family moved to London. While at least two remained in the British capital, a third, Christoph Frederick Pritzler, moved on to Zittau in Saxony to establish a business with one Christian Biedermann from Reichenhorst and a Johann Friederich Mölling (a relative of Pritzler) from Isselhorst, near Bielefeld, thus linking Saxony, the northwestern German territory, with London. Another example is that of the three Hasenclever brothers from Remscheid; one of them first went to Cadiz in order to establish a mercantile house there with a partner from Stralsund (on the Baltic Sea), before moving to London, where he entered a further partnership with two British merchants. In the meantime, one of his brothers went directly from Remscheid to Hirschberg (Jelenia Góra), in Silesia, while the other settled in Sedan, France.[11]

Those merchants who settled abroad permanently became points of contact for many more who stayed abroad for just a few years before returning home or settling elsewhere. Henry Voguell from Herford, one of the wealthy, London-based German textile traders of the first half of the century, became point of contact for many young merchants from Saxony and Silesia, who worked at his office either as employees or junior shareholders.

Besides emigration and temporary visits, 'travel and talk' practices, involving physical presence abroad and the pursuit of active personal, face-to-face interaction also contributed to creating links between regions, developing social relationships, overcoming uncertainty and generating trust. According to John Urry 'networks have to be performed', because lasting change can only occur when people meet and talk from time to time.[12] Travel and talk were thus generally practiced among merchants. Men such as Henry Voguell are frequently found travelling between London, the German port cities and the Silesian and Saxonian textile areas. For many merchants in Zittau Voguell was 'the best customer'.[13] He died unexpectedly in Bremen in 1746 during one of his journeys back to London, and he was buried in the city's cathedral, where his epitaph may still be seen.

Once a business was successfully established abroad, contacts with longstanding and trustworthy partners in distant regions were continued by the following generations. A balance sheet of 1772, pertaining to the successors of Voguell's linen firm, reveals that the firm maintained close business links with Saxonian and Silesian merchants, such as Böhl & Kaller in Glatz, Gottfried Bernds, Francis Hasenclever and Ernst Friedrich Schaeffer, in Hirschberg, as well as Chr. Freudiger in Zittau and Christian Gottlieb Frege in Leipzig.[14]

The South German network

German research on the period of the Hanseatic League and the merchant houses of the south German towns of Augsburg and Nuremberg consider the northern and southern networks as two separate entities. While the Hanseatic merchants traded in the north, the south German merchant families directed their trade towards the Mediterranean.

By the late Middle Ages, South German merchant families possessed a powerful trading organization in Venice, the *Fondaco dei Tedeschi*.[15] Originally, only Catholic merchants had traded in Venice, but from the mid-seventeenth century onwards, a Protestant community appeared that lived in the surrounding areas of the *Fondaco*. These Protestant merchants came from Nuremberg, Augsburg and other religiously mixed southern German cities. Following the shift of the financial centres towards north-western Europe, the *Fondaco* began to lose its economic pre-eminence, and trade flows began to expand and connect the southern and Mediterranean networks with the northern one. For instance, although the Langenmantel and Schorer firms, from Augsburg, kept their trading houses in Venice throughout the eighteenth century, by the last quarter of the seventeenth century they were already sending members to settle in London and acquire British nationality.[16]

Although the number of merchants in the *Fondaco* declined rapidly in the eighteenth century, trade with Italy remained important for the commercial elite of Augsburg and Nuremberg. Young members of the merchant families continued to go to Venice, but more and more often these stays were temporary, either during apprenticeship or junior employment, prior to moving on elsewhere. Again, as in the north we find the same migration pattern; that is, one son moved to London, and the other went to Venice, Trieste or, increasingly, Livorno. Moreover, we also find evidence of migration from the Hanseatic towns to the southern German trading centres and even further south, as will be shown later in this chapter.

The decline of German merchants in Venice was probably due to a concentration process. Only a couple of large businesses with far-reaching international trade links remained in the city, such as Benedict von Hermann. It was the largest German trading house in Venice in the 1770s, so by the time of Hermann's death in 1782 its main business connections ran between Amsterdam, London and Venice, trading with a variety of colonial goods. The firm belonged to those businesses that left the city later on. Only two years after von Hermann's death, it relocated to Trieste.[17]

Departure of the merchants from Venice was followed by a move to the new Italian commercial centres such as Livorno. The Grand Duke of Tuscany had made Livorno a free port at the end of the sixteenth century, granting free port privileges to Christians and Jews alike, but the growing presence of the British transformed Livorno into a crucial entrepôt between the eastern Mediterranean and the Atlantic. The town soon became an increasingly attractive destination for southern and northern German merchants. Some of them even took a detour via England before settling there.

A Dutch-German community, or 'nation', the *Congregazione Olandese-Alemanna*, was established in Livorno at the beginning of the seventeenth century.

Although originally founded as a Catholic community, Protestants soon began to enter the 'nation' and by the end of the century, they dominated membership. A change in the national composition of its membership also occurred. The congregation was originally dominated by Dutch merchants, but with the outbreak of the Anglo-Dutch Wars the number of Dutch members began to decline and by the mid-eighteenth century at the latest, the 'nation' had become predominantly German.

Beside those German merchants, who were members of the *Fondaco* in Venice and the Dutch-German congregation in Livorno, a certain number of German traders lived outside these societies or entered into partnerships with residents of these places without living there themselves. As a young man, Benedict Adam Liebert, one of the leading merchant-bankers of Augsburg, had temporarily lived in Livorno and Venice. After his return to Augsburg in the second half of the 1770s, he decided to enter the silk trade and establish a branch in Livorno under the name Leopoldi & Company in partnership with the Viennese banking house Fries & Company, and two Augsburg banking houses, Carli & Company and Köpff & Company.[18] It seems likely that, as with Liebert, many more Germans were non-resident shareholders in Italian firms than we are aware of. Due to the lack of sources, we have no means to estimate the scale of their commercial activities, but it was probably larger than suggested by the number of resident Germans.

Similar suggestions can be made concerning the commercial relations of South German mercantile houses with Amsterdam, Hamburg and London in the eighteenth century.[19] Despite London's dominant position, Amsterdam remained an important financial market for German trading houses. Many German firms, for example Förster & Schüler, from Augsburg, continued to conduct their credit and exchange transactions in the Dutch city.[20] A member of the Obwexer family, also from Augsburg, settled in Amsterdam in the first half of the century, and through contacts thus even opened a branch of the family firm in the Dutch colony of Curaçao.[21]

The financial crisis that followed at the end of the Seven Years War reveals how close commercial relations had become between Venice and the leading financial centres of Amsterdam, London and Hamburg. In 1763, the Amsterdam-based bank of de Neufville collapsed, sending a shock wave across Europe. In addition to grave effects in Amsterdam itself, more than 90 mercantile houses stopped payments in Hamburg alone, followed by many firms in Berlin, Stockholm and elsewhere. The bankruptcy wave even swept as far as Venice, where many German houses stopped payments.[22]

Trade relations intensified not only between north and south, but also between east and west; that is, between Germany and the Iberian Peninsula.[23] Following frequent travels to Spain and Portugal, Johann Georg Günther, of the Nuremberg-based firm of Förster & Günther, maintained business transactions with over 167 trading houses in Cartagena, Barcelona, Cadiz, Sevilla, Porto and other towns between 1791 and 1816. In the case of the three Rueprecht brothers from Memmingen, their migration led to the establishment of an international family network. One brother moved to Vienna, the other one opened a business in Palermo and the third brother, a business in Cadiz. The Cadiz-based house imported indigo, cochineal, cigars, cocoa and saffron, whilst it exported Bohemian, Saxonian and Lausitzer linen to Spanish America and the West Indies.[24]

Hanseatic merchants in European port cities

While merchants from the German hinterland connected their hometowns with the European port cities across the continent, merchants from the Hanseatic towns Hamburg and Bremen interlinked the European port cities from the middle of the seventeenth century onwards. After the Thirty Years' War, both towns experienced a high in-migration from the German hinterland and later generations of Hanseatic families opened branches in London, Bordeaux, Bilbao, Cadiz, Porto, Lisbon and Livorno.[25] However, a full account of the expansion of family and kinship relations to all European ports cities is well beyond the scope of this chapter. Links to Cadiz and Bordeaux have been described elsewhere.[26] Here I shall focus on the establishment of trade relations with Livorno.

Among the early arrivals in Livorno were Nicolo De Smeth and his business partner Günther Andrea Schulte, from Hamburg.[27] The De Smeth family were originally from Amsterdam, but in the early seventeenth century some of its members moved to Hamburg. In the 1680s, three De Smeth brothers left Hamburg; Raymond De Smeth to go to London, Nicolo to Livorno and Conrad to Frankfurt, while the fourth brother, Isaac, remained in the Hansetown. By having firms in London, Amsterdam, Hamburg, Frankfurt and Livorno, they operated from the leading financial centres of the period, giving them access to the non-European markets.

Nicolo De Smeth's business became an information centre for his brother Raymond, in London. Via Nicolo, Raymond sent goods and bills of exchange to his partners in Venice, Messina, Genoa and other places, where he maintained business relations with French, Dutch, German and Italian merchants.[28] After the end of the Spanish War of Succession, the De Smeths also opened business links with Cadiz, Bilbao and Seville, thereby gaining access to the Spanish colonial market. In the 1720s, at the latest, Raymond De Smeth sent ships via Cadiz to Veracruz, whence they returned laden with silver.[29] He was not the only Hamburg merchant in London who traded with Veracruz or Rio de Janeiro during this period.

Most of the members of the Dutch-German congregation in Livorno came from the Hanseatic towns of Hamburg and Bremen.[30] The growing pre-eminence of Hanseatic merchants can be attested by the fact that, in 1781, Hamburg appointed its first consul in the Italian port. Johann Heinrich Nolte began his career as an apprentice in the house of his uncle Otto Franck, owner of one of the largest firms in Livorno, which he took over after his uncle's death. After returning to Hamburg in 1787, he was appointed consul by the government of Livorno, in which he was eventually succeeded by his brother Octavio.[31] The close relations between Hamburg and England, and between the Noltes and the Barings may have played a role in their appointment to the consulate. Otto Franck himself had been married to an English woman, and Heinrich Nolte had been educated in Exeter through the initiative of his uncle. There he became friends with Francis Baring, the founder of the London bank. Later, Heinrich Nolte was to become one of the leading business partners of the Barings in Livorno.[32] He supplied them with dyed fabrics for their textile factory in Exeter, and with other products including oil, raisins and silk.[33]

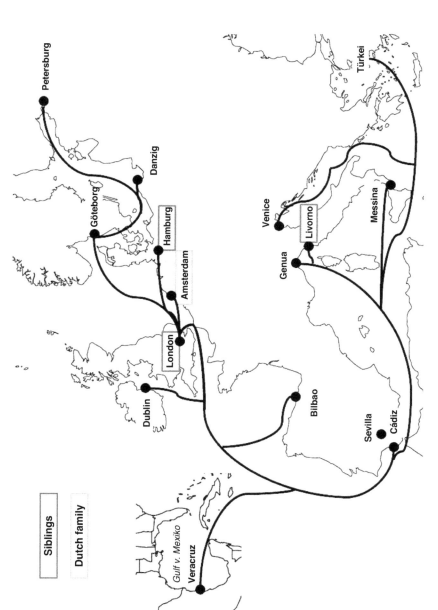

Map 8.2 Raymond De Smeth's trade (1690–1720).

Interestingly, some of the merchants from Bremen living in Livorno sided with the British factory. Religious affiliation may have been behind this, for they usually belonged to the Reformed or Calvinist Church, while Hamburg merchants were generally Lutherans. Economic factors should also be taken into account. Bremen's trade with Britain had grown considerably from the last quarter of the seventeenth century onwards, while its trade with the Mediterranean was negligible. The import for the port of Bremen, which began after the mid-eighteenth century, only mentions an occasional ship laden with wine or oil, arriving from Livorno or Gallipoli.[34] A significant factor was that shipping between the Hanseatic ports and Italy suffered greatly from North African piracy. Unlike the British merchants, they were not protected by a powerful navy. Following the failure of a treaty with the Barbary States in the early 1750s, the Hamburg Senate decided to stop sending ships under their own flag into the Mediterranean.[35] This does not mean, however, that the Hanseatic merchants ceased trade with the Mediterranean. Their goods were instead shipped in vessels sailing under foreign flags such as those of the Danish or the British. Similarly, the proximity of Amsterdam and the old and close business links between the Bremen trading families and the Dutch city may have directed a significant proportion of the city's Mediterranean trade to Dutch ports.

Furthermore, a considerable part of the trade also went via one of the British ports to the Mediterranean. From the seventeenth century onwards, Livorno turned into a hub of the British Mediterranean commerce and after the turn of the century, it became a leading international financial and insurance centre. British merchants made the port an ideal place of stopover for expanding trade to the eastern Mediterranean. The majority of ships that arrived at the port of Livorno in the eighteenth century carried English flags.

The first record of the British factory in Livorno dates from 1704, although it was probably already established in the late seventeenth century. British residents in the port city can be dated back to the early seventeenth century. The number of British merchants had risen to about 20 in the 1690s.[36] Attempts of the British community in Livorno to establish a chaplain date back to the period of the restauration of the English monarchy in 1660s, but only in 1705 did the Grand Duke of Tuscany allow the establishment of a chaplaincy.[37] Membership in the British factory varied a lot, due to the fact that members in British factories frequently were young men who worked abroad only for a couple of years – often as factors of a merchant house in Britain. After having gained sufficient knowledge and experience they returned home to open a merchant house themselves, only to send a young and trustworthy employee or partner again abroad. Few British merchants settled abroad permanently.[38] Partnerships with foreign Protestant merchants can also be found. Foreigners in partnership with British merchants of the British factory, generally had to acquire British nationality. Thus we find naturalised merchants of Huguenot descent, Swiss or German birth in the factory. Moreover, British nationality carried several commercial advantages. In the age of widespread piracy, especially in the Mediterranean, certainly most important was the privilege of becoming a shareholder or owner in a British vessel, which was protected by the British navy.

Likewise, the Bremish merchants in the British factory in Livorno had acquired British nationality. British law did not stipulate any residential or linguistic requirements, making it perfectly legal to live as a naturalised British subject elsewhere. Among those who availed themselves of that opportunity were members of the Wienholt family from Bremen. Several of them went to England, while one moved as a naturalised British subject to Livorno. George William Renner, from Bremen, also acquired British citizenship before arriving in Livorno. He became a prosperous banker and married an English woman in Florence in 1769. Renner died there in 1790 and was buried in the Old English Cemetery.[39]

Overall, German commercial communities existed in more or less all leading European ports from at least the mid-eighteenth century onwards. Moreover, these groups were connected through dense overland as well as maritime networks.

The ever-growing trade connections influenced perceptions of space and social relations. This was experienced not as the compression of space, but as an enlargement of personal horizons, before the time of trains and telegraphy. The changing spatial awareness was not restricted to travellers and migrants; information flows concerning foreign news and customs also reached those who stayed at home. Additionally, increased long-distance mobility fostered the internationalisation of social relations and marriage patterns.

Social and information networks

This expansion and densification of trade networks across Europe was intimately related to processes of social networking. Expatriate merchants were connected to a distant network of family, kin, coreligionists and compatriots, but they also engaged socially with the local commercial elite of their host cities through business transactions, friendship, membership of local clubs and parishes, and even marriage.

The example of the Uhthoff family, from Bremen, is illustrative. The Uhthoffs were originally from Hanover, but settled in Bremen in the second half of the seventeenth century; they were co-founders of the Bremish English Company. Their commercial relationship with Britain induced the Bremen-born Henry Uhthoff (b. 1728), a descendant of the original in-migrants, to move to London and become an apprentice in the house of his godfather, the aforementioned Henry Voguell of Herford.[40] Following Voguell's death, his firm was renamed Amyand, Uhthoff & Rücker.[41] In the following years the firm became the leading 'Russia house' in Europe, according to Walter Shairp, the British consul in Russia and a friend of Uhthoff.[42]

In London, Henry Uhthoff married into the Van Neck family (Figure 8.1). Gerard and Joshua Van Neck, naturalised British subjects born in Amsterdam, were regarded as the wealthiest merchants in Europe, after amassing a fortune in the American-French tobacco trade and other concerns. Thus, his business relations and marriage associated Henry Uhthoff with one of the most powerful and influential families in Europe. They not only had far-reaching international commercial links, but were also related to the British political elite, for one of the Van Neck daughters had married into the Walpole family.

Figure 8.1 Picture of the Van Neck-Uhthoff-Walpole family.

In the 1750s, Uhthoff left the firm of Amyand, Uhthoff & Rücker to enter into a new partnership with Nicolas Battier, one of the leading merchant bankers of Basle, thereby extending his business links to the Swiss States.[43]

The Bremen branch of the Uhthoff family expanded yet further, reaching Cadiz in the mid-eighteenth century. Johann Andreas Uhthoff was one of the partners in the Cadiz-based firm of Sylingk, Uhthoff & Kahler from 1764 onwards.[44] The firm still existed in 1790, when Ludolph Christian, a nephew of Johann Andreas Uhthoff (born in Bremen in 1776) entered it. He married into a Spanish family and later became Prussian consul in Cadiz.[45]

There are many more examples of expatriate merchants and their intertwining networks, including business partnerships, friendships, godparenthood and marriage, both locally and transnationally.

The chart in Figure 8.2 may be seen as a simplified version of what was at times a far more complex economic, ethnic and social interweaving of merchant families; this embeddedness and the multilayered nature of networks strengthened personal relationships and facilitated the flow of information and news. Furthermore, in times of crisis, when one link broke or was in danger of being cut off, other ties could be activated to reorganise the broken part. That possibility was of crucial importance in times of trade restrictions and war. In addition, the complexity of both long-distance and local relationships offered a variety of economic advantages; most importantly, they helped to overcome restrictions and obstacles to trade. Also, these links gave merchants access to commercial privileges from which they were otherwise excluded. During the eighteenth century the British concluded several commercial treaties, with the aim of securing economic privileges for their own inhabitants; for example, the British treaties with Portugal (1703), Spain (1713) and Russia (1734). Due to the interconnectedness provided by networks, family or friends at home could enjoy commercial privileges via their expatriate associates. For instance, the London-based Johann Abraham Korten, from Elberfeld, provided the means for his relatives in Elberfeld to enjoy the commercial privileges granted for British merchants in the Russian market.

Alongside family and business partners, brokers played a crucial role in expanding or reorganizing networks.[46] Brokers could be individuals in their home town or in expatriate communities (Figure 8.3). They were points of contact and information centres for compatriots at home who wished to expand their trade to previously unknown regions but who lacked the necessary language skills or were unaware

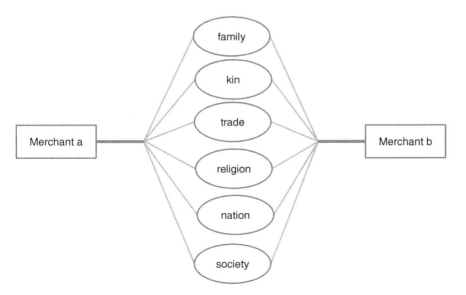

Figure 8.2 Multilayered relations.

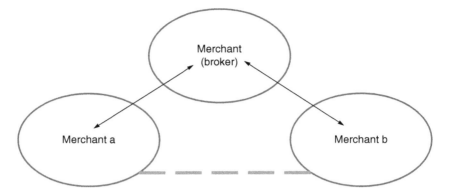

Figure 8.3 Role of agent (broker).

of local trade customs. Merchants with international business frequently possessed excellent long-distance communication systems based on travellers, brokers and correspondence that supplied them with information on market conditions and the reputation and reliability of known and unknown traders, thus providing instruments with which to expand, or to relocate trade or even to reorganise broken links following times of crisis.[47]

In order to assess the value of information or the reliability of a distant business partner, merchants did not rely on any single source of information; several sources were tapped and their information cross-checked. Trading partners abroad, whether related or not, were monitored and if they were unreliable they were then replaced, so that there was no need to sacrifice a distant but attractive market due to the failure of a partner.[48]

By the time of the outbreak of the Coalition Wars against Revolutionary France and Napoleon, a dense, multilayered geographical and social network of German merchants and expatriate communities spanned not only across Europe but also across the Atlantic. Their composition, scope and duration changed permanently over time. Their volatile character should not necessarily be taken as a sign of weakness, given these networks' inherent ability to regenerate. These regenerating properties came fully into their own during the French and Napoleonic Wars. Broken or interrupted trade links could be re-established elsewhere or if this was not possible, left in a dormant state until conditions improved again.

Heading for new shores: the French Revolution and the Napoleonic Wars

The prevailing opinion in historical research is that the French Revolutionary and Napoleonic Wars had a destructive effect on the emerging global markets. Using quantitative data, Ken O'Rourke has recently pointed out that the Coalition Wars had a devastating effect on market integration caused by rising prices and transportation costs.[49] Such effects will not be questioned here, nor will it be denied that the war destroyed long-established relations and that many economic agents suffered heavily. Rather, I aim to shed an alternative light on the period by emphasising the potential of commercial networks to regenerate, as well as their flexibility and resilience to external shocks.

Given the densely entangled, multilayered commercial networks previously described, merchants had multiple options for either circumventing the effects of the blockades or realigning their connections. At any rate, surging prices of certain commodities such as sugar and coffee raised staggering profit expectations if merchants could succeed in running the blockades despite the risk. It is certainly not possible to measure the volume of smuggling, for much of it remains invisible, but it is clear that the practice gained a new dimension during the Coalition Wars.

Classic works on the British and Napoleonic Blockades, such as those of Eli Heckscher and Freeman Galpin, have emphasised that the blockades were never fully effective.[50] The size of the Napoleonic Empire from 1806 onwards, for one, made holes in the Continental Blockade inevitable.

Moreover, for many merchants, such as the Italian-born Vincent Nolte, Napoleon was regarded a 'deadly foe of commerce' who drove merchants into the hands of the British.[51] Unlike Napoleon, the British government pursued a stick-and-carrot policy, and merchants thus preferred to collaborate with Britain despite her aggressive tendencies. Recent studies by James Davey, Christopher Hall and A. N. Ryan have shown that the British government was crucially dependent on the private sector for securing the import of necessary supplies for the navy and its population.[52] The surviving government records reveal that time and again, merchants successfully protested against war measures and forced politicians to mitigate or even withdraw them. Furthermore, the government actively supported merchants and mariners in breaking the Napoleonic Blockade. From 1798 onwards, the British Privy Council issued licences in rapidly increasing volume to protect merchant ships against privateering and allow them to pass the blockades.

Rapidly changing sites of warfare meant that for every loophole closed, another one would open unexpectedly elsewhere. This rapidly changing scenario forced merchants to increase mobility and to remain alert for new collaborators and partners abroad. When the French Revolutionary troops occupied the Netherlands, including Amsterdam in 1795, trade shifted to the North German ports of Hamburg and Bremen. Even small ports began to flourish. The blockade that the British navy imposed upon the Elbe and Weser after the 1803 renewal of war caused a further shift to even smaller ports such as Leer, Norden, Varel or Emden.[53] Many mercantile houses based in Bremen, Hamburg or Amsterdam opened branches in these small ports.

Furthermore, recent studies on the occupied regions of Germany have highlighted that trade and industry did not suffer entirely. The Continental Blockade protected young and nascent industries against British industrial power. Additionally, the new, extended borders of the French Empire led to some reorientation of trade in the enlarged occupied French empire. Westphalian merchants, among others, turned towards France, Italy or Spain. The textile entrepreneur

E. A. Delius from Bielefeld, for example, opened new markets in Italy and Spain. Spain evidently became such an attractive market that a family member opened a branch in Malaga in the early years of the nineteenth century. The situation only changed with the Treaty of Trianon in 1810.[54]

When Napoleon proclaimed the Continental Blockade at the end of 1806, a ring of smuggling nests developed around the European mainland. Islands, including Helgoland, Malta and the Canaries, as well as Gothenburg and other places, became entrepôts for the illegal entry of goods to the continent. The geography of the north German coast – that is, the tideland between the East and North Frisian island chains and the mainland – rendered difficult its control by French invasion forces. These conditions were favourable for clandestine operations; the locals knew the area well and could manoeuvre through the dangerous tideland with small ships, while the occupiers did not dare to enter it. Moreover, the British government yielded to the merchants' demands to let small ships under 60 tons pass the British blockade.[55]

Following the occupation of Helgoland by the British, the island became a port of turnover at which forbidden cargoes brought from Britain and elsewhere were reloaded onto smaller ships. The island was described by the father-in-law of Nathan Mayer Rothschild, the founder of the British Rothschild bank, as an 'infamous place'. In vain, he tried to dissuade his son-in-law from establishing an agent there. Nevertheless, for Nathan and for many others, the island became a valuable stopover for the thriving trade to the mainland. By 1809, three or four ships were leaving Hull for Helgoland every day, and the number of warehouses on the island had increased from 2 to 140.[56]

Similarly, Malta also became a flourishing smuggler's port for the entry of forbidden goods into Italy. From 1808, the number of Malta-based British-German and British merchant houses increased considerably. In 1809, the British alone had established 30 or 40 firms on the island, and they were not the only country to take advantage of its position.[57] England-based German merchants such as Nathan Mayer Rothschild, Isaac Aldebert from Frankfurt and John Anthony and Henry Rücker from Hamburg, sent agents to Malta in order to supervise the clandestine trade. The activities of Isaac Aldebert, John Anthony and Henry Rücker are revealing of the scope of the clandestine trade during these years.

Isaac Aldebert began his career in Frankfurt am Main, but settled in Manchester during the 1790s. He remained a shareholder in the Frankfurt house and also invested in a mercantile house in Milan, which was established by the son of his partner in Frankfurt, Enrico Mylius. Aldebert sent goods from England to Malta, where he had at least two agents. From Malta, his cargoes were reshipped to Trieste, Genoa or some other small ports, where his partner's son would supervise delivery. Aldebert also maintained excellent relations with the Swedish government and with Admiral Saumarez, who was stationed in the Baltic in 1808 for the protection of British merchant shipping. Through Saumarez, he received a large number of British government licences granting him permission to secretly transport goods to the Baltic German coast.[58]

Cooperation among European merchants of different countries became very close during this period. One of Aldebert's agents in Malta, for example, was a Danish subject. Similarly, Liverpudlian merchants engaged a German from Brunswick to supervise their business, first in Helgoland and later, in Malta, where he was responsible for organizing trade with the Levant.[59]

Throughout the blockade, the aforementioned Rückers regularly applied for shipping licences to the British government. Their applications reveal trading concerns on an even larger scale. As well as three mercantile houses in London, they had brothers and near cousins in Hamburg, St. Petersburg, Riga, Bordeaux and, temporarily, in New York. The London Rückers sent two factors to Malta, one from Hamburg and the other one was probably a Huguenot or of Huguenot descent.[60]

Their many licences are probably reflective of only a small proportion of their clandestine operations, but they reveal that trade with the Mediterranean increased considerably from about 1808 onwards. Given the enforced secrecy, licences do not always mention the actual ports of arrival or departure, but depending on the conditions of war, sometimes name only regions. The actual task of looking for loopholes was left in the hands of mariners and other agents on the ground. By 1810, the Rückers were granted licences for the transportation of goods from 'any Italian port south of Orbitello and Pesaro'.[61] Another licence allowed a ship to sail from Hamburg to 'Gallipoli or any port in Italy' to return with cargo containing oil, and to stop at Tunis or Algiers before returning to Britain.[62]

Besides trade licences for Italy, the Rückers received many permissions for Baltic and Canarian ports, as well as for the New World. From 1808 onwards, the number of import licences for Baltic goods rose considerably. Tar, masts and tallow were among the import goods from the Baltic. Licences for the Canary Islands were issued for the Rückers from at least 1804 onwards. They show that the Rückers used the islands as a stopover to obtain fresh clearances and probably to change flags before the ships sailed either to the Iberian Peninsula or to the New World. Although most licences simply name the islands without referring to the origin of the goods or the wares being transported, some offer a glimpse of the actual sailing routes. An 1804 licence, authorising the importation of goods from Tenerife to London, gives a detailed list of the wares carried by the ship, including cochineal, barilla, Spanish wool, indigo, skins, hides, silks, Castilian soap, wine and olive oil, among many others.[63] From time to time ships leaving Bilbao, Santander or Lisbon are mentioned. In all, the Rückers seem to have dealt intensively with Spain and Portugal.

Spanish wool was one of the main Spanish products entering Britain. Apart from sugar, coffee and cochineal, a variety of colonial products were transported across the Atlantic via the Canaries. These goods, shipped from St. Thomas and Brazil, but also from other regions, did not always have Britain as their final destination. Licences of ships inspected by the Royal Navy or British privateers also mention such destinations as Tönning, Denmark, Kiel, in the Baltic Sea, or Rotterdam.[64] In another case, a ship carrying logwood, Campeche and goatskins, among other wares, was to sail from Ystat in Sweden to St. Petersburg.[65] The ships of the Rückers usually sailed under the neutral flags of Denmark, Sweden and, most commonly, under the American flag.

On the whole, due to their neutrality over many years, the Americans became the big gainers in the Atlantic and Caribbean trade during the Napoleonic Wars.

Silvia Marzagalli has pointed out that most shipping between Bordeaux and the United States was in American hands.[66] The American flag became a common sight not only in Bordeaux but also in Tönning, Emden, Amsterdam, Rotterdam and even in small ports like Varel or Norden. This neutral flag, in any case, was not exclusively used by Americans; the American consul in Hamburg, John Forbes, frequently complained about the daily abuses of the flag by Prussians, Swedes and Britons.[67] Furthermore, many forbidden goods were routed via the United States, where new papers were produced to certify an American origin, before they were dispatched to Europe in bottoms displaying the American flag.

By the 1790s, the number of German merchants in the United States had already grown considerably, especially in Baltimore and Philadelphia.[68] A few young German merchants moved further south to New Orleans and some Caribbean Islands, such as St. Thomas and Caye (Haiti), in order to export colonial goods via Baltimore, Philadelphia and New York.[69] Similarly, German linen and other goods found their way from the German ports via the northern American states to the British and Spanish colonies in the Caribbean, Mexico and South America.[70] After the end of the Napoleonic Wars commercial relations with the Americas, whose foundations were laid down during wartime, gained new dimensions.

Conclusion

The networks that I have described can only be regarded as a sample of a much more comprehensive commercial network that also stretched into Russia, the Scandinavian countries, France and elsewhere. Similar patterns of mobility and settlement can also be attested for other European merchants. Given the political weakness of the German states and their geopolitical position in central Europe, it is possible that mobility was more common among German merchants than among merchants of other countries, but more research is needed to confirm this.

To sum up, migration and settlement abroad were essential and integral parts of commercial expansion. From the second half of the seventeenth century onwards, German merchants increasingly connected the northern and southern trade networks across the mainland as well as across the sea. By settling in port cities, relations were extended across the Atlantic.

Based on the interaction of local and long-distance economic, social and family ties, goods, information and customs flowed. Expatriate merchants maintained contacts to distant relatives and commercial partners, and at the same time, they tried to integrate with local elites through commercial partnerships, friendship and marriage. Thus, they did not only create multilayered networks, but generated a European and cosmopolitan elite which was variously linked across geographical, national and ethnic borders.

These dense commercially and socially interrelated layers, as well as the fluent and flexible structure of these relationships, made it easy to reactivate weak links, use well-trusted information channels, and find brokers or agents capable of using on-the-ground information. Moreover, as this century was a war-torn age in which trade interruptions were the order of the day, merchants quickly learned how to cope with the situation, and by the end of the century they could resort to a variety of slick strategies to circumvent restrictions. The long duration of the French Revolutionary and Napoleonic Wars and the harshness with which the belligerent countries behaved, however, forced merchants to increase their mobility and undercover cooperation in order to bypass or mitigate, if possible, the obstacles posed to trade. This, at any rate, gave merchants a good knowledge of new markets to which they were to turn anew after the end of the conflict. Obviously, some commercial channels were temporarily interrupted or even destroyed for good during the war, but on the whole, the trade links created during the conflict were easy to re-establish after the end of the wars.

Notes

1 M. Häberlein, *Brüder, Freunde und Betrüger. Soziale Beziehungen, Normen und Konflikte in der Augsburger Kaufmannschaft um die Mitte des 16. Jahrhunderts* (Berlin: Walter De Gruyter, 1998); M. Häberlein and M. Schmölz-Häberlein, *Die Erben der Welser. Der Karibikhandel der Augsburger Firma Obwexer im Zeitalter der Revolutionen* (Augsburg: Wißner, 1995).

2 For a good overview over the recent concept of 'spatial turn' in various academic fields see S. Rau, *Räume* (Frankfurt am Main: Campus, 2013) and on migration esp. E. Scheibelhofer, *Raumsensible Migrationsforschung. Methodologische Überlegungen und ihre empirische Relevanz für die Migrationssoziologie* (Wiesbaden: Springer, 2011), also the classic work of L. Febvre, *La terre et l'èvolution humaine* (Paris: Albin Michel, 1922).

3 J. Kulischer, *Allgemeine Wirtschaftsgeschichte des Mittelalters und der Neuzeit*, 2 vols (Berlin: Berlin Rütten & Loening, 1954), vol. 2, p.170.

4 E.K. Newman, *Anglo-Hamburg Trade in the Late Seventeenth and Early Eighteenth Centuries* (London: unpublished PhD, 1979), pp. 7–15, 64, 85, 102, 189 and 191.

5 See M. Schulte Beerbühl and K. Weber, 'From Westphalia to the Caribbean: Networks of German Textile Merchants in the Eighteenth Century', in A. Gestrich and M. Schulte Beerbühl (eds.), *Cosmopolitan Networks in Commerce and Society, 1660–1914* (London: German Historical Institute, 2011), pp. 53–98.

6 E. Schmitz, *Leinengewerbe und Leinenhandel in Nordwestdeutschland (1650–1850)* (Schriftenreihe zur Rheinisch-Westfälischen Wirtschaftsgeschichte 15, Cologne: Rheinisch-Westfälisches Wirtschaftsarchiv, 1967), esp. pp. 81–95. See also H.-W. Niemann, *Leinenhandel im Osnabrücker Land. Die Bramscher Kaufmannsfamilie Sanders 1780–1850* (Bramsche: Rasch, 2004).

7 K. Newman, *Anglo-Hamburg Trade*, p. 199, n. 1 and p. 205, table 42.

8 K. Weber, *Deutsche Kaufleute im Atlantikhandel 1680–1830* (Munich: Beck, 2004), pp. 53–54.; for linen in Africa see also H.S. Klein, *The Atlantic Slave Trade* (Cambridge: Cambridge University Press, 1999), p. 114.

9 M. Kossok, 'Die Bedeutung des spanisch-amerikanischen Kolonialmarktes für den Preussischen Leinwandhandel am Ausgang des 18. und zu Beginn des 19. Jahrhunderts', in *Hansische Studien* (FS Berlin: Heinrich Sproemberg, 1961), pp. 210–218, here, pp. 212–213.

10 See M. Schulte Beerbühl, *The Forgotten Majority. German Merchants in London, Naturalization, and Global Trade 1660–1815* (New York and Oxford: Berghahn, 2015), chap. 1.

11 A. Hasenclever (ed.), *Peter Hasenclever aus Remscheid-Ehringhausen, ein deutscher Kaufmann des 18. Jahrhunderts* (Gotha: Perthes, 1922); H. Gertmann, *Das Geschlecht Hasenclever im ehemaligen Herzogtum Berg und in der Provinz Westfalen und zeitweilig in Schlesien*, H. Hasenclever (ed.), 2 vols. (Remscheid and Leipzig: Hugo Gerstmann, 1922–1924).

12 J. Urry, 'Social Networks, Travel and Talk', *Journal of Sociology*, 54 (2003), pp. 155–175; idem, 'Small Worlds and the New, Social Physics', *Global Networks* 4 (2004) pp. 109–130.

13 A. Kunze, 'Der Zittauer Leinengroßhandel im 18. Jahrhundert', *Zittauer Geschichtsblätter* 6 (1930), pp. 43–48, here p. 44, see also M. Schulte Beerbühl, 'Internationale Handelsnetze westfälischer Kaufleute in London (ca 1660–1815)', in K.-P. Ellerbrock, N. Bodden and M. Schulte Beerbühl (eds.), *Kultur, Strategien und Netzwerke. Familienunternehmen in Westfalen im 19. und 20. Jahrhundert* (Dortmund, Münster: Ardey, 2014), pp. 153–174.

14 Amyand & Siebel, Herefordshire Record Office J56/VI/13; see also Schulte Beerbühl, Internationale Handelsnetze, pp. 153–174.

15 See H. Simonsfeld, *Der Fondaco dei Tedeschi in Venedig und die deutsch-italienischen Beziehungen*, 2 vols (Stuttgart: Cotta 1887), vol. 2, p. 164; the number of fully fledged members declined from 35 in 1723 to 12 in 1800.

16 The London port books mention David Langenmantel as an importer of metal wares E 190 156/3 7. October 1696, The National Archives Kew (hereafter TNA) Port Books.

17 W. Zorn, *Handels- und Industriegeschichte Bayerisch-Schwabens, 1648–1870* (Augsburg: Schwäbische Forschungsgemeinschaft, 1961), p. 92.

18 G. Seibold, *Wirtschaftlicher Erfolg in Zeiten des politischen Niedergangs* (Augsburg: Wißner, 2014), pp. 108, 211.

19 See M. Schmölz-Häberlein, *Die Erben der Welser*, p. 38.

20 G. Seibold, *Wirtschaftlicher Erfolg*, p. 419.

21 See G, Seibold, vol.2 Stammtafel no.37; also M. Häberlein, *Erben der Welser*, pp. 38 and 51–123.

22 M. Ressel, 'Failures of German Business Houses in Eighteenth Century Venice', in A. Cordes and M. Schulte Beerbühl (eds.), *Dealing with Economic Failures* (Frankfurt am Main: Peter Lang, 2015); for Stockholm see K. Nyberg and H. Jakobsson, 'Financial Networks, Migration and the Transformation of the Merchant Elite in 18th Century Stockholm, in T. Max Safley (ed.), *The History of Bankruptcy. Economic, Social and Cultural Implications in Early Modern Europe* (London and New York: Routledge, 2013), pp. 72–93.

23 For the migration of Bohemian glassmakers to Spain, see K. Weber, *Deutsche im Atlantikhandel*, pp. 142f.

24 W. Zorn, *Handels- und Industriegeschichte*, pp. 92f.

25 M. Reissmann, *Die hamburgische Kaufmannschaft des 17. Jahrhunderts aus sozialgeschichtlicher Sicht* (Hamburg: Christians, 1975); Ruth Prange, *Die bremische Kaufmannschaft des 16. und 17. Jahrhunderts in sozialgeschichtlicher Betrachtung* (Bremen: Schünemann, 1963).

26 K. Weber, *Deutsche Kaufleute im Atlantikhandel*; for the period of the Napoleonic Wars see also S. Marzagalli, *Les Boulevards de la fraude. Le négoce maritime et le blocus continental 1806–1813* (Paris: Septentrion, 1999); F. Crouzet, *L'économie Britannique et le blocus continental* (Paris: Economica, 1987).

27 G. Panessa and M. Del Nista, *La Congregazione Olandese-Alemanna* (Livorno: Debatte O., 2002), p. 163.

28 TNA, Probate Records (hereafter Prob) 31/52.

29 London Assurance MS 30488, 23. Oct 1720, 23 June and 28 July 1721, Guildhall Library London; Nicolo died without issue. In his will, he bequeathed his fortune to the three sons of his brother Conrad. At the time of his death, two of Conrad's sons were living in Livorno (TNA, Prob 11/778).

30 The list is published in Panessa and Nista, *La Congregazione Olandese-Alemanna*, pp. 162–165.

31 Consuls 111-1 CL.VI. No. 8b vol. 8 fasc 2, invol.2, fols.1–4, Staatsarchiv Hamburg.

32 V. Nolte, *The Memoirs of Vincent Nolte*, 1854 (reprint New York: Howard Watt, 1934), p. 18.

33 Baring Ledgers 1776–1791, Baring Archive London.

34 Angabebücher der Schlachte 2-SS.2.a.4.3, vols. 2-13, Staatsarchiv Bremen.

35 M. Ressel, *Zwischen Sklavenkassen und Türkenpässen. Nordeuropa und die Barbaresken in der frühen Neuzeit* (Berlin: Walter De Gruyter, 2012).

36 S. Villani, 'Protestanti a Livorno nella eta moderna', in U. Israel, M. Matheus (eds.), *Protestanten zwischen Venedig und Rom in der frühen Neuzeit* (Berlin: Walter de Gruyter, 2013), 129–142, here, p.132; for the British factory see also: H.A. Hayward, 'The British Factory in Livorno', *Atti del convegno Gli Inglesi a Livorno e all'Isola d'Elba* (Livorno: Bastogi, 1980), pp. 261–267; F. Trivellato, *The Familiarity of Strangers, The Sephardic Diaspora, Livorno, and Cross-Cultural Trade in the Early Modern Period* (New Haven: Yale University Press, 2009), pp. 80f.; G.P. De Divitis, *English Merchants in Seventeenth-Century Italy* (Cambridge: Cambridge University Press, 1990), pp. 114–125.

37 B.S. Sirota, 'The Church of England, the Law of Nations, and the Leghorn Chaplaincy Affair 1703–1713', *Eighteenth-Century Studies*, 48 (2015), pp. 283–306.

38 That residence pattern can also be perceived in British factories, for example, in Smyrna, or Russia.

39 H. Koehl and M. Giunti, 'A.E. Barry (1744–1835), ou quand Livourne décidait d'un destin de femme et d'écrivain', *Nuovi studi livornesi*, XIV (2007), pp. 95–118. The Renners were close friends of the English writer Thomas Smollett, and Renner was, in fact, Smollett's agent during his time in Italy.

40 The Voguells of Herford and Uhthoffs of Bremen were related by marriage several times.

41 George Amyand had also been apprenticed in the firm of Henry Voguell and become a partner already before Voguell's death. John Anthony Rücker came from Hamburg, and his original connection with Voguell is not clear. However, one of Henry Voguell's cousins was in Hamburg and it may be that the relationship derives from there.

42 George Amyand became one of the governors of the East India Company. All three partners were at times also members of the Russia Company's Court of Assistants.

43 Nicolas Battier had been a bookkeeper in the house of Abraham Korten from Elberfeld. Korten's daughter married George Amyand, which expanded the Herford-Bremen-London network to Elberfeld (current Wuppertal).

44 W. von Driesch, *Die ausländischen Kaufleute während des 18. Jahrhundert in Spanien* (Köln: Böhlau, 1972), p. 208.

45 The Uhthoff family (private collection of Rainer Uhthoff Berlin who kindly gave me a copy of the family history); Delius papers in the private possession of the Delius family Bielefeld: Sylingk, Uhthoff & Kahler, Cadiz to Gante & Delius jun. Bielefeld, 16 February, 27 August 1790 (I would like to thank Eberhard Delius for allowing me to access the family papers).

46 For the importance of brokers see S. Schaffer (ed.), *The Brokered World: Go-Between and Global Intelligence 1770–1820* (Sagamore Beach: Science History Publications, 2009).

47 D.E. Massey, 'Understanding Mexican Migration to the United States', in M. Casson and M. Della Giusta (eds.), *The Economics of Networks* (Cheltenham: Edward Elgar, 2007), pp. 186–217, here, p. 212.

48 On monitoring and the principle-agent theory see J. Ojala, 'The Principal Agent Problem Revisited: Entrepreneurial Networks Between Finland and "World Markets" During the Eighteenth and Nineteenth Centuries', in S. Beerbühl and J. Vögele (eds.), *Spinning the Commercial Web: International Trade, Merchants and Commercial Cities, c. 1640–1939* (Frankfurt am Main: Peter Lang, 2004), pp. 131–148.

49 K. O'Rourke, 'The Worldwide Economic Impact of the French Revolutionary and Napoleonic Wars', *Journal of Global History*, 1 (2006), pp. 123–149; similarly, see

K. Rönnbäck, 'Integration of Global Commodity Markets in the Early Modern Era', *European Review of Economic History*, 13 (2009), pp. 95–120.

50 E. Heckscher, *The Continental System. An Economic Interpretation* (Oxford: Clarendon, 1922); F.W. Galpin, *Grain Supply of England During the Napoleonic Period* (New York and London: Macmillan, 1925).

51 V. Nolte, *The Memoirs of Vincent Nolte*, 1854 (reprint), (New York: Howard Watt, 1934).

52 J. Davey, 'Securing the Sinews of Sea Power: British Intervention in the Baltic 1780–1815', *The International History Review* 33 (2011), pp. 161–184; C.D. Hall, *British Strategy in the Napoleonic War 1803–15* (Manchester: Manchester University Press, 1992); A.N. Ryan, 'Trade with the Enemy in the Scandinavian and Baltic Ports during the Napoleonic War. For and Against', *Transactions of the Royal Historical Society* 12 (1962), pp. 123–140.

53 See M. Schulte Beerbühl, 'Der Handel mit dem Feind. Verborgene Handelsnetze während der Napoleonischen Kriege', in R. Asch (ed.), *Hannover, Großbritannien und Europa. Erfahrungsraum Personalunion 1714–1837* (Göttingen: Wallstein, 2014), pp. 382–407, here, pp. 397–398.

54 For Delius see: H. Schmidt, *Vom Leinen zur Seide. Die Geschichte der Firma C.A. Delius & Söhne und ihrer Vorgängerinnen und das Wirken ihrer Inhaber für die Entwicklung Bielefelds 1722–1925* (Detmold: Wagener, 1926), also letter books of E.A. Delius (private archive of E. Delius Bielefeld); for his commercial transactions during the blockade see also W. Reininghaus, *Die Stadt Iserlohn und ihre Kaufleute (1700–1815)* (Dortmund: Sander, 1995), esp. pp. 388–402.

55 TNA Privy Council (hereafter PC) 2/173, 10 July 1807, 8 August 1807.

56 Rothschild Archive London, XI/112/05; L.B. Cohen to Nathan Mayer Rothschild 22. Oct 1807; B. Schmidt, *Hamburg im Zeitalter der Französischen Revolution und Napoleons (1789–1813)*, 2 vols (Hamburg: Verein für Hamburgische Geschichte, 1998), vol. 1, p. 297.

57 M. D'Angelo, Mercanti inglese a Malta 1800–1825 (Milano: Franco Angeli, 1990), p. 63.

58 His partner's son in Frankfurt, Enrico Mylius, had visited England several times before he settled in Italy. In 1796 he had already been arrested by the French for trading with British goods. For the Italian branch of the Aldeberts see M. Poettinger, *La tradizione rinnovata. Da Enrico Mylius alla Sesto San Giovanni del futuro* (Como: Villa Vigoni, 2006); for Saumarez and his activities see T. Voelcker, *Admiral Saumarez versus Napoleon in the Baltic 1807–1812* (Woodbridge: Boydell, 2008).

59 TNA HO 5/25 Register of Application 1810–1819; see also M. D'Angelo, *Mercanti inglesi*, p. 272. His house was in La Valetta Strada Zecca No 38.

60 The Hamburger was G. Haanwinckel and the other one Charles Grabau (see M. D'Angelo, *Mercanti inglesi*, pp. 70–72).

61 TNA PC 2/185 15. März 1810 p. 430

62 TNA PC 2/185 29. März 1809 p. 599; another licence allowed a vessel to depart from Naples or some place south of Orbitello and Pesara, and again to touch at Tunis or Algier before returning to Britain (TNA PC 2/186 10 April 1810).

63 TNA PC 2/165 p.5 7 March 1804.

64 TNA PC2/176 p.128f 14 March 1808, p. 182, 19 March 1808.

65 TNA PC 2/185, p.407 14 March 1810.

66 S. Marzagalli, 'Establishing Transatlantic Trade Networks in Time of War: Bordeaux and the United States, 1793–1815', *Business History Review* 79 (2005), p. 816.

67 Consular Despatches Hamburg, Forbes Kopenhagen 2. Feb. 1810 to Robert Smith, National Archives Washington. Forbes also mentioned that more than 90 American ships arrived in Tönning alone in 1809 (ibid. Forbes to Smith 29. Sept. 1809).

68 The membership of the German Society of Pennsylvania, founded shortly after the independence of the United States, increased sharply in the 1790s (see O. Seidensticker, *Geschichte der Deutschen Gesellschaft von Pennsylvanien* (Philadelphia: Graf & Breuniger, 1917), p. 54).

69 See Maryland Historical Society Edward Hall Papers MS 1300, letters of Carl Hopfengärtner (Caye) and H. Stricker (St. Thomas). In New Orleans the Germans F.H. Amelung, J.D. Pechten and V. Nolte established merchant houses to organise the trade to and from the Caribbean Islands and Veracruz. A relative of F.H. Amelung was living in Havana (see Clarke-von Kapff & Brune Baltimore, Maryland Historical Society, 1754).

70 M. Kossok, 'Die Bedeutung des spanisch-amerikanischen Kolonialmarktes für den Preussischen Leinwandhandel am Ausgang des 18. und zu Beginn des 19. Jahrhunderts', in *Hansische Studien*, (Berlin: FS Heinrich Sproemberg, 1961), p. 216.

Bibliography

Crouzet, F., *L'économie Britannique et le blocus continental*, Paris: Economica, 1987.

D'Angelo, M., *Mercanti inglese a Malta 1800–1825*, Milano: Franco Angeli, 1990.

Davey, J., 'Securing the Sinews of Sea Power: British Intervention in the Baltic 1780–1815', *The International History Review*, 33 (2011), pp. 161–184.

De Divitis, G.P., *English Merchants in Seventeenth-Century Italy*, Cambridge: Cambridge University Press, 1990.

Febvre, L., *La terre et l'évolution humaine*, Paris: Albin Michel, 1922.

Galpin, F.W., *Grain Supply of England During the Napoleonic Period*, New York and London: Macmillan, 1925.

Gertmann, H., *Das Geschlecht Hasenclever im ehemaligen Herzogtum Berg in der Provinz Westfalen und zeitweilig in Schlesien*, in Hasenclever, H. (ed.), 2 vols., Remscheid and Leipzig: Hugo Gerstmann, 1922–24.

Häberlein, M., *Brüder, Freunde und Betrüger. Soziale Beziehungen, Normen und Konflikte in der Augsburger Kaufmannschaft um die Mitte des 16. Jahrhunderts*, Berlin: Walter De Gruyter, 1998.

Häberlein, M. and Schmölz-Häberlein, M., *Die Erben der Welser, Der Karibikhandel der Augsburger Firma Obwexer im Zeitalter der Revolutionen*, Augsburg: Wißner, 1995.

Hall, C.D., *British Strategy in the Napoleonic War 1803–15*, Manchester: Manchester University Press, 1992.

Hasenclever, A. (ed.), *Peter Hasenclever aus Remscheid-Ehringhausen, ein deutscher Kaufmann des 18. Jahrhunderts*, Gotha: Perthes, 1922.

Hayward, H.A., 'The British Factory in Livorno', in *Atti del convegno Gli Inglesi a Livorno e all'Isola d'Elba*, Livorno: Bastogi, 1980, pp. 261–267.

Heckscher, E., *The Continental System. An Economic Interpretation*, Oxford: Clarendon, 1922.

Klein, H.S., *The Atlantic Slave Trade*, Cambridge: Cambridge University Press, 1999.

Koehl, H. and M. Giunti, 'Amelia Evans Barry (1744–1835), ou quand Livourne décidait d'un destin de femme et d'écrivain', *Nuovi studi livornesi*, XIV (2007), pp. 95–118.

Kossok, M., 'Die Bedeutung des spanisch-amerikanischen Kolonialmarktes für den Preussischen Leinwandhandel am Ausgang des 18. und zu Beginn des 19. Jahrhunderts', in *Hansische Studien*, Berlin: FS Heinrich Sproemberg, 1961, pp. 210–218.

Kulischer, J.M., *Allgemeine Wirtschaftsgeschichte des Mittelalters und der Neuzeit*, 2 vols., Berlin: Berlin Rütten & Loening, 1954.

Kunze, A., 'Der Zittauer Leinengroßhandel im 18. Jahrhundert', *Zittauer Geschichtsblätter*, 6 (1930), pp. 43–48.

Marzagalli, S., 'Establishing Transatlantic Trade Networks in Time of War: Bordeaux and the United States 1793–1815', *Business History Review*, 79 (2005), pp. 811–844.

———. *Les Boulevards de la fraude. Le négoce maritime et le blocus continental 1806–1813*, Paris: Septentrion, 1999.

Massey, D.E., 'Understanding Mexican Migration to the United States', in Casson, M. and Della Giusta, M. (eds.), *The Economics of Networks*, Cheltenham: Edward Elgar, 2007, pp. 186–217.

Newman, E.K., *Anglo-Hamburg Trade in the Late Seventeenth and Early Eighteenth Centuries*, (London: unpublished PhD), 1979.

Niemann, H.-W., *Leinenhandel im Osnabrücker Land. Die Bramscher Kaufmannsfamilie Sanders 1770–1850*, Bramsche: Rasch, 2004.

Nolte, V., *The Memoirs of Vincent Nolte*, 1854 (reprint), New York: Howard Watt, 1934.

Nyberg, K. and Jakobsson, H., 'Financial Networks, Migration and the Transformation of the Merchant Elite in 18th Century Stockholm', in Safley, T.M. (ed.), *The History of Bankruptcy. Economic, Social and Cultural Implications in Early Modern Europe*, London and New York: Routledge, 2013, pp. 72–93.

Ojala, J., 'The Principal Agent Problem Revisited. Entrepreneurial Networks Between Finland and "World Markets" During the 18th and 19th Century', in Schulte Beerbühl, M. and Vögele, J. (eds.), *Spinning the Commercial Web: International Trade, Merchants, and Commercial Cities, c.1640–1939*, Frankfurt am Main: Peter Lang, 2004.

O'Rourke, K., 'The Worldwide Economic Impact of the French Revolutionary and Napoleonic Wars', *Journal of Global History*, 1 (2006), pp. 123–149.

Panessa, G. and Del Nista, M., *La Congregazione Olandese-Alemanna*, Livorno: Debatte O, 2002.

Poettinger, M., *La tradizione rinnovata. Da Enrico Mylius alla Sesto San Giovanni del futuro*, Como: Villa Vigoni, 2006.

Prange, R., *Die bremische Kaufmannschaft des 16. und 17. Jahrhunderts in sozialgeschichtlicher Betrachtung*, Bremen: Schünemann, 1963.

Rau, S., *Räume*, Frankfurt am Main: Campus, 2013.

Reininghaus, W., *Die Stadt Iserlohn und ihre Kaufleute (1700–1815)*, Dortmund: Sander, 1995.

Reissmann, M., *Die hamburgische Kaufmannschaft des 17. Jahrhunderts aus sozialgeschichtlicher Sicht*, Hamburg: Christians, 1975.

Ressel, M., *Zwischen Sklavenkassen und Türkenpässen. Nordeuropa und die Barbaresken in der frühen Neuzeit*, Berlin: Walter De Gruyter, 2012.

———. 'Failures of German Business Houses in Eighteenth Century Venice, in Cordes, A. and Schulte Beerbühl, M. (eds.), *Dealing with Economic Failures*, Frankfurt am Main: Peter Lang, 2015, pp. 115–138.

Rönnbäck, K., 'Integration of Global Commodity Markets in the Early Modern Era', *European Review of Economic History*, 13 (2009), pp. 95–120.

Ryan, A.N., 'Trade with the Enemy in the Scandinavian and Baltic Ports During the Napoleonic War. For and Against', *Transactions of the Royal Historical Society,* 12 (1962), pp. 123–140.

Schaffer, S. (ed.), *The Brokered World: Go-between and Global Intelligence 1770–1820*, Sagamore Beach: Science History Publications, 2009.

Scheibelhofer, E., *Raumsensible Migrationsforschung. Methodologische Überlegungen und ihre empirische Relevanz für die Migrationssoziologie*, Wiesbaden: Springer, 2011.

Schmidt, B., *Hamburg im Zeitalter der Französischen Revolution und Napoleons (1789–1813)*, 2 vols., Hamburg: Verein für Hamburgische Geschichte, 1998.

Schmidt, H., *Vom Leinen zur Seide. Die Geschichte der Firma C.A. Delius & Söhne und ihrer Vorgängerinnen und das Wirken ihrer Inhaber für die Entwicklung Bielefelds 1722–1925*, Detmold: Wagener, 1926.

Schmitz, E., *Leinengewerbe und Leinenhandel in Nordwestdeutschland (1650–1850)*, Cologne: Rheinisch-Westfälisches Wirtschaftsarchiv, 1967.

Schulte Beerbühl, M., 'Der Handel mit dem Feind. Verborgene Handelsnetze während der Napoleonischen Kriege', in Asch, R. (ed.), *Hannover, Großbritannien und Europa. Erfahrungsraum Personalunion 1714–1837*, Göttingen: Wallstein, 2014, pp. 382–407.

———. 'Internationale Handelsnetze westfälischer Kaufleute in London (ca 1660–1815)', in Ellerbrock, K.-P., Bodden, N. and Schulte Beerbühl, M. (eds.), *Kultur, Strategien und Netzwerke. Familienunternehmen in Westfalen im 19. und 20. Jahrhundert*, Dortmund and Münster: Ardey, 2014, pp. 153–174.

———. *The Forgotten Majority. German Merchants in London, Naturalization, and Global Trade 1660–1815*, New York and Oxford: Berghahn, 2015.

Schulte Beerbühl, M. and Weber, K., 'From Westphalia to the Caribbean: Networks of German Textile Merchants in the Eighteenth Century', in Gestrich, A. and Schulte Beerbühl, M. (eds.), *Cosmopolitan Networks in Commerce and Society, 1660–1914*, London: German Historical Institute, 2011, pp. 53–98.

Seibold, G., *Wirtschaftlicher Erfolg in Zeiten des politischen Niedergangs*, Augsburg: Wißner, 2014.

Seidensticker, O., *Geschichte der Deutschen Gesellschaft von Pennsylvanien*, Philadelphia: Graf & Breuniger, 1917.

Simonsfeld, H., *Der Fondaco dei Tedeschi in Venedig und die deutsch-italienischen Beziehungen*, 2 vols., Stuttgart: Cotta, 1887.

Sirota, B.S., 'The Church of England, the Law of Nations, and the Leghorn Chaplaincy Affair 1703–1713', *Eighteenth-Century Studies*, 48 (2015), pp. 283–306.

Trivellato, F., *The Familiarity of Strangers, The Sephardic Diaspora, Livorno, and Cross-Cultural Trade in the Early Modern Period*, New Haven: Yale University Press, 2009.

Urry, J., 'Social Networks, Travel and Talk', *Journal of Sociolog*, 54 (2003), pp. 155–175.

———. 'Small Worlds and the New, Social Physics', *Global Networks,* 4 (2004) pp. 109–130.

Villani, S., 'Protestanti a Livorno nella eta moderna', in Israel, U. and Matheus, M. (eds.), *Protestanten zwischen Venedig und Rom in der frühen Neuzeit*, Berlin: Akademie Verlag, 2013, pp. 129–142.

Voelcker, T., *Admiral Saumarez versus Napoleon in the Baltic 1807–1812*, Woodbridge: Boydell, 2008.

Von Driesch, W., *Die ausländischen Kaufleute während des 18. Jahrhundert in Spanien*, Köln: Böhlau, 1972.

Weber, K., *Deutsche Kaufleute im Atlantikhandel 1680–1830*, Munich: Beck, 2004.

Zorn, W., *Handels- und Industriegeschichte Bayerisch-Schwabens 1648–1870*, Augsburg: Schwäbische Forschungsgemeinschaft, 1961.

9 Merchants between the Mediterranean Sea and the Atlantic Ocean

The Bouligny family case (1700–1762)[1]

Pablo Hernández Sau

Introduction

During the last 60 years, we have witnessed a historical rediscovery of the oceans and seas as socio-economic spaces. Braudel's studies on Mediterranean History created a new field of research on socio-economic maritime contexts which have developed an increasing interest for 'sea civilisations'. After the Second World War, the idea of an 'Atlantic civilisation' appears associated with the political context and the academic works of Charles Verlinden, Jacques Godechot or Robert R. Palmer.[2] As a result, multiple works about Atlantic slave systems, merchant networks, political and trade connections and the sociocultural exchange developed until now. Similarly, works about the commercial interaction in the Indian Ocean have demonstrated the liveliness of the 'multinational' commercial networks of the Atlantic. In all of these, an increasing attention to socio-economic links and agency has led to important research on commercial maritime systems. According to this approach, Peregrine Horden and Nicholas Purcell have recently proposed an alternative methodological approach, the *New Thalassology*,[3] which focuses on the study of 'water life'. For them, the landscape variety along the Mediterranean shores generated multiple links between micro-ecological regions which developed systems of necessities, commodities, ideas and cultural exchanges.[4] Peter N. Miller defined this methodological proposal as 'a kind of microhistory not about water, but about people',[5] a game of scale in which human experiences are the centre of the study, instead of geography. In line with it, Francesca Trivellato has reconsidered this reflection about the agency and the scale, developing a history *in* the sea/ocean[6] which shows the existence of commercial systems beyond geographical limits. All in all, a large number of 'sea' researchers have been covering the socio-economical life of the Mediterranean Sea, the Baltic Sea, the Atlantic Ocean, the Indian Ocean, the Pacific Ocean and the Chinese Sea.[7] Therefore a thorough monitoring of sea agents has given rise to understanding the history *of* the sea, instead of a history *in* the sea.[8] But has this research sufficiently explored the commercial maritime system in between seas and ocean?

This chapter tries to reclaim the importance of individuals in maritime history and the use of scale as methodological tool, while aiming to discover underestimated structures among different maritime spaces. I present here the first results of my research on the Bouligny family, a commercial family company in the Mediterranean–Atlantic commercial system. The Bouligny commercial company was inserted in some of the commercial flows between the Atlantic Ocean and Mediterranean Sea. As a French retailer merchant family living in Alicante, the Boulignys were part of a game of scale in which their local incorporation, the regional migration scale and the global commercial scale constituted part of one of the maritime systems which exceeded the geographical limitations of a single sea. Their study is essentially a microhistorical research in which I have underlined the agency of the family, their commercial links and their relation with Atlantic and Mediterranean products. A 'global microhistorical case'[9] which, from a thorough analysis of the combination of scales, digs into the maritime commercial systems between the Atlantic and the Mediterranean.

With this aim, the text is structured in four parts: first, a brief overview about the historiography on the Mediterranean–Atlantic commerce. Second, a contextualisation on the eighteenth-century commercial flows between the Mediterranean and the Atlantic, giving special attention to the southeast Iberian Peninsula region. Then, I examine the migration and commercial flows of the Marseille commercial community in southeast Iberian Peninsula, analysing the regional and the local dimension of some of these merchants. Fourth, I will present the Bouligny family case as an example of this commercial maritime system between the Mediterranean and Atlantic commercial flows. I will conclude with some remarks about how cases such as the Bouligny family help us to study the maritime system between the Mediterranean Sea and the Atlantic Ocean.

The historiography and the Atlantic–Mediterranean merchants

> For what boundaries can be marked when we are dealing not with plant and animals, relied and climate, but men, whom no barriers or frontier can stop? The Mediterranean (and the accompanying Greater Mediterranean) is as man has made it. The wheel of human fortune has determined the destiny of the sea, expanding or contracting its area (Braudel, 1972, pp. 168–169)

The most recent research about merchants and trade networks, regarding the study of the agency and the multiscale dimension, has brought about a redefinition of commercial maritime systems. These do not fix the previous conception of the Atlantic or Mediterranean systems. For instance, Francesca Trivellato's work about the Erga and Silvera family or Sebouh Aslanian's research about Armenian New Julfa merchant networks have informed us about the existence of merchant systems which linked, directly or indirectly, the Mediterranean and the Indian Oceans. Like Trivellato's and Aslanian's works on the Indo-Mediterranean commercial systems, the commercial maritime systems between the Atlantic and the Mediterranean still requires much more research.

One of the strongest faults of Braudel's work was his geographical determinism. However, his work also fostered a huge number of research works on Atlantic and Mediterranean maritime communities during the early modern period. Pierre Chaunu's book on sixteenth-century Seville's merchants, or Charles Carrière's work about eighteenth-century Marseille merchants, were the best example of a historiographical revival, which was extensively consolidated during the 1990s.[10] During this decade, an increasing number of historical studies about the Atlantic commercial networks were evolving by scholars like Jonathan Israel or Ana Crespo Solana.[11] These were followed by copious international literature about German, Irish, English, Dutch, Portuguese and Jewish commercial communities on the Atlantic coasts.[12] This revival also took place in the research about the Mediterranean commercial communities, developing important work on Jewish and Greek communities[13] or focusing on the commercial institutions and commercial maritime systems of the Inner Sea. As a result, a separate bibliography about the Mediterranean and the Atlantic commercial communities was developed in the international arena.[14]

Similarly, in the Spanish early modernist historiography, the studies on Atlantic and Mediterranean commercial communities has also developed without a comparative result approach. A geographical historiographical distinction materialised in three historiographical clusters: one among the recent works about the Basque elites; another among the studies on the foreign communities at Cádiz; and the last among the eighteenth-century Catalan merchants.[15] Three kinds of historiography which focused on similar topics have not linked and compared their results. However, some studies have already started to show commercial systems among the two seas. This is the case of the research about the Genoese socio-economical networks in which it is clear that Genoese agents did not find limitations in the geographical and state limitations, spreading their commercial networks in big maritime systems around the globe.[16]

In this chapter, we focus our attention, in some cases, on lesser work in the international and national bibliography, the Marseille commercial communities. A community which, during the eighteenth century, extended thick networks from Marseille to the rest of the Mediterranean Sea and Colonial America. Trivellato stressed for the eighteenth century the liveliness of the Mediterranean Sea:

> … A revival of European (and especially French) in the Mediterranean. European states waged war on one another in region and confronted the Ottoman Empire militarily and diplomatically, striving to extend their economic influence. … American goods and Asian products made their way to Leghorn via Lisbon, Cadiz, Seville, Bordeaux, Marseille, Amsterdam and London (Trivellato, 2009, pp. 6–7)

Her studies about the Ergas and Silveira family have refuted Braudel's idea of a Mediterranean commercial decay after 1650. This can be also supported in the 1970s and 1980s West Mediterranean Sea maritime studies,[17] and new research on the global commercial connections of Genoa, Leghorn, Marseille or Trieste for the post-1650 period.[18] A good example of the latest research about the global Mediterranean connection is the recent work of Manuel Pérez García. In this, he has stressed that:

> Spanish raw materials such as silk, cotton and wool were exported from Barcelona, Valencia, Alicante and Cartagena, and the same ports were the main sites of the reception of manufactured clothing and Asian textiles shipped from Marseille[19]

In addition to Pérez García's work, the recent studies of Catia Brilli and Klemens Kaps about the Genoese and Triestine commercial networks have also shown the active global connections of Genoa and Trieste with Cádiz after 1650.[20]

All these works show the intense Mediterranean commercial reality after 1650, and invite us to understand the Mediterranean trade in a global context, a global context in which new commercial maritime systems developed by agents who were not enclosed to geographical limitations.

The Mediterranean Sea and global commercial trends after 1650

During the second half of the seventeenth century and the first quarter of eighteenth century, the Great Sea suffered a structural readaptation and reorganisation, as consequence of numerous political and economic changes. Among these, the War of Spanish Succession changed the dynastic and political organisation of many Mediterranean states like Spain, Naples, Sicily and Sardinia. Most of these passed to the same royal family, the Bourbons, a change which also brought variation in the foreign and commercial policies, especially in relation to the Eastern and Southern Mediterranean states. As a result, the classical confrontation policy between Spanish Habsburgs and Ottomans swanned to a more 'friendly' political and commercial attitude.

Accordingly, during the eighteenth century different peace treaties and commercial capitulations were signed between 'new Bourbon' Western Mediterranean states and the Ottoman Empire. Among those states, it is important to analyse the case of Naples, which had been under Habsburg control between 1713 and 1734, but which was led by Philippe V's son, the future King of Spain, Charles III from 1734 onward. The first of these treaties was signed by Kingdom of Naples in 1740, which Mehmet Demirüyek has recently argued[21] had a special particularity: for the first time, the Ottoman argued the right to have a consul in the ports of cosigners.

In the same way, the Bourbon Spanish Empire approached the Kingdom of Morocco in the 1740s, with Jorge Juan's embassy establishing the first Spanish consulate in Morocco from 1740 to the 1760s.[22] A peace treaty and commercial capitulations were signed with the Ottoman Empire as a result of Juan de

Bouligny's efforts in 1782. This was followed by new treaties with the Barbary Regencies – Tripoli in 1784, Algeria in 1786 and Tunisia in 1791.[23]

This new political context implied new and broader maritime commercial systems. As a result, the classic preponderance of commercial communities such as the Jews, Venetians and Genoese, all who had played a prominent role in the Mediterranean commercial reality from the Middle Ages to the seventeenth century, were replaced by new communities. From the seventeenth century on, these were increasingly joined by the French, Flemish, English, Nordic and German merchant communities, who traded with raw material and manufactured products. They developed thick commercial networks in which the consulates and family companies had a central role.[24] Among them, the French and British commercial networks had already consolidated by linking the Mediterranean production and consumption with other commercial areas, such as the Atlantic or the Indian Oceans.[25] A context in which the Bouligny family inserted a base into their Marseille commercial chains, brought them to Alicante around 1714 to 1717.

This commercial turn brought an increasing entanglement of the markets placed in the Mediterranean Sea and the Atlantic Ocean, developing big commercial systems comprised of smaller commercial spaces interlinked among them. As a result, long-distance networks based on colonial products were coordinated with retailer networks.[26] In these, sugar, cacao or textiles were redistributed in Mediterranean ports like Marseille, Leghorn, Constantinople, Barcelona and Alicante. At the same time, these ports served as suppliers of other products of Mediterranean origin, like cotton, silk, wine, salt or *barilla* (saltwort). The Bouligny family played an important role in this complex process of exchange and cooperation on a local and regional scale.

Contextualizing the southeast Iberian Peninsula as a commercial region

In this global context, the southeast Spanish coast was a region in which trade flows from North Africa, Cádiz and Marseille spurred the development of an international commercial community which connected necessities and commodities. But was this as a commercial region inserted into global commercial systems? Pérez García has already researched, for Cartagena, how some manufactured goods, such as clothing, wool bedding, calico or cotton taffeta from Persia were manufactured in Marseille and imported to the eastern and southeastern Mediterranean. Where raw materials, like nonelaborated silk, caustic soda and *barilla* were exported to Provence, to be manufactured by Languedoc artisan industries, copying the Asiatic designs, and re-exported one more time to southeastern markets.[27] This circuit was not exceptional; Ricardo French Benavent's work about Valencian silk has shown the existence of similar commercial systems in Valencia.[28]

In all these works, a common commercial patron for the Spanish East seems to exist, a common French commercial zone between Valencia and Cartagena frequently represented in different maps as a geographical unit. From the seventeenth century onward, an increasing number of cartographers delineated Southeast Spain, the Balearic Islands and North Africa as part of a common area. In the National French Library (BNF), I have found different maps with a common patron in the Denia-Cape of Gata/Almeria zone.[29] Even though we cannot confirm the existence of an economically polarised region in Southeast Iberia,[30] a common consumption pattern in places like Valencia, Alicante or Cartagena did exist; the drawing of regional maps and thick commercial networks, especially French, lead us to see those ports connected on a regional scale, an internal connection which has been underlined in other works, but without connection to a global picture in which Marseille, Cádiz and the French community had a central role.

French commercial networks in eighteenth-century southeast Spain

The French commercial community, as suppliers and customers of local consumption, had a central role in the global Mediterranean trade.[31] From the Spanish Peninsula to the coast of the Ottoman Empire, the eighteenth century French community served as a supplier of raw materials, market goods and money loans. As illustrated, the *Roux Frères* Company, one of the most important Languedoc trade groups during the eighteenth century, specialised in buying and selling goods around the Mediterranean. They based their company in Marseille, connecting the Levantine routes with the Atlantic flows by attorneys in ports like Smyrne, Cairo, Alexandria, Aleppo, Cartagena and Cádiz.[32] These attorneys served as importers of Atlantic and Mediterranean products for local consumers, and exporters of regional products, like southeast Iberian *barilla*, wine, or Valencia silk to Marseille where these products were manufactured or re-exported.[33]

In the case of the eighteenth-century southeast Iberian Peninsula, the French community based its increasing importance on two main circumstances: first, the Spanish Dynastic Turn and the post-war reconstruction; and second, the existence of previous family commercial networks which encouraged labor migration chains.[34] Pérez Sarrión has underlined the positive conditions for French commerce in the Iberian Peninsula during the period of 1686 to 1709, even though this contrasts with the political circumstances of the Nine Year's War (1688 to 1697) and the French bombards of Alicante (1691), Malaga (1693) and Barcelona (1697).[35] In any case, the change of the Spanish royal dynasty and the reorganisation of the Spanish monarchy in a stronger centralised power structure allowed these commercial communities to develop stronger networks. The abolition of special regional privileges and rights (the so-called *fueros*) in Aragon, Catalonia, Majorca and Valencia facilitated an increase in French migration chains. As a consequence, the nature of the migrants changed in respect to the previous half century. In the second half of seventeenth century, the French migrant profile turned to a higher qualified profile characterised by a higher degree of urban origins, and in the case of the southeast, with a high percentage of Marseille origin.[36]

These appreciations are proven for Alicante's case, where the French community doubled their presence between 1700 and 1750, compared with the period of 1650 to 1700.[37] For instance, in 1754 the official list of Alicante residents[38] were 113 heads of households being French, with 75 per cent of them being engaged with long trade or retailer companies[39] and 26.1 per cent coming from Provence, from Marseille. These dates show the importance of maritime commercial networks in this southeast Iberian city, which had many similarities to the results about the French mercantile community of Valencia. There, the increasing power of the French community in the city ended up in a rising Francophobe sentiment during the second half of the century.[40] This French migration evolved with a common space beyond state borders, in which French merchants based in south-east Spain, contacts in Cádiz and familiars in Marseille formed part of the same commercial system.

French commercial networks developed important formal institutions – consulates or commercial guilds – and informal institutions – familiar bonds, friendship or fraternities – which ensured their Mediterranean–Atlantic commercial networks, regional moneylending and their local social-political positions. As Pérez García and Marta V. Vicente have defended, the merchants developed networks in the Mediterranean Sea and the Atlantic Ocean based on 'nationality' and family. Therefore, they depended on the social and familiar connections which allowed them to acquire information, credit or necessary products to maintain or improve their position. However, as Avner Greif has argued, the formal institutions also had an important role in those networks.[41]

Based on previous research, a deeper understanding of these Mediterranean–Atlantic commercial systems requires the study of specific cases, making it necessary to return to the agents. For this reason, I will introduce the case of the Bouligny family in this Mediterranean–Atlantic context, trying to understand this family in relation to the commercial systems evolved in the southeast over the course of time.

The Bouligny migration and their insertion in Alicante

The Bouligny family was a family of Marseille merchants who arrived in Alicante at the beginning of the eighteenth century. As a result of their chain migration, they established their center of business by the middle of the century, developing 'national links' which brought them to the port city on Spain's Levant coast. In Alicante between 1700 and 1749, the French community was not only the largest of all mercantile groups, but it was also dominated by merchants from Provence.[42] Their common origins and commercial nature generated supportive commercial-family networks, as was the case for Pedro Choly, Jaime Amorrich or Nicolas Larchier, who helped their familiars and Marseille neighbors emigrate and develop commercial companies.[43] It is difficult to specify the specific date (born in Marseille in 1654 and died in Alicante in 1734) when Joseph Bouligny Germain arrived in Alicante, but through a genealogical and socio-commercial network reconstruction, I have realised that his family and labor connections with

Nicolas Larchier were the first step toward settling in Alicante and developing his first clothing trade enterprise.

Joseph Bouligny was the only male child of François Bouligny and Cécile Germain, daughter of the Marseille merchant Pierre Germain.[44] His father had inherited Germain's commercial business around 1650, developing connections with Leghorn and Alicante which resulted in his sister's and his own marriage. While her sister, Claire Bouligny Germain, married Pietro Miccioni, a member of the Noble College of Leghorn, Joseph married Agnès Larchier, the niece of Nicolas Larchier who was resident in Alicante and founded a commercial textile company there.[45] Diverse notarial documents show the Bouligny relation with Luís Larchier Voligrana, his cousin-in-law. For instance, in 1718, Luís Larchier Voligrana is mentioned as Bouligny's attorney for collecting his rents and loadings in Marseille.[46]

The first evidence about Joseph Bouligny's presence points to his connection with the Marseille commercial community in 1717. For instance, at that time, he signed a common power of attorney with three other French merchants – Joseph Valiente, Joseph Benit and Joseph Binera – allowing Vicente Villegas, an Alicante lawyer, to defend them in the juridical tribunals of Alicante. During the 1720s and 1730s, the Bouligny family company intensified these relations with other French families in other ports of the Valencia region, Cádiz and Marseille. For instance, they established some contracts with the French Valencian families, such as the Debruges or Gautiers, and numerous commercial contracts with the French Alicante merchant families like the Bertholons, Amorrichs or the Rimbauds.[47] Similarly, I have found some cases of Bouligny empowerment of other French companies such as the Besson y Pascaly Company in Madrid, or the Claudio Chabri & Company in Lorca.

As a result, during the first years in Alicante, Joseph Bouligny's social and commercial links were concentrated in regional networks which facilitated his arrival. His notarial documents prove that Juan de Bouligny was already present right after the end of the War of the Spanish Succession, an era of internal reconstruction in which foreign commercial networks played a central role in supplying raw materials and manufactured goods. The previous historiography has analysed this migration and commercial communities only in relation to Alicante. But this approach does not include the multiscale work of these foreign merchants or their family and neighborhood connections which created multidirectional links in the region. In this respect, the commercial documents within the notary protocols allow reconstruction of a more complex global, regional and local reality, as we will explain in the next section.

The Bouligny business between the Atlantic Ocean and the Mediterranean Sea

At the beginning of 1720, Joseph Bouligny had already developed an established commercial network based in Alicante. Enrique Giménez, Henry Kamen, José Ignacio Martínez Ruíz and Perry Gaucci have already noted the importance of Alicante as one of the main Iberian scales for Atlantic vessels during the second half of the seventeenth century.[48] English convoys with salted products, the Nordic iron, the Dutch manufacturers and the South Italian wheat arrived at this port because of its commercial facilities. Enrique Giménez López's study about Alicante as a port city underlined Alicante's natural port conditions and its location in Vinalopo's Valley, the faster commercial route to Madrid, without any mountain system to cross. Therefore, Alicante was a proper hub for foreign commercial networks linking with Marseille, Leghorn, Naples, Valencia, Oran, Tripoli, Cádiz, Bristol, Newfoundland, etc.

Linked to the French commercial networks and the familiar textile commerce, the Bouligny Company developed connections with both shores of the Gibraltar Strait. In July 1720, Joseph Bouligny signed a testamentary codicil, in which he highlighted the inhabitance of the Bouligny-Larchier couple in Alicante and the settlement of their son in Marseille. Two years later, Joseph rented out a house on Main Street where most of the foreign and domestic traders settled.[49] The same house where Jean Bouligny Larchier (1696 to 1772) moved to constitute the first Bouligny family commercial company after his engagement with Maria Antonia Paret in 1724.[50]

In 1724 Joseph Bouligny Germain and Juan Bouligny Larchier created the 'Joseph Bouligny e hijo' Company, the first of three Bouligny's commercial companies that expanded in the Spanish Empire,[51] as a retail company dedicated to the importation and selling of textiles and raw materials.[52] This started very early to coordinate importations with moneylending to local producers, to whom they lent money for raw materials like clothes, fillet and other "genders and merchandise" which were resold or exported.[53]

The Alicante's customs from 1728 to 1733 clarified the kind of products that the Bouligny family imported and on some occasions re-exported, showing their role as an intermediary between seas. In line with this, in the Custom House – *aduana* – documents of 1728, under the name Boulini e hijo, listed: 42 pieces of *andinas* at 5 *pesos* for each piece; a white German canvas with directions to Valencia; 1 bale and 14 pesos of smoothing canvas, 12 serge stockings from Cádiz; and 3 *lanillas* and 4 scarlet textiles from Gines Palau of Seville. The customs account of that year records 111,242 *maravedíes*, an amount which, in 1731, increased to 231,176 *maravedíes*. This growth gives us an idea of the increasing influence of the Bouligny family on this Mediterranean–Atlantic system in which raw materials and textiles had a dominant role. For instance, in 1730, the customs account of 3 rolls with 321 sticks of *cotonina* arrived from Antonio Boacha Maltes; and 8 pieces of *lilas* textile products of divers colors made in Lille were sent by Giner Palau from Seville. This last product, the *lila* were also present in the 1731 account, and was joined by 5 camel furs. All this data requires still more thorough research but makes us intuit the Boulignys' links with Cádiz and Seville merchants, and at the same time they also had some contacts with Valencia and North Africa.

The customs data should be also coordinated with the products sold by Joseph and Juan Bouligny in their commercial house which I have been able to find in the Alicante Provincial Archive. Indeed, in 1741, they sold 175 pounds of cacao from

Caracas – 10 *sueldos* and 6 *dineros* per pound to the Alicante merchant Feliciano Canicia de Franqui. The same action was repeated in 1744, with a smaller amount, 92 pounds. During the same year, the Bouligny Company also sold to the same merchant 30 pieces of *zanalas* (canvas of gummed thread). As result of these documents, we can find the existence of a Bouligny continuous contact and interest for the products from the Atlantic, from the 1720s until the 1750s, which were sold to the Alicante population. These consumption circuits required a more-detailed study, but it should be part of the larger context of commercial maritime systems.

The Joseph Bouligny e hijo Company was substituted in 1746 by the Juan Bouligny e hijos. The second commercial Company was created by Juan Bouligny Larchier and his sons, Joseph Bouligny Paret (1724 to 1801) and Juan Bouligny Paret (1726 to 1798). Correlated to the nature of the individuals, the nature of the products changed a little, including supplement and supplier contracts of almonds, pepper, wine, rice, weath,[54] *barrilla* or filete.[55] All these products were connected with the Mediterranean flows, especially with the importation of materials for French manufacture production but especially wine and *barilla* (saltpower). These were sent to Marseille and in the case of the wine, its interest in Paris produced its re-exportation.

Among the examples of this product commercial turn, in 1745, Gerónimo Maricon sold Juan de Bouligny 37 *arrobas* and 8 pounds of pepper, for 560.55 Valencia *libras*, which were to be paid in fruits and wine.[56] The Bouligny interest of being paid in wine was correlated to their increasing investment in the *huerta alicantina*, the space dedicated to wine and vegetable production.[57] In relation to the case of saltpowder, this was used for the production of Marseille soap, and was a product whose exportation from Alicante to Marseille was all ready a fact in the sixteenth century. In 1752, the Bouligny Company was part of an important merchant judicial alliance against the merchant Móxica, who owed debts with ten foreigner merchants of Alicante.[58] In the Bouligny Company case, from 1736, Moxica owed 4.7111 *libras*, 5 *sueldos* and 2 *dineros* which were to be returned to Juan Bouligny in *saltpowder*.

The Bouligny's commerce between the Atlantic Ocean and the Mediterranean Sea developed commercial networks, which enlarged their economic and geographical radius of action in the 1750s. For instance, in 1755, Gerónimo Gambiani, the Genoese consul of Cartagena, loaned 3.425 *libras*, 7 *sueldos* and 7 *dineros*[59] (11.800 reales de vellón) to Bouligny. This loan was paid the same year, by the transfer of other three credits. But what makes it interesting is how the Bouligny had turned from local to regional loans which connected with more international action. Accordingly, in December 1755, the recently created Bouligny Hermanos Company empowered two Dutch merchants, Roquete and Vanteylingen to collect their Pedro Tunibart's debt in Rotterdam.[60] At the same time, Juan and Joseph Bouligny-Paret extended their commercial networks to Madrid where they empowered Pascual Escolano as their commercial agent, in August 1757.[61] That same year, they also empowered the company of Enrique Loubier, Lewis and Schweighauser to buy a ship in the London quays for 800 to 1.000 pound sterling.[62]

At the end of 1760s, the Bouligny family supposedly contributed to seven per cent of the total commercial transactions of Alicante.[63] However, in September 1762, Juan de La Rosa, the Spanish Consul in Marseille, stated that among the Spanish commercial companies most affected by the Seven Years' War, the Bouligny Company was one of them. In 1767, Bouligny still appeared in the Alicante records as the only company of Spanish commerce, and was defined as a company with dubious solvency and credit. The Seven Years' War, and what seems a familiar strategy of insertion inside the Spanish Imperial Administration, made the Bouligny family progressively change their family character.[64] It was the end of the retailer merchant company, which, during the previous 50 years, had been trading with products and networks from the Atlantic and the Mediterranean Sea.

Final remarks

In this chapter, I have used a 'global microhistorical practice' as a way to understand these Atlantic–Mediterranean merchants in their complexity. As a result, I played with the scale as a toll to reconstruct the socio-commercial world 'in between'. The reading of family commercial companies, like the Bouligny, can only be understood in context. This means, the need to study its connection with their global trade dimension, their regional commercial and migration context and their local socio-commercial insertion. With that aim, I have analysed the Mediterranean commercial reality in which the Bouligny were inscribed; the French regional migration chains and the commercial networks in which they were inserted; and the products and links that they developed.

The Bouligny family evolved from being foreigners to a Spanish commercial company; from the use of 'national' networks to 'multinational' networks; from commercial family networks to administrative family networks. Along this time and space, the Bouligny family networks evolved constantly. In 50 years, their commercial networks changed from a preponderance of the links with French networks to a heterogeneous commercial network in which the origins blur. Also the nature of their networks moved away from a textile commercial focus to a more diversified supply character. They started as exporters of cotton or *lillas* from the Atlantic Ocean areas, increasing their commerce with *barilla*, wine or money lending in the Mediterranean area during the 1740s and 1750s. These changes were the result of the concurrently global, local and regional processes, which changed their socio-economical spaces, but they maintained a maritime commercial system between the Atlantic and the Mediterranean Sea which was inserted into a global economy.

The Seven Years' War is the best example of this. The global war affected the French commercial networks around the world, while it increased British commerce in diverse parts of the globe. As a result, the Atlantic–Mediterranean commercial networks, as in the Bouligny family's case, suffered the need of being relocated and readapted to the new realities. Consequently, these companies, whose wills were linked to the commercial globalisation, were forced to look for new possibilities and new internal configuration in new spheres. Therefore, after 1762 the Bouligny family spread its household around the globe, associating themselves with the Spanish Empire's administration and its relations with the wars and diplomacy around the world.

This brief overview of Bouligny commercial and moneylending circuits has suggested the existence of commercial networks inserted in complex maritime commercial systems which exceeded the geographical limits of the Mediterranean and the Atlantic spaces. I have used a retailer family network showing the need to understand the Mediterranean commercial relations in their global dimension after 1650, running away from the geographical determinism and the idea of a post-1650 decaying Mediterranean Sea.[65] The Bouligny family's companies mixed the Atlantic Spanish networks of textile supplement with the Marseille Mediterranean commercialisation, manufacture and re-exportation from the 1710s to 1750s. This allows us to go deeper in the 'trans-sea' commercial systems, by seeing the multi-directional links of the Mediterranean–Atlantic merchants who were the smallest cellules of more complicate systems. The Atlantic–Mediterranean merchant families were part of thickly connected networks which still need more case studies to be clarified. In this chapter I have proposed a way to dig into these merchants in between, trying to preserve the complexity and the interconnectivity of these systems which still require further research.

Notes

1 The content of this article is part of my MA Thesis defended at the University Pablo de Olavide 'La familia Bouligny. Redes Complejas y mediterraneidad en el siglo XVIII' (2014). I would like to thank Manuel Herrero Sánchez for his help and supervision; he made me change my idea about the Mediterranean Sea.

2 Ch. Verlinden, 'Les Origines Coloniales de La Civilisation Atlantique: Antecedents et Types de Structure', *Journal of World History* 1:1 (1953), pp. 378–398; J. Godechot and R. Palmer, 'Le Problème de l'Atlantique du XVIIIe au XXe siècle', *Relazioni del X Congreso di szienze storiche. Vol.IV: Storia moderna* (Florence: Sansoni, 1955).

3 P. Horden and N. Purcell, 'The Mediterranean and 'the New Thalassology', *The American Historical Review*, 111:3 (2006), pp. 722–740, p.723. The concept of *thalassology* has been developed by Peregrine Horden and Nicholas Purcell, in base to the ancient Greek work *thalassa* 'sea'. The explanation of the alternativeness of this concept is related by Peter Miller in relation to the differentiation of the studies of the sea and the oceans, and the question of the maritime history focus in territorial history: P.N. Miller (ed.), *The Sea: Thalassography and Historiography* (Ann Arbor: University of Michigan Press, 2013), p. 5. For its application is clearer in the study of P. Horden and N. Purcell, *The Corrupting Sea: A Study of Mediterranean History* (Oxford: Blackwell, 2000).

4 D. Abulafia, 'Mediterranean History as Global History', *History and Theory*, 50:2 (2011), pp. 220–228.

5 Miller, *The Sea*, p. 19.

6 F. Trivellato, *The Familiarity of Strangers: The Sephardic Diaspora, Livorno, and Cross-Cultural Trade in the Early Modern Period* (New Haven: Yale University Press, 2009). Trivellato points to the importance of these studies sea as the context but not as the object of her study, following the microhistorical conclusions about the importance of the context, but not as the object of her study.

7 For more information about Mediterranean studies see: P. Horden and N. Purcell, *The Corrupting Sea* (Hoboken: Wiley-Blackwell, 2000); J.J. Norwich, *The Middle Sea: A History of the Mediterranean* (London: Chatto & Windus, 2006); G. Piterberg, T.F. Ruiz and G. Symcox (eds.), *Braudel Revisited: The Mediterranean World, 1600–1800* (Toronto: University of Toronto Press, 2010). On Atlantic studies: J.J. McCusker and K. Morgan (eds.), *The Early Modern Atlantic Economy* (Cambridge: Cambridge University Press, 2000); H. Pietschmann (ed.), *Atlantic History: History of the Atlantic System 1580–1830* (Göttingen: Vandenhoeck & Ruprecht, 2002); L. Putnam, 'To Study the Fragments/Whole: Microhistory and the Atlantic World', *Journal of Social History* 39:3 (2006), pp. 615–630; P. Gervais, 'Neither Imperial, nor Atlantic: A Merchant Perspective on International Trade in the Eighteenth Century', *History of European Ideas*, 34:4 (2008), pp. 465–473; R.L. Kagan, *Atlantic Diasporas: Jews, Conversos, and Crypto-Jews in the Age of Mercantilism, 1500–1800* (Baltimore: Johns Hopkins University Press, 2009). On Baltic studies: M.L. Hinkkanen and D. Kirby, *The Baltic and the North Seas* (London: Routledge, 2000); L. Bes, E. Frankot and H. Brand (eds.), *Baltic Connections: Archival Guide to the Maritime Relations of the Countries around the Baltic Sea (including the Netherlands) 1450–1800*, 3 vols. (Leiden: Brill, 2007); H. Brand and L. Müller (eds.), *The Dynamics of Economic Culture in the North Sea and Baltic Region: In the Late Middle Ages and Early Modern Period* (Hilversum: Verloren, 2007). On the study of the Indian Ocean: K.N. Chaudhuri, *Trade and Civilisation in the Indian Ocean: An Economic History from the Rise of Islam to 1750* (Cambridge, New York: Cambridge University Press, 1985, 2003); M.N. Pearson, *The Indian Ocean. Seas in History* (London, New York: Routledge, 2003); M.N. Pearson (ed.), *The World of the Indian Ocean, 1500–1800: Studies in Economic, Social, and Cultural History* (Aldershot: Ashgate, 2005); P. Gupta, I. Hofmeyr and M.N. Pearson (eds.), *Eyes Across the Water: Navigating the Indian Ocean* (Pretoria: Unisa Press, 2010); R.W. Harms, *Indian Ocean Slavery in the Age of Abolition* (New Haven: Yale University Press, 2013); P. Machado, *Ocean of Trade: South Asian Merchants, Africa and the Indian Ocean, c. 1750–1850* (Cambridge: Cambridge University Press, 2014). About the study of the Pacific Ocean: L. Laorden Jiménez, *Navegantes españoles en el Océano Pacífico: la historia de España en el gran Océano que fue llamado lago español* (Madrid: Luís Laorden Jiménez, 2013); F.J. Montero Llácer, *El océano Pacífico: conmemoración 500 años de su descubrimiento* (Madrid: Fundación Ramón Areces, 2014); R.F. Buschmann, E.R. Slack and J.B. Tueller, *Navigating the Spanish Lake: The Pacific in the Iberian World, 1521–1898. Perspectives on the Global Past* (Honolulu: University of Hawaii Press, 2014). About the China Sea: C. Guillot, D. Lombard and R. Ptak (eds.), *From the Mediterranean to the China Sea: Miscellaneous Notes* (Wiesbaden: Otto Harrassowitz, 1998); D. Lombard and J. Aubin (eds.), *Asian Merchants and Businessmen in the Indian Ocean and the China Sea* (New Delhi and New York: Oxford University Press, 2000).

8 P. Horden and N. Purcell, *The Corrupting Sea*, p. 9, "By contrast, history of the region presupposes an understanding of the whole environment. And the environment in question is the product of a complex interaction of human and physical factors, not simply a material backdrop or a set of immutable constraints".

9 The term has recently been used by T. Andrade, 'A Chinese Farmer, Two African Boys, and a Warlord: Toward a Global Microhistory', *Journal of World History*, 21:4 (2010), pp. 573–591; and F. Trivellato, 'Is There a Future for Italian Microhistory in the Age of Global History?', *California Italian Studies*, 2:1 at http://escholarship.org/uc/item/0z94n9hq.

10 P. Chaunu, *Seville et l'Atlantique (1504–1650): Partie Interpretative. Ports, Routes, Trafics*, Vol. 6 (Paris: SEVPEN, 1959); C. Carrière, *Negociants Marseillais Au XVIIIe Siecle: Contribution a L'etude Des Economies Maritimes* (Marseille: Institut historique de Provence, 1973).

11 J.I. Israel, *Empires and Entrepots: The Dutch, the Spanish Monarchy, and the Jews, 1585–1713* (London: Hambledon Press, 1990); A. Crespo Solana, *Entre Cádiz y los Paises Bajos: una comunidad mercantil en la ciudad de la ilustración* (Cádiz: Fundación Municipal de Cultura del Ayuntamiento de Cadiz, 2001); A. Crespo Solana, *Las comunidades mercantiles y el mantenimiento de los sistemas comerciales de España, Flandes y la República Holandesa, 1648–1750* (Córdoba: Universidad de Córdoba, 2002); A. Crespo Solana, *Mercaderes atlánticos: redes del comercio flamenco y holandés entre Europa y el Caribe* (Córdoba: Universidad de Córdoba, 2009).

12 Recently published works about national merchant communities - On German communities: M. Schulte Beerbühl, *The Forgotten Majority: German Merchants in London, Naturalization, and Global Trade, 1660–1815* (New York and Oxford: Berghahn Books, 2015); J.R. Davis, S. Manz and M. Schulte Beerbühl (eds.) *Transnational Networks German Migrants in the British Empire, 1670–1914* (Leiden: Brill, 2012); K. Weber, 'Intercambios mercantiles y culturales: Comerciantes alemanes en Cádiz, 1680–1830,' in A. Crespo Solana (ed.), *Comunidades transnacionales: Colonias de mercaderes extranjeros en el mundo Atlántico (1500–1830)* (Aranjuez: Doce Calles, 2010), pp. 101–122. In relation to the Irish and English commercial community; D. Worthington, *British and Irish Experiences and Impressions of Central Europe, c.1560–1688* (Burlington: Ashgate, 2012); D.T. Gleeson (ed.), *The Irish in the Atlantic World* (Columbia: University of South Carolina Press, 2010). For the Dutch case: J.I. Israel, *Empires and Entrepots: the Dutch, the Spanish Monarchy, and the Jews, 1585–1713* (London: Hambledon Press, 1990). For the French community see: K.J. Banks, *Chasing Empire Across the Sea: Communications and the State in the French Atlantic, 1713–1763* (Montreal and Ithaca: McGill-Queen's University Press; 2002). For the Portuguese commercial community see: D. Studnicki-Gizbert, *A Nation Upon the Ocean Sea: Portugal's Atlantic Diaspora and the Crisis of the Spanish Empire, 1492–1640* (Oxford and New York: Oxford University Press, 2007); F. Ribeiro da Silva, *Dutch and Portuguese in Western Africa: Empires, Merchants and the Atlantic System, 1580–1674*. Atlantic World: Europe, Africa and the Americas, 1500–1830, Vol. 22 (Leiden and Boston: Brill, 2011). In the case of Jewish commercial communities in the Atlantic context see: J.I. Israel, *Diasporas within a Diaspora: Jews, Crypto-Jews, and the World of Maritime Empires (1540–1740)*. Brill's Series in Jewish Studies, Vol. 30. (Boston: Brill, 2002); R.L. Kagan, *Atlantic Diasporas: Jews, Conversos, and Crypto-Jews in the Age of Mercantilism, 1500–1800* (Baltimore: Johns Hopkins University Press, 2009).

13 For the Jewish community in the Mediterranean see: F. Trivellato, 'Les juifs d'origine portugaise entre Livourne, le Portugal et la Méditerranée (c. 1650–1750),' *Arquivos do Centro Cultural Calouste Gulbenkian*, XLVIII: La Diaspora des 'Nouveaux-Chrétiens' (2004), pp. 171–182. For the Greek community see: M. Greene, *Catholic Pirates and Greek Merchants: A Maritime History of the Mediterranean* (Princeton and Oxford: Princeton University Press, 2010); M. Grenet, 'La Fabrique Communautaire: Les Grecs À Venise, Livourne et Marseille, v.1770-v.1830' (PhD Theses: European University Institute, 2010). In relation with the institutions, we should mention the new institutional studies J. Goldberg, *Trade and Institutions in the Medieval Mediterranean: The Geniza Merchants and Their Business World* (Cambridge and New York: Cambridge University Press, 2012).

14 One important exception is A. Greif, *Institutions and the Path to the Modern Economy: Lessons from Medieval Trade. Political Economy of Institutions and Decisions* (Cambridge and New York: Cambridge University Press, 2006).

15 For the Basque Social Network studies see J.M. Imízcoz Beunza and J. Ma (eds.), *Elites, Poder Y Red Social: Las Élites Del País Vasco Y Navarra En La Edad Moderna:*

210   Pablo Hernández Sau

Estado de La Cuestión Y Perspectivas (Bilbao: Servicio Editorial, Universidad del País Vasco, 1996); J.M. Imízcoz Beunzaand and O. Oliveri Korta (eds.), *Economía Doméstica Y Redes Sociales En El Antiguo Régimen* (Madrid: Sílex, 2010). In relation with the Cádiz-Dutch community see: A. Crespo Solana, *Entre Cádiz y los Países bajos*. In relation to Catalan commerce see: P. Molas Ribalta (ed.), *Comerç i estructura social a Catalunya i Valencia als segles XVII i XVIII*. Biblioteca de cultura catalana 27 (Barcelona: Curial, 1977); C. Martínez Shaw, *Cataluña en la carrera de Indias: 1680–1756* (Barcelona: Crítica, 1981); E. Martín Corrales, *Comercio de Cataluña con el Mediterráneo musulmán (siglos XVI–XVIII): el comercio con 'los enemigos de la fe'* (Barcelona: Bellaterra, 2001).

16 For more information about the Genovese merchants see: C. Brilli, 'Mercaderes genoveses en el Cádiz del siglo XVIII. Crisis y reajuste de una simbiosis secular', in A. Crespo Solana, *Comunidades transnacionales* (Aranjuez: Doce Calles, 2010), pp. 83–102; M. Herrero Sánchez, *Génova y La Monarquía Hispánica (1528–1713)* (Genova: Società ligure di storia patria, 2011); A. García-Montón, 'Génova Y El Atlántico (c.1650–1680): Emprendedores Mediterráneos Frente Al Auge Del Capitalismo Del Norte' (PhD Theses: European University Institute, 2014); C. Dauverd, *Imperial Ambition in the Early Modern Mediterranean: Genoese Merchants and the Spanish Crown* (New York: Cambridge University Press, 2015).

17 For more information about the history of Western Mediterranean maritime flows, see: Ch. Carrière, *Negociants Marseillais Au XVIIIe Siécle*; C. Martínez Shaw, *Cataluña en la carrera de Indias*; E. Giménez López, *Alicante en el siglo XVIII: economía de una ciudad portuaria en el Antiguo Régimen* (Valencia: Institució Alfons el Magnànim, 1981); R. Franch Benavent, *Crecimiento Comercial Y Enriquecimiento Burgués En La Valencia Del Siglo XVIII*. Estudios Universitarios 15 (Valencia: Institució Alfons el Magnànim, 1986); E. Martín Corrales, *Comercio de Cataluña con el Mediterráneo musulmán (siglos XVI–XVIII)*. In relation to Marseille see: M. Pérez-García, *Vicarious Consumers: Trans-National Meetings Between the West and East in the Mediterranean World (1730–1808)* (Farnham: Ashgate, 2013); J.T. Takeda, *Between Crown and Commerce: Marseille and the Early Modern Mediterranean*, The Johns Hopkins University Studies in Historical and Political Science (Baltimore: Johns Hopkins University Press, 2011).

18 F. Braudel, *El Mediterráneo y el mundo mediterráneo en la época de Felipe II*, Vol. 1., 2 vols. (México: Fondo de Cultura Económica, 2007), pp. 790–791.

19 M. Pérez-García, *Vicarious Consumers*, p.81

20 C. Brilli, 'Mercaderes genoveses en el Cádiz del siglo XVIII'; 'Crisis y reajuste de una simbiosis secular', in A. Crespo Solana (ed.), *Comunidades transnacionales* (Aranjuez: Doce Calles, 2010), pp. 83–102. K. Kaps, 'Entre Servicio Estatal Y Los Negocios Transnacionales: El Caso de Paolo Greppi, Cónsul Imperial En Cádiz (1774–1791)', in M. Aglietti, M. Herrero Sánchez and F. Zamora Rodríguez (eds.), *Los Cónsules de Extranjeros en la Edad Moderna y a principios de La Edad Contemporánea* (Aranjuez: Doce Calles, 2013), pp. 225–235.

21 M. Demiryürek, 'The Legal Foundations of the Commercial Relations Between the Ottomans and Neapolitans', *Bilig: Türk Dünyası Sosyal Bilimler Dergisi*, 69 (2014), pp. 53–74.

22 M. Arribas Palau, *Las relaciones hispano magrebíes en el siglo XVIII: selección de estudios* (Madrid: Agencia Española de Cooperación Internacional, Ministerio de Asuntos Exteriores y de Cooperación, 2007).

23 J.B. Villar and R. Lourido *Relaciones entre España y el Magreb, siglos XVII y XVIII* (Madrid: MAPFRE, 1992); E. Martín Corrales, *Comercio de Cataluña con el Mediterráneo musulmán (siglos XVI–XVIII)*; M. Conrotte, *España y los países musulmanes durante el ministerio de Floridablanca* (Sevilla; Espuela De Plata, 2006).

24 On a consular historiograpraphy review see G. Le Bouedec and J. Ülbert (eds.), *La Fonction Consulaire à l'Époque Moderne; L'affirmation d'une Institution Économique et Politique (1500–1700)* (Rennes: Presses universitaires de Rennes, 2006); A. Alimento (ed.), *War, Trade and Neutrality. Europe and the Mediterranean in Seventeenth and Eighteenth Centuries* (Milano: Franco Angeli, 2011); M. Herrero Sánchez, 'La Red Consular Europea Y La Diplomacia Mercantil En La Edad Moderna.' at J.J. Iglesias and M. Fernández Chaves (eds.), *Comercio y Cultura en La Edad Moderna* (Sevilla: Servicio de Publicaciones de la Universidad de Sevilla, 2015). In relation with the studies of the consulates at Mediterranean see M. Aglietti, M. Herrero Sánchez and F. Zamora Rodríguez, *Los Cónsules de Extranjeros*; F. Zamora Rodríguez, *La 'Pupilla Dell' Occhio Della Toscana' y la posición hispánica en el Mediterráneo Occidental (1677–1717)* (Madrid: Fundación Española de Historia Moderna, 2013); S. Marzagalli, M. Ghazali and Ch. Windler (eds.), *Les Consuls En Méditerranée, Agents D'information, XVIe-XXe Siècle* (Paris: Classiques Garnier, 2015).

25 E. Eldem, *French Trade in Istanbul in the Eighteenth Century* (Leiden: Brill, 1999); J.I. Martínez Ruiz and P. Gaucci, *Mercaderes ingleses en Alicante en el siglo XVII: estudio y edición de la correspondencia comercial de Richard Houncell & Co.* (Alicante: Universidad de Alicante, 2008); G. Pérez Sarrión, *La Península Comercial: Mercado, Redes Sociales y Estado en España en el siglo XVIII* (Madrid: Marcial Pons, 2012).

26 M. Pérez-García, *Vicarious Consumers*, pp. 135–153.

27 M. Pérez-García, *Vicarious Consumers*, pp. 111–192.

28 R. Franch Benavent, *Crecimiento Comercial Y Enriquecimiento Burgués.*

29 Three main maps: Willem Barents Beschryvinge vande Zeecusten van Spaengen beginnende van Cabo dagata tot de C. Martin, midschaders het eyland Yviça ende ooc de Barbarische custe van Caep de Hone tot de Stad van Alger, met alle havenen, reeden, bayen, ondiepten, clippe, Sanden, ende ander drooghten seer neerstigh, 1593, http://gallica.bnf.fr/ark:/12148/btv1b530570882 (Accessed 18 December 2015); Francesco María Levanto La Costa di Spagna da C. di Gata fino a C. S. Martin, et la Costa di Barbaria da C. di Hone a C. de Tenes, 1698, http://gallica.bnf.fr/ark:/12148/btv1b530570793 (Accessed 18 December 2015); H. Michelot, P. Grauver Starckman, and Jean Philippe de Orléans, Suite des Costes d'Espagne et de Barbarie, depuis Cartagene jusqu'a Denia, Et depuis Cap Falcon jusqu'au Cap Carbon, 1723, http://gallica.bnf.fr/ark:/12148/btv1b53064461w (Accessed 18 December 2015).

30 This hypothesis about a southeast Iberian commercial region requires deeper analysis, being necessary to corroborate it by a thorough analysis of market integration among cities like Valencia, Alicante, Cartagena and Malaga. It would be necessary to confirm this via a comparative study about the progressive approximation of prices, the synchronic price movement of different merchandise; the price deviation of the principle places; and the temporal serial differences in different port cities like Valencia, Alicante, Cartagena and Malaga. This method to confirm the existence of an economical polarized region is proposed in: G. Pérez Sarrión, *La Península Comercial*, p. 40.

31 G. Pérez Sarrión, *La Península Comercial*, pp. 202–212.

32 M. Pérez-García, *Vicarious Consumers*, pp. 111–122.

33 In the case of the wine, it was quite popular in the French court. See: E. Giménez López, *Alicante en el siglo XVIII*, p. 156.

34 J.A. Salas Auséns, *En busca de El Dorado: Inmigración francesa en la España Moderna*. Historia de la población 6 (Bilbao: Universidad del País Vasco, 2009), pp. 38–51.

35 G. Pérez Sarrión, *La Península Comercial*, pp. 190–203.

36 J.A. Salas Auséns, *En busca de El Dorado* pp. 46–50.

37 M.A. Rogles Hernández, 'La Inmigración En Alicante (1650–1799)', *Revista de Historia Moderna: Anales de La Universidad de Alicante*, 4 (1984), pp. 387–415.

38 During the 1760s and 1770s, the Spanish administration tried to develop increasing control of foreigner merchants settling in its Empire. As result, we have three foreign

merchant lists for the Valencia reign. These were developed in 1764 (Archivo Histórico Nacional (herafter A.H.N), Estado, leg.629-1), 1765 (A.H.N, Estado, leg.629-1) and 1773 (A.H.N, Estado, leg.629-3). Regarding the analysis of the 1764 Merchant List, out of 689 foreigners in the Valencia Reign, approximately 539 had French origin but have settled permanently in Valencia Reign (R. Franch Benavent and D. Muñoz Navarro, 'Minorías Extranjeras y Competencia Mercantil: Franceses Y Malteses En El Comercio Valenciano Del Siglo XVIII', *Minius. Revista do Departamento de Historia, Arte e Xeografia*, 20 (2012), pp. 69–92.) However, this data should be used carefully, as consequence of the incomplete nature of this document G. Pérez Sarrión, *La Península Comercial*, p. 210.

39 Among the 113 French household heads, we can mention '48 negociantes, 23 mozos de comercio, 12 escrituarios, 7 tratantes, 1 cónsul, 1 viceconsul, 1 cajero, 1 escribano, 1 fabricante de medias, 1 peluquero, 4 horneros, 4 caldereros, 4 criados, 1 estudiante y 7 personas sin oficio especificado'; see E. Giménez López, *Alicante en el siglo XVIII*, p. 67.

40 Franch Benavent, R. Muñoz Navarro, 'Minorías extranjeras y competencia mercantil: Franceses y malteses en el comercio valenciano del siglo XVIII Minius', *Revista do Departamento de Historia, Arte e Xeografia*, (number 20), pp. 61–92.

41 A. Greif, 'Reputation and Coalitions in Medieval Trade: Evidence on the Maghribi Traders', *Journal of Economic History*, 49:4 (1989), pp. 857–882.

42 "A diferencia de la italiana, la francesa es una inmigración más cualificada, por lo que respecta a Alicante, y su colonia mercantil tuvo en el siglo XVIII un peso específico incuestionable…Según nuestros datos referentes a 1754, la colonia francesa era la más numerosa: los varones franceses residentes en la ciudad y mayores de 15 años suman un total de 113 individuos, frente a los 66 genoveses, 7 piamonteses, 1 milanés y 1 napolitano ya citados, y 8 ingleses, 3 holandeses, 2 alemanes y 2 irlandeses." E. Giménez López, *Alicante en el siglo XVIII*, pp. 66–67.

43 Regarding the first two cases, see two chapters of Vicente Seguí Roma's Ph.D. thesis. There is also an article about Pedro Cholly's business in Alicante. L. Maldonado, 'Negocios e Integración Social Del Comerciante Marsellés Pedro Choly', *Revista de Historia Moderna: Anales de La Universidad de Alicante*, 11 (1992), pp. 79–94.

44 F. Martin. *A History of the Bouligny Family and Allied Families* (Lafayette: The Center for Louisiana Studies. University of Southwestern Louisiana, 1990), p. 102.

45 V. Seguí Romá, 'Comerciantes extranjeros en Alicante (1700–1750)', (PhD Thesis: Universidad de Alicante. Departamento de Historia Medieval, Historia Moderna y Ciencias y Técnicas Historiográficas, 2012).

46 Archivo Histórico Provincial de Alicante (hereafter A.H.P.A) Juan Bautista Hernández, Protocolo 782, 42 r.- 42 v. 06/05/1718

47 The two Amorich cases have been deeply analyzed in V. Seguí Romá, 'Comerciantes extranjeros en Alicante (1700–1750): hombres de negocios franceses y genoveses en una ciudad mediterránea' (PhD dissertation: Universidad de Alicante, 2012), pp. 11–94.

48 H. Kamen, *Spain in the Later Seventeenth Century: 1665–1700* (London: Longman: 1980); E. Giménez López, *Alicante en el siglo XVIII*; J.I. Martínez Ruiz and P. Gaucci, *Mercaderes ingleses en Alicante en el siglo XVII.*

49 A.H.P.A Antonio García, Protocolo 697, 321 r. -322 v. 26/07/1721 'Codicilio Joseph Bouligny'.

50 A.H.P.A Antonio García, Protocolo 700, 135 r. - 137 v., 17/04/1724 'Dote y recepción de María Antonia Paret' María Antonia Paret was also the daughter of other Marseille neighbor who had settled in Alicante some years before, getting the French bread provisions of Alicante V. Seguí Romá, 'Comerciantes extranjeros en Alicante (1700–1750)', p. 67.

51 The Bouligny family constituted three different family commercial companies: 1724 *Bouligny e hijo*, 1746 *Don Juan Bouligny Padre e hijos*; 1754 *Bouligny hermanos.*

52 In the primary sources they are defined as *comerciantes de puerta abierta*, Archivo Municipal de Alicante (hereafter A.M.A) Arm.7 Lib.3, ; Vezindario Integro de los vecinos de esta ciudad y huertos de regadío y secano por el orden de las clases; agencias que por sus facultades y oficios ganan; propiedades que estos tienen y Renta liquida, que al año 1731'; A.M.A Arm.7 lib.4. Repartimiento de Equivalente de Alcabalas, Cuentas, Millones y demás derechos expresados en el cupo despachado por la Intendencia General de este Reino señalado a esta Ciudad de Alicante en el presente año mil setecientos y veinte y nueve, en que se incluye la Contribuizion de Real de la Sal.

53 A.H.P.A, Antonio García, Protocolo 701, 201 r. -201 v. 23/06/1725; A.H.P.A, Antonio García, Protocolo 702, 2 r. -2 v., 05/01/1726; A.H.P.A, Onofre Savater, Protocolo 1063/1, 20r. – 20v, 06/01/1734; A.H.P.A, Francisco Hernández, Protocolo 707/1, 186r. – 188 v. 20/12/1732.

54 A.H.P.A, Onofre Savater, Protocolo 1294/2, 192r. – 192v.

55 A.H.P.A, Onofre Savater, Protocolo 1380/1, 170r.-170v.; A.H.P.A, Onofre Savater, Protocolo 1380/1, 170r.– 170v.

56 A.H.P.A, Onofre Savater, Protocolo 1292, 118r. – 118v. 13/07/1745; A.H.P.A Onofre Savater, Protocolo 1379, 164r. – 164v. 06/06/1746.

57 They bought different properties with vineyards, among which one will be their family home. A.H.P.A, Onofre Savater, Protocolo 1292, 248r.-254v. 25/11/1745. To see some of the vineyard properties bought A.H.P.A, Onofre Savater, Protocolo 1379, 88r.-91v, 20/04/1746; A.H.P.A, Onofre Savater, Protocolo 1293/2, 45r-47v, 25/04/1749.

58 A.H.P.A, Vicente Fons, Protocolo 606, 175r. - 175 v.; A.H.P.A, Vicente Fons, Protocolo 606, 287r.-288v.

59 A.H.P.A, Onofre Savater, Protocolo 1380, 171r-173v, 17/11/1755.

60 A.H.P.A, Onofre Savater, Protocolo 1380, 186r-186v, 16/12/1755.

61 A.H.P.A, Onofre Savater, Protocolo 1296/1, 71r.-71v, 16/08/1757.

62 A.H.P.A, Onofre Savater, Protocolo 1296/1, 74r.-74v, 23/08/1757.

63 I have not got enough dates to confirm or refute this but this is the reference which is given in the Bouligny family memoir. H.N.O.C, B.B.P 1997 F.118.

64 Some examples are Juan Buligny Paret (1726–1798) who was graced as honor adviser of *Consejo de Estado*, Francsico Bouligny y Paret (1736–1800), Coronel of Spanish Louisiana Regiment; Luís Bouligny Paret (1756–1793), Coronel of Regiment of Extremadura; Juan Heliodoro de Bouligny Marconié (1759–1803), Spanish ambassador in Batavia (Holland) and Sweden; Juan Ventura de Bouligny Marconié (1758–1826), Spanish consul in Leghorn; María Elena de Bouligny Marconié (1756–1817) marriage with José María Villavicencio de La Serna (1735–1830), general director of Spanish Navy; Elena de Bouligny Paret (1759–1802) married I Count of Yoldi (1764–1843), Spanish ambassador in Denmark; or Teófilo Bouligny Timoni (1795–1866), Knight of Charles III's Order.

65 F. Braudel *El Mediterráneo y el mundo mediterráneo en la época de Felipe II.* 2ª ed., Vol. 2 (Madrid: Fondo de Cultura Económica de España, 2001), p. 69.

Bibliography

Abulafia, D., 'Mediterranean History as Global History', *History and Theory*, 50:2 (2011), pp. 220–228.

Aglietti, D., Herrero Sánchez, M. and Zamora Rodríguez, F. (eds.), *Los Cónsules de Extranjeros en la Edad Moderna y a principios de la Edad Contemporánea*, Aranjuez: Doce Calles, 2013.

Alimento, A. (ed.), *War, Trade and Neutrality. Europe and the Mediterranean in Seventeenth and Eighteenth Centuries*, Milano: Franco Angeli, 2011.

Andrade, T., 'A Chinese Farmer, Two African Boys, and a Warlord: Toward a Global Microhistory', *Journal of World History*, 21:4 (2010), pp. 573–591.

Arribas Palau, M., *Las relaciones hispano magrebíes en el siglo XVIII: selección de estudios*, Madrid: Agencia Española de Cooperación Internacional, Ministerio de Asuntos Exteriores y de Cooperación, 2007.

Banks, K.J., *Chasing Empire Across the Sea: Communications and the State in the French Atlantic, 1713–1763*, Montreal and Ithaca: McGill-Queen's University Press, 2002.

Bes, L., Frankot, E. and Brand, H. (eds.), *Baltic Connections: Archival Guide to the Maritime Relations of the Countries Around the Baltic Sea (Including the Netherlands) 1450–1800*, 3 vols., Leiden: Brill, 2007.

Brand, H. and Müller, L. (eds.), *The Dynamics of Economic Culture in the North Sea and Baltic Region: In the Late Middle Ages and Early Modern Period*, Hilversum: Verloren, 2007.

Braudel, F., *El Mediterráneo y el mundo mediterráneo en la época de Felipe II*, Vol. 1, 2 Vols., México: Fondo de Cultura Económica, 2007.

Braudel, F., *The Mediterranean and the Mediterranean World in the Age of Philip II*, 2nd ed., London: Collins, 1972.

Buschmann, R.F., *Navigating the Spanish Lake: The Pacific in the Iberian World, 1521–1898. Perspectives on the Global Past*, Honolulu: University of Hawai'I Press, 2014.

———. *El Mediterráneo y el mundo mediterráneo en la época de Felipe II*. 2 ed. Vol. 2. 2 vols. Historia, Madrid: Fondo de Cultura Económica de España, 1972.

———. *El Mediterráneo y el mundo mediterráneo en la época de Felipe II*. Vol. 1. 2 vols. Historia, México, DF: Fondo de Cultura Económica, 2007.

Brilli, C., 'Mercaderes genoveses en el Cádiz del siglo XVIII. Crisis y reajuste de una simbiosis secular', Crespo Solana, A. (ed.), *Comunidades transnacionales*, Aranjuez: Doce Calles, pp. 83–102.

Carrière, Ch., *Négociants Marseillais au XVIIIe siècle: Contribution à l'étude des économies maritimes*, Marseille: Institut historique de Provence, 1973.

Chaudhuri, K.N., *Trade and Civilisation in the Indian Ocean: An Economic History from the Rise of Islam to 1750*, Cambridge and New York: Cambridge University Press, 1985.

Chaunu, P., *Seville et l'Atlantique (1504–1650): Partie Interpretative. Ports, Routes, Trafics*. Vol. 6, Paris: SEVPEN, 1959.

Conrotte, M., *España y los países musulmanes durante el ministerio de Floridablanca*, Sevilla; Espuela De Plata, 2006.

Crespo Solana, A., *Entre Cádiz y los Paises Bajos: una comunidad mercantil en la ciudad de la ilustración*, Cádiz: Fundación Municipal de Cultura del Ayuntamiento de Cadiz, 2001.

Crespo Solana, A. (ed.), *Comunidades transnacionales: Colonias de mercaderes extranjeros en el mundo Atlántico (1500–1830)*, Aranjuez: Doce Calles, 2010, pp. 101–122.

Dauverd, C., *Imperial Ambition in the Early Modern Mediterranean: Genoese Merchants and the Spanish Crown*, New York: Cambridge University Press, 2015.

Davis, J.R., Manz, S. and Schulte Beerbühl, M. (eds.), *Transnational Networks German Migrants in the British Empire*, 1670–1914, Leiden: Brill, 2012.

Demiryürek, M., 'The Legal Foundations of the Commercial Relations Between the Ottomans and Neapolitans' *Bilig: Türk Dünyası Sosyal Bilimler Dergisi*, 69 (2014), pp. 53–74.

———. *Las comunidades mercantiles y el mantenimiento de los sistemas comerciales de España, Flandes y la República Holandesa, 1648–1750*, Córdoba: Universidad de Córdoba, 2002.

———. *Mercaderes atlánticos: redes del comercio flamenco y holandés entre Europa y el Caribe*, Córdoba: Universidad de Córdoba, 2009.

Eldem, E., *French Trade in Istanbul in the Eighteenth Century. Ottoman Empire and Its Heritage*, v. 19, Leiden: Brill, 1999.

Franch Benavent, R., *Crecimiento comercial y enriquecimiento burgués en la Valencia del siglo XVIII*, Valencia: Institució Alfons el Magnànim, 1986.

Franch Benavent, R. and Muñoz Navarro, D., 'Minorías Extranjeras Y Competencia Mercantil: Franceses Y Malteses En El Comercio Valenciano Del Siglo XVIII', *Minius. Revista Do Departamento de Historia, Arte E Xeografía* 20 (2012), pp. 61–92.

García-Montón, A., 'Génova Y El Atlántico (c.1650–1680): Emprendedores Mediterráneos Frente Al Auge Del Capitalismo Del Norte', PhD dissertation: European University Institute, 2014.

Gervais, P., 'Neither Imperial, nor Atlantic: A Merchant Perspective on International Trade in the Eighteenth Century', *History of European Ideas*, 34:4 (2008), pp. 465–473.

Giménez López, E., *Alicante en el siglo XVIII: economía de una ciudad portuaria en el Antiguo Régimen*, Valencia: Institució Alfons el Magnànim, 1981.

Gleeson, D.T. (ed), *The Irish in the Atlantic World*, Columbia: University of South Carolina Press, 2010.

Goldberg, J., *Trade and Institutions in the Medieval Mediterranean: The Geniza Merchants and Their Business World*, Cambridge; New York: Cambridge University Press, 2012.

Godechot, J. and Palmer, R., 'Le Problème de l'Atlantique du XVIIIe au XXe siècle', *Relazioni del X Congreso di szienze storiche. Vol.IV: Storia moderna*, Florence: Sansoni, 1955.

Greene, M., Catholic Pirates and Greek Merchants: *A Maritime History of the Mediterranean*, Princeton, Oxford: Princeton University Press, 2010.

Greif, A., 'Reputation and Coalitions in Medieval Trade: Evidence on the Maghribi Traders', *Journal of Economic History*, 49:4 (1989), pp. 857–882.

Guillot, C., Lombard, D. and Ptak, R. (eds.), *From the Mediterranean to the China Sea: Miscellaneous Notes*, Wiesbaden: Otto Harrassowitz, 1998.

Gupta, P., Hofmeyr, I. and Pearson, M.N. (eds.), *Eyes Across the Water: Navigating the Indian Ocean*, Pretoria: Unisa Press, 2010.

———. *Institutions and the Path to the Modern Economy: Lessons from Medieval Trade*, Cambridge, New York: Cambridge University Press, 2006.

Herrero Sánchez, M. (ed.), *Génova Y La Monarquía Hispánica (1528–1713)*, Genova: Società ligure di storia patria, 2011.

———. 'La Red Consular europea y la Diplomacia Mercantil en la Edad Moderna', in J.J. Iglesias and M. Fernández Chaves (eds.), *Comercio y Cultura en la Edad Moderna*, Sevilla: Servicio de Publicaciones de la Universidad de Sevilla, 2015.

Hinkkanen, M.L. and Kirby, D., *The Baltic and the North Seas*, London: Routledge, 2000.

Horden, P. and Purcell, N., *The Corrupting Sea: A Study of Mediterranean History*, Hoboken: Wiley-Blackwell, 2000.

———. 'The Mediterranean and "the New Thalassology"', *The American Historical Review*, 111:3 (2006), pp. 722–740.

Iglesias, J.J. and Fernández Chaves, M., *Comercio y Cultura en La Edad Moderna*, Sevilla: Servicio de Publicaciones de la Universidad de Sevilla, 2015.

Imízcoz Beunza, J.M. (ed.), *Elites, Poder Y Red Social: Las Élites Del País Vasco Y Navarra En La Edad Moderna: Estado de La Cuestión Y Perspectivas*, Bilbao: Universidad del País Vasco, 1996.

Imízcoz Beunza, J.M. and Oliveri Korta, O. (eds.) *Economía doméstica y redes sociales en el Antiguo Régimen*, Madrid: Sílex, 2010.

Imízcoz Beunzaand, J.M. and Oliveri Korta, O. (eds.), *Economía Doméstica Y Redes Sociales En El Antiguo Régimen*, Madrid: Sílex, 2010.

Israel, J.I., *Empires and entrepots: the Dutch, the Spanish monarchy, and the Jews, 1585–1713*, London: Hambledon Press, 1990.

Israel, J.I., *Diasporas within a Diaspora: Jews, Crypto-Jews, and the World of Maritime Empires (1540–1740)*, Brill's Series in Jewish Studies, Vol. 30, Boston: Brill, 2002.

Kagan, R.L., *Atlantic Diasporas: Jews, Conversos, and Crypto-Jews in the Age of Mercantilism, 1500–1800*, Baltimore: Johns Hopkins University Press, 2009.

Kamen, H., *Spain in the Later Seventeenth Century: 1665–1700*, London: Longman, 1980.

Kaps, K., 'Entre Servicio Estatal Y Los Negocios Transnacionales: El Caso de Paolo Greppi, Cónsul Imperial En Cádiz (1774–1791)', in Aglietti, M., Herrero Sánchez, M. and Zamora Rodríguez, F. (eds.), *Los Cónsules de Extranjeros en la Edad Moderna y a principios de La Edad Contemporánea*, Aranjuez: Doce Calles, 2013, pp. 225–235.

Laorden Jiménez, L., *Navegantes españoles en el Océano Pacífico: la historia de España en el gran Océano que fue llamado lago español*, Madrid: Luís Laorden Jiménez, 2013.

Le Bouedec, G. and Ülbert, J. (eds.), *La Fonction Consulaire À L'époque Moderne; L'affirmation D'une Institution Économique et Politique (1500–1700)*, Rennes: Presses universitaires de Rennes, 2006.

Lombard, D. and Aubin, J. (eds), *Asian Merchants and Businessmen in the Indian Ocean and the China Sea*, New Delhi and New York: Oxford University Press, 2000.

Machado, P., *Ocean of Trade: South Asian Merchants, Africa and the Indian Ocean, c. 1750–1850*, Cambridge: Cambridge University Press, 2014.

Maldonado, L., 'Negocios e Integración Social Del Comerciante Marsellés Pedro Choly', *Revista de Historia Moderna: Anales de La Universidad de Alicante* 11 (1992), pp. 79–94.

Martin, F., *A History of the Bouligny Family and Allied Families*, Lafayette: The Center for Louisiana Studies. University of Southwestern Louisiana, 1990.

Martín Corrales, E., *Comercio de Cataluña con el Mediterráneo musulmán (siglos XVI–XVIII): el comercio con 'los enemigos de la fe'*, Barcelona: Bellaterra, 2001.

Martínez Ruiz, J.I. and Gaucci, P., *Mercaderes ingleses en Alicante en el siglo XVII: estudio y edición de la correspondencia comercial de Richard Houncell & Co.*, Alicante: Universidad de Alicante, 2008.

Martínez Shaw, C., *Cataluña en la carrera de Indias: 1680–1756*, Barcelona: Crítica, 1981.

Marzagalli, S., Ghazali, M. and Windler, Ch. (eds.), *Les Consuls En Méditerranée, Agents D'information, XVIe–XXe Siècle*, Paris: Classiques Garnier, 2015.

McCusker, J.J. and Morgan, K. (eds.), *The Early Modern Atlantic Economy*, Cambridge and New York: Cambridge University Press, 2000.

Miller, P.N., *The Sea: Thalassography and Historiography. Bard Graduate Center Cultural Histories of the Material World*, Ann Arbor: University of Michigan Press, 2013.

Molas Ribalta, P., *Comerç i estructura social a Catalunya i Valencia als segles XVII i XVIII*, Barcelona: Curial, 1977.

Montero Llácer, F.J., *El océano Pacífico: conmemoración 500 años de su descubrimiento*, Madrid: Fundación Ramón Areces, 2014.

Norwich, J.J., *The Middle Sea: A History of the Mediterranean*, London: Chatto & Windus, 2006.

Oostindie, G. (ed.), *Dutch Atlantic Connections, 1680–1800: Linking Empires, Bridging Borders*, Atlantic World: Europe, Africa and the Americas, Vol. 29, Leiden and Boston: Brill, 2014.

Pearson, M.N., *The Indian Ocean. Seas in History*, London and New York: Routledge, 2003.

Pearson, M.N. (ed), *The World of the Indian Ocean, 1500–1800: Studies in Economic, Social, and Cultural History*, Aldershot: Ashgate, 2005.

Pérez-García, M., *Vicarious Consumers: Trans-National Meetings Between The West and East in the Mediterranean World (1730–1808)*, Farnham: Ashgate, 2013.

Pérez Sarrión, G., *La Península Comercial: Mercado, Redes Sociales Y Estado en España En El Siglo XVIII*, Madrid: Marcial Pons, 2012.

Pietschmann, H. (ed.), *Atlantic History: History of the Atlantic System 1580–1830*, Göttingen: Vandenhoeck & Ruprecht, 2002.

Piterberg, G., Ruiz, T.F and Symcox, G., *Braudel Revisited: The Mediterranean World, 1600–1800*, Toronto: University of Toronto Press, 2010.

Putnam, L., 'To Study the Fragments/Whole: Microhistory and the Atlantic World', *Journal of Social History,* 39:3, 2006, pp. 615–630.

Ribeiro da Silva, F., *Dutch and Portuguese in Western Africa: Empires, Merchants and the Atlantic System, 1580–1674.* Atlantic World: Europe, Africa and the Americas, 1500–1830, Vol. 22, Leiden and Boston: Brill, 2011.

Rogles Hernández, M.A, 'La Inmigración En Alicante (1650–1799)', *Revista de Historia Moderna: Anales de La Universidad de Alicante,* 4 (1984), pp. 387–415.

Salas Auséns, J.A, *En busca de El Dorado: Inmigración francesa en la España Moderna,* Historia de la población 6, Bilbao: Universidad del País Vasco, 2009.

Schulte Beerbühl, M., *The Forgotten Majority: German Merchants in London, Naturalization, and Global Trade, 1660–1815,* New York, Oxford: Berghahn Books, 2015.

Seguí Romá, V., 'Comerciantes extranjeros en Alicante (1700–1750): hombres de negocios franceses y genoveses en una ciudad mediterránea', PhD dissertation: Universidad de Alicante, 2012, pp. 11–94. http://rua.ua.es/dspace/handle/10045/27146.

Studnicki-Gizbert, D., *A Nation Upon the Ocean Sea: Portugal's Atlantic Diaspora and the Crisis of the Spanish Empire, 1492–1640,* Oxford, New York: Oxford University Press, 2007.

Takeda, J.K., *Between Crown and Commerce: Marseille and the Early Modern Mediterranean.* The Johns Hopkins University Studies in Historical and Political Science, Baltimore: Johns Hopkins University Press, 2011.

Trivellato, F., 'Les juifs d'origine portugaise entre Livourne, le Portugal et la Méditerranée (c. 1650-1750)', *Arquivos do Centro Cultural Calouste Gulbenkian,* XLVIII: La Diaspora des "Nouveaux-Chrétiens", (2004), pp. 171–182.

———. *The Familiarity of Strangers: The Sephardic Diaspora, Livorno, and Cross-Cultural Trade in the Early Modern Period,* New Haven: Yale University Press, 2009.

———. 'Is There a Future for Italian Microhistory in the Age of Global History?', *California Italian Studies,* 2 (1), 2011. http://escholarship.org/uc/item/0z94n9hq

Verlinden, Ch., 'Les Origines Coloniales de La Civilisation Atlantique: Antecedents et Types de Structure', *Journal of World History* 1:1, 1953, pp. 378–398.

Villar, J.B. and Lourido, R., *Relaciones entre España y el Magreb, siglos XVII y XVIII,* Madrid: MAPFRE,1992.

Worthington, D., *British and Irish Experiences and Impressions of Central Europe, c.1560–1688,* Burlington: Ashgate, 2012.

Zamora Rodríguez, F., *La 'Pupilla Dell' Occhio Della Toscana' Y La Posición Hispánica En El Mediterráneo Occidental (1677–1717),* Madrid: Fundación Española de Historia Moderna, 2013.

Part IV

The complexity of networks

Formal and informal exchange
mechanisms and rupture of
merchant cooperation

10 Hides and the Hispanic monarchy

From contraband to royal privilege[1]

Bethany Aram

Cattle hides have been scorned as 'virtually the offal of the Indies' and relatively neglected in the historiography.[2] Among exceptions to a common disdain for hides, Lorenzo López y Sebastián and Justo L. del Río Moreno have emphasised the importance of their production on Hispañola,[3] and Carla Rahn Phillips has called attention to the value of American skins registered in Atlantic trade, as recorded by Pierre and Huguette Chaunu, Eufemio Lorenzo Sanz and others.[4] The importance of the extension of livestock production in the conquest of the Americas – from the availability of meat to the transformation of ecosystems and the propagation of crowd diseases – is increasingly recognised,[5] as is the growing demand for leather in early modern European and American markets.[6]

American hides played multiple roles. In addition to 'bulking up' ships laden with high-value, low-weight products, bovine hides provided ready packaging for a range of goods, and even a coveted commodity themselves. Capable of 'hiding' the goods they conveyed, raw or cured skins from the Caribbean, New Spain and South America could facilitate contraband in a variety of genres. While transporting products including tobacco, ginger and indigo across the Atlantic, these cattle hides also proved attractive loot and valuable merchandise in their own right. Hides were used to make a variety of products including saddles, saddlebags, furniture, tablecloths, parchment, decorated wallpaper and shoes, and constituted an important export from Spanish America to Italy, France, England and the Low Countries.[7] Officially, they had to be registered and taxed in Seville, where the crown established its House of Trade in 1503 to regulate commerce between Europe and the Americas.[8]

This chapter will explore some of the Hispanic monarchy's efforts to regulate and profit from a healthy, if potentially hidden, commerce in American cattle skins. Specifically, in an attempt to curtail contraband, the government of Philip II began a policy, continued under Philip III, of issuing licences to re-export American hides from Iberian ports (particularly Sanlúcar de Barrameda and Cádiz) to markets in Florence, Antwerp, London and Rouen. After a brief look at the Caribbean cradle for American hides, which attracted corsairs and fostered the emergence of buccaneers, this chapter will analyse official licences to export hides and the effects of Spanish policies that contrasted with those pursued by the

English crown. In an attempt to regulate the redistribution of American leather, the Hispanic monarchy drew upon a multigenerational network of patronage in the royal service, rewarding and compensating loyal servants with export licences. In this way, permissions to export hides from Castile offer a case study of efforts to regulate and reinforce an informal economy of favours. While potentially detrimental to royal income, the distribution of licences to export hides bolstered royal authority in other ways.

The Caribbean cradle

European animals, especially cattle, reproduced themselves throughout Spanish America with devastating success. The inexorable propagation of livestock in the Americas after Christopher Columbus transported cows from the Canary Islands to Hispaniola in 1493 is well known, especially in the case of Mexico.[9] Drawing upon an important tradition from the Iberian Peninsula, Hispaniola's colonial elite readily invested in ranches and livestock, and began exporting cattle hides.[10] As early as 1526, Gonzalo Fernández de Oviedo recorded the spectacular growth of Iberian bovine stock on Hispaniola: 'for, in truth, the land has the best pastures in the world for this type of livestock, with very lovely waters and temperate airs, so that the cattle are bigger and more beautiful than in all of Spain; and since the weather in those parts is not cold, they are never weak or bad-tasting'.[11] An English participant in the seizure of San Juan de Puerto Rico in 1597 reported the great value of the island's hides, given the steers' greater size than those raised in England.[12] Corroborating such testimony, the Dutch sailor A.O. Exquemeling described the hides industry on Hispaniola in the 1670s, and the skill of 'hunters and butchers' in 'flaying the beasts that are killed'. On Hispaniola, Exquemeling observed: 'The wild bulls are of a vast corpulency, or bigness of body', producing hides from 11 to 13 feet, or 3.4 to 4 meters long.[13] According to such testimony, their size distinguished American cattle and, consequently, hides, from the European varieties. Indeed, while the costs of trans-Atlantic transport and insurance would have been significant, the size of American skins could further explain why 'West Indian hides' were worth 0.31 to 0.58 guilders/pound, or two to three times more than 'native salted hides' (0.12 to 0.18 guilders/pound), in Amsterdam from 1624 through 1654.[14]

Because of the importance of stock raising to Hispaniola's economy, its elites regularly requested and received royal intervention to protect their investment. In response to the pleas of the ubiquitous Gonzalo Fernández de Oviedo on behalf of Santo Domingo and its Royal Tribunal (Audiencia) in 1548, the crown allowed hides to be tanned on the island and exported from it.[15] By the mid-1570s, another royal official, the licentiate Alonso Estevez, asked the crown to renew prohibitions of the slaughter of female cattle to protect the industry from over-exploitation,[16] declaring: 'beef in this land is like bread and wine in Castile', and 'hides are money here and in Castile'.[17] Estevez, who had resided in Santo Domingo for some 28 years, suffered from gout,[18] which was widely attributed to the excessive consumption of meat. Like Fernández de Oviedo, Estevez expressed concern at the decline in cattle, which sustained the island's irreversibly transformed population and economy. Beef, he argued, had become a basic necessity on Hispaniola. Moreover, with the island's supply of gold exhausted by the 1520s, skins served as a kind of currency.[19] Sailors were sometimes remunerated in hides,[20] and one delegate to the court from Santo Domingo's Municipal Council and Royal Tribunal even litigated to have his salary paid against taxes on exports of hides and sugar.[21]

American delegates to the King and Royal Council, while seeking protectionist measures on Hispaniola, decried them in Seville. In 1554, Santo Domingo's Municipal Council and Royal Tribunal sent another representative, Baltazar García, to seek royal favour in Brussels and Castile. Five out of twenty nine points the town council instructed García to press at court decried the effects of royal attempts to centralise trade in Seville. On the one hand, García argued that foreigners should be permitted to settle on Hispaniola and trade for hides and sugar in Santo Domingo, 'without having to pass first through the hole of the river of Seville for no reason'.[22] According to García's instructions, Seville's municipal restrictions, which only allowed the sale of hides to the city's tanners and shoemakers, kept their price artificially low and prevented their redistribution. Exacerbating this situation, laws passed in the Cortes of Castile prohibited the export of leather from the kingdom, so that Caribbean hides sent to Seville could no longer proceed legally to Venice, Florence, Barcelona and Valencia by sea or to Portugal and Aragon by land. Opposing the 'tyranny' of the merchants of Triana (Seville), Santo Domingo's town council argued that the English, Dutch and Genoese should be permitted to trade freely along the coast of Hispaniola, as they did in the Canary Islands.[23] According to García, Hispaniola produced more than 100,000 hides per year and suffered annual damages worth more than 100,000 ducats due to Seville's restrictions. Finally, the Tribunal and City Council requested exemption from the requirement of passing through Seville for cargoes containing hides and sugar 'and other merchandise of the land' without precious metals.[24] In response to this petition, Charles V decreed that ships from Hispaniola and San Juan de Puerto Rico could unload hides and other merchandise in Cádiz as long as it was registered and any precious metals were sent on to Seville. Without going so far as to allow foreigners to trade directly with Hispaniola, the crown exempted merchandise designed for re-export from the obligation of passing through Seville as early as 1558.[25]

The monarchy's early measures to facilitate the re-exportation of hides from Cádiz or Sanlúcar offered an alternative to contraband or direct trade between Hispaniola and hide-hungry French, English and Dutch merchants or privateers who plagued the early modern Caribbean. Even official sources reveal local dependency upon these foreigners and collaboration with them based on different degrees of coercion and need. For example, in 1548 the *Audiencia* of Santo Domingo informed the Emperor that corsairs lurked in the area, while the island's inhabitants, having awaited ships from Castile for over eight months, lacked bread and wine, and could obtain other goods only at excessive prices.[26]

Under such circumstances, it seemed hard to imagine that prohibitions on trade with corsairs would be heeded. The following year, Santo Domingo's Royal Tribunal reminded the Emperor that foreigners habitually sought to trade along the coasts of Hispaniola and Jamaica. Although the port of Yaguna, on the north of Hispaniola, usually resisted them, the corsairs had allegedly 'landed by force and made the householders buy their cloth and wine and other things they brought, constrained by necessity'.[27] The island's residents mainly traded hides for European goods otherwise unavailable or prohibitively expensive.[28] The *Audiencia*'s reports suggest that illegal trade continued and even increased. Regardless of the restrictions in place in Seville, the 'high price' of Caribbean hides in 1553 allegedly led to meat shortages. According to the Royal Tribunal at Santo Domingo, too many young bulls had been slaughtered simply for their hides, requiring further measures to prevent their extinction.[29]

Merchant-corsairs in the sixteenth-century Caribbean sought hides for the expanding tanning industries, particularly in Northern Europe, offering African slaves and European goods in exchange.[30] These adventurer-interlopers obtained hides through a combination of intimidation and cooperation. One of their beneficiaries and victims, a stock-raiser from Santo Domingo, Lázaro Bejarano, reported an encounter with John Hawkins in 1565.[31] The coercive yet conciliatory privateer demanded hides and offered to pay for them, indicating that he could also barter slaves from Guinea, silks or gold. Hawkins nevertheless held Bejarano hostage on his ship until he received the hides.[32] According to C. Harding, Hawkins invested the proceeds from the sale of 300 slaves from Sierra Leone in the acquisition of additional hides, sending half of them to England and the other half, remarkably, to Seville in Spanish vessels.[33]

Hides lured contrabandists and privateers to Hispaniola. Direct commerce in hides between Santo Domingo and Rouen has been documented as early as 1572.[34] A royal investigator (*visitador*) sent to Hispaniola in 1584 advised the King that French traders and privateers loaded hides on the island's northern coasts and from its rivers with impunity, 'sending them all to France'.[35] Wild cattle and their hunters, the original buccaneers, proliferated on west and northwest Hispaniola. Indeed, the word 'buccaneer' derives from the term used to refer to the animal's smoked flesh or 'boucan'.[36] Eventually, the corsairs who traded with the original buccaneers and, more generally, the French, Dutch and English privateers who raided Spain's overseas possessions were also described as 'buccaneers'.

These privateers were far from the only, or even the main threat facing vessels bound for Seville. Beginning in the late sixteenth century, the city's Consulate regulated the enforcement of insurance policies, some of which covered cargoes of hides, and often in combination with ginger, sugar or tobacco. A sample of claims on insurance for hides presented between 1590 and 1623, indicate that most of the losses were attributed to Turkish, Dutch, French and English corsairs, with a growing threat from the Turkish privateers, in particular, after 1616. In the sample overall, pirates who robbed insured ships, identified simply as 'enemies' on one occasion, were described as 'Turks' five times, as 'English' only three times,

'French' twice and 'Dutch' once. On the other hand, 40 per cent of the insurance claims recorded bad weather, shipwrecks and even bad luck as motives for the losses, as seen in the Appendix at the end of this chapter.[37]

In addition to claims on insurance policies, the archive of the Chamber of Commerce/Consulate of Seville contains visits to ships as well as the denunciations and seizures of goods that arrived unregistered.[38] Seizures of goods by the officials at Seville's House of Trade indicate that hides often were among the articles impounded as contraband.[39] Indeed, the seizures of unregistered hides recorded in the General Archive of the Indies invites the suspicion that many more may have gone undetected. One historian has even suggested that goods (Pacific slaves, in the case she examined) were embargoed mainly when their owners refused to pay the bribes that officials requested in order to facilitate contraband.[40]

Insurance claims also can be complemented by the reports of sailors who survived pirate attacks. In 1561, the mariner, Tomé Jorge lost 40 hides when French corsairs boarded and robbed a ship from Santo Domingo commanded by Gaspar Hernández, who allegedly had issued hides to the crew as part of their pay.[41] Another mariner, Juan Estevan, reported being seized by the English with the vessel he accompanied from Cuba, and forced to sail to Falmouth on a ship originally from Santo Domingo and laden with sugar, hides and ginger, along with 50 other Castilians and Portuguese. The English took Estevan with these ships to the port of Falmouth, where they sold the merchandise and permitted him to escape. Returning to his home in Sanlúcar de Barrameda via Saint-Malo, France and Lisbon, the mariner informed the Duke of Medina Sidonia that he had observed the English preparing a large fleet.[42] War with the English and Dutch magnified the threat posed by their privateers. Meanwhile, officials on Hispaniola insisted that the French continued trading with impunity on the island's north shore, disseminating Protestant propaganda and sending over 50,000 hides directly to France each year.[43] In February 1601, captains sailing from Santo Domingo reported eleven Flemish ships on the same island's coast, 'trading with the locals as securely as if in their own land, and even dispersed in the rivers, awaiting their cargoes of hides and ginger.'[44] Such Caribbean contraband appeared almost comfortable for northern European corsairs. At the same time, English State Papers for colonial affairs adopted references to Atlantic products to code correspondence that might be intercepted. Specifically, the term 'raw hides' was used to refer to ships, Scots were denoted as 'shoemakers', Spain called 'Mr Steward', 'religion' coded as 'ginger', 'sugar' as 'heresy', and 'Holland cheese' invoked to signify 'money'.[45] Whatever their uses, such commodities had become ubiquitous.

As in the case of slave labour, European expansion facilitated new sources of bovine hides and unprecedented demands for them. Merchants, like pirates, discovered that American hides sold well throughout Europe. Specifically, the merchant Simón Ruíz and his agents in Seville found it useful to trade debts for hides and export the skins to Italy, where they could be redeemed in cash, undoubtedly at a profit.[46] In marked contrast to English policy, rather than prohibiting the re-exportation of hides, the Hispanic monarchy sought to regulate and benefit from their redistribution. Drawing upon precedents from licencing the exportation of slaves and other 'prohibited merchandise', the Hispanic monarchy took steps to make the export of hides a privilege dependent upon the royal will. In this way, royal licences to re-export American hides made them more visible and useful for the monarchy. The monarchy used licences to export hides to reinforce and reward the loyalty of cities, monasteries, servants and families. The decision to issue such licences showed that the crown needed and valued these networks of supporters more than the fees due on the export of a specific commodity. Rather than imposing its norms on these networks, the monarchy nourished them with the fruits of overseas expansion. The imperial venture required their allegiance.

From hiding out to outing hides

The demand for leather in Renaissance Europe made the re-exportation of bovine hides from Seville, Cádiz and Sanlúcar a lucrative business.[47] By licensing the export of hides, Philip II sought to combat corsairs and contraband, while garnering revenues for the royal treasury. From 1563 through the 1620s, however, licences to re-export American hides also became a source of rewards and, specifically, cost-of-living supplements (*ayudas de costa*) for royal servants. Servants' demands for licences, recorded in the *Cámara de Castilla* section of the General Archive of Simancas, suggest that the alleged 'offal of the Indies' offered royal servants a stake in the redistribution of colonial products. By 1617, questions emerged about whether or not adopting the *asiento* system of licencing the export of hides to a single merchant or company might prove more efficient. The ensuing debates cast light on the interests and loose ties crucial to informally regulated sectors of the economy. In 1563, as well as 1617, with respect to hides the crown of Castile favoured 'exceptional' permissions and the informal ties they reinforced instead of monopolistic regulations.

Although Hispaniola obtained royal authorization in 1556 to re-export half of its hides 'for a limited time', the permission quickly became a pretext to re-export many more hides than allowed, not only from Hispaniola, but also from Puerto Rico, New Spain and Cuba. According to one report, American hides were redistributed from Cádiz with the collusion of the city's governor, who charged one *Real* for every hide dispatched for Italy, Catalonia, France or other territories. In this way, the exportation of over 60,000 cattle hides from Cadiz each year led to an illicit annual profit of the same number of *Reales*.[48] To make matters worse from the standpoint of royal revenues, these hides may have wrapped and concealed or, quite literally, hidden, other merchandise from tobacco to ginger. Informed of such practices and aware of the potential for fraud, the crown attempted to exert greater control over export licences.

In 1569, Philip II began remunerating servants with licences to re-export hides from Seville and Cadiz, a practice that would flourish into the seventeenth century.[49] Although the subject requires more systematic study, a sample of 136 licences preserved in the Cámara de Castilla section of the General Archive of Simancas from

1569 through 1615, clearly among many more issued, indicates that recipients of licences to export hides ranged from mid-level servants of the royal household (17 guards, 12 lodgers or *aposentadores*, 4 archers, stablemen, fur-makers, soldiers, etc.) to more elite members of the bureaucracy (2 accountants). Retainers were granted licences to export 1,000, 2,000, 3,000, or up to 9,000 skins, in accordance with their social status and needs.[50] Most recipients of the licences to export hides alleged years of loyal service and debts incurred, for example, to accompany Philip II to Portugal in 1580 (in eight cases). In addition to (relative) poverty and necessity, candidates for hide licences often invoked illnesses, injuries or dependent spouses and children to win royal favor. A number of servants requested hides when other privileges turned out 'uncertain' or had first sought different grants, favors or positions, but turned to hides when advised to seek an alternative.[51] Such was the case of Hernán Arias, a householder who requested licences in order to pay ransom for a captive son;[52] or the royal chefs, Francisco de Cubille and Francisco de Jatalán, who initially had requested offices in the Indies to complement their salaries, yet had been told to 'find something else'.[53] Other servants sought to recover costs incurred in the royal service, as in the case of *guarda mangiers* who had been charged for spoiled food.[54] In a modest way, licences to export hides enabled members of the royal household to engage in commerce that connected the court to mercantile activities and ports where it thrived.[55]

Licences to export hides also became a form of grace or favor that the crown could bestow upon retainers to remedy their travails. Within the context of restricted exports, servants' needs justified exceptions to the protectionist goal of keeping American leather in Castile. Permissions to export hides to reward servants reinforced their place in the hierarchy of the court as well as their ties to each other and to the crown itself, not to mention connections with the American colonies where the hides were produced and the European territories where they were marketed. Not surprisingly, petitioners for hide licences reported service to the crown in Flanders, Portugal, England and Italy and multigenerational traditions of sacrifice for the monarchy. Service and necessity proved the common denominator in grants to export hides.

The largest grants of licences examined went to the Convent of Nuestra Señora de la Merced in Madrid and to the city of Seville. The Madrid convent requested 10,000 licences to restore its sacristy and ornaments after a fire, and subsequently 30,000 more to finance continued repairs.[56] By far the largest block of export permissions issued – for no fewer than 70,000 hides – went to the city of Seville in 1569 to compensate the costs of its recovery from the plague as well as that of sending 2,000 foot soldiers against the *Morisco* uprising in Granada.[57] The export of so many hides, overseen by the count of Barajas, could not be achieved in two years, and required an additional term.[58] Such extensions, when requested and granted, reveal the degree to which the demand for hides and licences to export them could exceed the American supply reaching Cádiz and Seville.

On the other hand, most grants to export hides from 1569 through 1615 were conceded to servants based on particular hardships in the royal service. Debts were among the most frequent causes and calamities cited, even leading to imprisonment in one case.[59] Grants in hides could also compensate authors for their expenses: The mule driver Juan de Valverde requested 6,000 hides for 'his efforts to compose and print a book about working the land with oxen and other things regarding the government and growth of these kingdoms' and the licentiate Lara (possibly Juan de Mal Lara) requested 4,000 licences to compensate him for the effort of writing 'diverse books' (in addition to an illness that he suffered) in 1580, whereas the doctor D[o]uay requested permission to export 3,000 or 4,000 hides in order to print books of Herodotus that he had translated in 1605.[60] Like the crown, its servants had recourse to hide licences in the absence of other sources of funds.

Although the licencing system reinforced ties of service and loyalty to the crown, it also entailed disadvantages that became apparent in the 1610s. In particular, royal officials denounced the potential for fraud in the unlicenced export of hides through Vizcaya, Galicia and Portugal. Opportunities for fraud emerged when merchants were permitted to export hides after depositing sums in Seville, which they redeemed upon presenting testimony from the authorities of San Sebastián, Pontevieja, Bayona in Galicia, or other ports, that the hides had, in fact, gone there.[61] Some local authorities proved more rigorous than others, and insisted on having the hides disembarked from the ships in order to register them on the docks.[62] After signing the requisite papers, however, the same officials could do little to prevent and much to ignore or simply permit the same cargoes' continuation to France, Flanders or England without export licences. In the midst of concerns about fraud and its impact upon crown finances, figures offered by the royal official in charge of recording leather exported from Seville, Juan Ramírez de Rivera (in the office previously held by his father, Sebastián Ramírez), pointed to a rather limited and declining phenomenon. According to Ramírez de Rivera, the number of hides sent to Galicia from Seville had decreased from 3,356 in 1610 to 300 in 1614, rising only slightly to 520 in 1615. When consulted on the matter, the local governor upheld the scribe's allegations that no more than 840 hides had been sent to Galicia and Vizcaya between 1614 and 1616.[63]

Ramírez de Rivera and a royal informant asked to study the matter, Juan de Samaniego, attributed a decline in royal revenues from the licensing and export of hides not to fraud, but rather to a new 10 per cent tax on the export of 'prohibited goods' through Portugal and the granting of too many licences. The practice of including leather in a new tax on prohibited goods sent from Castile through Portugal, the *diezmeño*, facilitated hides' redistribution without the purchase of licences worth two *Reales* for each hide.[64] Yet the *diezmeño* alone could not be blamed for the drastic drop in the sale (and value) of export licences.[65] In addition to the new outlet for hides through Portugal, Samaniego pointed to another problem: The crown went from issuing 50 or 60 of these licences per year in the 1570s to granting 400000 licences annually by the 1610s. Samaniego argued that the King could not expect to profit from the sale of additional licences if the number issued already exceeded the demand for hides in France and Flanders. Given the worthy and deserving nature of most recipients, the inspector observed that granting so many licences led to embarrassing situations.[66]

Anonymous recommendations sent to the King from 'a well-intentioned person' in 1617 corroborated the idea that grants in licences to export hides no longer benefitted royal servants. Perhaps exaggerating the situation, the anonymous person claimed that the crown had assigned its servants cost-of-living supplements (*ayudas de costa*) in hides to the point that some 600,000 licences had been granted that could not be used in many years, so that some recipients were forced to sell the licences, which had once been worth up to 2.5 *Reales*, at 12 or 14 *maravedies* each. In order to overcome the 'confusion and delays' that marked the re-export of American hides from Seville, the anonymous projector or *arbitrista* offered to purchase a contract or *asiento* to export hides from Seville for 16,000 ducats at the start, followed by 5,000 ducats per year. According to this projector, the crown would enjoy the advantage of a fixed rent, which could also prove more beneficial to its servants. Specifically, the investor requested the right to sell 6,000 licences per year in exchange for 5,000 ducats, offering to withhold one-fourth of the licences until those that the crown already had granted could be used. Otherwise, the projector argued, licences to export hides garnered 'poor servants' more frustrations than rewards.[67] The move to an *asiento* or single grant would offer more efficient and rational management, while potentially removing one fringe benefit available to royal servants. No evidence of the implementation of such an *asiento* for hides has been encountered, although grants in licences to export them barely appear in the archives after 1621.

Whether or not the Hispanic monarchy turned to fixed grants, it had acted to foment and profit from rather than to restrict the re-exportation of bovine hides. On the other hand, the sovereign of England, while also concerned about fraud, refused to licence such exports. Instead, given the 'great scarcity and extraordinary dearness of leather', James I banned the removal of 'any raw hydes or any leather, either into any foreign countries beyond the Seas or into Scotland'. The English king emphasised that 'extraordinary provisions' for the navy included hides, since they were essential for making boots and shoes. Given its strategic importance, James I refused to licence the export of leather and prohibited any attempt to transport it 'secretly, and by stealth' to other kingdoms.[68] Hence, the English crown, having encouraged the seizure and even the purchase of Spanish hides, prohibited the exportation of its homegrown stock.

Large bovine hides produced in Spanish America offered merchants and monarchs benefits. Rather than imposing monopolistic or proto-mercantilist policies, from the midsixteenth century, and in contrast to the English monarch, the King of Spain took measures to facilitate the re-exportation of American hides. Remarkably, the crown of Castile authorised the redistribution of leather from Hispaniola that reached Cádiz without passing through Seville in the 1550s. At the end of the following decade, Philip II began using licences to export hides as rewards for loyal servants who reported a range of particular hardships from debts to illnesses, which they requested support to affront. The licences granted reinforced these servants' multigenerational loyalty to the crown, which in some cases included service in hide-hungry areas such as England, the Low Countries and Italy, and strengthened their commercial connections. Rather than hoarding hides, the monarchy took advantage of the European-wide demand for them. By the 1610s, however, it had licenced the export of more skins than reached the Iberian Peninsula and confronted signs that its attempted largess had become counterproductive. Although the system of individual licences broke down, no evidence has been found to date for the adoption of a single concession or *asiento* system for hides. However inefficiently, the monarchy had issued small-scale grants to reward personal service.

When the Hispanic monarchy considered more profit-oriented policies, the English crown insisted on protectionism. A clear contrast between Spanish and English measures to regulate the circulation of hides suggests that their abundance in Spanish America made them potentially more of a commercial, and less of a strategic, product in Spain. Philip II and Philip III facilitated the export of hides to raise revenues and to reinforce servants' loyalty. James I, on the other hand, insisted that leather be retained for the navy. Yet all three monarchs considered hides a crucial commodity and regulated their use accordingly. In the process, they reinforced the loyalty of mobile servants and articulated strategic priorities.

Appendix

Motives for insurance claims on cargoes of hides registered in Seville's Chamber of Commerce (Cámara de Comercio)

Record of claim	Vessel	Year	Cargo	Motive for claim
Consulados, 431, N.6	Santa Ana	1590	sugar, ginger, hides	bad weather, shipwreck
Consulados, 432, N.11	el filibote nombrado la Fortuna	1595	hides, ginger, sugar	English corsairs
Consulados, 437, N.9	El Unicornio	1595	hides, sugar, ginger	overcome in battle with Dutch
Consulados, 434, N.2	el navío El Espíritu Santo	1596	hides, Campeche wood	bad luck ("caso fortuito")
Consulados, 434, N.7	navío nombrado Nuestra Señora de Candelaria	1598	sugar and other merchandise	English corsairs
Consulados, 437, N.5	não San Antonio	1606	hides, sugar, ginger	water

(*continued*)

Record of claim	Vessel	Year	Cargo	Motive for claim
Consulados, 437, N.6	San Luis	1606	hides, sugar, ginger	bad weather, shipwreck
Consulados, 437, N.2	El Espíritu Santo, El San Luis, Nuestra Señora de la Concepción	1606	sugar, hides, ginger	enemies
Consulados, 437, N.4	San Miguel	1606	hides, ginger, other merchandise	shipwreck
Consulados, 422, N.3	la não del maestre Bartolomé de Medina	1612	hides, other merchandise	seized by English
Consulados, 424, N.7	Nuestra Señora del Rosario	1615	tobacco, hides, ginger, sugar	robbed by French
Consulados, 424, N.11	Nuestra Señora del Rosario	1616	hides, ginger, palos, tabacco	seized by Turks
Consulados, 417, N.12	Nuestra Señora de la Concepción	1621	hides, sugar, other merchandise	Turkish corsairs
Consulados, 418, N.6	el navío Nuestra Señora de la Limpia Concepción	1622	hides, ginger, Reales	seized by Turks
Consulados, 418, N.9	la não nombrada San Joan Bautista	1622	hides, ginger, Reales	storm
Consulados, 418, N.21	Nuestra Señora de Atocha y San Antonio	1622		shipwreck fleeing from Turks
Consulados, 418, N.3	la não San Ignacio	1623	hides	storm
Consulados, 419, N.17	Santa Catalina	1623	hides	bad weather, shipwreck
Consulados, 419, N.20	não Consolación	1623	hides, sarsaparilla, tobacco	seized by French corsair
Consulados, 419, N.22	navío San Francisco	1623		Turkish attack

Notes

1 Work on this chapter has been financed by Spain's Ministry of Science and Innovation through the Ramón y Cajal program, RYC-2012-10358 and, initially, by the Junta de Andalucía's Proyecto de Excelencia, P09-HUM 5330. The author is grateful to Marina Alfonso Mola and the members of the Early Modern History seminar at Cambridge University, particularly Melissa Calaresu and Ulinka Rublack, as well as the editors, for their suggestions.

2 K.R. Andrews, *The Spanish Caribbean: Trade and Plunder 1530–1630* (London: Yale University Press, 1978), p. 195.

3 L.E. López y Sebastián and J.L. del Río Moreno, 'La ganadería vacuna en la isla Española (1508–1587)', *Revista Complutense de Historia de América* 25 (1 January 1999): 11.

4 C.R. Phillips, 'Trade in the Iberian Empires, 1450–1750', *The Rise of Merchant Empires: Long-distance Trade in the Early Modern World, 1350–1750*, J.D. Tracy (ed.) (Cambridge: Cambridge University Press, 1990), pp. 34–101, esp. p. 79 and Table 2.4. See also E. Lorenzo Sanz, *El comercio de España con América en la época de Felipe II* (Valladolid: Servicio de Publicaciones de la Diputacion Provincial, 1979), vols. I and II.

5 A.W. Crosby, *Ecological Imperialism: The Biological Expansion of Europe 900–1900* (Cambridge: Cambridge University Press, 1986), p. 177; idem, *The Columbian Exchange: Biological and Cultural Consequences of 1492* (Westport: Praeger, 2003); F. Chevalier, *La Formación de los latifundios en México: Haciendas y sociedad en los siglos XVI, XVII Y XVIII* (Mexico: Fondo de Cultura Económica, 1999), esp. pp. 117–142.

6 U. Rublack, 'Matter in the Material Renaissance', *Past and Present* 219, no. 1 (2013): 41–85. On the Dutch demand for hides, see C.Ch. Goslinga, *The Dutch in the Caribbean and on the Wild Coast, 1580–1680* (Gainesville: University of Florida Press, 1971), pp. 53–55.

7 See G. Anes Álvarez de Castrillón, 'Tejidos, Corambre y Leyes en la Castilla del Siglo XVI', *Anuario de Estudios Atlánticos* 50, no. 1 (2004): 457–476 as well as R. Córdoba de la Llave and P. Hernández Íñigo, 'El Utillaje de los Transportes en la Andalucía del descubrimiento', *Historia, Instituciones, Documentos* 30 (2003): 159–179.

8 For a critical view of the 'Seville monopoly' over trade, see J.M. Oliva Melgar, 'Realidad y ficción en el Monopolio de Indias: Una reflexión sobre el sistema imperial español en el Siglo XVII', *Manuscrits: Revista d'història moderna* 11(14) (1992): 34–47 and, more recently, idem, 'El Monopolio de Indias en el siglo XVII y la economía Andaluza: Un apunte sobre el origen del atraso económico en Andalucía', *Archivo hispalense: Revista histórica, literaria y artística*, 95, 288 (2012): 167–194.

9 E.G.K. Melville, 'Land Use and the Transformation of the Environment', in *The Cambridge Economic History of Latin America* (Cambridge: Cambridge University Press, 2006), pp. 109–142; idem, 'Conquest Landscapes. Ecological Consequences of Pastoralism in the New World', in *Le Nouveau Monde-Mondes Nouveaux. L'Experience Americaine* (Paris: Ecole des Hautes Études en Sciences Sociales, 1996), pp. 99–113; A.S. Sluyter, 'The Ecological Origins and Consequences of Cattle Ranching in Sixteenth-Century New Spain', *Geographical Review*, 86:2 (1996): 161–177.

10 L.E. López y Sebastián and J.L. del Río Moreno, 'La ganadería vacuna en la isla Española', pp. 13–45.

11 '… y la verdad es que la tierra es de los mejores pastos del mundo para semejante ganado, y de muy lindas aguas y templados aires; y así, las reses son mayores y más hermosas … que todas las que hay en España; y como el tiempo en aquellas partes es suave y de ningún frío, nunca están flacas ni de mal sabor.' G. Fernádez de Oviedo, *Sumario de la Natural Historia de las Indias* (México: Fondo de Cultura Económica, 1950; orig. Toledo, 1526), ch. 2, f. 4v.

12 C. Coll y Toste, (ed.), 'La Toma Del Capital Por Cumberland', *Boletín Histórico de Puerto Rico*, V (1918): 40–70, esp. p. 65.

13 A.O. Exquemelin, *The Buccaneers of América* (New York: Dover Publications, 1967), pp. 18–19, 38.

14 Later on, hides from Brazil would also be worth more than those from Denmark, suggesting a greater value ascribed to American skins in general rather than to West Indian hides in particular. The Medieval and Early Modern Data Bank, incorporating the work of Posthumus and others, is based at Rutgers University. http://www2.scc.rutgers.edu/memdb/result_postpr.php?start=200, consulted 23 January 2014. N.W. Posthumus,

Inquiry into the History of Prices in Holland. Wholesale Prices at the Exchange of Amsterdam, 1585–1914; Rates of Exchange at Amsterdam, 1609–1914 (Leiden: E.J. Brill, 1946), Vol. I, pp. 162–164.

15 Archivo General de Indias (AGI), Justicia, 19, N.1, Accounts of Alonso de Peña, royal treasurer, undated. AGI, Indiferente, 1964, L.11, f.111, 'Real cédula al concejo de Sevilla para que, a petición de Gonzalo Hernández de Oviedo y el capitán Alonso de Peña, en nombre de la isla Española, dejen curtir los cueros que vienen de allí', 24 October 1548.

16 L.E. López y Sebastián and J.L. del Río Moreno, 'La ganadería vacuna en la isla Española', p. 30.

17 AGI, Santo Domingo, 71, L. 3, f. 44–49, Memorial by the Lic. Alonso Estevez, 31 March 1574.

18 AGI, Santo Domingo,71, L. 3, f. 50-53v, Alonso Estevez to the king, 15 March 1574.

19 C.H. Haring, *The Buccaneers in the West Indies in the XVII Century* (London: Methuen, 1910), pp. 45–66. Horses, donkeys, sheep and goats, certainly less abundant on the island, were also more carefully guarded. The use of leather and spices as currency has also been recorded among merchants associated with the Fuggers and the Hochstetters. J.A. Goris, *Étude sur les colonies marchandes méridionales (Portugais, Espagnols, Italiens) à Anvers de 1488 à 1567. Contribution à l'histoire des débuts du capitalisme moderne* (New York: Burt Franklin, 1971), p. 198.

20 AGI, Contratación 135A, N. 3, El fiscal vs. Tomé Jorge, mariner, who requested 40 hides proceeding from his salary. Four out of five other mariners paid in hides were identified as Portuguese.

21 AGI, Justicia, 19, N.1, 'Testimonio de la flota que partió de Santo Domingo que iba por capitán Juan Franco,' 20 April 1552.

22 AGI, Justicia 1002, N.1, R. 3, f. 29v-42v, 'Instrucciones del cabildo y regimiento de Santo Domingo al capitán Peña thesorero y a Baltasar Garcia vecino della de lo que había de suplicar y negociar ante Su Magestad en su real consejo de Yndias,' 13 April 1554.

23 The Audiencia of Santo Domingo reiterated this argument, stated in the 1554 instructions, two years later. See G. Rodríguez Morel (ed.), *Cartas del cabildo de Santo Domingo en el siglo XVI* (Santo Domingo: Editora Búho, 2011), p. 174, citing AGI, Santo Domingo 49, R.25, N.152, Audiencia to Philip II, 10 June 1556.

24 AGI, Justicia 1002, N.1, R. 3, f. 29v-42v. Difficulties in the re-export of hides from Seville are discussed in E. Lorenzo Sanz, *El Comercio de España con Amércia en la Época de Felipe II* (Valladolid: Servicio de Publicaciones de la Diputacion Provincial, 1979), I, p. 622.

25 AGI, Indiferente, 425, L.28, f.325v-327, Provision of Philip II, 3 April 1558; AGI, Indiferente,1966, L. 14, f. 104-106, Privileges to unload in Cádiz confirmed, 16 November 1561.

26 G.R. Morel, (ed.), *Cartas del cabildo de Santo Domingo*, p. 57 (AGI, Santo Domingo 49, R.18, N.114, The Audiencia of Hispañola to the Emperor, 16 October 1548).

27 G.R. Morel, (ed.), *Cartas del cabildo de Santo Domingo*, p. 70 (AGI, Santo Domingo 49, R.18, N.117).

28 For an account of the relationship between corsarism and contraband trade on Hispañola and the role of the Royal Tribunal, see E. Mira Caballos, *La Española, Epicentro del Caribe en el Siglo XVI* (Santo Domingo: Academia Dominicana de la Historia, 2010), pp. 543–555.

29 AGI, Santo Domingo 73, N. 107G, Chapters that the Visitor to Santo Domingo sent to his Magesty, 1584. G.R. Morel (ed.) *Cartas del cabildo de Santo Domingo*, p. 153 (AGI, Santo Domingo 49, R.18, N.142, Lic. Maldonado to the King, 13 November 1553).

30 M. Caballos, *La Española*, p. 548. On the importance of Dutch and English piracy for 'Sourcing' African Slaves, see J. Adelman, 'Mimesis and Rivalry: European Empires and Global Regimes', *Journal of Global History* 10, no. 1 (2015): 77–98, esp. 87.

31 G.R. Morel, (ed.), *Cartas del cabildo de Santo Domingo en el siglo XVI*, pp. 211–215. (AGI, Santo Domingo 50, R.3, N.5a, Information sent from the Audiencia of Santo Domingo to the King, 28 May 1565).

32 G.R. Morel, (ed.), *Cartas del cabildo de Santo Domingo en el siglo XVI*, pp. 211–215.

33 C.H. Haring, *The Buccaneers*, p. 37.

34 K.R. Andrews, *The Spanish Caribbean*, p. 181.

35 AGI, Santo Domingo 73, N. 107g, Chapters from the letter from the 'lord visitor' to the King, 1584.

36 C.H. Haring, *The Buccaneers*, p. 66.

37 The data provided in the Appendix at the end of this chapter comes from the 'Consulado' section of the Archivo General de la Cámara de Comercio de Sevilla (AGCOCINS), which the archivist, María del Carmen Maestre, kindly facilitated for consultation.

38 Archivo de la Cámara de Comercio de Sevilla (AGCOCINS), Consulados, 424, N. 11, 'Autos formados contra Francisco de Aspe, capitán y maestre, contra Alonso de Cepeda, capitán de la não San Francisco de Padua, Hernán Sánchez y otros por la aprensión de 444 cueros en la não Nuestra Señora de la Asunción y Diego de Segovia, artillero, y Francisco de la Torre Ayala', 1619–1620. AGI, Justicia, 870, N.2, The royal attorney vs. Francisco de Paradas, *vecino* of Cuba, 'sobre la entrega de 192 cueros que le trajeron de Santo Domingo,' 1564-7, and AGI, Justicia, 939, N. 10, The royal attorney vs. Sebastián Nieto, *vecino* of Seville, 'sobre comiso de 29 cajas de azúcar y 1.552 cueros', 1575. AGI, Contratación, 5738, N.1, R. 7, 'Comiso de 500 cueros, los 250 de toros y los otros 250 medianos desembarcados en San Lúcar,' 1635–1636.

39 AGI, Indiferente 1961, L.3, f. 287-288v, Royal instructions to the city and governor of Seville, regarding a case of contraband in hides, 16 June 1535.

40 T. Seijas, *Asian Slaves Colonial Mexico. From Chinos to Indians* (Cambridge: Cambridge University Press, 2014), pp. 88, 94.

41 AGI, Contratación 135A, N. 3, Tomé Jorge, mariner, vs. the royal attorney, 28 September 1562.

42 AGI, Indiferente 743, N. 5, Declaration of Juan Estevan, mariner, 22 December 1594.

43 AGI, Santo Domingo 74, N. 112, Royal officials at Santo Domingo to the King, 28 April 1579.

44 AGS, Estado 2636, f. 89, Consultation regarding a letter from the Duke of Medina Sidonia and Dutch trade in Santo Domingo, 17 February 1601.

45 'A collection of certain intercepted intelligence since Michaelmas', *Calendar of State Papers, Domestic Series of the Reign of Elizabeth, 1595–1597* (London: Longmans, Green, & Co., 1869), vol. CCLX, p. 118.

46 Archivo Histórico Provincial de Valladolid, Archivo Simón Ruiz, 7–150, Gonzalo de Villamizar to Simón Ruiz, 15 July 1568 and C 173-35, Pedro de Tolosa to Simón Ruíz, 22 May 1595.

47 G. Anes Álvarez de Castrillón, 'Tejidos, corambre y leyes en la Castilla del Siglo XVI,' pp. 453–454; E.M. Caballos, *La Española*, esp. p. 548. On the other hand, although English pirates in the Caribbean often seized hides, Kenneth Andrews did not consider them a 'valuable commodity'. K.R. Andrews, *The Spanish Caribbean*, pp. 181, 195.

48 AGS, CJH 49–58, 'Memoria de los cueros que se sacan', 16 March 1563.

49 Licenses to export American hides from Seville and Cadiz have been identified in the Archivo General de Simancas, Cámara de Castilla, legs. 496, 890 and 1059.

50 The sample is taken from AGS, Cámara de Castilla, legs. 496 and 1059.

51 AGS, CCA 496-182-2-34, 74, 71 y 46, Licenses for Juan de Croysi, Pedro Gonzalo de Sayavedra, San Juan de Liaño, y Cristóbal de Rivero, 1580.

52 AGS, CCA 496-182-2, Licenses to export 8000 hides to eight guards of the palace's front door (*porteros de cadena*), 1580.

53 AGS, CCA 496-182-2-37, Licenses for two cooks to export 4000 hides, 1580.

54 AGS, CCA 496-182-1 and 496-182-1, Licenses for Juan Fernández de Yzaguerre and Luis Carrera, *guardamangiers*, and Luis de Madrigal, *ayuda de guardamangier*, 1580.

55 Manuel Herrero Sánchez has pointed out that these licenses provided a nexus between historiographies that tend to ignore each other: those of court, on the one hand, and the urban mercantile elites, on the other.

56 AGS, CCA 496-182-2-51 and 76, Licenses for the Monastery of Nuestra Señora de la Merced of Valladolid and Madrid, 1580.

57 AGS, CCA 496-53, License for Seville to export 70,000 hides, 1571.

58 AGS, CCA 496-75, Extension on license granted to Seville and the count of Barajas, 23 December 1573.

59 AGS, CCA 496-182-2-24, Licenses for Juan Moriz, 1580.

60 ....'lo que ha travajado en componer e imprimer el libro que trata de labrar con los bueyes y otras cosas del gobierno y acrescentamiento de los reynos'. AGS, CCA, leg. 496-182-1 and leg. 890, N. 3.

61 AGS, CCA, leg. 1059, N. 78, The city of Seville, 'sobre los fraudes en la saca de cueros,' 20 August 1610.

62 AGS, CCA, leg. 1059, N. 78, Juan Hortego de Lansos, *alcalde hordinario de la villa*, 'testimonios y diligencias', 10 June 1613.

63 AGS, CCA, leg. 1059, N. 78, 'Información sobre el fraude en la saca de cueros', 1 March 1616.

64 AGS, CCA, leg. 1059, N. 78, Juan de Samaniego, 'Información sobre el fraude en la saca de cueros', 1 March 1616.

65 Ibid.

66 Ibid.

67 AGS, CCA, leg. 1082, N. 61, 'Arbitrio de "una persona bien intencionada" sobre los cueros', 1617.

68 James I, *By the King: A Proclamation to Restraine the Vnlawfull Transportation of Hides and Leather* (London: Bonham Norton and Iohn Bill, 1626).

Bibliography

Adelman, J., 'Mimesis and Rivalry: European Empires and Global Regimes', *Journal of Global History* 10, no. 01 (2015), 77–98, esp. 87.

Andrews, K.R., *The Spanish Caribbean: Trade and Plunder 1530–1630*, London: Yale University Press, 1978, p. 195.

Anes Álvarez de Castrillón, G., 'Tejidos, Corambre y Leyes en la Castilla del siglo XVI', *Anuario de Estudios Atlánticos*, 50, no. 1 (2004): 457–476.

Caballos, E.M., *La Española, Epicentro del Caribe en el Siglo XVI*, Santo Domingo: Academia Dominicana de la Historia, 2010, pp. 543–555.

Castillo Martos, M., 'El Uso del cuero en la minería de época moderna', in *Mil Años de Trabajo Del Cuero. Actas del II Simposio de Historia de las Técnicas*, R. Córdoba de la Llave (ed.), Córdoba: Litopress, 2003, pp. 373–394.

Chevalier, F., *La Formación de los latifundios en México: Haciendas y sociedad en los siglos XVI, XVII Y XVIII*, Mexico: Fondo de Cultura Económica, 1999, esp. pp. 117–142.

Coll y Toste, C. (ed.), 'La Toma Del Capital Por Cumberland', *Boletín Histórico de Puerto Rico*, V (1918), pp. 40–70, esp. p. 65.

Córdoba de la Llave, R. and Hernández Iñígo, P., 'El Utillaje de los Transportes en la Andalucía del Descubrimiento', *Historia, Instituciones, Documentos*, 30 (2003): 159–179.

Crosby, A.W., *Ecological Imperialism: The Biological Expansion of Europe 900–1900*, Cambridge: Cambridge University Press, 1986, p. 177.

———. The Columbian Exchange: *Biological and Cultural Consequences of 1492*, Westport: Praeger, 2003.

Exquemelin, A.O., *The Buccaneers of América*, New York: Dover Publications, 1967.

Fernádez de Oviedo, G., *Sumario de la Natural Historia de las Indias*, México: Fondo de Cultura Económica, 1950; orig. Toledo, 1526, ch. 2, f. 4v.

Gil-Bermejo García, J., *Panorama histórico de la agricultura en Puerto Rico*, Seville: Escuela de Estudios Hispano-Americanos, 1970.

———. *La española: anotaciones históricas (1600–1650)*, Seville: Escuela de Estudios Hispano-Americanos, 1983.

Goris, J.A., *Étude sur les colonies marchandes méridionales (Portugais, Espagnols, Italiens) à Anvers de 1488 à 1567. Contribution à l'histoire des débuts du capitalisme moderne*, New York: Burt Franklin, 1971.

Goslinga, C.Ch., *The Dutch in the Caribbean and on the Wild Coast 1580–1680*, Gainesville: University of Florida Press, 1971.

Haring, C.H.,*The Buccaneers in the West Indies in the XVII Century*, London: Methuen, 1910.

James, I., *By the King: A Proclamation to Restraine the Vnlawfull Transportation of Hides and Leather*, London: Bonham Norton and Iohn Bill, Printers to the Kings most Excellent Maiestie, 1626.

López y Sebastián, L.E., and del Río Moreno, J.L., 'La ganadería vacuna en la isla Española (1508–1587)', *Revista Complutense de Historia de América*, 25 (1 January 1999): 11–49.

Lorenzo Sanz, E., *El Comercio de España con Amércia en La época de Felipe II*, Valladolid: Servicio de Publicaciones de la Diputacion Provincial, 1979. 2 vols.

———. 'La Producción y el comercio de las plantas medicinales, alimenticias, maderas preciosas, cueros vacunos y productos diversos recibidos de Indias en el reinado de Felipe II', *Boletín Americanista*, no. 28 (1978), pp. 137–164.

Melville, E.G.K., 'Conquest Landscapes. Ecological Consequences of Pastoralism in the New World', *Le Nouveau Monde-Mondes Nouveaux. L'Experience Americaine*, Paris: Ecole des Hautes Études en Sciences Sociales, 1996, pp. 99–113.

———. 'Land Use and the Transformation of the Environment', *The Cambridge Economic History of Latin America*, Cambridge: Cambridge University Press, 2006, pp. 109–142.

Michaelmas, *Calendar of State Papers, Domestic Series of the Reign of Elizabeth, 1595–1597*, vol. CCLX, London: Longmans, Green, & Co., 1869.

Morel, G.R. (ed.), *Cartas del cabildo de Santo Domingo en el siglo XVI* , Santo Domingo: Editora Búho, 2011, p. 174, citing AGI, Santo Domingo 49, R.25, N.152, Audiencia to Philip II, 10 June 1556.

Oliva Melgar, J.M., 'Realidad y ficción en el Monopolio de Indias: Una reflexión sobre el sistema imperial español en el Siglo XVII', *Manuscrits: Revista d'història moderna*, 11:14 (1992), pp. 34–47.

———. 'El Monopolio de Indias en el siglo XVII y la economía Andaluza: Un apunte sobre el origen del atraso económico en Andalucía', *Archivo hispalense: Revista histórica, literaria y artística*, 95, 288 (2012), pp. 167–194.

Phillips, C.R., 'Trade in the Iberian Empires, 1450–1750', in Tracy, J.D. (ed.), *The Rise of Merchant Empires: Long-Distance Trade in the Early Modern World, 1350–1750*, Cambridge: Cambridge University Press, 1990, pp. 34–101.

Posthumus, N.W., *Inquiry into the History of Prices in Holland. Wholesale Prices at the Exchange of Amsterdam, 1585–1914; Rates of Exchange at Amsterdam, 1609–1914*. Vol. I., Leiden: E.J. Brill, 1946.

Rodríguez Molina, J., 'Tenerías de Andalucía a Finales de La Edad Media', in *Mil Años de Trabajo del Cuero*, Córdoba de la Llave, R. (ed.), Córdoba: Litopress, 2003, pp. 9–65.

Seijas, T., *Asian Slaves Colonial Mexico. From Chinos to Indians*, Cambridge: Cambridge University Press, 2014.

Sluyter, A.S., 'The Ecological Origins and Consequences of Cattle Ranching in Sixteenth-Century New Spain', *Geographical Review*, 86:2 (1996), pp. 161–177.

11 Structural holes and bad ideas

Liverpool's Atlantic trade networks in
the early-eighteenth century[1]

Sheryllynne Haggerty

Historians have been complicating their understandings of networks, and especially mercantile networks. Moving on from a rather positivistic approach based on family, religion and ethnicity, research has now started to stress the problems inherent in networks.[2] Furthermore, researchers have started to stress the problems in constructing and maintaining networks of any type.[3] However, far less work has been conducted on the problems encountered in developing and under-developed networks, where key actors may be unduly influential because they have access to new and/or highly prized information. Such key actors (often but not always, Mark Granovetter's 'weak ties') can help bridge what Ronald Burt has called structural holes in networks; that is, 'the separation between non-redundant contacts'.[4] He argues that actors standing near structural holes are 'at a higher risk of having good ideas' through the ability to better synthesise the varied and new information to which they have access.[5] Moreover, that information is likely to be seen as high value and credited because it is considered rare. Therefore, actors bridging structural holes are often perceived as positive players within a network.[6] However, the very fact that these bridging actors have information arbitrage to their advantage means they are also in a great position to act *against* the interests of the principal(s), especially where there is a lack of good governance.[7] These opportunities could be seen as 'bad ideas', the opposite of Burt's good ones. This situation could lead to bad decision making simply due to a lack of competency, through positive adverse selection, or even fraud.[8]

Either of these behaviours could be seen as a type of network failure, which Andrew Schrank and Josh Whitford define as 'the failure of a more or less idealized set of relational-network institutions to sustain 'desirable' activities or impede 'undesirable activities'.[9] They posit two types of network failure: absolute and relative – the latter of which is more relevant to the discussion here.[10] They argue that relative failure occurs when networks fail due to a lack of competencies (involuted), or due to opportunism (contested). The first is due to ignorance and a failure to absorb enough information, and the latter occurs where there is sufficient competence, but safeguards against mistrust and opportunism are absent. The clear, if colloquial way that Schrank and Whitford sum this up is: the difference between a partner 'screwing up' and 'screwing you'.[11] However, this chapter will argue that both types of this relative network failure can occur within the same network and at the same time. Furthermore, it will argue that this does not necessarily mean that the network has failed or is failing in a developmental or underdeveloped context.

Bridging actors are clearly not going to have perfect information in a developmental context. Therefore, it is quite possible that adverse selection may occur, but without intentional moral hazard (involuted failure). It is equally true that fraud could occur on a large scale (contested behaviour). At the same time, such bridging actors, or middlemen, play a key part in market integration, despite the 'significant difficulties' they face in a context of new and developing markets, both in terms of geography and commodities, and indeed changing and/or new institutional contexts.[12] However, without a developed network to oversee or correct these behaviours, they could go undetected for a long period of time. It is also quite possible that a network would continue and be (relatively) profitable, even if both these behaviours were present. The other actors (especially the principals) might not realise that the adventure could be even *more* profitable because they do not realise that such behaviours are present. Actors might also trust strong ties, or those with rare or valuable information, because they want to believe it, or perceive that they have no other options.[13] As long as the venture was successful to a *certain* extent, a positive affect could cause relational cohesion and moral obligation, leading to a sense of group. This would become more reinforced over time with frequent exchange, because attachments can arise simply from the 'idiosyncratic investment of learning to work together' that produces pleasure over and above the economic profit.[14] We know that economic actions are hardly ever taken by a mythical 'rational economic man', but occur within 'ongoing systems of social relations'.[15] Therefore, actors may not feel that the network is failing if they are making *some* profit and good feelings are being produced from the transaction(s). Moreover, in the long term, a developing network should improve the quality of information by diffusing competence, which infers that lacking competence is simply part of the process.[16] We might say therefore, from a broader perspective, that in a developing international trading environment a network with involuted and contested behaviours was performing as well as it could, or could be expected to do. In order to investigate the problems with developing networks, these ideas are applied to a case study of Liverpool's developing Atlantic trade in the early eighteenth century. Whilst Europeans had been trading (and conquering) in the Atlantic world for over two centuries, Liverpool was still a minor, if developing port. It therefore provides an excellent prism for examining the problems with developing or under-developed networks. The next section outlines the context and the trading network. The following analyses the behaviour of two bridging actors; one of whose behaviour can cause the network to be characterised as involuted (relative failure due to lack of competency), and the other to cause it to be termed as contested (failure due to opportunism). The conclusion argues that despite the presence of lack of competencies *and* opportunism, this network was not failing, but was simply at one point in a process of development. Bad ideas were present, but did not represent failure.

The *Providence*

This case study derives from a voyage of the brigantine *Providence*, from 1711–1713 which produced a case in the equity jurisdiction of the Court of Exchequer from 1714–1716.[17] This side of the Exchequer was established in the sixteenth century and whilst not as important as Chancery, it assumed its doctrines, and thereafter the two developed side by side. Many cases also came to this court that would have been under the jurisdiction of the Court of Admiralty in the seventeenth century.[18] People often used the equity side of the Exchequer when the payment of debt to the crown was involved, in this case, customs duties.[19] The *Providence* was supposed to go from Liverpool, to Belfast, to New York, to one of the Leeward Islands (St Kitts, Antigua, Montserrat and Nevis) and then return to Liverpool. The voyage was therefore a sophisticated if peripatetic one, which seems to have been normal practice at this stage of the development of the Atlantic economy for the Dutch and the English.[20] Liverpool was then still a relatively small port of around 6,500 persons, but was building on its coastal and Mediterranean trade (with ports such as Livorno) by joining in the expanding Atlantic commerce.[21] Indeed, at the very same time of the *Providence's* voyage, Liverpool's proactive merchants were constructing the port's, and indeed, the country's, first wet dock, which opened in 1715.[22] This was built specifically to cope with Liverpool's increasing trade with the continental colonies and the West Indies which had begun by 1665.[23] Belfast was also an important port in the Irish trade, a mainstay of the Liverpool commerce at this time.[24] New York, taken from the Dutch in 1664, was a major entrepôt port on the Eastern Seaboard.[25] The Leeward Islands, having become independent from Barbados in 1670 were starting to show their potential following years of laggard growth in the seventeenth century.[26] This was also a period of war, with the War of Spanish Succession (1701–1714) mainly in Europe, and Queen Anne's War (1702–1713) in the Americas. From 1711–1712, the war was being fought mainly in Europe and was to some extent 'on hold' during the peace negotiations of those years, even if many of them were in secret.[27] However, whilst the new Tory government in Britain was more concerned with reconstructing trade and the colonies, there were still plenty of privateers for the sailors to contend with.[28] There were therefore a number of elements making the voyage of the *Providence* developmental as well as potentially dangerous. This was especially true in the commercial context of the Caribbean where no chartered or regulated companies had overall (supposed) control of the trade from England.[29]

The sole owner of the *Providence* was John Cunningham, a nonconformist, which meant that he could not serve on the town council.[30] However, this did not stop many elite Anglican merchants of the period from adventuring goods on his vessels and under his management. These included Richard Gildart and William Clayton, both of whom served on the town council at various points like many Anglican merchants, who dominated the Council.[31] The *Providence* sailed from Liverpool laden with coal and salt in addition to a wide variety of textiles such as hats, linens, woollens, nails and iron for sale in New York and the Leeward Islands, with a stop in Belfast.[32] The *Providence* returned from the West Indies with sugar and molasses.[33] The crew also purchased provisions in Belfast and flour, pork, beer and other supplies in New York for sale in the West Indies, but the precise details are not recorded.[34] However, the voyage did not go as planned, and the resultant case in the Court of Exchequer provides us with wonderful evidence of the problems of developing and underdeveloped networks during this formative period of Liverpool's Atlantic trade.

The *Providence* sailed from Liverpool on 9 March 1711 and arrived in the Belfast Lough the next day. She was supposed to sail to New York on 21 March, but did not leave for that port until 28 March 1711. The *Providence* arrived in New York on 16 May 1712 (the Julian calendar still being in operation), after a journey of five weeks. She sailed from there on 4 August 1712 (46 days later than planned).[35] It was rumoured on board that she was bound for Antigua, which was sighted on 31 August (as was Barbados), but instead they sailed to Nevis, where they arrived on 1 September 1712. They eventually left the island on 3 July 1713 (250 days later than planned), arriving in Liverpool on 6 August 1713.[36]

Much of the evidence as part of the case in Exchequer relating to this long and extremely delayed voyage concerns the existence or otherwise of a charter party, and moreover, the dead freight and demurrage payments deriving from any such charter party, if it existed.[37] There is also a lot of evidence given about exactly what a charter party was and how they should be enacted. This is rather strange as charter parties had been in 'common usage' for centuries, and so it is likely that this evidence was given as part of an effort to try and find out whether a charter party did in fact exist for the *Providence*, and if so, who knew about it.[38] Indeed, some leading merchants who were 'very well skilled and experienced' in such matters, were chosen to arbitrate the case.[39] The arbitrators were John Earle, William Pemberton, Edward Tarleton, William Webster, Lewis Jenkyns, Jonathon Livesay and Thomas Seddon.[40] Although the outcome of the case is unknown, they assessed that a further 96 hogsheads of sugar and 80 bags of cotton wool, each bag containing 200 weight, could have been freighted over and above what was imported (and for which freighters would have had to contribute if there had been a charter party). As the freight for sugar from Nevis to Liverpool was 3s 6d per hundred weight, this only amounted to £28. Furthermore, demurrage was estimated at £1590, and portage at £1575.[41] The Liverpool arbiters decided that in satisfaction of all of Cunningham's demands as well as for the cost of the freight of the goods on board, as for dead freight and 'all their Clayms' they should receive £1260. Therefore a lot of money was at stake.[42] It is not surprising then that the case documentation is filled with technicalities regarding charter parties, dead freight and demurrage. However, the evidence given by the litigants in their attempts to apportion blame for the delays encountered on the voyage (i.e. who caused the demurrage charges) tell us a lot about the behaviour of the ship's captain Joseph Pearson, and the supercargo John Whiteside. Quite apart from the money at stake, the court case may have been a way of unearthing information about these two men, without accusing them directly, which may have been difficult in a close-knit socially embedded trading network such as in Liverpool. The merchants may have been concerned about the financial outcome of the case, but finding out whether these men could truly be trusted may have been equally important to them.

Figure 11.1 outlines the network as constructed from the Exchequer records. The cluster on the top right is the dense network of Liverpool merchants exporting and importing on the *Providence*. The group on the bottom right are those giving evidence on the case, but not involved in the voyage. The network to the left of centre is the ship's crew (or at least those that gave evidence). From the far left of Figure 11.1, it is clear that the records show very little evidence of networks in New York and the Caribbean. This could be due to the nature of the sources, but the evidence within them suggests that there were in fact few developed networks on the Western side of the Atlantic, despite the fact that some of the adventurers had traded to the West Indies before.[43] John Cunningham, the owner, is in the middle, but it is clear that Joseph Pearson, the captain, and John Whiteside, the supercargo, were extremely important bridging actors both geographically and within terms of the trading network in which there seems to have been plenty of structural holes. They were therefore likely to be trusted and their information valued, but they also had opportunities for moral hazard and fraud. In fact, their respective behaviour could easily be characterised as lacking in competency (involuted) or fraudulent (contested) and therefore be termed as a case of relative failure within the network. As mentioned previously, the embedded nature of the relations within this network may have made it impossible to accuse either of these men directly. This does not necessarily mean that the network failed however. By looking more closely at their reported actions and behaviour we can better analyse their role as bridging actors in this network. These records, whilst flawed and incomplete, tell us a lot about how and with what problems mercantile networks were developed in the early modern Atlantic trade.

Joseph Pearson: involuted failure due to incompetence?

Joseph Pearson was the captain of the *Providence*. He was also a joint complainant with John Cunningham (the sole owner) in the original case in the Exchequer, and therefore in opposition to the majority of the merchants involved in trading on the vessel (as shown in Figure 11.1). It would therefore appear that he was on the same side, or at least, Cunningham continued to trust him after the *Providence*'s voyage. However, there are several aspects of his behaviour that others in the network thought worth commenting upon in answer to the preset questions posed to them.[44]

The first was regarding the delayed sailing from Belfast Lough by a week. Henry Bibby, the foremastman (who gave evidence for the defendants in the original case), said that the originally planned sailing date of 21 March had been good for sailing, that the ship had been ready and therefore the delay was due to the 'neglect and omission' of Pearson.[45] Other ships had sailed at this time without a problem, he added. Bibby further commented that Pearson had said that he was waiting for a signal or ensign – but that he [Bibby] did not know the real reason for the delay. John Marsden was a merchant in 1715, but was the captain of the *Tabitha and Prescilla*, also in Belfast in March 1711. He confirmed that Pearson was due to sail from the Lough on 21 March in the company of the *Tabitha and Prescilla*, the *Elizabeth and Ann* and the *Three Sisters*, the latter two of Liverpool, for 'the greater safety' of all ships, as the first had guns to combat privateers.[46]

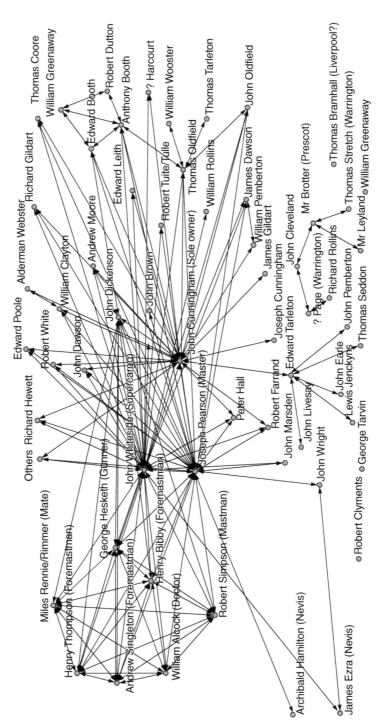

Figure 11.1 Interrogatories, 16 November 1714, E134/1Geo1/Mich 37; Interrogatories, 8 April 1715, E134/1Geo1/East21; Decree, 1716.

Pearson stayed behind though he could have sailed, but Marsden did not know why he chose to either. Only one person, Henry Thompson, another foremast-man, gave an explanation as to why Pearson did not sail with the other vessels. He reported that the *Providence* was hindered and retarded in her passage because of the mistake of a pilot, and therefore, lost the company of the other ships.[47] This was not confirmed by any of the other deponents, however.[48] It is difficult to say why Pearson delayed so long. It is unlikely that he was waiting for information from Liverpool – that was only a day's sailing away, and we have no further clues as to the signal for which he was purportedly awaiting.

Bibby, who appeared to have plenty to say about Pearson (perhaps because he had allegedly refused him permission to put some sugar on board at Nevis), thought that this late sailing had serious repercussions.[49] When the *Providence* arrived in New York on 16 May 1712, they found that a London ship had come in two weeks before and 'lower'd the Markett'[sic].[50] He believed that if the *Providence* had sailed for New York on 21 March they would have come to a better and higher market, and that 'the Adventurers or persons who were Concerned in freighting the Said Ship were considerable loosers[sic] by the Said Ship not Sailing from Belfast when ready as aforesaid'.[51] Although trade was still rather peripatetic, a May arrival would have been late compared to other vessels arriving for the spring trade after the Hudson River had melted. Therefore, it is worth noting that the vessel had left Liverpool quite late in the first place for a good spring arrival in New York.

A second matter mentioned by several deponents was the seizure of the *Providence* in New York by customs officers. This was due to coal being taken on board by Pearson without the proper certification. Bibby said that the vessel lay under condemnation for one month during which time the coal and other goods were sold by the customs officers. However, Henry Thompson argued that the officers only pretended 'to have authority', and that the coal was only seized for four or five days, after which time the vessel was entirely discharged of her cargo.[52] It is not clear whether any correct documentation was eventually produced, whether this omission was explained away or whether there was an error on the part of the customs officials. Either way, it seems that Pearson's error was due to lack of experience, rather than being fraudulent.

The third matter of some confusion was the intended destination in the West Indies. Bibby, yet again ready to give evidence against Pearson, reported the rumour on board was that the *Providence* was bound for Antigua, and that this was confirmed by the sailing course.[53] Indeed, the vessel came in sight of St. John's harbour on 31 August 1712, but according to Bibby, Pearson ordered the sailors to make for Nevis, which was indeed where they made land. Bibby thought this hazardous due to the privateers in the area. Indeed the Leeward Islands were all attacked by the French in periods of war, and St Kitts and Nevis particularly so.[54] Andrew Singleton, another foremastman on the *Providence*, also reported that Whiteside had wanted to go to Antigua but that Pearson said that he could not justify this to the owner unless Whiteside could confirm the vessel would be fully loaded there, which the supercargo could not.[55] This is strange because of all the

Liverpool adventurers that traded in the West Indies during 1709–1710, Antigua was the most popular destination, and only William Clayton had exported to Nevis that year.[56] According to Bibby, the decision to go to Nevis was a bad one, because when they arrived at the island on 1 September 1712, sugar was very scarce. This was not surprising since the harvest would have begun in January and continued until May.[57] There were also several other ships there, including some from New York, which had no doubt pushed up the price of sugar and made sales of the Liverpool and New York exports more difficult. Bibby learned that the ship's doctor, William Alcock, had been told that prices were better in Antigua, which he suggested confirmed the losses for the adventurers.[58] This indecision over the destination in the Leeward Islands caused friction, but Pearson once again appears to have been acting in a trustworthy manner.[59]

As we shall see later in this chapter, Whiteside was accused of not acquiring freight for the return voyage to Liverpool as he should have done, but according to Bibby (yet again) Pearson also discouraged some factors from putting freight on board. Apparently Pearson (who clearly thought there *was* a charter party) told Archibald Hamilton and several others not to put goods on board because the charter party determined that their goods would be seized on arrival in Liverpool because of 'deadfreight and demurrage'; that is, the cargo would be seized until the extra costs were paid.[60] This is indeed what happened, but this behaviour is strange. Perhaps Pearson was trying to create a good reputation for the Liverpool merchants he represented by being so honest. Certainly it hurt them financially in the short term. Alternatively, Pearson may have been building up his own good reputation for when he might become a merchant in his own right in the future.

The last aside that Bibby made against Pearson was to report that he boarded the *Jolly*, a man-of-war. His tone was accusatory, yet this was a time of war, and Pearson could simply have been getting the latest information to protect the vessel and its crew.[61] Given that the Leeward Islands lay near Martinique and Guadeloupe, the bases of French power in the eastern Caribbean, an attack was a very real danger at this time – Nevis having been attacked in 1706.[62]

John Whiteside: contested failure due to opportunism?

In contrast to Joseph Pearson, the supercargo, John Whiteside, was one of the defendants in the original case. It would appear that he had had some falling out with the owner, John Cunningham, but he was on the same 'side' of the case as the other merchants who were involved with the venture. However, his behaviour does seem far more suspect than that of Pearson.

Whilst Pearson had held up the *Providence* for a week or so in Belfast, Whiteside was accused of holding up its progress from New York for three weeks. In fact, in all, they stayed there 46 days longer than specified in the [alleged] charter party. Henry Thompson, the foremastman, gave evidence that on arrival in New York in May, the crew was busy following Whiteside's orders in delivering the cargo, including the coal that had been temporarily seized on arrival. Once the vessel was completely cleared, the crew then applied themselves to reloading the vessel according to Whiteside's orders, apparently as per their instructions in the charter party.[63] Once loaded, the *Providence* sailed into the North River and had the 'Jack and Antiant'[sic] flags flying as signals of readiness to sail from New York.[64] However, Whiteside was not then on board, and it was only when he came on board three weeks later that the *Providence* and its crew finally set sail for the West Indies. Andrew Singleton, another foremastman, confirmed this delay, adding that the 'ship continued waiting for the defendant [Whiteside] who as reported had not finished his business thereabout', though there was no comment as to what this business might have been.[65] It seems strange that the vessel was made ready to sail and so was therefore presumably fully loaded (or as full as possible) so long before the supercargo was ready; what was Whiteside doing in New York for so long? In holding up the vessel for such a long time for no apparent reason, Whiteside was surely negligent. As the vessel was in the river ready to sail he could not have been arranging more freight. It is possible that he could have been conducting legal business for Cunningham or one of the other venturers, but this long delay was clearly against the remit of any charter party. It was not good practise to hold up such heavily capitalised equipment as a sailing vessel. Whether he was working for the adventurers or on his own agenda during this time, this had serious repercussions on their [late] arrival in the West Indies, and far more so than Pearson's delay in Belfast.

It would seem that Whiteside was also to blame for the extraordinarily long stay in Nevis. Andrew Singleton reported that it was commonly known on board that Whiteside had an opportunity to sell all the cargo to one person residing on the island.[66] John Dickenson, the ship's carpenter, confirmed this. The fact that Whiteside had lost an opportunity to dispose of the cargo he thought 'delatory and negligent' especially as he had refused a reasonable 'markett[sic] Price for his Goods'.[67] Henry Thompson, the other foremastman, concurred. He said that Whiteside could have disposed of the cargo within six weeks of their arrival at Nevis, and at a better price than he later received. No doubt, any buyers on the island realised he was getting desperate to dispose of his goods.[68] To further stress Whiteside's culpability, Thompson added that he never knew of any fault in the master or the crew of the vessel, and that they had worked as fast as they could for the supercargo. John Dickenson agreed that Pearson and the crew were not at fault, and further noted that whilst the *Providence* was at Nevis [for over ten months] several other ships had been laden and sailed, including the *Samuel*, the *Union* from London and the *Anvill* from Bristol. Indeed, the latter had sailed from Nevis to Bristol and returned, and re-laden all whilst the *Providence* was there.[69] Even William Rollins, the one person who supported Whiteside on this issue by stating that Whiteside had been 'very diligent and industrious in his efforts', conceded that it would have been better for him to take the opportunity of the early sale.[70] It is possible that Whiteside was simply trying to get the best price for Cunningham and the other merchants. The selling of goods, and the purchase of sugar, so far ahead of the harvest was bound to be slow. Perhaps he had wanted to go to Antigua as some of the adventurers may have had better networks there, but as mentioned previously, he did not feel able to ensure full sales even there to Pearson. However, the fact that so many deponents mentioned that he could have sold the goods earlier and for a better price, does appear to put the blame firmly on Whiteside. He seems to have been working on his own agenda.

Whiteside, whether or not he was acting for the good of the ship, its crew and the adventurers, seems to have made some other poor decisions. During their stay at Nevis, Whiteside ordered cable and a 'considerable quantity of cordage' to be brought on board by a sloop from the island of St Thomas, which then belonged to the Dutch. Henry Thompson clearly thought these items were stolen, or at the very least put on board illegally. He reported that when the 'Queen's officers were preparing to come on board' to search the vessel, the cable and cordage were thrown overboard to prevent seizure of the vessel.[71] Andrew Singleton also reported the same event.[72] Even if the vessel was in desperate need for these items, stolen or not, and if Whiteside was acting in the best interests of the crew, it surely would have been better to purchase the cable and cordage legally at Nevis, or from another vessel. However, the *Providence* seems to have sailed home successfully without these items, suggesting that Whiteside was working for his own advantage.

A last possible hint at some fraud by Whiteside came from Henry Thompson. Thompson mentioned that he had seen Whiteside ordering or instructing Miles Rimmer, the mate, how to write the 'markes' of several hogsheads then on board.[73] Subsequently, Rimmer assisted Whiteside in changing the marks accordingly. Unfortunately, the source does not tell us more about this incident, so we cannot know why this was done.

Discussion

Pearson's failures, the delay of the *Providence* for a week in Belfast and the taking on of coal without certification, caused delays in the voyage which had financial repercussions for the adventurers. However, his actions point to a lack of competence and knowledge rather than fraudulent activity. The decision to discourage people from freighting in the vessel from Nevis appears strange, but he does seem to have been acting honestly. His actions, no doubt part of socially embedded behaviours, were possibly part of a long-term business strategy, even if it caused even higher dead freight charges for the Liverpool adventurers.[74] They were certainly not the actions of a (short-term) rational economic man. It is also worth noting that much of the evidence against Pearson comes from Bibby, who seems to have held a grudge against him – although his accusations were corroborated by other deponents.[75] The fact that Pearson was a plaintiff in the original case with Cunningham also suggests that their relationship had not broken down as a result of his actions. Pearson's case therefore points to an involuted failure on part of the network, due to lack of knowledge and skills or competency.

By contrast, in holding up the vessel for such a long time in New York and Nevis, Whiteside was surely negligent, and possibly fraudulent. Both delays were clearly against the remit of any charter party (if it existed). In not accepting an early offer for his cargo in Nevis, Whiteside was perhaps waiting for a better price, which he may have received nearer the harvest period. However, the *Providence* did not leave Nevis until well after the next harvest had finished, which was inexcusable. Taking on board (apparently) illegal cable and cordage also seemed to have cost money, which may have been his own money as part of a private venture. Certainly the *Providence* seemed to have sailed back to Liverpool safely without these items. Whiteside definitely caused the most delays, and instigated the high demurrage charges that became due by the adventurers. The fact that Whiteside was a defendant in the case brought by Cunningham suggests that he was not acting on his behalf, or according to instructions. He was also co-defendant and co-plaintiff with the majority of the other merchants involved in the venture. However, he may have been acting along with them in arguing that there was no charter party in order to divert blame from himself because of the high costs involved in dead freight and demurrage if it were judged that there was a valid charter party. Whiteside's behaviour does appear fraudulent or suggests that he was at least acting on his own behalf, and therefore represents a contested part of the network.

The decision about which island to go to in the Leeward Islands, which was clearly a matter of dispute, was supposed to have been agreed to in New York by both Pearson and Whiteside.[76] The orders to delay this decision until they (presumably) had better or later knowledge available in New York came from Cunningham. This delayed decision seems to have been normal in the peripatetic trade of this period; however, he should have given the decision to one or other of the men to avoid such arguments. Both Pearson and Whiteside contributed to the lengthy nature of the voyage. However, the voyage never left Liverpool at a good point in time for either a New York or a West India arrival. So we could place the blame on Cunningham as ship's husband and owner, because the original planning was not good either. Therefore, it was not just Pearson and Whiteside who were to blame for the problems related with this adventure.

It was not possible to establish whether Pearson or Whiteside worked with Cunningham or any of the other merchants before or after this case from the port books, because the captain is not always listed, and the supercargo not at all – unless importing on his own account. This means that without further evidence, we cannot assess the long-term nature of Pearson and Whiteside's relationship with the rest of the Liverpool network, although some of the merchants imported on the same vessels previous to this voyage. Neither is it possible to say to what extent Cunningham's nonconformity and exclusion from the town council isolated him. He was certainly isolated in terms of the court case from the majority of the merchants, but whether this was religious politics or simply down to the others not wanting to pay dead freight and demurrage is unknowable with the available sources. At the same time, the arbiters, many of whom were on the town council, seemed to have found in his favour, perhaps because as merchants they would have liked a similar finding for themselves; but again, we cannot tell whether politics or economics was the driving force.

Conclusion

The case study of the *Providence* shows that relative failure of both types, involuted and contested, can be present in one network at the same time. The behaviour of Pearson and Whiteside had serious financial repercussions for the owner Cunningham, as well as the other merchant adventurers. However, the voyage was not well planned or timed from the start, for which failure we need to look to Cunningham. Nor did Cunningham or Pearson make the existence of any charter party sufficiently clear to the others freighting on the vessel from Liverpool. However, this venture occurred early in Liverpool's Atlantic trade. Although some of the merchants had traded to the West Indies beforehand – and collectively Liverpool merchants had been trading to the West Indies since at least 1665, it appears that the networks on the western side of the Atlantic were still developing and under-developed. This meant that clearer or more precise instructions could not be given to the captain and supercargo, leaving the requirement for this journey to be rather peripatetic. Moreover, this lack of networks meant that there were no actors in place to advise, govern and/or report on the behaviour of Pearson and Whiteside in the Americas. Although the institution of the Exchequer was available to resolve this issue, transaction costs would have been much lower had good governance networks been in place.

This does not necessarily mean that this network failed. This venture may have been only partly successful, but it did not deter Cunningham or the other merchants investing in similar voyages afterwards, so they must have considered it at least partly successful, if only in gaining new information and experience (developing competence) as part of a learning process. Furthermore, other merchants in the wider Liverpool trading community ventured into the West Indies in the decades that followed. Indeed, Liverpool became the leading Atlantic out port during the 1740s. Therefore, incompetency and fraud caused both Pearson and Whiteside to have 'bad ideas' within the structural hole(s) they were bridging, but this does not mean that the network failed; just that it was one in which both involuted and contested elements existed. The behaviour of Pearson and Whiteside should be seen as a 'best case scenario' within the context of a developing and as yet under-developed network.

Notes

1 My great thanks to S. Talbott and D.E. Ascott for very helpful discussions on earlier versions of this paper, and especially to the latter for pointing me to references concerning John Cunningham.

2 For a positivistic approach see: P. Mathias, 'Risk, Credit and Kinship in early Modern Enterprise', in J.J. McCusker and K. Morgan (eds.), *The Early-Modern Atlantic Economy* (Cambridge: Cambridge University Press, 2000), pp. 15–35; M.B. Rose, 'The Family Firm in British Business, 1780–1914', in M.W. Kirby and M.B. Rose (eds.), *Business Enterprise in Modern Britain from the Eighteenth to the Twentieth Century* (London, 1994), pp. 61–87; A. Prior and M. Kirby, 'The Society of Friends and the Family Firm, 1700–1830', *Business History*, 35:4 (1993), pp. 66–85. On the inherent problems with networks see D. Hancock, 'The Trouble with Networks: Managing the

Scots' Early-Modern Madeira Trade', *Business History Review*, 79, Special Edition on Networks in the Trade in Alcohol (Autumn 2005), pp. 67–91.

3 See for example, A. Popp, 'Building the Market: John Shaw of Wolverhampton and Commercial Travelling in Early Nineteenth-Century England', *Business History*, 49:3 (May 2007), pp. 321–347; T. Crumplin, 'Opaque Networks: Business and Community in the Isle of Man, 1840–1900', *Business History*, 49:6 (2007), pp. 780–801; A. Forrestier, 'Risk, Kinship and Personal Relationships in Late Eighteenth-Century West Indian Trade: The Commercial Network of Tobin & Pinney', *Business History*, 52:6 (2010), pp. 912–931. For ascribed trust see L.G. Zucker, 'Production of Trust: Institutional Sources of Economic Structure, 1840–1920', *Research in Organizational Behaviour*, 8 (1986), pp. 53–111.

4 M.S. Granovetter, 'The Strength of Weak Ties', *American Journal of Sociology*, 78:6 (May, 1973), pp. 1360–1380; R.S. Burt, *Structural Holes: The Social Structure of Competition* (Cambridge and London: Harvard University Press, 1992), p. 19.

5 R.S. Burt, 'Structural Holes and Good Ideas', *American Journal of Sociology*, 10:2 (2004), pp. 349–399, p. 349.

6 Structural holes can only last for so long. Due to the fact that they offer high rewards, entrepreneurs can get into a 'network race' to fill them, at the end of which it is unlikely that anyone will be in a privileged position. V. Buskens and A. van de Rijt, 'Dynamics of Networks if Everyone Strives for Structural Holes', *American Journal of Sociology*, 114:2 (September 2008), pp. 371–407, p. 375.

7 R.S. Burt, *Structural Holes*, p. 354.

8 On adverse selection and moral hazard see N. Strong and M. Waterson, 'Principals, Agents and Information', in R. Clark and T. McGuiness (eds.), *The Economics of the Firm* (Oxford: Basil Blackwell, 1987), pp. 18–41.

9 A. Schrank and J. Whitford, 'The Anatomy of Network Failure', *Sociological Theory*, 29:3 (2011), pp. 151–177, p. 155.

10 Under absolute failure they, demarcate between the non-appearance of networks (network stillbirth) and the breakup of existing networks (network devolution). A. Schrank and J. Whitford, 'The Anatomy of Network Failure', p. 153, and *passim*.

11 A. Schrank and J. Whitford, 'Anatomy of Network Failure', p. 161.

12 R. Grabowski, 'Market Evolution and Economic Development: The Evolution of Impersonal Markets', *American Journal of Economics and Sociology*, 58:4 (October 1999), pp. 699–712, pp. 707–708. J.M. Podolny and K.L. Page also argue that networks should help synthesise information, confer legitimacy and status, and reduce information and transaction costs, 'Network Forms of Organization', *Annual Review of Sociology*, 24 (1998), pp. 57–76.

13 M.S. Granovetter, 'The Strength of Weak Ties: A Network Theory Revisited', *Sociological Theory*, I (1983), pp. 201–233, p. 213. On wanting to believe information that suits us see R.T. Stillson, *Spreading the Word: A History of Information in the California Gold Rush* (Lincoln and London: University of Nebraska Press, 2006).

14 S.R. Thye, E.J. Lawler and J. Yoon, 'The Emergence of Embedded Relations and Group Formation in Networks of Competition', *Psychology Quarterly*, 74:4 (December 2011), pp. 287–413; E.J. Lawler, and Y. Yoon, 'Commitment in Exchange Relations: Test of a Theory of Relational Cohesion', *American Sociological Review*, 61:1 (February 1996), pp. 89–108; M.S. Granovetter, 'Economic Action and Social Structure: The Problem of Embeddedness', *American Journal of Sociology*, 91:3 (November 1985), pp. 481–510, p. 498.

15 M.S. Granovetter, 'Economic Action and Social Structure', p. 487.

16 M. Casson, 'Entrepreneurial Networks in International Business', *Business and Economic History*, 26:2 (Winter 1997), pp. 811–823.

17 Interrogatories taken on behalf of John Cunningham, Merchant and Joseph Pearson, Mariner, for HM Court of Exchequer by English Bill ..., April 1714, E 134/1Geo1/ Mich 37; Interrogatories taken on behalf of ..., E134/1Geo1/East21, 18 April 1715;

Decree, Whereas John Cunningham and Joseph Pearson ..., E 190/30, f.18, 1716, The National Archives, Kew (hereafter TNA). The case appears to have gone on longer, but the Decree of 1716, which is not conclusionary, is the last evidence found at the time of submission.

18 G.F. Steckley, 'Freight Law in the Seventeenth-Century Admiralty Court', *Journal of Legal History*, 27:2 (2006), pp. 175–197.

19 W.H. Bryson, *The Equity Side of the Exchequer: Its Jurisdictions, Procedures and Records* (Cambridge: Cambridge University Press, 1975), introduction and pp. 10–11.

20 C.J. Koot, *Empire at the Periphery: British Colonists, Anglo-Dutch Trade, and the Development of the British Atlantic, 1621–1713* (New York and London: New York University Press, 2011).

21 D.E. Ascott, F. Lewis and M. Power, *Liverpool, 1660–1750: People, Prosperity and Power* (Liverpool: Liverpool University Press, 2006), p. 34.

22 M. Power, 'Creating a Port: Liverpool 1695–1715', *Transactions of the Historic Society of Lancashire and Cheshire*, 149 (1999), pp. 51–71.

23 Exchequer, Port Books, Chester, Liverpool, Customer Overseas (hereafter Port Books), E190/1337/16, ff. 13, 58, TNA.

24 M.K. Stammers, 'Ships and Port Management at Liverpool Before the Opening of the First Dock in 1715', *Transactions of the Historic Society of Lancashire and Cheshire*, 156 (2007), pp. 27–50.

25 C. Matson, *Merchants and Empire: Trading in Colonial New York* (Baltimore and London: Johns Hopkins University Press, 1998).

26 N.A. Zacek, *Settler Society in the English Leeward Islands, 1670–1776* (Cambridge: Cambridge University Press, 2010), p. 18.

27 J.B. Hattendorf, *England in the War of the Spanish Succession: A Study in the English View and Conduct of Grand Strategy, 1701–1713* (London: Routledge, 1987), ch. 12, 'English Conduct of the War During the Search for Peace, 1710–1713', pp. 231–272. There had been more conflict in the Caribbean at the turn of the century, though occasional raids continued until the end of the war. N. M. Crouse, *The French Struggle for the West Indies, 1665–1713* (New York: Columbia University Press, 1943). Neither Jamaica nor Barbados were attacked, although the French mounted a successful raid on Nevis in 1706 which allegedly led to loss of circa one million pounds. B.P. Lenman, 'Colonial Wars and Imperial Instability, 1688–1793', in P.J. Marshall (ed.), *Oxford History of the British Empire, Vol. II, The Eighteenth Century* (Oxford: Oxford University Press, 1998), pp. 151–168.

28 J.A. Lynn, *The Wars of Louis XIV, 1667–1714* (Longman: London and New York, 1999), p. 341. Privateering had perhaps been a bigger issue during the first decade of the eighteenth century for Liverpool traders. B. Poole, *Liverpool's Trade in the Reign of Queen Anne* (unpublished MA Thesis, University of Liverpool, 1961), pp. 101–109. See also D.J. Starkey, *British Privateering Enterprise in the Eighteenth Century*, Exeter Maritime Series No. 4 (Exeter: University of Exeter Press, 1990). The interest in the mixture of trade and colonies could be called part of a 'Blue-Water Policy'. D.A. Baugh, 'Britain's Blue Water Policy, 1689–1815', *International History Review*, 10:1 (February 1988), pp. 33–58.

29 The East India Company took control of the *Asiento* in 1713, but they never had a monopoly on the trade to the Spanish colonies, nor did the Royal African Company in the British Atlantic slave trade. R.B. Sheridan, *Sugar and Slavery: An Economic History of the British West Indies, 1623–1775* (Kingston: Canoe Press, 1974), pp. 218, 259–260, 317. See also E. Mancke, 'Chartered Enterprises and the Evolution of the British Atlantic World', in E. Mancke and C. Shammas (eds.), *The Creation of the British Atlantic World* (Baltimore and London: Johns Hopkins University Press, 2005), pp. 237–262.

30 Deposition of Henry Orme, 16 November 1714, Interrogatories, E134/1Geo1/Mich37. John Cunningham was involved in 128 various shipments with regard to all his

trading career. Ascott et al, *Liverpool, 1660–1750*, p. 153. This did not include the slave trade however. http://www.slavevoyages.org/tast/database/search.faces, accessed 14 May 2015.

31 Deposition of Richard Norris, 16 November 1714, Interrogatories, E134/1Geo1/ Mich37; Ascott et al, *Liverpool, 1660–1750*, p. 154. Richard Gildart had exported to Antigua on the *Elizabeth* during 1709/10, and William Clayton had traded to and from Antigua, St Christopher, Nevis and Barbados in the same year, on the *Tyger*, *Goodspeed, Content, Neptune* and *Cleaveland*, Port Books 1709–1710, E190/1377/11, *passim*. M.J. Power, 'Councillors and Commerce in Liverpool, 1650–1750', *Urban History*, 24:3 (1997), pp. 301–323. There were no merchant guilds in Liverpool.

32 Deposition of George Tarvin, 16 Nov 1714, Interrogatories, E134/1Geo1/Mich37; Deposition of Henry Bibby, 18 April 1715, Interrogatories, E134/1Geo1/East21.

33 Deposition of Edward Tarleton, 16 November 1714, Interrogatories, E134/1Geo1/ Mich 37.

34 Decree, 1716, E 190/30, f. 18, p. 1.

35 The vessel was supposed to stay '45 days running' whereas this stay was ninety–one days long, Decree, 1716, p. 1.

36 Deposition of Henry Bibby, 18 April 1715, Interrogatories, E134/1Geo1/East21; the vessel was only supposed to stay at the Leeward Islands for 'sixty five days', Decree, 1716, p. 3.

37 Charter parties are voluntary agreements wherein a number of traders contract for a vessel to make a certain journey in a certain time. Extra charges are shared for space not taken up (dead freight) and for delays on the voyage (demurrage). See T. Mortimer, *A New and Complete Dictionary of Trade and Commerce: Containing a Distinct Explanation of the General Principles of Commerce …* (London, 1766).

38 G.F. Steckley, 'Freight Law in the Seventeenth-Century, pp. 175–197.

39 Deposition of Thomas Oldfield, 18 April 1715, Interrogatories, E134/1Geo1/East21, TNA.

40 Deposition of Edward Tarleton, 16 November 1714, Interrogatories, E134/1Geo1/ Mich 37.

41 Decree, 1716, p. 4. Portage is getting a vessel or its cargo from one navigable place to another.

42 Deposition of Thomas Oldfield.

43 For example, John Cunningham imported c. 200 Cwt of sugar on the *Happy Entrance*, 13 September 1705. Robert Tuite had imported muscovado sugar on the same vessel, 26 September 1705, Port Books 1704–1705, E190/1337/16, f. 13, TNA. Cunningham also imported 40 Cwt of sugar during 1709–1710, Port Books, E190/1377/11.

44 These 'interrogatories' are all listed on the first page(s) of each of E134/1Geo1/Mich37 and E134/1Geo1/East21.

45 Deposition of Henry Bibby.

46 Deposition of George Marsden, 18 April 1715, Interrogatories, E134/1Geo1/East21.

47 Deposition of Henry Thompson, 15 April 1715, Interrogatories, E134/1Geo1/East21.

48 Support from the Crew was very important in these freight cases. Steckley, 'Freight Law', p. 181.

49 Deposition of Henry Thompson.

50 Deposition of Henry Bibby.

51 Deposition of Henry Bibby.

52 Thompson was formerly sworn in 'on the Defendant's Part' but was this time sworn and Examined on the Complainant's part.

53 John Cunningham did import from Antigua in later years. See for example, the *Susanna* in January 1714, Port Books, 1714–15, E190/1387/7, f. 24, TNA. His brother-in-law, Samuel Danvers, was the firm's representative in Antigua at some point but as yet, it has not been possible to discover which years. My thanks to D.E. Ascott for this information. If Danvers was in Antigua at this point it is strange that Cunningham did not direct the vessel there.

54 N.A. Zacek, *Settler Society*, p. 19.
55 Deposition of Andrew Singleton, 15 April 1715, Interrogatories, E134/1Geo1/East21.
56 Anthony Booth traded with Antigua; Edward Leeth, Barbados; Robert Tuite, Antigua mainly, but also Jamaica and St Christopher; William Clayton, Antigua mostly, but also St. Christopher, Barbados and Nevis. Port Books, 1709–10, E190/1377/11.
57 On the cultivation of sugar see R.S. Dunn, *Sugar and Slaves: The Rise of the Planter Class in the English West Indies, 1624–1713* (Chapel Hill and London: University of North Carolina Press, 1972), ch. 6, 'Sugar', pp. 188–223.
58 Deposition of Henry Bibby.
59 Some of the blame regarding this can be apportioned to Cunningham, see the discussion below.
60 Deposition of Henry Bibby.
61 Deposition of Henry Bibby.
62 Zacek, *Settler Society*, pp. 41–42; Lenman, 'Colonial Wars', p. 155.
63 Decree, 1716, pp. 1–2.
64 Deposition of Henry Thompson.
65 Deposition of Andew Singleton.
66 Deposition of Andrew Singleton.
67 Deposition of John Dickenson, 16 November 1714, Interrogatories, E134/1Geo1/Mich37.
68 Deposition of Henry Thompson.
69 Deposition of John Dickenson.
70 Deposition of William Rollins, 16 November 1714, Interrogatories, E134/1Geo1/Mich37. Even Andrew Singleton allowed that he had taken the long boat to St. Christopher's to enquire into the market there. Deposition of Andrew Singleton.
71 Deposition of Henry Thompson.
72 Deposition of Andrew Singleton.
73 Deposition of Henry Thompson.
74 See S. Haggerty, *'Merely for Money'? Business Culture in the British Atlantic, 1750–1815* (Liverpool: Liverpool University Press, 2012).
75 Bibby claimed that Pearson had not allowed him to put sugars on the *Providence* at Nevis, but Henry Thompson stated that those refused were because Bibby had already reached his allowance as a sailor on board. Deposition of Henry Thompson.
76 Decree, 1716, p. 1.

Bibliography

Primary sources

The National Archives

HM Court of Exchequer.
Interrogatories, E 134/1Geo1/Mich 37 April 1714.
Interrogatories, E134/1Geo1/East21, 18 April 1715.
Decree, Whereas John Cunningham and Joseph Pearson ..., E 190/30, f. 18, 1716.
Port Books, Chester, Liverpool, Customer Overseas, E 190/1337/16 (1664–1665); E290/1377/22 (1709–1710); E190/1387/7 (1714–1715).

Printed

Mortimer, T., *A New and Complete Dictionary of Trade and Commerce: Containing a Distinct Explanation of the General Principles of Commerce ...* (London, 1766).

Secondary literature

Ascott, D., Lewis, E.F. and M. Power, M., *Liverpool, 1660–1750: People, Prosperity and Power*, Liverpool: Liverpool University Press, 2006.

Baugh, D.A., 'Britain's Blue Water Policy, 1689–1815', *International History Review*, 10:1 (February 1988), pp. 33–58.

Bryson, W.H., *The Equity Side of the Exchequer: Its Jurisdictions, Procedures and Records*, Cambridge: Cambridge University Press, 1975.

Burt, R.S., *Structural Holes: The Social Structure of Competition*, Cambridge and London: Harvard University Press, 1992.

———. 'Structural Holes and Good Ideas', *American Journal of Sociology*, 10:2 (2004), pp. 349–399.

Buskens, V. and van de Rijt, A., 'Dynamics of Networks if Everyone Strives for Structural Holes', *American Journal of Sociology*, 114:2 (September 2008), pp. 371–407.

Casson, M., 'Entrepreneurial Networks in International Business', *Business and Economic History*, 26:2 (Winter 1997), pp. 811–823.

Crouse, N.M., *The French Struggle for the West Indies, 1665–1713*, New York: Columbia University Press, 1943.

Crumplin, T., 'Opaque Networks: Business and Community in the Isle of Man, 1840–1900', *Business History*, 49:6 (2007), pp. 780–801.

Dunn, R.S., *Sugar and Slaves: The Rise of the Planter Class in the English West Indies, 1624–1713*, Chapel Hill and London: University of North Carolina Press, 1972.

Forrestier, A., 'Risk, Kinship and Personal Relationships in Late Eighteenth-Century West Indian Trade: The Commercial Network of Tobin & Pinney', *Business History*, 52:6 (2010), pp. 912–931.

Grabowski, R., 'Market Evolution and Economic Development: The Evolution of Impersonal Markets', *American Journal of Economics and Sociology*, 58:4 (October 1999), pp. 699–712.

Granovetter, M.S., 'The Strength of Weak Ties: A Theory Revisited', *Sociological Theory*, 1 (1983), pp. 201–233.

———. 'Economic Action and Social Structure: The Problem of Embeddedness', *American Journal of Sociology*, 91:3 (November 1985), pp. 481–510.

Haggerty, S., *'Merely for Money'? Business Culture in the British Atlantic, 1750–1815*, Liverpool: Liverpool University Press, 2012.

Hancock, D., 'The Trouble with Networks: Managing the Scots' Early-Modern Madeira Trade', *Business History Review*, 79, Special Edition on Networks in the Trade in Alcohol (Autumn 2005), pp. 67–91.

Hattendorf, J.B., *England in the War of the Spanish Succession: A Study in the English View and Conduct of Grand Strategy, 1701–1713*, London: Routledge, 1987.

Koot, C.J., *Empire at the Periphery: British Colonists, Anglo-Dutch Trade, and the Development of the British Atlantic, 1621–1713*, New York and London: New York University Press, 2011.

Lawler, E.J. and Y. Yoon, 'Commitment in Exchange Relations: Test of a Theory of Relational Cohesion', *American Sociological Review*, 61:1 (February 1996), pp. 89–108.

Lenman, B.P., 'Colonial Wars and Imperial Instability, 1688–1793', in P.J. Marshall (ed.), *Oxford History of the British Empire, Vol. II, The Eighteenth Century*, Oxford: Oxford University Press, 1998, pp. 151–168.

Lynn, J.A., *The Wars of Louis XIV, 1667–1714*, London and New York: Longman, 1999.

Mancke, E., 'Chartered Enterprises and the Evolution of the British Atlantic World', in Mancke, E. and Shammas, C. (eds.), *The Creation of the British Atlantic World*, Baltimore and London: Johns Hopkins University Press, 2005, pp. 237–262.

Marshall, P.J. (ed), *Oxford History of the British Empire*, Vol. II, The Eighteenth Century, Oxford: Oxford University Press, 1998, pp. 151–168.

Mathias, P., 'Risk, Credit and Kinship in Early Modern Enterprise', in McCusker, J.J. and Morgan, K. (eds.), *The Early-Modern Atlantic Economy*, Cambridge: Cambridge University Press, 2000, pp. 15–35.

Matson, C., *Merchants and Empire: Trading in Colonial New York*, Baltimore and London: Johns Hopkins University Press, 1998.

Podolny, J.M., and Page, K.L., 'Network Forms of Organization', *Annual Review of Sociology*, 24 (1998), pp. 57–76.

Poole, B., *Liverpool's Trade in the Reign of Queen Anne*, unpublished MA Thesis: University of Liverpool (1961), pp. 101–109.

Popp, A., 'Building the Market: John Shaw of Wolverhampton and Commercial Travelling in Early Nineteenth-Century England', *Business History*, 49:3 (May 2007), pp. 321–347.

Power, M., 'Creating a Port: Liverpool 1695–1715', *Transactions of the Historic Society of Lancashire and Cheshire*, 149 (1999), pp. 51–71.

Prior, A. and Kirby, M., 'The Society of Friends and the Family Firm, 1700–1830', *Business History*, 35:4 (1993), pp. 66–85.

Rose, M.B., 'The Family Firm in British Business, 1780–1914', in Kirby, M.W. and Rose, M.B. (eds.), *Business Enterprise in Modern Britain from the Eighteenth to the Twentieth Century* (London, 1994), pp. 61–87.

Schrank, A. and Whitford, J., 'The Anatomy of Network Failure', *Sociological Theory*, 29:3 (2011), pp. 151–177.

Sheridan, R.B., *Sugar and Slavery: An Economic History of the British West Indies, 1623–1775*, Kingston: Canoe Press, 1974.

Stammers, M.K., 'Ships and Port Management at Liverpool Before the Opening of the First Dock in 1715', *Transactions of the Historic Society of Lancashire and Cheshire*, 156 (2007), pp. 27–50.

Starkey, D.J., *British Privateering Enterprise in the Eighteenth Century*, Exeter Maritime Series No. 4, Exeter: University of Exeter Press, 1990.

Steckley, G.F., 'Freight Law in the Seventeenth-Century Admiralty Court', *Journal of Legal History*, 27:2 (2006), pp. 175–197.

Stillson, R.T., *Spreading the Word: A History of Information in the California Gold Rush*, Lincoln and London: University of Nebraska Press, 2006.

Strong, N. and Waterson, M., 'Principals, Agents and Information', in Clark, R. and McGuiness, T. (eds.), *The Economics of the Firm*, Oxford: Basil Blackwell, 1987, pp. 18–41.

Thye, S.R., Lawler, E.J. and Yoon, J., 'The Emergence of Embedded Relations and Group Formation in Networks of Competition', *Psychology Quarterly*, 74:4 (December 2011), pp. 287–413.

Zacek, N.A., *Settler Society in the English Leeward Islands, 1670–1776*, Cambridge: Cambridge University Press, 2010.

Zucker, L.G., 'Production of Trust: Institutional Sources of Economic Structure, 1840–1920', *Research in Organizational Behaviour*, 8 (1986), pp. 53–111.

Index

For Product Safety Concerns and Information please contact our EU
representative GPSR@taylorandfrancis.com
Taylor & Francis Verlag GmbH, Kaufingerstraße 24, 80331 München, Germany